HUDDERS IN WORLD WAR I

Brian Heywood
with
Laurence Brammer
David Gronow
Joe Hopkinson
Martin Richardson
Luke Russell
Jacqui Smith
Joe Taylor
Adam West

Edited
by
Brian Heywood

Upper Calder Valley Publications
in association with
Huddersfield Rugby League: A Lasting Legacy

First published in 2014
by
Upper Calder Valley Publications
in association with
Huddersfield Rugby League: A Lasting Legacy

Copyright ©
Upper Calder Valley Publications
and
Huddersfield Rugby League: A Lasting Legacy

ISBN 978-0-9547146-7-3

Printed by
The Amadeus Press, Cleckheaton BD19 4TQ

Contents

Acknowledgements

Glossary

Introduction

References

Index

Acknowledgements

Heritage Lottery Fund Grant

Huddersfield in World War I originated from an application to the Heritage Lottery Fund (HLF) to finance the project Huddersfield Rugby League: A Lasting Legacy (HRL: ALL). This project was the brainchild of **Laura Hanson**, then head of Huddersfield Giants in the Community, and of **Dr Rob Light**, the project's first manager. We, the authors, are grateful to them for their ideas.

We express out gratitude to the **HLF** for its support in funding the project, including this book, and for the encouragement and guidance of their staff at Leeds.

HRL: ALL would like to thank those who supported their application for the grant that made the project and this book possible: **Professor Tony Collins**, Director, International Centre for Sports History and Culture, De Montfort University, Leicester; **Ken Davy**, Chairman, Huddersfield Giants RLFC; **John R Rawlinson**, Chairman, Huddersfield Local History Society; **Dr Robert Ellis**, Senior Lecturer, Division of History, University of Huddersfield; **Janet Pearson**, Area Manager, Kirklees Culture and Leisure Services; and **Julie Swift**, Junior Club Secretary, St Joseph's Sharks ARLFC.

Larchwood Homes Sponsorship

HRL: ALL would like to thank **Larchwood Homes** for their sponsorship of HRL: ALL, which has enhanced the quality of the project and of this publication.

Advice and Guidance

The authors are privileged to have had the advice and guidance of all those who have read drafts of various chapters, suggested corrections and improvements, and assisted with the quality of images:

Clive Cranston, **Janette Martin** and **John Rumsby**, Huddersfield Local History Society;
Freda and Malcolm Heywood, Upper Calder Valley Publications;
David Gronow, **Jacqui Smith**, **Angela Sykes**, **Charles Sykes** and **David Thorpe** (HRL: ALL);
David Tattersfield, Western Front Association;
David and Barbara Wyles, Huddersfield Civic Society;
Sue Hanson, University of Huddersfield;
Jane Chesworth, BBC Radio Leeds.

Research and Authorship

The editor is grateful to the following contributors:
Laurence Brammer for extensive researching of information from the *HDE* from 1914 to 1916, and for writing the drafts of Chapter 5: 1914-15 The U-Boat Menace, and Chapter 7: Gallipoli.
Martin Richardson for adapting and developing his feature about Royds Hall War Hospital, originally written for the Local History Society journal, in writing Chapter 11: War Hospitals.
Joe Hopkinson for researching additional information for and writing Chapter 12: Recruitment and Conscription.
The late **David Gronow** for supplying northern union rugby information and images for Chapter 15: Sport and Leisure and for Chapter 22: Transition and Legacy. David also accessed from the Imperial War Museum and painstakingly transcribed Douglas Clark's War Diary which features prominently in Chapter 18: 1917: Passchendaele. David passed away in August 2014 shortly before this book was published.
Adam West for writing the draft of Chapter 15: Sport and Leisure.
Jacqui Smith for writing the draft of Chapter 16: Women: Vindication for Emancipation.
Luke Russell for extensive researching and recording of information from the 1918 editions of the *HDE*, and for writing the draft of Chapter 20: 1917-18: Rationing
Joe Taylor for extensive researching and recording of information from the 1919 editions of the *HDE*, and for writing the draft of Chapter 22: 1918-19: Transition and Legacies.
Jonathan Morris for extensive researching of information from the *HDE* from 1917 to 1919

General Assistance

HRL: ALL is especially grateful to **Dr Robert Ellis**, **Janette Martin** and **Sarah Bastow** of the **University of Huddersfield** who facilitated the work-placements of seven students to assist with researching and writing this book: Laurence Brammer, Joe Hopkinson, Jonathan Morris, Martin Richardson, Luke Russell, Joe Taylor and Adam West.

We also thank the staff of the following organisations for their help in accessing archives and images:

Clayton West Parish Church

Duke of Wellington's West Riding Regiment

Huddersfield Local Studies Library

Huddersfield Giants RLFC

Huddersfield Examiner

Imperial War Museum

Kirklees Archive Service

National Football Museum

Rugby Football League Archive

South Crosland Junior School

University of Huddersfield

West Yorkshire Archive Service

Original Source Materials

We are grateful to **Caroline Courtney** for allowing us to read, research from and reproduce letters and WWI artefacts of her Great Uncle, Wilfred Greenfield (pp140, 141 and 143).

We thank **Kirklees Archive Service** for allowing access to letters written from the front line by Private Freddie Smith (quoted pp44-55 and 187) and by Lieutenant Roland Hely Owen (quoted pp4 and 12).

We thank **Kirklees Archive Service** and the **Duke of Wellington's West Riding Regiment** for permission to reproduce images and documents, including several from the scrapbook of Captain Keith Sykes who served on the western front with the 5th (Huddersfield) Battalion from April 1915 to May 1919.

We thank **Huddersfield Local Studies Library** for providing access to microfilm of local newspapers, particularly the *HDE* from 1914 to 1919, to numerous local history publications, and for providing copying facilities.

We are grateful to the **Kirklees Images Archive** for supplying numerous high resolution images.

Secondary Source Materials

The books and websites accessed for research are all included in the reference section, but the authors are particularly grateful to the following local authors:

Laurie Magnus (*The West Riding Territorials in the Great War*; 1920)

Cyril Pearce (*Comrades in Conscience: The story of an English community's opposition to the Great War*; 2014)

David Tattersfield (*A Village Goes to War: A History of the Men of Ravensthorpe who fell in the Great War*; 2000).

Their works provided valuable background, context and additional detail to many of the stories that we found.

We are particularly grateful to the *Huddersfield Examiner* and its predecessors the *Huddersfield Daily Examiner* and *Huddersfield Weekly Examiner*, and to their wartime proprietor and editor **Ernest Woodhead**, for the newspapers' extensive coverage of the war. We are also indebted to **Charles Lunn**, some of whose locally-flavoured contemporary wartime poems are reproduced in this book, having first appeared in the *HDE*'s weekly 'In and About' column.

Images

The following have allowed us to reproduce illustrations, for which we thank them:

Tony Allen (www.worldwar1postcards.com) pp7, 8, 35, 47, 48, 51, 52, 54, 57, 85, 105, 113, 115, 189

Caroline Courtney pp140, 141, 143

Chappell and Co Ltd (1920) p138

Christ Church Staincliffe, Batley (staincliffe.weebly.com/priests) p35

Clayton West Parish Church p150

Digital Poster Collection (http://digitalpostercollection.com/propaganda/1914-1918-world-war-i) p 172

Duke of Wellington's West Riding Regiment pp12, 43, 45, 203, 245, 252

Duke of Wellington's West Riding Regiment and Kirklees Archive Service pp52, 103, 107, 108, 189, 211, 241, 242, 246, 249, 255, 256, 273, 274

Encyclopedia Titanica (www.encyclopedia-titanica.org) p35

David Gronow pp78, 124, 159, 162, 196, 198, 199, 202, 204, 267

Brian Heywood pp57, 66, 125, 170, 182

Huddersfield Examiner pp2, 4, 5, 10, 17, 24, 31, 37, 58, 73, 82, 88, 97, 103, 111, 118, 122, 168, 170, 174, 176, 178, 180, 183, 185, 187, 196, 219, 231, 251, 254, 259, 273

Kirklees Images Archive (www.kirklees images.org.uk/) pp27, 28, 70, 77, 90, 91, 99, 100, 103, 106, 112, 117, 152, 157, 163, 183, 184, 272

National Railway Museum/Science and Society Picture Library, Science Museum Group p105

Photos of the Great War: World War I Image Archive (www.gwpda.org/photos/) pp21, 62, 64, 69

We are grateful to the following sources for making available images in the public domain. Every effort has been made to contact and thank them.

Benfleet Community Archive (www.benfleethistory.org.uk) p29

'The Story of 25 Eventful Years in Pictures', Odhams Press Ltd (1935) pp146, 225, 226, 228

Illustrated London News Digital Archive pp109, 261

The Dawlish Chronicles (dawlishchronicel.com/hms-aboukir-cressy-and-hogue-disaster-1914/) p29

The 4 Funnel Liners (www.raeth.ch/teh_4_funnel_liners) p34

Bettmann/Corbis (www.theguardian.com/world/2008/nov/12/gallipoli-diary-dardanelles-campaign) p60

http://commons.wikimedia.org/wiki/File:Ww1pddBroke.jpg p151

http://commons.wikimedia.org/wiki/File:HMSWarspitesidedamage1916.jpg p149

http://commons.wikimedia.org/wiki/File:HMS_Warspite_No7_6_inch_gun_after_Jutland.jpg p149

http://commons.wikimedia.org/wiki/File:Destruction_of_HMS_Queen_Mary.jpg p148

http://www.museumsyndicate.com/item.php?item=43181 p67

http://www.gracesguide.co.uk/L._B._Holliday_and_Co p80

http://images.1233.tw/zeppelin-airship-ww1/ p93

http://www.rememberscarborough.co.uk p94 (Images in public domain, originators unknown)

Patrick Brennan (www.donmouth.co.uk/womens_football/huddersfield_atalanta.html) p269

Imperial War Museum (http://www.iwm.org.uk/collections/item/object/205194706) p247 image Q9534**, (http://www.iwm.org.uk/collections/item/object/205215580)** p214 image Q46932

The Long Long Trail website (www.longlong trail.co.uk/PIX/post-7367-1132676608.jpg) p214 (photograph by unknown German photographer, 1917)

http://Hospitalship.tripod.com p37

Glossary

Abbreviations

ASC	Army Service Corps	**NCO**	Non-Commissioned Officer
BEF	British Expeditionary Force	**NMV**	National Motor Volunteers
BRCS	British Red Cross Society	**NRFU**	Northern Rugby Football Union
CO	Conscientious Objector	**RAMC**	Royal Army Medical Corps
FC	Football Club	**RFA**	Royal Field Artillery
HDE	Huddersfield Daily Examiner	**RFU**	Rugby Football Union
HWE	Huddersfield Weekly Examiner	**VAD**	Voluntary Aid Detachment
KOYLI	Kings Own Yorkshire Light Infantry	**YMCA**	Young Men's Christian Association
MST	Military Service Tribunal	**YWCA**	Young Women's Christian
MT	Motor Transport		Association

Terms

salient

A salient is an area of land that juts out into enemy territory, vulnerable to attack as the enemy borders it on three sides. Such territory usually arises because one or both sides occupy strategically valuable land, such as high land that borders the salient, and/or are protecting a strategically important position.

British Expeditionary Force (BEF)

Often used to describe the first 100,000 troops who fought through the autumn of 1914, BEF refers to the entire British force in France and Belgium through the duration of the war. Its infantry comprised:

i) **Regulars**, the professional soldiers who went out in August 1914

ii) **Territorials**, part-time troops based and trained locally, over 90% of whom volunteered to serve overseas when war was declared. They enabled the numbers of the British Army to be maintained whilst Kitchener's New Army of volunteers was raised and trained. Huddersfield had two **territorial battalions**, the 5th (Huddersfield) and 7th (Colne Valley) of the **Duke of Wellington's West Riding Regiment**, commonly referred to as the **5th Dukes** and the **7th Dukes**. They crossed to the continent in April 1915 as part of the **49th (West Riding) Division**. Both battalions spent the entire war on the western front. Like most other territorial battalions they doubled, then trebled their numbers, designated the 1/5th, 2/5th and 3/5th; 1/7th; 2/7th and 3/7th. The 3/5th and 3/7th stayed at home as training battalions supplying reinforcements for the first and second line battalions, trainees being transferred when required. The 2/5th and 2/7th formed part of the **62nd (2nd West Riding) Division** which comprised the Territorial Force second line battalions of the 49th Division and transferred to the western front in January 1917. Owing to shortage of numbers the 1/5th was disbanded in January 1918. Their remaining troops were either merged with the 2/5th Dukes, then renamed the 5th Dukes, in the 62nd Division, or redistributed among the remaining battalions of the 49th Division, most of them into the 1/6th (Skipton) battalion. Only 39% of the local troops served in the local battalions. The rest were allocated to other battalions, most of them in other regiments.

iii) **New Volunteers**, recruits to the army, who eventually formed the vast majority of the BEF. They made new lines of existing territorial battalions, or formed new battalions. The **Duke of Wellington's West Riding Regiment** eventually raised 8th, 9th, 10th and 11th service battalions and Huddersfield men probably served in all of these. Until February 1916 all new soldiers were volunteers from civilian life. In February 1916 conscription was introduced, after which new recruits were a combination of volunteers and conscripts.

Voluntary Training Force

Comprising overage, underage and unfit men, they were the 'Home Guard'. Some provided military transport using their own vehicles. They included the **National Motor Volunteers**, who used their own vehicles to provide a free taxi-service, usually from Huddersfield Railway Station, for wounded troops and troops home on leave.

Equivalent Military Ranks in the British Army, Navy and Air Force in World War I

Army	Navy	Air Force
Field-Marshall	Admiral-of-the-Fleet	
General	Admiral	
Lieutenant-General	Vice-Admiral	Lieutenant-General
Major-General	Rear-Admiral	Major-General
	Commodore 1st Class	
Brigadier-General	Commodore 2nd Class	Brigadier-General
Colonel	Captain	Colonel
Lieutenant-Colonel	Commander	Lieutenant-Colonel
Major	Lieutenant-Commander	Major
Captain	Lieutenant	Captain
Lieutenant	Sub-Lieutenant	Lieutenant
Second-Lieutenant	Chief Commissioned Warrant-Officer	Second-Lieutenant
	Commissioned Warrant-Officer/Midshipman	
Sergeant	Petty-Officer	Sergeant
Corporal or Lance-Corporal	Leading-Seaman	Corporal
Private	Seaman	Aircraftman

Structure of the British Army

Command Group	Rank of Commanding Officer	Approximate Number of Men
Army Group	Field-Marshal	2,000,000
Army	General	300,000
Corps	Lieutenant-General	60,000
Division	Major-General	12,000
Brigade	Brigadier-General	4500
Regiment	Colonel	4000
Battalion	Lieutenant-Colonel Major (second-in-command)	1000
Company	Captain	200
Platoon	Lieutenant or Second-Lieutenant Sergeant (second-in-command)	50
Section	Corporal or Lance-Corporal	12

N.B. A Brigade usually comprised the four battalions of a regiment plus a machine gun company and a trench mortar battery allocated by Divisional command.

Hierarchy of Awards

Award	Abbrev.	Origin Date	Eligibility	Royal Warrant
Award Level 1				
Victoria Cross	V.C.	29 Jan 1856	All ranks	For most conspicuous bravery, or some daring or pre-eminent act of valour or self-sacrifice, or extreme devotion to duty in the presence of the enemy
Award Level 2				
Distinguished Service Order	D.S.O.	6 Sept 1886	Army and naval officers, usually Major or equivalent rank (RAF from 1 April 1918)	Meritorious or distinguished service in wartime
Distinguished Conduct Medal	D.C.M.	4 Dec 1854	Other ranks of the armed forces	Gallantry in the field in face of the enemy
Conspicuous Gallantry Medal	C.G.M.	1855	Other ranks in the navy	Gallantry against the enemy in the sea or in the air
Award Level 3				
Distinguished Service Cross	D.S.C.	15 June 1901	Naval officers	Gallantry at sea in presence of the enemy
Military Cross	M.C.	28 Dec 1914	Commissioned officers ranked captain or below	Gallantry during active operations in presence of the enemy
Distinguished Flying Cross	D.F.C.	3 June 1918	RAF officers and warrant officers	Acts of valour, courage or devotion to duty while flying on active operations against the enemy
Distinguished Service Medal	D.S.M.	14 Oct 1914	Other ranks in the navy	Bravery while on active service at sea
Military Medal	M.M.	25 Mar 1916	Other ranks in the army	Gallantry and devotion to duty when under fire in battle on land
Distinguished Flying Medal	D.F.M.	3 June 1914	Other ranks in the air force	Acts of valour, courage or devotion to duty while flying on active operations against the enemy
Award Level 4				
Air Force Cross	A.F.C.	3 June 1918	RAF officers and warrant officers (all ranks from 1993)	Acts of valour, courage or devotion to duty while flying though not in active operations against the enemy
Air Force Medal	A.F.M.	3 June 1918	Other ranks in the RAF	Acts of valour, courage or devotion to duty while flying though not on active operations against the enemy
Meritorious Service Medal	M.S.M.	1845 (Army); 1849 (Royal Marines); 1918 (RAF); 1919 (Navy)	Non-commissioned officers	Gallantry, meritorious or distinguished service
Bar to any award			As above	A second award of any of the above

Award	Abbrev.	Origin Date	Eligibility	Royal Warrant
			Other	
Mentioned in Despatches (Certificate)	M.I.D.	6 Oct 1898	All ranks	Senior commander's official commendation for act of gallantry or service

N.B. In 1993 the D.S.O., D.C.M. and C.M.G. were replaced by the Conspicuous Gallantry Cross as Level 2 gallantry award for all ranks in the British Armed Forces.

Money Conversion Table

Imperial Amount 1915	Decimal Conversion	Approximate Decimal Value 2014
1d	½p	£0.29
2d	1p	£0.58
6d	2½p	£1.45
1s	5p	£2.90
2s	10p	£5.80
2s 6d	12½p	£7.25
5s	25p	£14.50
7s 6d	37½p	£21.75
10s	50p	£29.00
15s	75p	£43.50
20s (£1)	£1	£58.00
£2	£2	£116.00
£5	£5	£290.00
£10	£10	£580.00
£20	£20	£1,160.00
£25	£25	£1,450.00
£30	£30	£1,740.00
£40	£40	£2,320.00
£50	£50	£2,900.00
£75	£75	£4,350.00
£100	£100	£5,800.00
£150	£150	£8,700.00
£200	£200	£11,600.00
£300	£300	£15,960.00
£400	£400	£20,320.00
£500	£500	£29,000.00
£1000	£1000	£58,000.00
£2000	£2000	£116,000.00
£5000	£5000	£290,000.00
£10,000	£10,000	£580,000.00
£20,000	£20,000	£1,160,000.00
£50,000	£50,000	£2,900,000.00
£100,000	£100,000	£5,800,000.00
£200,000	£200,000	£11,600,000.00
£500,000	£500,000	£29,000,000.00
£1,000,000	£1,000,000	£58,000,000.00
£2,000,000	£2,000,000	£116,000,000.00

This is neither an academic book nor a military history. It is a collection of wartime stories about the people of Huddersfield and its surrounding districts, put into context. It has not been possible to include all the stories we have found, but those selected are intended to be representative, reflecting the lives of local people during World War I.

Huddersfield in World War I

Introduction

The First World War was the most devastating conflict in history. Blood was shed on a scale seen neither before nor since. Over ten million lost their lives. Many more were scarred, physically and psychologically, for life. Beyond the battlefield, the war and its consequences touched the lives of everyone in Europe and in many countries beyond, causing immense material hardship and emotional suffering.

This book considers how the war impacted on the people of Huddersfield and its surrounding districts. Comprehensively researched from the *Huddersfield Daily Examiner* and the *Huddersfield Weekly Examiner* from 1914 to 1919, from numerous other publications, and from original diaries and letters, it recounts the experiences of the courageous local servicemen, taking you to the heart of the action through the personal stories of many who served on the Western Front, at Gallipoli, at sea and in the air.

It also relates tales of resourcefulness, conflict and humour on the home front as local people adjusted to the extraordinary social, industrial and economic wartime demands. The district's wool, dye and steel industries were adapted to the mass production of khaki and munitions. Blessed by outstanding civic leadership, dedicated voluntary organisations and incalculable generosity, Huddersfield contributed fully to recruitment, fundraising and caring for the injured. Women, including many migrant factory workers, grasped long-overdue opportunities to prove their capabilities in the workplace, wartime necessities accelerating their progress towards equal rights and freedoms. Entertainment through sport, film, drama, music and variety provided oases of morale-boosting relief, and comforting communal links to happier times.

Amidst the spirit, energy and patriotic fervour, Huddersfield's characteristic radical and socialist convictions surfaced in vehement opposition to conscription, in support for conscientious objectors, and in conflicts between unions and employers over excessive government demands.

All was played out against the unrelenting, debilitating anxiety, stress and upset of awaiting news about friends and loved ones from afar.

The length and brutality of the war exceeded the most pessimistic expectations. By 1918, supplies of manpower, food and materials had become critical. In the *Huddersfield Daily Examiner*, the local battalions' increasingly frequent and heroic deeds were accompanied by casualty lists that became little more than that, just lists. Death, with the epitaph 'killed in action', 'missing', or 'died from wounds', had lost the power to shock.

For those who paid the ultimate price, the stories in this book represent the world as they last saw it. The free world continues to owe a debt of gratitude to all who fought, and suffered, and sacrificed, abroad and at home. This story, of a town at war, is dedicated to all of them.

Are <u>YOU</u> in this?

Chapter 1

1914: War is Declared

By the summer of 1914 Europe was a powder-keg of international alliances. A complex web of treaties, built over many years and motivated mainly by suspicion and fear of isolation, had evolved into two major groups, the Triple Entente, comprising Great Britain, Russia and France, and the Central Powers, comprising Germany, Austria-Hungary, Turkey and, initially, Italy, before her defection to the Allies in May 1915. Economically and militarily, these were the most powerful international alliances the world had ever seen.

Mistrust and apprehension was particularly fuelled by Germany's intimidating militarisation. France and Britain had discussed the protection of French borders from German attack. Britain, meanwhile, felt that Germany was becoming a threat to her naval supremacy. The result was an escalating European arms race.[1]

There were foreboding references in the local press, which covered national and international news extensively. On 2 January 1914, the *HDE* reported:

> The increase of Continental armies ... has been used as a reason for increasing both our fleet and our army ... The growth of the German navy has been talked of as a menace ... Mr Lloyd George [Chancellor of the Exchequer] deplores the mad competition in armaments.

Although arming on a smaller scale than Germany, on 19 January the War Office revealed that Britain had, in twelve months, increased its number of 'Voluntary Aid Detachments' by 50% to 2276, with the number of personnel up from 57,000 to 68,000.[2] The numbers in the 5th (Huddersfield) Battalion of the Duke of Wellington's West Riding Regiment (the 5th Dukes) had increased by 80 to 850.[3]

On 10 March 1914 the dreadnought HMS *Iron Duke*, the world's most powerful warship, became the first to be equipped with anti-aircraft guns and was commissioned into the British fleet as its flagship.[4] As military preparations gathered momentum, the *HDE* of 13 May reported:

> Everywhere on the continent of Europe ... may be observed signs of the intense anxiety lest war should of a sudden break out and find one or other of the great nations ill-prepared for the gigantic struggle ... enormous sacrifices are being made to increase the strength and efficiency of the armies.

Many events might have broken the fragile peace. The one that did came in Bosnia. Since 1908, when Bosnia and Serbia were annexed from the crumbling Ottoman Empire by Austria, this volatile and fragmented region had festered widespread resentment against Austrian rule. On 28 June 1914, Archduke Franz Ferdinand, the 51-year-old nephew of Austrian Emperor Franz Josef and heir to the Austrian throne, visited the Bosnian capital Sarajevo. There, the Archduke and his wife were assassinated by 19-year-old Gavrilo Princip, a fanatic of the Serbian Black Hand Gang.[5]

On 6 July, Germany opportunistically pledged to support Austria-Hungary in crushing the Serbs and in repelling any support for the Serbs from Russia. Emboldened by this 'blank cheque' from Berlin, Austrian officials manufactured an excuse for a short war to crush Serbia. They demanded outrageous control of the Serbian judicial process regarding the assassination. When this was refused, Moltke, head of the German army, exceeded his authority by sending a telegram urging Austria to act, and on 28 July Austria declared war on Serbia. The dreaded chain of alliance-honouring action and reaction had begun. The momentum would prove impossible to stop.[6]

On 29 July Austria bombed Belgrade. Russia mobilised her army to protect her beleaguered Serbian ally, and Austria-Hungary looked to Germany for support. On 31 July Russia refused Germany's ultimatum to withdraw and Germany mobilised, declaring war on Russia on 1 August.

Headline from the *HDE*, 3 August 1914

Germany asked France to remain neutral but, with one eye on Alsace-Lorraine which the Germans had annexed following the Franco-Prussian War in 1871, the French refused. On 3 August Germany declared war on France. German troops were, however, already marching westwards as part of the Schlieffen Plan, devised in 1905 in anticipation that France would honour her alliance with Russia. The German strategy was to quickly defeat the French before transferring troops to the east to confront the Russians, thus avoiding a war on two fronts.[7]

Despite her alliances, Britain had no duty to enter the war. The next few hours would present Prime Minister Herbert Asquith and his Liberal government with the gravest of decisions. The days of Asquith's youth, growing up in Morley and Mirfield, and his first year of schooling – 1860-61 – as an eight-year-old at Huddersfield College, must have seemed a world away. Germany hoped that Asquith's government would be preoccupied with the seemingly interminable problem of Home Rule for Ireland. But as her Triple Entente allies tumbled into the conflict, pressure on Britain escalated.[8]

Escape from the Continent

Meanwhile, the speed of developments on the continent had caught many people out. On Thursday 30 July, Herbert Brook, a Huddersfield elementary school teacher holidaying with German friends in Cologne, saw a notice that 'all foreigners without reason for staying in Germany are advised to leave the country within 24 hours.' On enquiry to the local police, Brook was told there was no urgency and he could leave as planned. This proved to be incorrect. Within two days transport routes were guarded and everyone was 'closely scrutinised.'

Assisted by his friends, Brook left Cologne by train on 3 August. During the next two increasingly fraught days, he was refused permission to cross the border at both Dolheim and Neuss, and was eventually arrested and imprisoned at Munchengladbach. Along with two Belgians and two Englishmen in the same predicament, he was released the following morning and travelled to Dusseldorf to locate the British Consul.

By now the German authorities had decreed that no Englishman or Frenchman of 'military age', defined as 16 to 43 years old, may leave Germany. Joined by ten more compatriots, Herbert Brook lay low in lodgings for nine days, but on Friday 14 August secret service officers knocked on their door and they were arrested. Fortunately, 'no suspicion' was found against any of them, and the Oberburgermeister (Lord Mayor) reluctantly endorsed their passports to cross the Dutch border at Emmerich.

Locations on the escape of Huddersfield citizens from the continent in August 1914

Their train was in open country when it was stopped for an inspection. The nerve-wracked group passed themselves off as Dutchmen, but to their horror were transferred to a military train packed with German troops. Mistaking them for comrades-in-arms, the Germans heartily cheered them aboard, but once underway they were thankfully left alone. It was a temporary reprieve. On reaching the border they were arrested again, German customs officers telling them that they would never reach England. Their one ray of hope was a local policeman who seemed very unhappy at their rough treatment.

Moved to a nearby cottage, they were kept under guard as civil prisoners overnight. Then, at sunrise, the policeman appeared and quickly released them. Within ten minutes they had crossed the Dutch border. Their ordeal was over, and the Englishmen immediately vented their frustrations with a full-throated rendition of the National Anthem. Travelling via Arnhem, Utrecht, Rotterdam and Harwich, Herbert Brook arrived home in Huddersfield on Monday 17 August, a fortnight and three arrests after leaving Cologne.[9]

Others were a little more fortunate. Mrs Hellawell Carter of Marsh returned from holiday in Frankfurt on a train 'so overcrowded that she and other passengers travelled part of the journey in the cattle truck.' She was disconcerted to see that the Rhine had several new bridges which were heavily guarded.[10]

Tom Pitts of Lindley, who was working in Aachen, was advised to leave the country by 1 August or to sign up for the German army. As several of his work colleagues were called to arms, he made his escape, held up only at Antwerp where, on 3 August, the docks were so overcrowded that only women and children were allowed onto boats heading for England.[11]

John Dyson from Marsh, who worked as a power loom weaver in Silesia, and Mr Eastwood, a native of Longwood whose family moved to Germany in his youth, decided to remain in Germany. In November 1914 both were arrested and interned at a Prisoner of War Camp in Ruhleben, Berlin. 53-year-old Dyson was returned to England after 12 months, but Eastwood, who was of military age, was held until January 1918.[12]

Such problems were not one way. There were 'thirty aliens of enemy origin' in Huddersfield. Of these, 16 were interned, one of whom died, six were eventually exempted from internment, and the rest were dealt with 'in various ways.'[13]

The Moment of Decision

On 30 July, as these dramas began to unfold, Prime Minister Asquith addressed a special meeting of Parliament, referring to 'circumstances of almost unparalleled gravity ... the issues of peace and war are hanging in the balance, and ... there is the risk of an almost immeasurable catastrophe ... England is working earnestly for peace in the interests of all the powers.' On the same day, mobilisation of the military across Britain suggested that 'the public were not in possession of all the facts about the commitments of this country.' The Special Reserves of the Territorials were called out, all leave was stopped in the army and navy, and men on leave were recalled to barracks. Locally, news spread that the 'Special Service' men of the 4th (Halifax) Dukes were on their way to Grimsby. The collection and transportation of military supplies was another giveaway.

In Huddersfield, 'here and there one met an extremely serious face, and one was greeted with the query "Is it right that we are mobilised?" ... By midday on 30 July rumours began to take shape ... whispers of "Jack's for it" and "Billy's going".'[14]

On Sunday 2 August, Albert I, the King of Belgium, refused a German ultimatum demanding passage through Belgium for her armies. He appealed to Britain for help in guaranteeing Belgian neutrality, as agreed by the Treaty of London (1839). Simultaneously, there was an anti-war demonstration in London's Trafalgar Square. Locally, a resolution passed by a well-attended meeting of the Huddersfield branch of the Independent Labour Party in St George's Square expressed ...

> ... serious alarm [at] the prospects of a European war, into which every European power will be dragged owing to secret alliances and understandings, which in their origin were never sanctioned by the nations. We stand by the efforts of the international working class movement to unite the workers of the nations concerned in their efforts to prevent their Governments from entering upon a war, as expressed in the resolution passed by the International Socialist Bureau.

In Huddersfield, anti-war unity with the workers of other nations was largely accepted as a legitimate point of view. Two thousand supporters of a local strike by engineers' labourers passed their own prescient resolution:

> ... this meeting of Huddersfield citizens views with horror the acts of war ... which threaten to involve the whole Continent of Europe in an orgy of bloodshed unparalleled in the history of mankind. We protest in the strongest possible terms against this country being embroiled in this insane conflict.[15]

Rowland Owen, captain of the Huddersfield Old Boys Rugby Union Football Club and a regular soldier took the opposite view. On 2 August he wrote home from army camp in Kent:

> If we stay out, whoever wins, we shall presumably take it in the neck soon ... if we don't start now, it will be all over, and we shall have disgraced ourselves.[16]

At 11.20pm on Monday 3 August the territorials of the 5th Dukes returned early from camp at Marske. The battalion band dispelled any remaining doubts that the country was on the brink of war, cutting the night air with the brassy strains of *Under the Banner of Victory* and *To the Rescue* as they marched from the railway station to their Drill Hall headquarters. The following morning rumours were rife that they were 'being kitted out for war.'[17] Later that day a socialist peace meeting at New Mill near Holmfirth sent a telegram to the Prime Minister's office urging British neutrality. At least their opinions and distress were on record, but the tipping point had arrived.[18]

All countries, including Germany, had guaranteed Belgian neutrality in the event of war, but the Schlieffen Plan prescribed German troops taking the quickest route to Paris. On 4 August news arrived that the German army was marching into the heart of Belgium. Britain's allies were under attack. There was a perceived threat to her navy. If Germany gained control of the channel ports, she would dominate the trade routes, negate any immediate possibility of Britain landing and supplying an army on the continent, and have a launch pad to invade Britain. By controlling Europe Germany would control international finance. Kaiser Wilhelm was anxious that Britain should stay out of the conflict, but Germany had misread Britain's position. The breech of Belgium's borders was a test of Britain's legal, moral, military and economic resolve. At 4pm Asquith gave a last ditch ultimatum that Germany remove her armies from Belgium. As expected, this was ignored. At 11pm on 4 August 1914 Britain declared war on Germany.[19]

An 'Examiner Special' cartoon from 21 August 1914
sardonically reflects Kaiser Wilhelm's misreading of Britain's position.

Europe's web of alliances, spun over decades, had crystallised into conflict between the Central Powers and the Triple Alliance. Amid a great deal of British excitement, euphoria and over-confidence, Foreign Secretary Sir Edward Grey reflected the magnitude of the crisis:

The lamps are going out all over Europe; we shall not see them lit again in our lifetime.[20]

Chapter 2

1914: Raising an Army

Mobilisation

On the morning of Wednesday 5 August, schoolgirl Vivien Hurst was walking through Huddersfield with her father, when a 'newsboy' ran towards them shouting: 'War! England declares War on Germany. War!'

> … all else faded from my mind. Daddy beckoned the boy over to buy a paper, his look grave and preoccupied, and almost snatching it he turned to the huge headlines across the front page. 'So,' said Daddy, 'it has come.'[1]

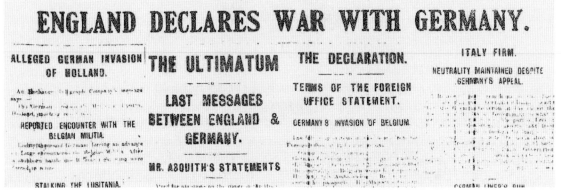

Headline from the *HDE*, 5 August 1914

The proclamation of war was posted in front of the Town Hall, where a portly old gentleman was asked 'Do you expect to be called to the front?' 'Well, I might make a good target,' he jested. It was also posted at the Market Cross, where a large crowd gathered and cheered on reading it. There was an extra bustle around town. Postmen delivered summons to reservists, young women accompanied military boyfriends to the Drill Hall, and the police were despatched to guard railway bridges and tunnels. All excursion trains were cancelled to divert extra carriages for troop transport.

The news had reached 450 Territorials of the 5th Dukes at the Drill Hall during the previous evening. The order to mobilise came at 8.15pm, almost three hours before the public declaration of war. They were medically examined by Major Louis Petro Demetriadi, the battalion's medical officer, who declared a few men and three officers 'not fit.' When the official announcement reached them just after midnight 'the men rose and cheered very enthusiastically.'

They slept on the floor at the Drill Hall, paraded at 8.15am the following morning and then marched through the town via Ramsden Street, New Street and John William Street to the railway station. Hundreds lined the streets, but the initial excitement had abated. The mood was pensive. There were polite and sincere goodbyes and wishes of 'Good Luck', but only occasional cheers and little of the jingoism that accompanied similar departures elsewhere. At the station they were joined by the 7th (Colne Valley) Dukes, taking the number of local men who left that morning to 1100.[2]

The local Territorials left behind in this first wave were 'bewailing the fact' but didn't have long to wait. Amid 'extensive preparations … for war', a further 120 officers and men of the 7th Dukes marched away to the strains of 'Auld Lang Syne' the following Sunday, hundreds lining the streets from Milnsbridge Drill Hall to see them off.[3]

The country's Territorials had signed up pre-war to serve at home. During this first week of the war they were telegraphed to request that they serve abroad. It was likely that most would agree. They were volunteers with presupposed military and patriotic leanings, trained in military drills and open to military expectations and influence. The pressure to conform, spoken or unspoken, was considerable. Across the country, 92% of the Territorials immediately agreed to fight abroad, rising to 96% in the first year. They would be vital in maintaining and developing the numerical strength of the British Army.

By 9 August all of Huddersfield's regular and volunteer troops had gone. The professional soldiers of the small but well-trained British Army were heading for France in the first wave of the British Expeditionary Force (BEF). The two local Territorial Battalions, the 5th and 7th Dukes, were beginning months of arduous training in camps at Doncaster and in Lincolnshire. One evening, approaching camp in near darkness after a particularly gruelling route march, they were challenged at the gate: 'Are you the West Riding?' 'No', came a voice from the ranks. 'We're the Dukes, walking.'[4] They would eventually cross to the continent as part of the 49th Division of the British Army in April 1915.[5]

WHICH IS THE QUICKEST WAY TO THE HOSPITAL MY BOY ?

STAND IN THE ROAD AND SHOUT 'THREE CHEERS FOR THE KAISER', SIR.

True to her liberal traditions, Britain was the only major combatant nation that did not conscript her troops, and was ill-equipped for a land war. Within a month Germany had deployed one and a half million troops to the western front, with a further two and a half million combating the Russians to the east or in reserve. The French army numbered close to one and a half million. By comparison, the BEF of 1914, described by Kaiser Wilhelm as 'a contemptible little army', numbered just 150,000, comprising about 70,000 well-drilled full time troops, plus part-time territorials.[6]

The regulars and territorials of August 1914 represented only a fraction of the numbers Britain would eventually need. For the next year, the BEF, supplemented by more territorials and joined by an increasing number of troops from the Commonwealth, assisted the French in keeping the Allies in the war, primarily on the western front. But, without a massive recruitment campaign, the British army would, sooner or later, be decisively outnumbered.[7]

Recruitment

In Huddersfield there was a brief initial rush to recruit for the forces. Many young men, anticipating excitement, an escape from industrial drudgery or, if trade collapsed, unemployment, needed little incentive to go to war. By 6 August, before any national appeal for volunteers had been made, the Huddersfield Recruiting Office had processed 600 new applications for the regular army or the special reserve.[8]

The national appeal began with the appointment of Lord Kitchener as Secretary of State for War on 7 August. By 11 August his stern features adorned the most famous, enduring poster of the war, fronting a propaganda campaign that achieved its first target of 100,000 men in three weeks. In Huddersfield a further 140 local men joined the colours during the next fortnight. Consistent with the national pattern, as the international situation developed and stories of atrocities in Belgium emerged, more local men rushed to join.[9]

Lord Kitchener, Secretary of State for War, glowers from the recruitment poster
that remains the most enduring image of World War I.
Satirists enjoyed rich pickings at the expense of the authoritarian establishment.

The volunteers would swell the ranks of many of the territorial battalions. The 5th Dukes eventually formed second (2/5th) and third (3/5th) lines. Likewise, the 7th Dukes formed (2/7th) and (3/7th) lines. The 3/5th and 3/7th stayed in England, training and transferring reinforcements as required. Nationally, by January 1915 one million men had volunteered, rising to two and a half million by January 1916.[10]

The famous Kitchener recruitment poster led a powerful propaganda campaign that challenged men's patriotism and virility, and appealed to their senses of adventure, duty and responsibility. Simultaneously, the campaign targeted powerful emotions of love, guilt, pride, shame, fear, anger and hate. The ruthless plundering of Belgium by the German army offered a particularly rich seam. The ransacking of Louvain, and the burning of the priceless collections in its famous library on 25 August, was interpreted as a powerful symbol of German barbarity. The killing of 6500 Belgian hostages, many in cold blood, confirmed them as heartless murderers. The atrocities were so shocking that for many years historians believed them to be exaggerated British propaganda.[11] Numerous posters simply presented an image and asked variations of the question: 'What are you going to do about it?'

The testimonies of local servicemen were consistent with national reports about the plight of many Belgians. Lance-Corporal Thomas Webb wrote of:

> much devastation … A lot of the houses had their roofs blown off, and the country people, with the children … carrying bundles were fleeing to the coast.[12]

Gunner Cyril Pusey described:

> … the Belgian people having to leave their homes and everything they possessed to the Hun. It made our blood run cold for we were longing to get at them. Every place they got to they turned upside down after bombarding it.[13]

On 13 September, a 'Huddersfield officer' wrote:

> All the villages where the Germans have been are completely wrecked and ransacked. Everything they could not take they have destroyed. I saw about six cows lying dead, and just one little calf alive, standing looking at them. Also several dogs lying on the roadside skinned. The roadside is absolutely paved with empty bottles and also fowls' feathers. All the way along there are dead horses …[14]

In Huddersfield those who had not volunteered, or who opposed the war, were subjected to a frenzy of criticism. A letter from EA Beaumont, printed in the *HDE* on 24 August, reflected the mood.

> Stern facts should impress themselves upon the mind. Germany has levied a tax on Liège for two million pounds, Brussels eight million pounds. Bring it home to yourselves. Suppose they got to Huddersfield, demanded five millions in cash within twenty-four hours, made householders feed one or more soldiers and if the lodger took a fancy to anything you had in the house he could take it without asking permission. Every man who is physically fit should volunteer at once to help in defeating Germany, the ruler of which has let hell loose upon Europe.

In a society without public radio or television and a fledgling film industry, poetry was an influential propaganda medium. Publicity about the first of many large local recruitment meetings appeared alongside the following poem in the *HDE* of 24 August.

AN APPEAL TO ARMS
by
W.J.S.

Brave youth of England, flower of every shire,
From cottage, homestead, and from palace, too,
Answer the call to arms with zealous fire,
Yet in the ranks we look in vain for you.

Don't rank with scallywags and corner scum,
Think a bit higher than this poltroon crew,
Your nation's welfare should be yours, now come,
Remember our appeal is meant for you.

The need is urgent and the cause is just
For England's honour and your own be true,
The sands are running, yours a solemn trust,
Let Nelson's signal now appeal to you.

The clichéd stereotyping of non-volunteers as 'scallywags and corner scum' would endure alongside the recruitment campaign's romantic characterisation of the country's past military glories. Nelson's nostalgic pre-battle signal, 'England expects that every man will do his duty', was a particular Godsend, as were the impending commemorations of 1915, the centenary of the Battle of Waterloo and the 500th anniversary of the Battle of Agincourt. On 5 August the *HDE* added *Henry IV Part I* to the mix, praying that:

> … out of this nettle danger, we may pluck the flower safety, as the men of Agincourt, of Crecy and Poitiers, of Trafalgar and Waterloo, faced the danger and won the safety, power and influence of England in days gone by.

Fuelled by news of defeat for the BEF at Mons in the first battle of the war, Huddersfield's first major recruitment event, at the Town Hall on Tuesday 25 August, reflected the growing national mood.

> Never before in the history of Huddersfield have there been such memorable meetings representative of all parties and clashes of the community as took place last night. In order to help in the recruiting of a new battalion of the Duke of Wellington West Riding Regiment the … town seemed to rise as one man to the 'Call to Arms' … Not only was the Town Hall packed to its utmost capacity long before the hour fixed for the meeting, but hundreds vainly clamoured to gain admission. As a consequence an overflow meeting was hurriedly arranged for in the 'Milton Church' Schoolroom. This was soon filled in its greatest capacity, so that a move had to be made to the Drill Hall. Here an audience of some 4,000 people listened to the speeches made from the balcony.[15]

A further 290 volunteers enlisted over the next two days and by 2 September the territorials of the 5th Dukes had 800 men.[16] The meeting's success encouraged a repeat on 3 September, at which Lord Robert Cecil MP moved:

> That we, the citizens of Huddersfield … pledge ourselves to do all in our power to obtain recruits for the army and navy in our town and district, and … hereby express … conviction that …, it is the duty of every young, unmarried, able-bodied man to follow without delay the example of those who, with an enthusiasm and without thought of self, have gone to take their part in the defence of their King and country.[17]

The 'Huddersfield Civilian Recruitment Committee', which covered the borough of Huddersfield and 26 neighbouring urban districts, was inaugurated by 'influential townsmen', which meant mainly professionals, with no working class representatives. Based at the Albany Hall under Captain WG Wrigley, its duties were to recruit '… feed, house, clothe, pay, and drill … men … for the service battalion of the West Riding Regiment', to recruit for the regular army and, ominously, '… to register all eligible men likely to be required later.'

During the next few weeks a further 300 recruitment meetings were held in various workplace, social and leisure venues, covering 'every village and hamlet in the district.' Prominent throughout were Chairman and Vice-Chairman of the recruitment committee, Sir William Raynor and Mr Arthur P Crosland. As part of this campaign a tramcar, illuminated in red, white and blue and decorated with propaganda, 'ran on every route for fourteen nights', frequently halting for open air meetings to rally support, particularly from those who could not attend the town centre events.[18]

Employees in companies that were fulfilling government contracts were particularly targeted. Many single men were told that volunteering guaranteed their job on their return, but failing to volunteer risked redundancy.

In addition to recruitment for the regular forces, the committee aimed to raise a Volunteer 'Citizens'' Battalion from those debarred by age, infirmity or occupation from joining the regular forces – a 'Home Guard.'[19]

THE WAR.

LORD KITCHENER WANTS ANOTHER 100,000 MEN

Young Men of Huddersfield and District,

Answer the Call of Your King and Country.

Having regard to the immediate need for further recruits to His Majesty's Army, I, as Deputy Mayor of this Town, have been requested to and do hereby convene another

MASS MEETING,

to be held in the

TOWN HALL, HUDDERSFIELD,

on **THURSDAY EVENING NEXT,**

the 3rd inst., at 7-30 p.m., which will be addressed by

LORD ROBERT CECIL, M.P.,
Mr. A. J. SHERWELL, M.P.,
Mr. WILL CROOKS, M.P.,
Mr. F. V. HARCOURT,

and other Gentlemen,

Advertisement in the *HDE* on 2 September 1914 for the recruitment meeting in Huddersfield Town Hall the following evening.

As well as attracting the adventurous spirits, the local recruitment campaign's success in August and September owed a little to a slump in trade, particularly in woollen goods. From the outbreak of war, many foreign markets were cut off. Almost immediately, raw materials were scarce, demand slowed and local workers were laid off or had their hours reduced. Within a few weeks this bleak outlook was transformed by huge government orders for khaki, and by the end of November local woollen mills had more orders than they could cope with. Reflecting on the war on 30 March 1919, the *Supplement to the HWE* commented:

> … the pressure of orders for Government clothing became so insistent no complaint could be made as to the members enlisting ... The shortage of labour and the pressure brought to bear upon local manufacturers by Government inspectors for the supply of clothing led to a falling off in the numbers of recruits towards the end of 1914.

A similar boom across much of the West Riding largely explained why recruitment tailed off more quickly in the 'khaki towns' than elsewhere. In Huddersfield, other major industries were beginning to convert to a war footing. Steel factories began to make bomb casings and war-related machinery, and the chemical/dye works were selected and adapted to manufacture explosives as dye and gunpowder are both derivatives of coal tar. There were plenty of legitimate reasons to stay at home, but this did not prevent a great many questions, largely unfounded, about the commitment of local men. The *HWC* even advocated rounding up the local drunks and conscripting them![20]

Many men were simply being pragmatic. They had businesses to run and families who relied on them. For millworkers, the hours of work available offered better remuneration than the shilling per day paid by the army. They had an economic imperative to stay. Not all felt the same spirit of adventure.

The main opposition to the war was on moral grounds, but added to this in Huddersfield were beliefs derived from some of the district's deep-rooted, radical political and religious traditions. Socialist, non-conformist, and anti-imperialist convictions were all aligned with pacifism. Some socialists regarded war as state-sanctioned, capitalist violence against the workers, regardless of nationality. A socialists' mass meeting in St George's Square on Sunday 9 August passed a resolution that:

> We, the workers of Huddersfield, send greetings to our comrades in Germany, France, Russia, Austria, and Serbia, and declare that we have no quarrel with them. We call upon the general Federation of Trade Unions in Britain to communicate at once with the similar organisations in France, Germany, and Russia, with a view to the presentation of a joint demand to the respective Governments that the war shall cease forthwith. We further demand that when the war is ended an international congress of workers shall be held to prevent the further manufacture of war material and to make arrangements for the employment of all people thus displaced.[21]

Later that day in St George's Square, a Trades Council demonstration in support of striking engineers' labourers also condemned the war.

There were also considerable elements in Huddersfield to whom co-operation with the authorities was anathema, particularly if it meant going to war. The district had a history of dissidence and non-cooperation. In 1812, for example, 1000 troops were stationed in Huddersfield to counter repeated Luddite attacks on manufacturing premises and new machinery that was replacing manpower and putting men out of work.[22] Such radical independence was still to the fore in the Great War. There was a hard core who sympathised with those who did not volunteer and, later, supported those who resisted conscription. The national tide of socialism had been rising for several years pre-war, but the vehement left-wing opposition to the war in Huddersfield was very unusual and possibly more extreme than anywhere else.

Some socialists objected to killing other working men irrespective of nationality, and some religious objectors refused to participate in taking life. Others were disinclined to cooperate with a Government they did not vote for. With an electorate of 7.7 million from a population of about 40 million, most of the working class was not enfranchised in 1914.[23]

Opposition to the war from the left was far from unanimous and there were those who reluctantly concluded that, however discontented they were with the pre-war establishment, they would be much worse off should the war be lost. Guest speaker JB Hudson, of the Manchester branch of the Marxist British Socialist Party, shocked his comrades by declaring his support for the war at a meeting in St George's Square on 22 August.[24]

Entrenched political views, combined with industrial and economic factors, complicated and hampered the recruitment campaign in Huddersfield. Local volunteer numbers dropped towards the end of 1914, invoking some public tongue-lashings from recruitment officials, but in the longer term the figures would recover and hold up quite well. For all its home front commitments and political convictions, the local population would collectively fulfill government expectations.

Sport: 'This is not the time to play games.'

Whilst various local issues muddied the recruitment waters, the pro-war patriots had perfect clarity about the role of sport and leisure. It was a waste of time, energy, manpower and resources. A sense of duty pervaded, defined as hard work, requiring personal and collective sacrifice and eschewing enjoyment. Aligned with the Protestant Work Ethic – a term coined by German sociologist Max Weber in 1904 – patriotic commitment was espoused with almost religious fervour.

'Frivolous' activities were pounced upon, almost regardless of whether they deflected young and middle-aged men from enlisting. The *HDE* printed numerous vitriolic letters condemning sports clubs, in particular association and rugby football clubs, that continued to fulfil their usual engagements. Their matches were, after all, played and watched by precisely the demographic group required by the forces.

The critics took succour from an announcement by the secretary of Kent-based Blackheath Rugby Union FC on 31 August:

Rowland Owen

> all matches arranged by us for the coming season … are hereby cancelled. My committee are of the opinion … that it is the duty of every able-bodied man of enlistable age to offer personal war service to his King and country and that every Rugby footballer of the present day comes within the scope of Lord Kitchener's appeal.

Locally, Huddersfield Old Boys RUFC did likewise, eighteen of their players joining the forces, perhaps encouraged by their captain, Yorkshire County star and army officer, Rowland Owen. Laurie Hickson, President of Yorkshire RFU urged other clubs to follow these examples, stating: 'This is not the time to play games.'[25]

In November 1914 Roland Owen wrote to the secretary of Huddersfield Old Boys RUFC, frustrated at the number of sportsmen who had not enlisted.

REPRINTED FROM
"THE WEEKLY DISPATCH"
November 22nd, 1914

This was going to be our great year. Well, so it will be if we send as many on to the field of battle as we send on to the field of play.

Inspired by Rowland Owen's sentiments, on 22 November *The Weekly Dispatch* printed a composite picture of a wounded soldier standing over a fallen comrade in Flanders, with a photograph of a large crowd watching a football match behind them. The War Office adapted it, adding the caption 'Will they <u>never</u> come?' it became one of the most successful recruitment posters of the war.[26]

Cancelling the season was more straightforward in the strictly amateur game of rugby union than it was in the professional ranks of association football and northern union rugby football, where players depended on the game for their living. By continuing their activities, Huddersfield Town FC, Huddersfield Northern Union Rugby FC and their professional leagues were pariahs in the eyes of many. After heavy losses at the Battle of Mons increased the desperation for volunteers to enlist, even the *HDE*'s football correspondent commented:

Footballers are always of necessity the most physically fit of our population. The Blackheath club have taken the lead in the matter, and have cancelled all their fixtures, and other Rugby Union clubs have followed suit. Will the Northern Union and the English [Football] League follow this patriotic example?

Francis H Knaggs, an ophthalmic surgeon, concurred:

It is in appalling thought, when this country's very existence is at stake, that our young men should be spending their time training for sports, when they should be training for the defence of the motherland and their own homes ... there is a time for everything, and ... the present is not one for playing games before thousands of spectators, who should be more usefully employed in their country's cause.[27]

Knaggs practised what he preached, joining the RAMC and rising to the rank of Captain. In 1917 he returned, wounded and weakened by pneumonia. He never recovered, dying at home on 24 June 1917.[28]

An old Honley resident, Walter Knott, now living in Connecticut, wrote after the German navy had bombed Hartlepool, Whitby and Scarborough.

… we all wished the shells could have dropped on some football field with a game in progress. Are Yorkshiremen waiting till the Germans get their guns mounted on Castle Hill or the Standedge before they wake up or has their blood turned to water?'[29]

Thomas P Crosland, who had been Conservative MP for Huddersfield 1892-95, added:

I think you and your readers will agree with me that a football match held at Fartown, and witnessed by some thousands of young fellows, who ought to be at the front, would be a disgrace to the fair name of Huddersfield.[30]

Arthur Hardisty responded with a vigorous defence:

Is it to be understood that in keeping with Mr Crosland's suggested cancellation of all football engagements, the same stricture should be applied to cricket, lawn tennis, golf, bowling, theatres, music halls, picture houses, motoring; to, in fact, any and every form of amusement or pleasure? I put this question because if the stricture is applied to one it should be applied to all. Perhaps Mr Crosland would go further, and suggest that we should draw on all the blinds, and sit in sackcloth and ashes while our gallant soldiers are fighting for their King and country ...

… Then supposing football matches were cancelled, what reason is there to suppose that this would lead to those "thousands of young fellows, who ought to be at the front" actually going to the front? I must also point out that the average football match – whether it be at Fartown or at Leeds Road, is attended by thousands of men who, for many and various reasons, cannot serve their country at the front.

Rightly or wrongly, many football players – as also cricketers, golfers etc. – play as professionals ... The cancellation of matches would therefore lead to considerable shortage in means of sustenance, not to mention the loss to ground staff, caterers, tradesmen etc. ... I certainly do not think it "would be dangerous to the fair name of Huddersfield" if the matches are played at Fartown as usual, as far as circumstances will permit.[31]

Another correspondent, 'Spectator' cited the difference between professional sportsmen and less physical employment:

I should like to learn how many men have given up salaries of £4 per week to join the colours? … In industrial spheres the promise of re-instatement has been made to recruits, but this is not altogether practicable in the case of men whose living depends on their physical fitness and soundness of limb. Even a slight wound might debar them from attaining their former skill with the ball. Hence, the obvious unfairness of comparing footballers with other professions or employments.[32]

The Chief Constable of Bradford valued sport as a distraction in his city where, as in Huddersfield, many woollen industry workers were enjoying increased disposable income.

> … unless they have attractive football matches on Saturday afternoons to attend there is certain to be a deplorable increase in drunkenness.[33]

In February 1915 Prime Minister Asquith received a protest from 'many ministers of religion and the mayors of numerous boroughs, condemning professional football and the playing of cup finals during the present crisis.' He told Parliament that, following negotiations between the War Office and the FA, international matches had been abandoned but that the FA 'did not see their way to stop the playing of cup ties.'[34]

The counter-arguments and the Prime Minister's statement seemingly ended the local feud. In March 1915 the *HDE*'s weekly Golf Chat column reflected the consensus:

> … when you have done what you can for the soldier at the front there would appear to be small reason why you should not follow your normal course in all the ordinary affairs of life, for abstinence from any particular form of pastime will not help at all, and the soldier himself would be the first to counsel the pursuit of ordinary diversions.[35]

Sport had a valuable ally in Lord Derby, who was heavily involved in the Government's recruitment campaign and is credited with originating the concept of the Pals' Battalions. In October 1915 he would became 'Director of Recruiting.' The Epsom Derby was named after his ancestor, the 12th Earl of Derby, he was a racehorse owner, President of the Jockey Club, and, in later life, would become President of the Rugby Football League.[36] In March 1915, the immediate future of horse racing was threatened by legitimate questions about feed and fuel. Lord Derby, emboldened by the Prime Minister's statement, pinned his sporting colours firmly to the mast in a speech at Southport:

> Please understand if racing is stopped, you are going to stop all – races, football, cricket, and all the theatres. I say, 'No, do not stop them.'
>
> As far as the troops in the field are concerned, they like to hear the results of football and cricket… Sport of all kinds is absolutely engrained in every single Englishman. All our similes are taken from sport, and the ideal of a soldier is taken, surely, from sport. The best you can say of a soldier is that he has played the game right well.[37]

A letter from Private J Roebuck of Lockwood, expressing pleasure that 'Town … had beaten Barnsley' was one of several in the *HDE* supporting Lord Derby's view. In May 1918, the *HDE* made a request for cricket clubs to send in their scores, as 'the boys who are far away … are always anxious to see how their old clubs are faring … anything we can do for the boys at the front should receive first consideration.'[38]

Huddersfield Town FC and the Huddersfield Northern Union Rugby Club FC were understandably keen for the public to see them supporting the war effort, and their matches were frequently used to recruit volunteers. On 5 September 1914, after Huddersfield Town had entertained Bury, Arthur P Crosland made an appeal to the Leeds Road crowd:

> The duties of citizenship … did not end in enjoying its privileges, but also included the obligation of defending those privileges.[39]

On 14 November, before a Fartown crowd swollen by numerous wounded soldiers from the battles of Mons, the Marne, Aisne and Ypres, there were several recruitment speeches on behalf of the 232nd Company Royal Engineers at half time, and a further meeting after the match, when GL Paton of the Parliamentary Recruiting Committee commented:

> … the West Riding of Yorkshire stands at the bottom so far as numbers per head of population joining the ranks of recruits ... that is a stain upon their patriotism ... Those men with their wounds are far more eloquent than … I am capable of. Huddersfield have won the game by a margin of 61 points, and I appeal for at least that number of recruits. We must score against the Huns as well as Huddersfield have scored against Hunslet.

The meeting's chairman, W Fillens, scathingly described the locals as 'a cold and undemonstrative people, apparently afraid of waving the Union Jack.' The Huddersfield club's president, Harry Lodge, countered with some propaganda of his own. The Northern Union had granted £250 to the War Relief Fund, and carried out its resolutions to offer players …

> … every encouragement to join the colours ... football should be continued so long as it is not a hindrance to recruiting ... if the playing of any single match prevents even one man from joining the colours that match should not be played …

He highlighted that a great local deterrent to recruitment was the indifference and, in some cases, hostility towards volunteers.

> … some lads who had so bravely joined the colours were almost heartbroken by the callous reception that they had had in the streets. The Fartown crowd showed enthusiasm for football and their magnificent players. That enthusiasm ten times magnified should be shown for those brave chaps who are willing to fight our battle at the front.[40]

The *HDE* eventually committed itself on the issue in its editorial of 22 April 1915.

> Those who have taken such a strong line against recreation during the period of the war have overlooked two important facts – the need of the workers for relaxation and the interest of the soldiers themselves in the various competitions.

Despite all the flak fired at football and rugby, it was probably fortuitous for recruitment officers that the start of the war coincided with the start of the football and rugby seasons. Local volunteer Arthur Barraclough sensed an affinity for the war effort from players of all the football codes.

> If you played football or rugby you were a sportsman, and if anything like this came along you'd go without argument but if you were a yellow-belly you'd do anything to get out of it.[41]

To be called a 'yellow-belly' was second only to 'cheat' as the ultimate sporting insult. Soldiering demanded the qualities that sportsmen respected the most – physical and psychological courage, speed, strength, stamina, skill, toughness, perseverance, determination, teamwork, camaraderie, honesty and loyalty. As the *HDE*'s weekly rugby columnist, 'Rouge', commented:

> I can imagine no men more likely to cause the Germans more trouble than a number of Rugby footballers; hard as nails and trained to take advantage of the slightest opening that presents itself, our footballers are bound to make splendid soldiers.[42]

An anonymous poem in the *HDE*'s Golf Chat column appealed to the masculinity of potential volunteers.

> When you return to the Links again,
> Having answered duty's call,
> What pride we shall feel in our splendid zeal,
> That prompted the giving of all.
>
> From the ends of the earth you will gather –
> From the West and mystic East –
> The joy you will find, in those left behind,
> You will share, and be "none of the least."
>
> Your hands we will grip, with a warmth that will nip,
> As your features we proudly scan;
> Your grit we'll extol, from the depth of our souls,
> And thank God that you acted the "Man."[43]

Players and supporters from association, northern union and rugby union football contributed an estimated 100,000 of the first 700,000 volunteers to join Kitchener's army. Huddersfield Town's left back, Fred Bullock, and centre forward, Jack Cock, both joined the 'Footballers' Battalion.' Several such battalions were formed, the professional players acting as role models for supporters lured by the prospect of serving alongside their sporting heroes.[44]

For now, professional association and northern union rugby football continued at Leeds Road and Fartown, but the impact on local amateur sport was immediate. Mot football clubs of both codes suspended operations. Northern Union clubs Almondbury and Marsden Villa had disbanded before the end of August, Almondbury citing the collapse in local trade and Marsden, as one of the outlying clubs, transport costs.[45] On 24 September, the Huddersfield and District Northern Rugby Union announced:

> Owing to the great European War, and the consequent resignation (for the present season) of several clubs … through players being either in the Territorials or having joined Kitchener's Army, it has very reluctantly been found necessary to suspend the Intermediate League for 1914-15.[46]

By 20 November, the Huddersfield Amateur Football League had just three teams left and also abandoned its season.[47] Many local teams had played their last football of the war.

Even Huddersfield Golf Club, with many members over military age, had its lowest-ever entry for its annual Challenge Bowl in September 1914. All sports tried to balance 'relegating their pastime to the back seat', maintaining their clubs' facilities and finances, and providing healthy recreation to sustain spirits and distract from the incessant anxieties.[48]

By the end of November 1914 between 7000 and 8000 Huddersfield men had joined the armed forces, and were serving abroad or in training. Up to 3000 of them were with the two local battalions, the majority were with battalions in other regiments, some were in the navy and a handful had joined the Royal Naval Air Force.[49] As the seriousness, horror and scale of the war became apparent, all would feel the increasing warmth of public admiration and approval.

On 14 December the *HDE* reported that local recruitment had dropped to its lowest in weeks. Speculation that many must have decided to spend Christmas at home was seemingly confirmed by signs of improvement in January 1915. Over succeeding months, it wasn't so much fluctuating recruitment numbers as the sheer scale of the war and the number of casualties that brought the dreaded prospect of conscription, and related public tension, increasingly to the fore.[50]

Chapter 3

1914: To War

The recruitment campaigns would count for little if the Schlieffen Plan was successful and Germany forced a quick victory over France. The gallant Belgian army bought valuable time, holding up the Germans for ten days at Liège. They also sabotaged their own rail network to delay the transportation of German troops, horses, ammunition, weaponry and food to the fields of battle. It was a shrewd move. Whilst the road network across Europe was in its infancy, the railways would never be more extensive. Prosecution of the war on such an industrial scale would have been impossible without rapid, mass transportations by rail.

Despite Belgian resistance, Brussels fell to the Germans on 20 August. On the same day, the BEF of just 120,000 marched through Belgium to Nimy, north of Mons.[1] Among them were Corporal Thomas Webb, Private Victor Rayner and Gunner Cyril Pusey, all of Huddersfield, and Private Fred Walker of Slaithwaite.

WELL TACKLED!

An 'Examiner Special' cartoon from, 27 August 1914,
representing the gallantry of Belgium against the might of the Kaiser's army

The Battle of Mons

On 23 August Corporal Webb's part of the line moved to a canal bank at Mons where they held the German advance in check, both sides suffering heavy losses under severe fire. A first class shot, Webb believed he 'may have accounted for one or two Germans.' Tired, having no food all day, they were withdrawn five miles back to the support lines, but the Germans broke through their replacements at the front, located the support lines and shelled them again.[2] As Gunner Pusey of the 117th Battery Royal Field Artillery (RFA) put it, 'they were too many for us.'[3]

On 24 August Webb's battalion was ordered to fall back, but their retreat disintegrated into chaos when, '... marching down a road they saw German cavalry coming up another.' Before they could seek cover the Germans spotted them, and chased them into a Wood. In the skirmishes that followed, Webb's sergeant, named Carney, had a 'muscle of one arm torn by a bullet.'

They were told to make their way through the wood as best they could, but Webb became separated from the others. With Germans lying in wait beyond the trees, he found escape impossible. He hid in the wood for two days and nights, with 'nothing to eat except a small cake of chocolate' from his haversack.

Lying 25 yards from the main road, Webb watched with increasing horror as a German transport column, about 30 miles in length, advanced unhindered towards France. This immense German force was now between him and his regiment.

Eventually hunger forced him to leave his refuge. Around 3pm on 26 August he buried his rifle and equipment and set out for the nearest Belgian house. There he was given food and drink, and his hosts confirmed that the Germans had 'overrun the district.'

Carefully avoiding the roads, Webb moved on to a public house, where he was given shelter for the night. Using sign language, he persuaded the locals to provide him with civilian clothes as a disguise, and at breakfast the next morning he was joined by three men of the 15th Hussars. One of them was wounded, and after walking for five miles they left the wounded man at a hospital. There, Webb acquired a map and planned a route to the French frontier to re-join their regiments, but local people convinced them that they would be captured and persuaded them to head for the coast.

Treated with consistent kindness by the Belgians, they travelled via Atha and Lessines to Ghent, picking up three more survivors from the Mons retreat along the way. Using train passes supplied by the local Belgian Commandant, they travelled to Ostend, witnessing much devastation in the Belgian villages. After a night in barracks, they crossed to Folkestone, and journeyed home, Webb arriving in Huddersfield still wearing the clothes given to him by the Belgians. Indicative of Britain's shortage of troops, Corporal Webb was granted just two days' leave before reporting to the Halifax Depot. The *HDE* reassuringly concluded that he was 'anxious to get back to the front again to have another "go" at them.'[4]

Private Rayner may have been close to Webb in the Mons retreat. In a letter to his father, printed in the *HDE* on 10 Sep 1914, he explained:

> Ten of us were cut off from our regiment by the Germans, and we met the German Cavalry in a wood and we had to fight them. It was like 10 to 1. All my comrades were killed with the exception of a Lance-Corporal. We were taken prisoners after being wounded. They took away our rifles and equipment, but fortunately we managed to escape the same night. We walked about for a long time. When we were picked up we were on the Belgian frontier, and were taken to a hospital, where I am now writing from. We have been told that our regiment has been cut up, and there are only about 20 left. If I am reported missing you must take no notice of it, as I shall be out of hospital, and shall join some British troops at Havre, on the coast, and then have another 'go' at them.'

Not all the troops cut off behind German lines were as fortunate as Webb and Rayner. Private Fred Walker of Slaithwaite, a Bandsman with the 2nd Dukes, was captured on 24 August and transported to Germany along with about 150 other prisoners. For four days they were marched through the streets of Doberitz with their hands bound behind their backs, propaganda for the 'gratification of the German public.' At night they were initially compounded in a huge tent, where one of their number unwisely struck a German sentry and assaulted a German officer. When no one would admit to this, all 150 prisoners were marched to the top of a nearby hill and told no one would leave until the culprit's name was divulged. They were held there all day without food until, in the evening, Private Lonsdale from Leeds stepped forward and confessed. He was given two death sentences and executed by firing squad.

Bandsman Walker's war was effectively over. He faced four years of hard manual labour and atrocious food – 'coffee made from water, black bread fit to poison you, and cabbage water for soup' – punctuated by moments of terror, the sentries occasionally firing 'at random amongst the prisoners of the camp.' Without the Red Cross parcels from home, he did not think anyone would have survived. 'We shall never forget the goodness and kindness of our own people sending food and clothing.'[5]

At Doberitz, Fred Walker was joined by Clifford Appleyard of Hillhouse, and Oswald Beaumont from Horbury, who were among 936 British sailors taken prisoner at the fall of Antwerp on 9 October.[6]

Seaman Beaumont and 71 crewmates had spent the first 65 hours after capture in a van where, periodically, German Red Cross nurses threw hot coffee over them.[7] Despite their early capture, they had played a valuable part in the outcome of the war. Weeks of stubborn Belgian and British resistance at Antwerp occupied substantial numbers of German troops who might otherwise have tipped the precarious balance in the first battles of the war.[8]

Whilst others were isolated or captured, Gunner Pusey retreated with his battery.

I don't think I had ten hours' sleep on the retreat, and it lasted a good week ...[9]

Locations of battles of 1914 – Mons, Le Cateau, Marne, Aisne and Ypres.

The Battle of Le Cateau

The major stand during the British retreat came on 26 August at Le Cateau, where Sir Horace Smith-Dorien organised an artillery-based rearguard against overwhelming odds. Supported by French cavalry, they endured a fierce German bombardment, stalling their advance for a day before retiring to St Quentin. The British suffered almost 8000 casualties. Lieutenant Rowland Owen of the 2nd Dukes was one of the 32,000 survivors. Smith-Dorien was criticised for his decision, but it would be five invaluable days before the Germans in this part of their advance were ready to engage in further combat.[10]

The British and French forces re-grouped on the eastern outskirts of Paris. There, they awaited the Germans and seemingly inevitable defeat. Amidst much panic in the French capital was a Fartown man, 27-year-old Archibald MacDonald Scott, who had worked for several years on the educational staff of *The Times* in Paris. Whilst the rest of the newspaper's staff left for their homes or other places of safety, Archibald volunteered to remain at the offices to 'receive messages and send important wires to London.' For several days he was 'in entire charge of the Paris edition of *The Times*.' In December 1915, still in Paris, Archibald enlisted as a private with the Northumberland Fusiliers. He went on to earn promotion to sergeant in just seven weeks and a reputation as 'one of the finest leaders' in his regiment.[11]

To the surprise of the Allies, the Germans delayed their final assault and lost their potentially decisive forward momentum. Private Harry Mulleague from Outlane had retreated with the 2nd Dukes. The belief among their troops was that Von Kluck, Commander of the German First Army, 'either out of deference to the Crown Prince or acting on orders received, halted for some hours ... to enable the Crown Prince to come up and have the honour of taking the city.'[12] In fact, Von Kluck had advanced to within 13 miles of Paris, then wheeled south eastwards to support the more cautious Karl von Bulow, who had underestimated the strength of the German position and halted the German Second Army's advance. This exposed the First Army's right flank. French commander, General Joseph Joffre, seized the opportunity to re-group. French troops flooded into the Paris region by train, enabling him to launch a counter-attack against the vulnerable German flank, breaking their line and driving the invaders back to the River Marne.[13]

The First Battle of the Marne

The week-long Battle of the Marne began on 5 September. There, the Allies enjoyed their first and strategically crucial success. The cost, however, was huge. Any illusions local people had about the glory of this victory were dispelled by a letter from Driver James McKenzie of the Army Service Corps (ASC) to Andrew Wadsworth, a Holmfirth butcher, published in the *HDE* on 22 Sep 1914:

> I saw a full train load of wounded coming from the front, some with half their faces blown away, others with bullets in their arms, hands and legs. I can tell you that your slaughter-house never looked worse. I saw one fellow of the Gordon Highlanders trying to get a bullet out of his knee with a jack knife.

In glorious late-summer weather, the Germans retreated from the Marne with the Allies literally in hot pursuit, many of the British troops naively throwing away their greatcoats. Bombardier Anthony Greenwood from Huddersfield, a reservist with the Ammunition Supply Column, had several narrow escapes as the retreating Germans shelled their wagons.[14]

The Battle of the Aisne

On 12 September the Germans crossed the River Aisne and waited. When the British tried to cross they came under heavy fire, Private Harry Mulleague describing it as one of the fiercest bombardments he had seen.[15] Occupying the Allied forces by the river, the Germans controlled the last part of their retreat and entrenched on the high ground beyond. The British camped for the night close to the river, but the weather suddenly changed for the worse. One Huddersfield officer of the 2nd Dukes suffered ...

> ... a wretched night ... simply out in the open in the pouring, cold rain. It was the first night we have not had to get up at 3am. Just luck. The night before I was in a lovely hayloft.

Gunner Pusey recalled that all of his Battery 'were wet through to the skin and ... it was three weeks before he had a chance to dry himself.'[16]

The British assault on the German positions began the following day. The experiences of another Huddersfield soldier, Sergeant Arthur Guest, were reported in the *HDE* of 14 October 1914.

> The next morning we marched up a hill, and instantly came under heavy artillery fire. Our advance then lay across a number of level fields, affording but little cover. Gradually the fire became hotter and machine guns and rifles began to "pop" at us. A thick mist lay in front, and we could see nothing to fire at. A few hundred yards further and the volume of fire was terrible, shells and bullets dropping like rain. I quickly lost my officer and then took charge of the platoon, about 50 men. We advanced by short rushes for about a half mile and then came to a road with a shallow bank at the edge, which gave us a little cover. Here we re-organised and I had 32 men left. We again advanced, this time for about a mile, which took about three hours to cover ... we could not get more than 15 or 20 yards at a time. We were ordered to halt here and hold the ground we had gained, and this we did ... I did not hear the number of casualties among the rank and file of the battalion, but in my own company [of 100] we lost 76. I seemed to bear a charmed life that day, and began to think I should never be hit, men continually dropping on my right and left the whole day. At night we again re-organised, and then entrenched ... The enemy had retired about half a mile and were also "digging in" ...
> We stayed in the trenches for about six days after this, being shelled by heavy artillery from

day-break till sunset every day. Once or twice they would send a few over in the night and we would man the trenches expecting a night attack, but nothing happened until about midnight – 19th [September] – when they commenced a heavy bombardment. This was a night attack in earnest and we stood up and lined the trenches. It was a dark night and we could see nothing. While looking over the top a shell burst in front, and something hit me in the eye. It seemed like a blow from a sledgehammer and down I went. When I came to about an hour after I found our chaps had beaten the enemy off, though the shells still came over. I had a bandage round my head, also a terrible aching … rain started falling heavily, but I could not be moved till daybreak. I was then taken to the nearest field hospital, had my wound bathed and dressed, and then was moved by motor ambulance to another field hospital about ten miles away ... I believe this battle still continues … I hope our boys are not in the same old trenches.

Arthur had been in the trenches for a week. He was taken to a French hospital where, endeavouring to save his left eye, surgeons removed his right one. He survived with limited vision, but his war as a combatant was over.

Private Norman Townend of Huddersfield described the first trenches dug at the Battle of the Aisne.

You will wonder what trenches are. Well, they are a long line dug in the field, about 3 feet wide and about 5 feet deep, and we put the dirt up in front just high enough to look and fire over.[17]

With neither side advancing or retreating, the trenches needed to offer more shelter and protection. An officer from the 2nd Dukes organised construction of one of the first dug-outs.

Yesterday I was told to put in props to the covering of the shelter trenches, so I went to my platoon and said I wanted some detailers. Two of them came and took a tremendous interest and pride in the job, and did it extremely well. One of them guaranteed that when he had finished the job he would undertake to drive a wagon and horses over the trench. I suppose he really meant that he would undertake to sit inside while somebody else drove the wagon; that would be a fairer test.[18]

Private Townend continued:

We can see the Germans all day a few 100 yards in front, and we keep having a pop at them; also they do the same to us. We get a few killed and wounded every day. There was a fellow shot in the head and killed about six yards off me yesterday morning. We buried him at night. You can't do it before it gets dark, or you would share the same fate. There is no service here – just dig a hole and place him in as well as you can. We get a bit of wood and make a cross and put his name on. There he is left. Me and my mate Fred thought we were shot the other morning. We were digging our hole a bit deeper, when bang; we were both shocked for a bit, but when we came round we saw it had hit just in front and sent the dirt and powder all in our face and made a lot of little marks. It is all right in the day but it is cold at night in these trenches. We do not do much fighting during the day but sleep and eat and do our fighting at night. It is all artillery firing during the day. They fire hundreds of shells. They are deafening and airships are flying round all the day. They are playing a great part in this war, and there are some brave fellows among them. They go right over the enemy's lines and we watch them fire up at them.[19]

Gunner Pusey had a similar narrow escape. During a nighttime barrage, he was moved from his

Battery's Number 3 to Number 4 gun, and took shelter behind it '... for pieces of shell and shrapnel bullets were flying in all directions.' The following morning they found Number 3 gun virtually severed in two. Its gunners 'could only be identified by the discs ... hung around the neck, and in some cases even these were blown off.' The solemn duty of burying them had to wait until evening. Their 'daily ration of three or four hours' shellfire,' continued to take a heavy toll, Gunner Pusey, commenting:

> It was nothing ... to see infantrymen passing ... minus some part of their bodies.[20]

Like so many, he was becoming desensitised to the sight of human slaughter. It was the only way to cope.

A Huddersfield officer of the 2nd Dukes found:

> ... the danger of these shells is that when one does at length come under a bit of rifle fire in one's delight one treats it as child's play although it must be far more dangerous really. Some of the enemy are only about sixty yards away from our position and the rest are about three hundred yards away. There are snipers all over the place – in the woods and up trees – and they carry on a hearty old shoot all day. I always wish I understood German when I hear the enemy in their trenches, talking in the evenings.[21]

Trench warfare, first endured at Aisne, would characterise the war on the western front. Entrenched on the steep northern slopes of the Aisne Valley, the British were shielded from most of the German shells, but found attacking the Germans' higher positions very difficult. With both sides occupying defensible territory, the first, mobile, phase of the war was over. The war of attrition had begun. From this point, dislodging the enemy would be extremely hazardous. Any move above or beyond the cover of the trench wall was fraught with danger, and charging the enemy was suicidal. It would be more than three years before a major attack by either side yielded more casualties than it cost.[22]

The stalemate at Aisne cost 12,000 British casualties. One of them was Huddersfield Town full back, Larrett Roebuck. Reported 'missing in action', his death was confirmed in January 1916.[23] The Aisne offensive was abandoned on 28 September.[24]

Both sides now began to extend their lines of trenches north and south in what is misleadingly known as 'The Race to the Sea.' In fact, each was attempting to outflank the other. The British were particularly keen to protect their northern flank to avoid being cut off from the Channel ports, their supply routes for reinforcements, ammunition, equipment and food. The Germans were equally keen to capture the ports to eliminate Britain from the war.[25]

The First Battle of Ypres

On 20 October 1914 the Germans attacked the British at Ypres, aiming to break through to Calais and Dunkirk. The Ypres Salient – where the British line bulged into enemy territory – was strategically very important as it drove a wedge between the German troops, leaving those at one side disconnected from those at the other. But, with three sides to defend, it was also a vulnerable part of the British line.[26]

The First Battle of Ypres lasted for a month. Bombardier Anthony Greenwood's Ammunition Supply Column drove horse-drawn trucks of shells, bullets and replacement rifles to the front line day and night, surviving frequent attacks to stop them.

> ... we could see shells blowing the fronts of houses into the roadway. The shock of the bursting shells lifted some of the drivers clean out of their saddles.[27]

Despite justified concerns from British Commander Lord John French that his forces were running dangerously short of ammunition, the fighting was intense.[28] Almondbury Police Constable, Lance-Corporal Walter Bentley, serving with "A" Company, King's Shropshire Light Infantry, 6th Division, wrote:

> ... spending a few cruel weeks in the trenches. Oh, my word, it was worse than awful! Never have I experienced any such thing like it. We fought on, charged with bayonets, and they tried to shell us all out of our trenches. Shrapnel was bursting all around us ... I am sorry to say our casualties were about -------- (The number is blotted out by the Censor) ... If during the day

one pops his head up above the trenches, a sniper will shoot at him.

> When shrapnel bursts at night it illuminates the whole sky and trenches and it … scatters after and spreads for fully 200 yards … [shrapnel] has accounted for the majority of our wounded. I have now had a good taste and fully realise what fighting is – mighty thuds of guns, terrific roars of rifles worse than an earthquake, which I cannot better name than hell upon earth.[29]

Several times the Germans almost broke through the British lines. By 1 November even British cooks, grooms and drivers were pressed into front line action.

On 8 November German troops captured a trench occupied by a company of the Duke of Wellington's West Riding Regiment. Their officer was killed and Company Sergeant-Major Albert E Taylor of Paddock took command. Supported by Lance-Sergeant E Pogson of Primrose Hill, who commanded the right half of the company, Taylor led a counter-attack. A fierce skirmish ensued but, with 'conspicuous skill and gallantry,' they recaptured the trench and handed it over to a relieving company. This courage and initiative earned Taylor and Pogson the DCM, the first awards received by Huddersfield soldiers in the war.[30]

Just over a week later, on 15 November, Taylor was critically injured.

> … about noon ... I was with my company in the trenches, and just on my right was a big chateau, which required holding at all costs, as the enemy had tried several times to capture it. I went into the house to see how some men of my company were going on when a severe bombardment took place. Shell after shell came pouring into the upper rooms of the house, and at last one of the floors gave way. I was hit on the head by the bullets [shrapnel] from a shell, and then buried by the fall of the building. How I was extricated I don't know. I eventually found myself on my way to the divisional hospital. From there I was sent to a hospital in Boulogne.

Taylor was then transferred to a hospital ship back to England.[31]

The battle took a heavy toll on Gunner Pusey's battery. After three weeks in the thick of it nearly all had been wounded or killed and the survivors were withdrawn to reorganise and re-equip. Pusey …

> … was lucky enough to draw a grey shirt out of the hat, which was the only change I had for three months. The old shirt nearly walked away on its own when I took it off.

He was soon back in the action. On 17 November, evading sniper-fire, he took shelter in a farmhouse and awaited the cover of darkness. The snipers waited too, and in the evening he emerged to another hail of bullets. Darting for some haystacks, he was shot in the leg. Now on all fours, he 'dragged himself through the mud until he came to some infantry' who helped him back to a field hospital. He was immediately operated upon, then moved to Boulogne for three further operations before returning to England. Five weeks in Manchester Royal Infirmary followed, and he eventually returned to his Huddersfield home in late January 1915.[32]

The Allied line, strengthened by the arrival of the first Canadian troops, held at Ypres, but the back of the original BEF had been broken. Sergeant Guest, Sergeant-Major Taylor and Gunner Pusey were among 90,000 British casualties since the Battle of Mons. Of those who had landed in August, an average of one officer and 30 men of the 100 comprising each company remained. The need to recruit and train volunteers was paramount. French losses were also very heavy. Germany had made some minor gains, but had suffered 170,000 casualties.[33]

Many British casualties were patched up and returned to the front. Sergeant Major Albert Taylor was back in Belgium by the spring of 1915, but he had not suffered the last of his injuries.[34]

Ypres was the last major battle of 1914. Both sides now concentrated on fortifying and extending their trenches. By the end of the year, the front line of trenches stretched almost 500 miles, north to the Belgian coast at Nieuport, and south to the Swiss border. In many places there were lines of reserve trenches, connected to the front line trenches by communication trenches.[35] Both sides zig-zagged their trenches so that the trench walls would absorb the blast and shrapnel from shells, rather than channelling them along the trench.[36] Before the winter was over, 20,000 British troops would be treated for trenchfoot caused by permanently wet feet. In the worst cases infection turned to gangrene, requiring amputation.[37]

In the month prior to the Battle of the Marne, there had been more troop mobility and more land lost and gained, than there would be for over three years. For now, the stalemate suited the Allies more than the Germans. The Schlieffen Plan had failed. France had not fallen. Although the Russians had been out-manoeuvred and their Second Army routed at the Battle of Tannenberg, their First Army had dug in at Warsaw, committing Germany to a war on two fronts. Proportionately, Britain had lost far more troops than the other nations. She needed time to recruit, to train her replacements, and to integrate further forces from the Commonwealth.[38]

''BUNKERED!''

Satirising the failure of the Schlieffen Plan to secure a quick victory on the western front, thereby avoiding war on two fronts, the caption reads:
Francis Joseph: "For Heaven's sake, William, hurry up and get out of that bunker!
That Russian fellow's on the tee already, and he'll be playing through in a minute!"

As the lines of trenches lengthened, so did the likely duration of the war. Christmas came and went, and the war was not 'over.' The Christmas Day Armistice of 1914, when troops exchanged gifts and played football with the enemy in No Man's Land, 'allayed all rumours' that the Germans were 'stricken in morale, poorly clothed and underfed.'[39] As the major combatant nations continued to pour men and arms into the combat zones, it became increasingly clear that this was war on an unprecedented scale – and it had only just begun.

Chapter 4

1914: Kindling the Home Fires

Excitement, Panic and 'Spy-mania'

In Huddersfield, the declaration of war left patriotism, excitement, panic and consternation in its wake. Members of 'a well-known club in the town … broke into cheers,' except for one gentleman who …

> … stood out of the demonstration, and when asked by his … boisterous companions why he did not cheer replied, "This is much too serious a matter for cheering. I will cheer with the best of you when peace is proclaimed."[1]

A rush to stock up on food was nipped in the bud by local shopkeepers, who prevented a shortage by 'refusing orders for more than a reasonable quantity of goods.'[2]

As people braced themselves for Britain's first European war for a century, they were captivated by information from newspapers, public meetings and gossip. There was widespread uncertainty about the methods and reach of the German war machine, and as news and opinion merged with gossip and rumour, 'spy-mania' swept the country. On 14 August, the *HDE* reported:

> There have been spies and rumours of spies these past few days sufficient to satisfy the most ardent lover of such excitement. But the prize for spy hunting must be given to Crosland Moor. The other day … great excitement was caused in the vicinity of the tram terminus in this lovely suburb of the borough. There dismounted from the car a party of foreign-looking individuals, the appearance of whom was not at all to the liking of the peaceable inhabitants of the district.
>
> Apprehension quickly grew into the most intense excitement and alarm when it was seen that members of the party began to chalk a curious message on the flags outside a local shop. They were Germans! What could they be seeking in this part of the world? They were up to no good, at all events! Immediately the answer was supplied. They were going to poison the water in the Blackmoorfoot reservoir, or else blow up the banks and create suffering and devastation in that way. People began to draw supplies of water before the evil work could be accomplished. The wildest rumours existed.
>
> The police were telephoned for, and pending their appearance the mysterious message in chalk was jealously guarded.

The rumours 'gained strong credence in the Honley and Berry Brow district' when a couple actually fell ill. Was it true that people had 'been poorly through the water being poisoned'? An 'old man in Honley' put the record straight.

> Now ot isn't lad. But ther' wormonny a one badly wi' t' thowts on it; an' they worfetchin' watter thre' t' wells here, asteed o' usin' aat o' t' taps. Why … ther' wor' one couple just finishin' gettin' the'r breakfast when th' next door neighbour coom in to tell 'em they worn't to use onny tap watter. It 'ad been 'pooisined'. Well they booath began o' feelin' right poorly in a toos-three minuite. They gain a gooid doose a' salt an' water, an' then they felt war, an' thout they wor baat to dee straight off. Yahivver, they lingered on an aar or two, an then t' wahfe – shoo's a careful sooart – bethourt her they'd plenty o' summat to eyt i' th' haass, an' Aw expect shoo felt a biot empty lahk after t' salt an' watter an' shoo sed,
>
> "Well, Ben, lad, if we're baan to dee we'll 'ave a gooid dinner, fust at onny rate." Soa shoo set to an' cooked a first-rate dinner, an' it acted laik magic. They mended right away after they'd etten it. But they didn't feel right fair comfortable till they'd yard it wor all fake.

The hysteria subsided, along with the self-inflicted upset stomachs, once someone 'more intelligent and learned than the rest' translated the chalked message. It was in Esperanto, the writers were Dutch Esperantists on holiday, and the message was to the remainder of their party, who were arriving by a later tramcar. Two weeks into the war, Blackmoorfoot Reservoir wasn't quite so high in the Kaiser's priorities after all. The *HDE* concluded:

> The reservoir has neither been blown up nor poisoned. The people of Crosland Moor are again satisfied with the normal supplies from the taps, and are once more able to sleep at nights. The moral is – and it has been emphasised since the outbreak of hostilities – keep cool.[3]

Beginnings of the Great Fundraising Initiatives

In 1914 there was no National Health Service, a meagre state pension for the over 70s, and modest benefits limited to wage earners who became unemployed or ill. Communities helped themselves. Collections, fundraising events and philanthropy from the better off were essential and integral to local life. Wartime took this to new levels. Memories of the community's response to the Boer War, which ended in 1902 and had impacted on the families of local servicemen, were still fresh.

Huddersfield's response to the declaration of war on 4 August 1914 was swift and impressive. On Friday 7 August the Huddersfield Insurance Committee met to prevent and alleviate distress in families of those called up, and also of those who had already lost their jobs through 'the dislocation of industry.'[4]

By 12 August, at the behest of the Mayoress, Mrs Mary Blamires, Mrs Kilner Clark had inaugurated the 'Huddersfield Women's Fund for Sick and Wounded Soldiers and Sailors.' This was initially based at the Guild of Help Office in Ramsden Street before moving to the Parochial Hall in George Street. Later its headquarters moved to Westgate and, in January 1916, back to Ramsden Street. This magnificent organisation operated far beyond its original brief, working for the benefit of all servicemen, sick, wounded or able bodied, and their families. Sustaining its efforts for the duration of the war, it raised £34,761 through entertainments, whist drives, garden parties and flag days. About half was spent on wool and other materials from which an army of volunteers created comfortable clothing for the troops. 'Never in history has there been so much activity in knitting,' commented the *HDE* on 3 October 1916, as the Committee dispatched its 200,000th garment. The Fund's Committee coordinated the efforts of over 2000 women, including prolific groups such as the 'Needlework Guild' and the 'Women of the Colne Valley.'

Supplemented by donated goods, the Committee dispatched over half a million items by the end of the war. They sent out regular supplies of 'bandages, including skillfully made Davis slings', plus 'socks, mittens, sun shields, casualty bags, other garments and pillow cases,' and responded to specific requests for recreational items such as 'magazines, books, games and footballs.'

All manner of shortages arose and the Huddersfield women were unfailingly quick to respond. Their resourcefulness was apparent as early as September 1914 when, learning that the soldiers on the Western Front had few if any bathing facilities, they ran a successful 'Tubs for Tommies' campaign.[5] Simultaneously, as the weather turned suddenly colder prior to the Battle of Aisne, they collected and sent out thousands of blankets, and supplied almost 1000 greatcoats to the Halifax depot.[6]

Children were inspired to emulate their efforts.

> …cases are on record of little children of the poor going into the Bureau and announcing shyly, but proudly, "Please we have had a little stall in our yard and charged a ha'penny to come in, and there is eighteen pence for the soldiers."[7]

In the same week that the women's fund was founded, the national Prince of Wales Distress Fund was announced. Local collections for this were coordinated through the Town Hall office of the Mayor, Alderman Joseph Blamires. Boxes were distributed among shopkeepers and in its first week the district raised £8867 11s, including several three figure sums from local dignitaries.[8]

This fund for assisting the needy grew quickly, boosted by regular initiatives such as a 'Drop Something into the Box' appeal over Christmas 1914, which raised £294 despite several boxes being stolen.[9] Given the frequency of fundraising, and the numbers of volunteers and locations involved, reports of such pilfering are rare.

The Mayoress,
Mrs Mary Blamires
and the Mayor,
Alderman Joseph
Blamires, who both
worked tirelessly for
various war funds

Local organisations further swelled the Prince of Wales Fund. On 25 August Huddersfield Northern Union Rugby FC donated £100, stung by criticism that receipts from its pre-season practice matches had been given to the local District League and not to the war fund.[10] On 31 August, a special cricket match between Slaithwaite and Marsden raised £4.[11]

Other organisations gave assistance in kind. Members of Huddersfield Automobile Club offered their cars, at their own expense, 'for the use of the Government', an arrangement later formalised, primarily for the transport of wounded troops.[12] The Huddersfield and District Rifle Club 'received many applications' for practice on its range at Brockholes and, to facilitate this, announced on 10 August that all club competitions had been suspended.[13] South Crosland National School repeated their operetta *Princess Chrysanthemum* with proceeds going to the war funds.[14] The Hippodrome Theatre began a wartime trend for local places of entertainment by giving free seats to the wives of soldiers or territorials called away.[15]

War-themed propaganda abounded in the theatres, usually in the guise of 'stirring military dramas', and in the cinemas, where censored newsreels showed footage from the front.[16] Huddersfield's various music societies helped to allay fears about their futures by committing some or all of their profits to various war relief funds.[17]

Responding to reports of the humanitarian disaster in Belgium, Huddersfield's 'Belgian Relief Fund' was founded at the end of August and raised £178 12s in its first week, rising to £2333 18s by the end of the year. By then a 'Belgian Famine Fund' had also raised £100 specifically to send food to the beleaguered country.[18]

The First Belgian Refugees

On 7 October, Huddersfield saw the human suffering first-hand. That afternoon the local Refugee Committee heard that 60 Belgians – 19 men, 17 women and 24 children – would be on the 5.34pm train from Kings Cross, part of a national distribution by the 'overwhelmed' Belgian Refugees Committee in London. Word spread quickly and a crowd of about 5000 turned up to greet them. It was …

> …a typical Yorkshire welcome although there was more than a tinge of sadness about it. They are the guests of the town of Huddersfield, and Huddersfield will see that they are made comfortable until the war cloud has lifted from their unhappy land. But the sight of the refugees with the bundles containing all their worldly possessions was very pathetic. It brought tears to the eyes of many among the thousands gathered in St George's Square and along the route to Royds Hall. A lump arose in many a throat as the refugees were driven away, and altogether the reception, though cordial and hearty, had a very sad side.

The Belgians had fled from districts around Brussels and from Malines where, after five bombardments, there was scarcely a building left. Most of the men were skilled tradesmen – plumbers, joiners, wood-turners and chair-makers.[19]

A week later two Belgian children were admitted to Crow Lane School.[20] Local schools continued to accept refugees, the South Crosland National School Log Book for 8 February 1915 recording:

> Admitted two Belgian children Jan and Anna de Coster aged respectively 9 and a half and 10 and a half.

Royds Hall was only temporary accommodation for the refugees. Most of them were taken in by local families, and many lifelong friendships were formed. Huddersfield Golf Club deflected criticism for vetoing use of their clubhouse by donating £418 for the Belgian Relief Fund, £200 from the club and the rest from members' donations.[21]

The First Wounded Soldiers

At teatime on Friday 30 October, three weeks after the first Belgians arrived, there were further harrowing sights at Huddersfield Railway Station – the district's first convoy of 100 wounded soldiers.

> The arrangements which have been made in Huddersfield and District for the accommodation of wounded soldiers have at last been taken advantage of by the authorities and the first contingent, numbering 100, is due to arrive this evening.[22]

The troops, representing many different regiments from various parts of the country, were heartily cheered by a large crowd as they emerged. The encouragement melted to pathos as the blood-splattered, broken bodies hobbled, or were carried on stretchers, into St George's Square, some of them missing a limb. Sympathy for the suffering in front of them was accompanied by a shocking realisation. This was what modern weaponry could do. Their friends and loved ones were equally vulnerable.

Huddersfield, along with other towns and cities, had spent several weeks preparing for this moment. The four divisions of the Huddersfield Corps of the St John Ambulance Brigade – Huddersfield Central, Honley, Huddersfield Railway and Huddersfield Nursing – were supplemented by the Automobile Club's private cars and vans, a handful now converted into private motor ambulances. The Corporation and various firms and individuals added to the assortment of vehicles. This impressive coordination of local resources saw all the casualties transported to various care locations in just over an hour.[23]

Official ambulances and motor volunteers await a convoy of wounded soldiers outside Huddersfield Railway Station

Fifty five were driven to the Royal Infirmary and the rest were distributed among three nursing homes, 30 to Durker Roods at Meltham, under the care of trained nurses supervised by Matron, Mrs Wrigley, ten to Trinity Street Nursing Home and five to Bradley Lane. The cost of accommodation and treatment was met by the Local Board, assisted by the ever-adaptable Women's Committee which supplied 'a consignment of shirts, bed jackets and dressing gowns, pillows and other useful articles.'[24]

Continuing to improvise its medical and humanitarian measures, Huddersfield adapted resourcefully, generously and sincerely. Sustaining such efforts for the duration of the war would stretch even the most resilient. For the next four years, the demands on everyone – professional or artisan, skilled or unskilled, employed or volunteer – would be unrelenting, as the tendrils of the war crept remorselessly into every aspect of life.

Chapter 5

1914-15: The U-Boat Menace

Whilst Belgium, Britain and France were surprising Germany by their stubborn resistance on land, Germany struck a serious blow to British confidence and morale at sea. The sinking of HMS *Pathfinder* by the German submarine U24 off the Berwickshire coast on 5 September could be viewed as an isolated incident, until disaster struck three old armoured cruisers just over a fortnight later.[1]

The Sinking of HMS *Aboukir*, HMS *Hogue* and HMS *Cressy*

HMS *Aboukir*

On 22 September 1914, HMS *Aboukir*, HMS *Hogue* and HMS *Cressy* were on routine patrol in the North Sea, 22 miles off the Dutch coast. Leading Stoker of the *Aboukir* was John Pascall of Huddersfield. At 6.25am, asleep in his hammock, John was suddenly awoken by a loud explosion and a juddering through the ship. A torpedo fired by German submarine U9 had broken the ship's hull.

Many men were trapped in the flooding lower decks, but John found a route to the open deck, joining other crew who had calmly assembled there. Captain John Drummond, gave the order, 'Abandon ship, every man for himself.'

HMS *Aboukir* keels over, sailors lining its port side

As the ship keeled to starboard John clambered over the railings onto its port side. He waited until it sank a little deeper then, as its side became almost horizontal, walked down it and plunged into the chilling water. Three times he tried to swim away from the wreckage, but the suction dragged him back hard against the hull, injuring his back and his left foot. As the *Aboukir* disappeared beneath the waves, the suction eased and he was strong enough to swim clear. Many others were not so lucky.

Removing most of his clothing, he started to swim towards the approaching *Hogue*, where the captain had launched the lifeboats and ordered wooden objects to be thrown into the water. John had almost reached the *Hogue* when two torpedoes struck her, causing a huge explosion. The *Hogue* too began to sink rapidly. John and the other survivors began to swim towards their last hope, the *Cressy*.

Although tiring, he 'helped another man who was beginning to feel the effects of the struggle in the water.' As he dragged him towards the *Cressy* he saw the periscope of submarine U9 break the surface. The *Cressy* fired, but the submarine replied with two torpedoes. John was just a few yards away when one of these exploded into the *Cressy's* starboard side. Then a second torpedo struck home. The bow of the stricken ship dipped and its starboard propeller spun crazily out of the water. For twenty minutes the *Cressy* became ever more vertical until it plunged, bow first, beneath the waves.

With crew from all three ships in the water, the sea was 'a struggling mass of humanity.' Many had already drowned, a few were aboard lifeboats and others, including John and his colleague, clung to timber. More were drowning by the minute, either exhausted, unable to move with cramp, or losing consciousness through hypothermia. Somehow, John kept himself and the crewmate he was rescuing afloat until they were pulled into one of the *Hogue's* lifeboats. Some were passed from lifeboats to the *Hogue's* picket boat and steam pinnace, which had been launched before the main vessel sank.

One of John's crewmates from the *Aboukir* had scrambled aboard the *Hogue* immediately before it was sunk, escaped again, and was hauled onto the *Cressy* only to be sunk again. He survived and remained the only man in the entire war to be sunk on three different ships.

After several hours, a ship was sighted. It was a Lowestoft trawler. Dutch steamers *Flora* and *Titan*, followed. John clambered aboard the trawler where, along with other survivors, he removed his wet clothing and was wrapped in fishing nets for warmth. Taken to Lowestoft, he was treated by the ambulance corps. He was one of 850 survivors, but 1459 lost their lives.

A court of inquiry blamed the senior officers. John Drummond, Captain of the *Aboukir*, was at fault for not zigzagging, a standard strategy to evade submarine attack, and for not calling for the assistance of destroyers. Rear Admiral Christian had not told Drummond that he could summon destroyers. The bulk of the blame was directed at the Admiralty which, against the advice of senior officers, persisted with a dangerous patrol which was of limited value. Germany had superior armaments in submarines, torpedoes and mines. The U-boat threat had been anticipated, but the warnings unheeded. The incident had shown that a U-boat only had to sink one boat to earn easy strikes at others as they stopped to pick up survivors.

The U9's captain and crew returned to Germany as heroes. Just seven weeks into the war, the German U-boat had proved an effective weapon against Britain's warships. The implications for Britain's security, and for the transportation of men and supplies to and from the continent, were grim, and the incident had a profound effect on naval strategy for the rest of the war.

The North Sea became a virtual No Man's Land. British dreadnoughts, based at the heavily fortified Scapa Flow, patrolled its northern edge between the northern isles and Scandinavia. To the south, the Dover Patrol controlled the English Channel, protecting British troop, supply and hospital ships on their daily voyages. After numerous German ships were sunk in the first weeks of the war, it was clear that this blockade prevented the German Navy from getting out, and many of her imported goods from getting in. Sustained for the next four years to great effect and with relatively low loss of life, it was arguably the most successful tactic of the war. Germany was largely reduced to occasional, risky forays against Britain's east coast, and opportunist, but nevertheless devastating U-boat sinkings for the rest of the war.

The *HDE* concluded its report by emphasising the local man's bulldog spirit. John Pascall's 'one wish' was 'to get into active service again … on a destroyer or submarine, as he thinks he might have a better opportunity of satisfaction for the loss of his ship.'[2]

Design for an allegorical group to be presented to Admiral Von Tirpitz, founded on the famous statue of "Laocoon" in the Vatican.

Cartoon from the *HDE*, 25 February 1915, depicting three leaders of the Central Powers, Emperor Franz Josef of Austria, Kaiser Wilhelm of Germany and Enver Pasha of Turkey, tied up by Britain's blockade of the North Sea and naval control of the Mediterranean.

Locations of sinkings of HMS *Aboukir*, HMS *Formidable*, Cunard Liner *Lusitania* and HMHS *Anglia*

The Sinking of HMS *Formidable*

U-boat attacks were less frequent in stormy seas, and the crew of battleship HMS *Formidable* were not expecting one in the turbulence off Portland Bill in the early hours of New Year's Day 1915. Manning one of the guns on this Channel patrol, many miles from his Brighouse home, was Able Seaman Cameron Robert Smith. Suddenly, at 2.20am, 'he heard an explosion ... underneath the casement of the gun.' The casement was knocked lop-sided, trapping Cameron and his mates against the hull. A torpedo from German submarine U24 had struck one of the boilers on the port side. The *Formidable*'s captain, Noel Loxley, headed for the coast, but within 20 minutes the battleship was listing 20° to starboard and he gave the order to abandon ship.

Extricating themselves from the gun casement, Cameron and his colleagues helped to launch the lifeboats but, buffeted by large waves and high winds, some of these toppled on release and hit the water upside down. Cameron dropped into an upright boat and vigorously began to row away when he was struck by a jumping crewmate and knocked overboard. Cold and wet, he 'managed to scramble back again, and helped to rig up signals of distress.'

At 3.05am, 45 minutes after the torpedo strike, Cameron and his colleagues were rowing around picking up survivors when there was another explosion. A second torpedo had struck the *Formidable*'s starboard side. Locating survivors had become even more urgent, but the lifeboat started shipping water.

> ... two holes were found in the boat, and the men took off their trousers and filled up the holes with them. They had to bail the water out with their sea-boots.

They were still baling out at 4.50am when, to their horror, the *Formidable* finally keeled over on top of men who were still in the sea. For the next four hours Cameron and the lifeboat crew worked flat out to stay afloat. Then, 'in a state of great exhaustion', they sighted the Brixham trawler, *Providence*.[3]

Brixham Trawler Providence

by

A.W.K.

The Brixham trawler Providence
Stood boldly out to sea,
Her freightage was but fifty tons,
Her crew but numbered three.
Her captain was of Devon's breed –
A skilful man was he.

Anon a furious gale arose,
The waves ran mountains high.
Said Seaman Clark, "Above the roar
Methinks I hear a cry."
He up the rigging nimbly swarmed
And leeward cast his eye.

"I see," he cried, "In desperate strait
A launch with shipwrecked men.
Their signal is a broken oar,
With scarf tied round its stem.
They're baling water with their boots,
But fast it gains on them."

The captain wore his ship about,
And with supernal skill
A line was thrown, and thrown again,
And yet again, until
Those numb, half-naked mariners
Caught it and gripped it still.

And then ensued a wondrous feat,
For, spite of wave and blast,
The cutter to the trawler's side
Was limbered and made fast,
And one by one those sailormen
From death to safety passed.

Oh! right named was the Providence,
Whose four saved seventy-two,
And 'mid the stars of noblest fame
That meet our mental view,
Resplendent in the firmament,
Shine Pillar and his crew.[4]

The *Formidable* was the third British battleship to be sunk in the war, but the press accentuated the *Providence* and its crew as national heroes. The 72 sailors on Cameron's lifeboat were among 233 survivors. 547 men lost their lives. A number of these were on a life-raft blown ashore up the coast at Lyme Regis, where the landlord of the Pilot Boat pub opened his cellar as a mortuary. His collie, Lassie, nuzzled one of the bodies, warming it with his fur for over half an hour. To everyone's amazement, Able-Seaman John Cowan revived and went on to make a full recovery. Re-told many times, the story of Lassie eventually reached Hollywood and a film legend was born.[5]

Salvaging the *Empress of Ireland*

Whilst military vessels were fair game, attacks on civilian vessels broke the rules of warfare and aroused the strongest feelings, particularly with two transatlantic disasters, the *Titanic* (1912) and the *Empress of Ireland* (1914) still fresh in the mind.

In May 1914 the *Empress of Ireland* was en route from Quebec to Liverpool when the Norwegian Collier *Storstad* ploughed into her on a foggy St Lawrence River. The loss of life was greater than that on the *Titanic* – 1012 out of 1477 passengers and crew – and it remains Canada's greatest maritime catastrophe.

In August 1914 the *Empress of Ireland* hit the headlines again during a perilous salvage operation to retrieve bodies, cargo and mail. All contact was lost with the lead diver, Edward Cossaboom from New York. A second American dived to investigate but couldn't find him. Third to descend was 25 year-old Leading-Seaman Wilfred Whitehead of Marsden, a diver of four years' experience who was serving aboard HMS *Essex*.

Grasping Cossaboom's lifeline, Wilfred lowered himself hand-over-hand, resisting the force of the St Lawrence's sweeping currents against his cumbersome canvas suit and diving bell helmet. Peering through 'the cold, pitch darkness', he found the *Empress of Ireland* on a sloping bank, listing at 45° on its starboard side, its highest point 13 fathoms deep. At 17 fathoms, he touched a body with his feet. It was Cossaboom, prostrate on the river bed. The American had fallen, passed out with the sudden increase in pressure, and was lying on his airline. Feeling 'no air in his suit', Wilfred concluded that he 'must be in a bad way' and informed the salvage vessel. Both were hauled to the surface, but Cossaboom was already dead. Wilfred Whitehead gained 'international prominence on account of his bravery.'

The salvage operation, unprecedented in scale, went on to recover scores of bodies, all the mail pouches, and silver bullion worth $150,000 – over $2 million today – but in Edward Cossaboom, the *Empress of Ireland* disaster had claimed another victim.

The Sinking of the *Lusitania*

Against the sensitive backdrop of the *Titanic*, the *Empress of Ireland*, and abhorrence at the bombarding of defenceless British civilians by German warships and Zeppelins, the Cunard Liner *Lusitania* set sail from New York to Liverpool on 1 May 1915. Aboard were 2160 passengers and crew, and a cargo that included a legitimate consignment of rifle cartridges and shrapnel shell cases. Notwithstanding significant U-boat activity off southern Ireland, and a warning from the Imperial German Embassy in Washington that passengers on the *Lusitania* sailed 'at their own risk', no one expected the Germans to attack an unarmed liner.[7]

Among the passengers was 49 year-old Tom King, a woollen manufacturer and a native of Shepley. He had emigrated to America in the mid-1880s and was returning to visit his family. Also aboard was former Kirkburton curate, the 32-year-old Reverend Herbert L Gwyer, who was returning to England after three years as a missionary, based at Saskatoon, Canada. With him was his Canadian bride, Margaret.[8] The couple had married on 15 April.

At 2.10pm on 7 May, six days into the voyage, the *Lusitania* was eleven miles off the Old Head of Kinsale, southern Ireland. Herbert and Margaret were in the dining room with a couple of passengers they had befriended, Archie Donald and Lorna Pavey. Suddenly there was a muffled thud and a shudder through the ship which lurched to starboard. Herbert recalled:

I shall never forget the crash of all the crockery from the tables.

Everyone knew they had been torpedoed. The *Lusitania* had crossed the path of submarine U20. The missile unleashed by Kapitanleutnant Schwieger had struck the liner's starboard bow underneath the wheelhouse.[6] A second explosion in the hull followed. Smoke and cinders rose from the starboard side and water flowed in through numerous open portholes, causing the ship to list quickly. They didn't have much time.

In the dining room the lights went out. Amidst the stumbling and screaming, Herbert suggested to Archie that they should 'quieten the people.' Locating the door, they shouted, as convincingly as they could, that everything would be all right and that there was 'no need to panic.' Calmed, the passengers in that area made their way up to the open deck. Herbert and Margaret discussed retrieving their lifebelts from their cabin, but feared becoming trapped on the flooding lower decks.

RMS *Lusitania*

Among the last to leave the dining room, Herbert and Margaret teetered along the sloping deck on the starboard side. They could see that a good number of the *Lusitania*'s 48 lifeboats had overturned on hitting the sea, or remained stubbornly tethered to the ship. The deck was rapidly approaching sea level when Herbert located the last of the six lifeboats that had successfully launched. Six feet four inches tall and powerful, he helped Margaret, three other women and a baby aboard, before jumping aboard himself, the last of the lifeboat's 80 or so passengers. Hundreds were now in the sea, the majority drowning or slowly perishing from hypothermia.

At that moment the *Lusitania* heaved and toppled. Looking up, Margaret saw one of the funnels plummeting towards them and jumped back towards the deck, just as Herbert began to row away. A broken Marconi radio wire attached to a funnel whipped downwards, but the ship's purser, William Harkness grabbed and diverted it. As the wire grazed the end of the lifeboat, the funnel crashed down on one side of them and the main mast on the other, 'smothering' them with water. Grabbing an oar, Herbert rowed furiously, helping to power the lifeboat beyond the undertow as the *Lusitania* disappeared beneath the waves. It was just 18 minutes since the torpedo strike. Only then did Herbert realise that Margaret was not aboard. Emmie Hill from Peterborough recalled:

> We continued to keep our heads. In less than five minutes from the ship's disappearance beneath the waves, the water was like a sea of glass and nothing was to be seen; only chairs, trunks and other loose articles from the ship. When we got a little way off, we saw the German submarine come to the surface, and the crew hoisted their flag, staying a short time above the water to witness the awful scenes of which they were the cause.

Another survivor, Willie Inch, had admiration for the way the 'persons in this boat' worked together, some rowing, whilst others 'rendered great service by reviving those who were picked up half dead.'

Four hours later they were rescued by the trawler *Flying Fish*. Herbert sobbed quietly and prayed for Margaret. What had happened to her?

Seconds after Margaret jumped back to the *Lusitania*, its deck reached sea level. Battling the turbulence, she swam away as the ship began to slip beneath the surface, but after only a few yards she and two men were sucked backwards, straight down one of the funnels. Margaret briefly lost consciousness. When she came to, she was floating in pitch blackness, except for a pool of light somewhere ahead. Suddenly there was an explosion behind her. A boiler had burst. The force expelled the sea water from the funnel, shooting Margaret and the two men back into open water.

She splash-landed close to a flimsy, collapsible lifeboat commandeered by Massachusetts bookseller Charles Lauriat and his fellow passenger, Leslie Morton. Margaret was covered in oil and soot and they helped the 'African' lady aboard.

Five hours later, aboard the *Flying Fish*, Margaret, still coated in oil and soot, found Herbert, who was overjoyed once he realised who she was.

'Never mind, we've lost all those awful wedding presents,' she said.

Margaret kept the oil and soot-stained camisole she had been wearing for the rest of her life.

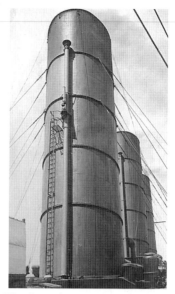

The Reverend Herbert Gwyer

The funnels, support wires and radio wires of the *Lusitania*

The Gwyers were among 762 survivors. Tom King was one of 1198 who died. There wasn't time for all to escape. It was the biggest single maritime disaster of the war and bodies were washed up on the Irish coast for weeks afterwards.[9] Reverend Gwyer went on to become the chaplain of the Huddersfield War Hospital at Royds Hall and in 1936 became the Second Bishop of George in South Africa.[10]

Propaganda from the sinking of the *Lusitania* was among the most effective of the war.

In July the enquiry found flaws in the *Lusitania*'s emergency procedures but concluded that the U20 was 'acting under the directions of the German government', no warning had been given, '… it was a murderous attack.'[11] There was an outpouring of anti-German feeling across the nation. The *HDE* reported that, by running up the German flag as the victims floundered in the water, the U20's captain behaved 'as though it were necessary to claim this supreme degradation for a nation already thoroughly dishonoured ... They are gloating over this fiendish crime.'[12] Huddersfield cyclist RF Machiey, who was attached to Number 8 Platoon Army Cycling Corps, 49th West Riding Division, wrote from France:

> … after the sinking of the *Lusitania* it leaves us no alternative but to exterminate the German race, for it is nothing but wholesale murder.[13]

Littlewood Hoyle, who had emigrated from Holmfirth to Massachusetts, was so incensed that he returned to re-enlist, serving as a driver with the 168th Holme Valley RFA.[14] He was among a rush of volunteers to join the forces. Elsewhere, there were widespread riots and attacks on German shops and individuals. The Royal Family changed their name from the House of Saxe-Coburg to the House of Windsor. The deaths of 128 U.S. citizens had significantly soured American opinion against Germany and increased the pressure on the U.S. government to side with the Allies. For Germany, it was a propaganda disaster.[15]

Bucking the national trend and the sentiments expressed in the *HDE*, Huddersfield experienced no reported instances of anti-German riots or violence akin to the 'the crude and violent jingoism of the carefully managed mobs of London, Cardiff, Leeds, Keighley and Bradford.' Cyril Pearce, in *Comrades in Conscience* attributes this, at least in part, to the sizeable socialist groups in the district, which were strongly anti-war.

Attacks on hospital ships also aroused *Lusitania*-like anger. Diplomatic rows between Britain and Germany about such attacks littered the war. The aggressor's justification was invariably that ships hadn't been showing their flag, or were carrying arms or able-bodied troops.

The Sinking of HMHS *Anglia*

On 17 November 1915, Privates Harry Longbottom from Huddersfield and Robert Morrison of Berry Brow, respectively serving with the 5th and 9th Dukes, were among 385 wounded troops sailing from Calais to Dover aboard the hospital ship HMHS *Anglia*. Harry was incapacitated with a leg injury and Robert had septic poisoning. Harry recalled:

> It was about 12.50 and we were three or four miles off Dover, when the explosion took place. I was not in the part of the ship where it occurred, but heard from some chaps who were, that it blew some of the bed cots to bits.

The *Anglia* had struck a German mine portside forward of the bridge. The bridge was destroyed, along with the two wards underneath it, which flooded instantly. There were no survivors from that part of the ship. All surviving sisters, orderlies and patients donned their lifebelts. The majority of cases had fractured limbs, severe wounds and amputations, and the staff began to remove splints to prevent bodies going under whilst the splints floated uppermost. Harry continued:

> Everyone seemed cool and the nurses, doctors, and R.A.M.C. men helped the patients up on to the deck, and put some overboard … I was not a cot case and I managed to walk, or rather limp, up the steps on to the deck, and waited till the ship was nearly down.

> They set the buzzer or siren … for help, and in about fifteen minutes some destroyers and tugs arrived. They let the [life]boats down and made for us. The ship was sideways, and the low part took us nearly into the sea. The nurses, doctors and ambulance men were throwing all sorts of things overboard for us to cling to. When the final lurch came there was a rope down the side, and some of us slid down into the sea, and then did the best we could. Others jumped overboard and were picked up.

Harry was fortunate that his wounds did not prevent him from swimming.

> … the salt-water made our wounds smart for a minute. I made my way to a boat which was not far off, and the sailors helped us in. They were champion … and handled the wounded gently. I was in the water about fifteen minutes ... They lifted us out of the boat and put us on the tug. There we took off our wet things and they gave us blankets. Our wet dressings were taken off and our wounds dressed again.

Whilst Harry was being rescued, the nurses continued to half-carry helpless soldiers from below to the upper deck, ignoring cries from the lifeboats to save themselves. Sister Alice Meldrum recalled:

> Unfortunately, in some cases, the struggling patients hung on to the sides of a boat and capsized it, and once again all were thrown into the sea. It was a never-to-be-forgotten sight to see armless and legless men struggling in the water, very many of whom were eventually saved.

Prominent in the rescue were gunboat HMS *Hazard* and the collier SS *Lusitania*, which launched two lifeboats then itself struck a mine and sank. Harry was taken to the Royal Herbert Hospital, Woolwich, where he received a telegram of sympathy from the King:

> His Majesty the King desires that a special message of sympathy be conveyed to all patients ex S.S. Anglia and has expressed the hope that they may quickly recover from their trying experience.

The stricken HMHS *Anglia* goes down; in the background are the collier *Lusitania* and HMS *Hazard*

Another to be rescued was Private Hilton Furness of Slaithwaite, one of the original members of the Colne Valley Territorials. Promoted to Second Lieutenant, he went on to earn the Military Cross in 1917, when he led his platoon 'with great dash and determination against very heavy hostile machine-gun and rifle fire ... until brought in at dusk by a stretcher bearer.'

As the *Anglia* sank so rapidly, it was only possible to lower one of its lifeboats. Ten medical staff, 25 crew, four officers and 125 other ranks were lost. For Private Robert Morrison's parents there was an anxious wait. On 13 November, four days before he boarded the *Anglia*, they had learned that he was on his way home.

An *Examiner* Cartoon Special from 15 March 1915; the caption reads:

The Gorilla: "Well, if that doesn't take the monkey-nut! I've never been so insulted in all my life! I may be an ape, but I hope I'm a gentleman."

Nothing further was heard concerning the lad until Wednesday morning (24 November),when a communication was received from the military headquarters at York stating that he was ... amongst the missing ... it is assumed that Morrison has gone down with the ill-fated vessel.[16]

Notwithstanding all these calamitous sinkings, there were no major sea-battles in 1915. The British fleet controlled much of the North Sea and, like the German fleet, was wary of the enemy's strength. Caution by both fleets negated a major strategic opening.

Meanwhile, both sides impeded deliveries of commercial overseas supplies. Attacks on merchant shipping would bring increasing misery and hardship to civilians in Britain and in Germany, profoundly affecting their way and quality of life. The long-term strategy of starving the opposition into submission was chilling, both in its inhumanity, and as an admission that this was a war with no end in sight.

Chapter 6

1915: A Bloody Stalemate

On the western front, the retreat of 1914 had allowed the Germans to choose where to dig in. They occupied much of the higher, more easily defendable ground. An unsuccessful French-led attack in Artois and Champagne at the beginning of 1915 showed how difficult they would be to dislodge. For much of 1915 the Germans defended this ground with the fewest possible men and superbly positioned and well-fortified machine-gun positions, releasing troops to attack the Russian army in the east where there was greater room for mobility. Russia suffered two million casualties in 1915.

Germany's defensive strategy allowed the British Army time to train volunteers and introduce them to the front line. By April 1915 the British Army had 900,000 men organised into 28 divisions. Amongst them were the 49th West Riding Division which included the 1/5th (Huddersfield) and 1/7th (Colne Valley) Battalions of the Duke of Wellington's West Riding Regiment – the 5th and 7th Dukes. Not all would participate in every major battle, but all took their turn in the day-to-day manning of the trenches, where the next deadly shell or sniper bullet was never far away.

Winter in the Trenches

Conditions in the trenches during the wet, freezing winter of 1914-15, frequently described in letters to the *HDE*, were utterly grim.[1] Private James Milligan of the 7th Dukes bewailed 'Our trenches are half full of water, and the sides keep falling in upon us.'[2] A private from Fartown …

> … woke up in a little dug-out … and found a comrade and I were lying in water about four inches deep, and wet to the skin … The dug-out was about 5½ feet long, 2 feet wide, and about 2½ feet high. Two of us in this, cuddled up, and often sleeping like logs … No visitors allowed – but they come, whether you like it or not, in the shape of frogs, mice, rats, and millions of insects, flies, and other vermin too numerous to mention. We do not get much sleep in the trenches and in the last firing we had no sleep whatsoever during night time.[3]

Corporal G Plowright described a 400-yard wade through a communication trench:

> All the way through we were up to the thighs in thick clay mud. Some of the chaps were stuck for hours and all the time the Germans were sniping over the top … the place stunk of dead bodies of Germans and Frenchmen who had been buried there.[4]

Writing on 7 April 1915, Private W Haigh of Marsh was thankful for the recent distribution of gum boots. He explained that any forays from the trenches had …

> … to be done at night and in utter darkness, and it is no unusual thing to find oneself in a Jack Johnson hole full of water, or to go sprawling full length in the mud …[5]

As Private Frank Dean from Newsome, put it:

> When a fellow has done twenty-four hours in the front line, he comes out looking like a crumpled up sick report.[7]

Among the popular songs of 1915 was *The Little Grey Home in the West*, which was adapted to describe the trench experience by Private C Garthwaite of Dalton, serving with the 1st Battalion, Gordon Highlanders.

My Little Wet Home in a Trench
by
Private C Garthwaite

I've a little wet home in a trench,
Where the rainstorms continually drench,
There's the sky overhead,
Clay or mud for a bed,
And a stone that we use for a bench.

Bully beef and hard biscuits we chew,
It seems years since we tasted a stew.
Shells crackle and scare,
Yet no place can compare
With my little wet home, if you knew.

Our friends in that trench o'er the way
Seem to know that we've come here to stay.
They shoot and they shout,
But they can't get us out,
Thought there's no dirty trick they won't play.

They rushed us a few nights ago;
But we don't like intruders, and so
Some departed quite sore,
Some were left evermore
Near my little wet home. Now you know.

Yes. We think of the cold, slush and stench
As we lie with the Belgians and French;
There'll be shed yet, I fear,
Redder stuff than a tear,
For my little wet home in the trench.[6]

Different Roles in the Front Line

On 26 September 1915 Frank Dean was part of a daring bomb-throwing raid in a damaged mine, for which he was awarded the 'Distinguished Conduct certificate' in early November. The award was timely. On 13 November Sapper G Winterbottom reported seeing Frank and a colleague carrying a box of explosives, when …

> … one of them slipped and caused the bombs to explode. His mate was killed outright. We were working about 50 yards away, and saw the flash … We could not get to him very quickly because of the state of the roads ... We did all we could to help him. One of us got a stretcher, then we took him to a first aid dressing station and got a doctor to him.

Frank was taken by ambulance to hospital but died soon afterwards.[8]

The perilous occupation of the sapper was just one of the surprisingly varied roles undertaken by local troops. One of the most despised roles, according to a Huddersfield private, was…

> ration carrying at night time – often four journeys a night, frequently under rifle and shell and shrapnel fire, sometimes in pouring rain, with communication trenches six inches in water and sludge. Our total mileage is often twelve miles a night … carrying as much as … possible on our backs. You can imagine we are somewhat exhausted at the finish.[9]

Quartermaster Sergeant Ernest Cook of the 5th Dukes was responsible for overseeing the preparation of food and other supplies and for delivering them to the front line. He described one such suspense-filled journey.

NIGHT JOURNEY TO THE TRENCHES

It was almost black darkness … I gathered my ration party of 40 men together and set off for the trenches with the rations in little bags. We set off up a road. I am leading and picking the way and our path is swept with rifle fire … As we move slowly along picking our way … a German star shell suddenly goes up and lights up the country for miles around. We drop flat on the ground and lie motionless just as we drop. A heavy fire always follows as a flare enables the Germans to see what they are firing at. Our pace is slow and as we advance again another flare goes up and so on. I should think we dropped fifty times on our way up. When we reach the top of the road we turn to the left along a road that runs behind our trenches. Our men have named it 'Death's Corner.' We are halted by a sentry who demands to know who we are. I answer the challenge and advance to be recognised. As we pass on, bullets whistling along … we turn down a … by-path to the trenches. This by-path is a crazy little railway running beside a ditch – stinking as usual – and we crouch down and wait. Theoretically it is impossible that the journey could be made in safety … we should be silhouetted to the German marksmen. On the slippery ground we should stumble and fall and the noise of our falling would betray us, and then we lie flat and wait… On our journey we get a minute or two to think and the thoughts are not of fear. I was not afraid; my only sensation was one of rage. "Why should I be called upon to use my life like this?" I was being shot at and it was impossible to shoot back. I wanted to get at somebody … The animal part of me was uppermost. I found myself cursing my men, quite unnecessarily too.

Time is no object, but life is. Again we crawl along getting gradually nearer and nearer to our trenches and, judging by the noise of rifle fire and machine gun fire, we are quite close. To gain the trench we have to pass quickly over a stream by means of a crazy wooden bridge (consisting of a plank) … Twenty yards more and we are safe in the trench with our load of coke, wood, straw and food, and among friends who quickly relieve us of our loads. The return journey is the same, only a little quicker, as we are relieved of our burdens.

It's all strange. And this life is exciting, but we shall be glad when it's over. This journey I have described has to be done four times a week.[10]

Gunner F Kyne from Huddersfield, attached to the 92nd Brigade RFA, described his role of signaller as 'a fairly risky job', but essential in technological warfare in which, unlike previous wars, the military leaders made their decisions from well behind the front line.

I am writing this in a dug out at 4a.m., with a row of telephones in front of me, so I have a fairly busy time. We laid about five miles of telephone wire out, and all has to be kept in good working order. It does not matter what is going on, the repairing of wires and keeping up of communications must be done, or the battery is of no use. We may be called out at any time during the night to repair the wires.

Writing in November 1915, he described a bombardment:

Our guns began to roar all along the line, smashing the German trenches to bits. I was in one of our observing stations, and practically one could see all that was going off on a two-mile front. I saw our boys make the charge through clouds of smoke and gas. The German artillery answered us back and we got a few in the observing station – one signaller killed and four wounded. There was many a brave deed done that day. At last darkness came and we settled down for the night after a hard day, holding what we had won.[11]

Bandsman Albert Wood from Moldgreen was a stretcher bearer with the 7th Dukes.

Stretcher bearing is a very unthankful job, especially for long lads like myself for we have to crouch when carrying anyone out of the trenches, which makes it a strain on the back … I have just about got used to the noise of the bullets whistling overhead. On Sunday … the Germans shelled our trenches, and we had a few casualties. As soon as they passed the word on for stretcher bearers we were there in a minute and set to bandaging them up. I am glad to say that it never entered our heads that they might drop another shell in the same place. We only thought of making the poor fellows as comfortable as we could. … Our worthy colonel … thanked us for the way in which we had attended to our duties.

… Tommy Broadbent, from Diggle, is in the same stretcher squad as myself, and the other day he had a narrow escape in the trenches. He was stood talking to me when a bullet came over the parapet and went through the top of his hat and came out of the side without hurting him.[12]

The 'ordinary Tommy' also had many varied experiences, as described by a Fartown private.

We have to dodge aerial torpedoes, and it is a good job you can see these coming, both day and night, and it is your duty to warn your comrades of these and trench mortars by telling of their direction as soon as you spot one coming. It pays you to be alert.

One of our chaps was shot through the head on Monday, and two of us had the unpleasant task of digging his grave at night, amidst shot and shell, and every time a flare light went up and a searchlight was flashed we had to lay flat. We afterwards helped to carry and put him in the grave, and it was a gruesome job …

… One time we were asleep on the (Yser) canal side, and a shell dropped in the centre of the canal, and the back splash covered us in sludge. Even when out on rest we have had to go a five-mile tramp and fill sandbags, dig new trenches, and do navvying generally, and then walk back at three in the morning. When last on this job we had a "joy ride" on motor buses of the London type … first bit of fun for some time, and we made the best of it …

Our last firing line was only about fifteen yards from the Germans, and fighting was mostly done by rifle fire and hand grenades, and our bombers did good work.

We keep losing good comrades, to our sorrow, and wish they could be restored to their parents. It is the hardest part in this war. Must close this quick as am due on sentry duty in a few minutes.[13]

Laying, checking and repairing the barbed wire that protected the Allies' trenches, and cutting that of the enemy, required regular, precarious nighttime sorties into No Man's Land, as H Burton and W Thornton of Skelmanthorpe recounted.

We were … repairing the barbed wire when the Germans saw us. They opened fire on us. We dropped down and stayed there for a while. It was … very dark … and misty … and somehow we got parted from the rest of the party. We did not quite know whether we were making for our trenches or the German trenches, but we kept on until we got to a parapet. Then we kept quiet and listened, and we found ourselves under the German's parapet, so we made our way across the wires back again. We came across our listening post and they took us in with them. You can imagine our feelings when we found out we were under the German parapet, but luckily for us they never heard a sound, otherwise it would have been all up.[14]

The troops needed regular training in the use of new 'bombs, rifle-grenades, and other similar engines of war', as both sides pursued a decisive technological advantage. Such training was not always fully understood, as 'Old Volunteer' explained.

… the brand new infantrymen began to imagine that these new forms of ancient weapons were intended to supersede the rifle … men began to turn instinctively to the bomb … the ridiculous spectacle of a British soldier, carrying his rifle, running after a German and trying to stop him by throwing bombs at him was seen more than once. It is now recognised that bombs have their uses, but the infantryman's chief weapon is the rifle.[15]

The Battle of Neuve Chapelle

The first major British attempt to break through the German lines in 1915 began on 10 March. The targets were the village of Neuve Chapelle and Aubers Ridge beyond, which was only 20 feet higher than the surrounding land but strategically valuable. The operation would also straighten the front line west of Lille where the Germans held a small salient.

The attack began with a massive artillery barrage over a front of 2000 yards. In 35 minutes, 342 guns unleashed more shells than in the entire Boer War.[16] Private Joseph Oates wrote:

> I will never forget it as long as I keep on this weary globe. The bombardment was awful. Thunder is like a whisper compared to it. When we advanced on the enemy trenches they opened such a fire on us that it was like going through a hailstorm, and our chaps were dropping like ninepins … a shell burst among a dozen of us, three being killed and the rest being wounded, some of them badly. I drew a lucky number and escaped with a wound in the foot …
>
> … We stuck it despite this fire, and captured the trench, with a few hundred prisoners thrown in. I can tell you they were glad to surrender, for the shelling had fairly driven them silly.[17]

Locations of major battles involving British forces in 1915

Neuve Chapelle
by
Barry Connor

The following lines are inscribed to my friend Sergeant Thomas Churchill, 2nd Northampton Regiment, who was wounded at the battle of Neuve Chapelle on March 10th, 1915.

I

We slept within our trenches
As men sleep when in a trance,
Till the bugle sound awoke us
And we heard the word "Advance,"
"Advance, boys," cried our Colonel,
Mid the whirl of shot and shell,
Be our watchword, death or glory,
Forward, boys, to Neuve Chapelle.

II

Death or glory was our watchword,
And we used it not in vain,
As we thought of Rheims and Antwerp,
And the sacking of Louvain
Death or glory, swelled the chorus,
Like some mighty magic spell,
As we rushed to meet the foemen
Face to face at Neuve Chapelle.

III

In spite of wire entanglements
We steadily press on,
While gallant comrades right and left
Are falling one by one.
The invaders far outnumber us,
But we give them shot and shell,
We drive them from their stronghold
Till we capture Neuve Chapelle.

IV

Death or glory still the watchword,
As we trod the village street,
Over scores of gory helmets,
With their owners at our feet.
In the hand to hand encounter
Many dauntless heroes fell
Ere our cause was crowned with glory
In the streets of Neuve Chapelle.[18]

The fighting was brutal. It took four hours for the British to advance just 300 yards and capture Neuve Chapelle village. In that time 11,200 British troops were killed, wounded or missing. The Germans also lost 11,000 men, with a further 1200 captured.

The opportunity to push on to Aubers Ridge dissipated. Delayed by German barbed wire, the need to reorganise, and poor weather, the British spent 12 March repelling a German counter-attack. The following day 1100 British troops attacked the town of Aubers. None survived. It was time to regroup and secure Neuve Chapelle. The British would hold this village until the German spring offensive of 1918.[19]

Back to Blighty
by Charles Lunn
I'm just an old "contemptible" who fought at Neuve Chapelle,
And my heart is sad and woeful when I think of those who fell
Defending our great Empire with their loyal British blood,
And dying in their hundreds in the slime and stench and mud.[20]

The World War I Memorial at Le Touret, beyond the military cemetery, commemorates the combatants who died in this area but have no known grave. These include the many missing troops from the Battle of Neuve Chapelle.

Attack on Aubers Ridge

Eight weeks later, on Friday 8 May, British troops gathered for another assault on Aubers Ridge. Among them was Lance Corporal J Slater of Moldgreen. A cleaner on the Huddersfield trams and veteran of the Boer War, he was serving with the 1st Battalion King's Own Royal Lancaster Regiment on the British Army's southern flank near La Bassée. On the eve of the battle he wrote to his wife and children to thank them for a recent parcel.

> This is Friday, your birthday, so I wish you many happy returns.... I am hoping to be home for mine, if I am lucky enough to get through. I and several of my comrades had a narrow escape this morning when the Germans were shelling this place. They dropped one through a house not five yards away from where we were, but there was no one hurt, thank goodness.
>
> … it is to be hoped it won't be much longer before we see each other again. We must look on the bright side, if there is a bright side to this war. Do not upset yourself about me. Try and keep at your best, and keep the children the same. Keep telling them that their daddy will be coming home one day, and bring them something home as well. You keep on asking me if there is anything I want. Well, there are plenty of things I want, but I don't want to put you to any expense. I daresay I could write to plenty of places for different things, but I don't want to humble myself to anyone. I keep managing with things I get. I don't like to see things sent out here at the prices you have to pay for sending them, so don't bother about sending anything until I ask you. Don't think that I don't value anything you send, but I don't want you to spend money on things for me.

During the attack on Aubers Ridge the following day, Lance Corporal Slater was killed. The attack failed.[21]

The Second Battle of Ypres

Whilst the British eyed Aubers Ridge, the Germans had designs on the Ypres Salient, a landscape which still bore gaping wounds from the First Battle of Ypres the previous autumn, as described by a Huddersfield private:

Zone of the Dead

The aspect of the narrow strip between the hostile lines in the woods round Ypres almost defies description. If the reader can imagine what a wood would look like with most of the trees either felled altogether or half-sawn through and lying with their tops on the ground. If he can further imagine this wood standing in soft, muddy clay, in which every few yards there is a pit several feet deep, and if he can further picture to himself the whole of this tangle of dead vegetation, mud, and deep pits heaped from end to end with thousands of German corpses, the majority of whom have lain there since November, he will then gain some idea of the appearance of this awful zone of the dead that lies between us and the enemy.[22]

Here, Germany launched their only major offensive of 1915 with sustained bombing on 14 April.

On the same day, the Huddersfield Territorials of the 5th Dukes travelled to France, leaving their Doncaster barracks at lunchtime, departing Doncaster Station at 2.15pm and arriving in Boulogne at 11.30pm. They were part of the 49th Division which was transported south on 84 trains over five days from 12 to 16 April. 18-year-old Huddersfield private, Freddie Smith, recorded many of his experiences in letters to his parents. On 15 April he described the journey from Boulogne to their base:

… a pretty stiff march of 10 miles in the boiling sun to the station ... this time we were not enjoying cushion seated carriages. Instead of these we travelled in freight trucks no less than 20 in each.

This seven-hour train journey was followed by a '5 mile tramp.' Freddie was struck by the number of military aircraft.

I remember people paying 5/-, even pounds in order to see an aeroplane ... they should come over here.[23]

Hill 60

Meanwhile, British sappers were preparing to detonate explosives packed into mines under the German lines close to Hill 60, a 60-feet high strategic mound of 'railway earthwork' spoil, 100 yards in front of the British trenches two and a half miles south east of Ypres. Although it would be several days before Freddie and his comrades in the 5th Dukes would enter the fray, numerous Huddersfield lads were at the heart of the first British charge at Hill 60 as part of the 2nd Dukes.[24] They included Corporal AE Wilkinson, a tram conductor from Moldgreen, who wrote:

… it was general knowledge … that a very important tactical mole hill (one could not flatter it by calling it a hill) was to be blown sky high with dynamite along with its attendant trenches, rifle pits and dug outs our enemy had established there since 11th November 1914.
... on Saturday [17 April] at tea time an air duel … which the Britisher won, was the prelude in the blowing up of the hill. [We] saw the "tornado" burst. "Dante's Inferno" must have been very mild compared with this treat …the Germans had … received a blowing up with a vengeance and they were just like a hornets nest and fully prepared to give full vent to their uncontrolled rage.

The Germans unleashed a tornado of artillery and rifle fire, grenades, hand bombs and trench mortars with their 'fear-inspiring whizz bangs.'[25] The British charge at 6pm 'was perfect and the courage and morale of the men … of the best',[26] but before dawn …

… casualties were increasing most alarmingly. During the whole of Sunday we were subjected to a most pitiless fire from all sorts of short range guns, bombs, and shells, with disastrous effect.

Among the officers in Corporal Wilkinson's platoon was Lieutenant Roland Hely Owen, the outstanding Huddersfield Old Boys rugby union footballer.[27] At 5.30pm on Sunday afternoon, as the platoon sheltered in a crater, Lieutenant Owen called together the few NCOs left alive to tell them the plan of action.

> Mr Owen said we were to attack the enemy's trenches over the crest of the craters at 6pm, making a bayonet charge and pinching a few more trenches from them. … The Bayonet charge was to be carried out by our own regiment with the K.O.Y.L.I. on our left ably supporting us.

> Mr Owen patted me on the shoulder just prior to the charge, saying as he did so, with a smile, "Well, corporal, Huddersfield's going to see this through." He was enough to oil anyone with courage. He was simply brimful of it. He revelled in danger … and such men inspire the less courageous. When the whistle blew, we kicked off, and put the fear of God into them, and they fled down the communications trenches – those that could get away. Mr Owen and myself were over the parapet from our crater like a shot …

Suddenly, Corporal Wilkinson saw Lieutenant Owen 'reel as if hit in the neck.'[28] A shell had burst, flooring Owen and Lance-Corporal WJ Coates of Thurstonland, who 'fell helpless on the lieutenant's body ... "Come on, Coates, we shall have to stick it; it is going to be a warm job,"' encouraged Owen. They were his last words.

Lifted from the Lieutenant's corpse, Coates was carried from the battlefield, severely wounded. He was operated upon at Northern General Hospital, Lincoln, adding to his catalogue of scars from Mons and the First Battle of Ypres.[29]

Corporal Wilkinson, unaware that Owen and Coates were no longer with them, pressed on to confront the Hun in hand-to-hand combat:

Lieutenant Roland Hely Owen

> I received a bullet through the left hand at point blank range … whilst I was putting sandbags in their faces. About half an hour later I received a shrapnel wound in the head … I brought one or two badly wounded men out of the danger zone, dressed them (as I am used to first aid), and assisted them to a clearing hospital.

The Corporal suffered sharp pain and dizziness for six days until the shrapnel was removed from his head at a Rouen hospital. He was expected to be fit for duty in a fortnight.[30]

The Battalion took the German frontline trenches and blocked the communication trenches as protection against counter-attack. Despite the 'terrible cost' of 35 killed, 345 wounded and 43 missing, Company Sergeant-Major Albert Taylor viewed the Battle of Hill 60 as a success:

> Although our casualties were great, we gained a decisive victory ... the 2nd Dukes made a name for themselves that will live forever in history.[31]

The First Chlorine Gas Attack

Four days later, on Wednesday 22 April, the entire war took a sinister turn. Albert Taylor experienced it first-hand. French and Algerian troops were manning the front line east of Ypres when a veil of green and yellow mist began to roll across No Man's Land towards them – chlorine gas – 168 tons of it. Far more deadly than the tear gas employed in 1914, it destroys lung tissue, effectively drowning the victim, and was banned by the Hague Convention's rules of warfare. Terrified Allied troops fled towards Ypres. Not all could escape. The gas crept over the parapets and clogged the trenches, claiming 10,000 casualties. Half of them died within ten minutes and 2000 were taken prisoner. The 2nd Dukes were brought forward in support but found it impossible. Sergeant-Major Taylor was one of those 'compelled to leave our trenches for safety.' He had inhaled the gas and had to make his escape, one of 3000 who did so. He was once again hospitalised … 'nothing serious, but it would have been if I had not had a good respirator.'[32]

Within days of returning to action Sergeant-Major Taylor was wounded at St Eloi, south of Ypres, and invalided home to recuperate. Back in Huddersfield he 'took part in many recruiting meetings', making 'forcible' and 'telling' appeals as 'one who had had actual experience of German methods at the front.' He also married Mary Lumb of Paddock, but like many wartime brides she was soon a widow. Returning to his regiment, Albert Taylor was commissioned to Second-Lieutenant. He was killed during the attack on Vimy Ridge on the first day of the Battle of Arras, 9 April 1917.[33]

The chlorine gas attack opened a 7km gap in the Allied lines. Ypres, the gateway to the channel ports, was wide open to the two German corps that advanced, protected by respirators. But even the German leaders were unprepared for the degree of devastation and, lacking back-up, the two corps risked being cut off if they advanced too far from their front line. After 3km they were halted by an improvised counter-attack.

During the next couple of days the Allies distributed respirators, but gas remained a major fear for the troops on both sides because of the painful, lingering death it could cause.[34] The Germans soon experienced first-hand the effects of their chlorine gas. Lieutenant-Colonel Louis Petro Demetriadi, the Huddersfield doctor in charge of the 49th (West Riding) Division's Casualty Clearing Station, translated a document found on an injured German officer:

> ... the gas was put over the English lines at 4 o'clock this morning, but within three minutes of the gas being discharged from the cylinder the wind changed direction and the whole of the gas was blown back onto the German lines – the British never knew that any gas had been sent over, but ... at 10 o'clock [we] found 1100 suffocated Germans in the first line trenches.[35]

Coming shortly before the sinking of the *Lusitania*, the illegal, indiscriminate use of gas contributed to the hardening of attitudes against Germany among neutral countries, not least the United States.

The heavy toll of casualties from Hill 60 was soon felt in Huddersfield. On 3 May a train brought 100 wounded soldiers, 80 of them on stretchers, for hospitalisation.[36] The top brass of Northern Command descended on the Huddersfield Recruiting Committee with details of the alarming numbers that ...

> ... would be required to make up the "wastage" ... to keep the numbers of the local Territorial battalions at full strength ... they would need to recruit 400 to 500 men per month.[37]

As the Second Battle of Ypres raged on through May, the proliferation of obituaries in the *HDE* reflected not only family tragedies, but a growing number of gaps in community life left by talented young men. One such was 23-year-old Lance-Corporal Lewes Walker. Held 'in high esteem locally', he was a 'baritone and soloist of great promise' and leading chorister in the Armitage Bridge Church Choir. On 14 May 1915 he was struck by shrapnel between the eyes and killed instantly. At his funeral service in Armitage Bridge Church, Major GP Norton read a tribute to him. He had been 'picked from a large number of available men to be a Lance-Corporal, and has been a splendid help all through.' Buried not far behind the trenches by nine comrades from the Dukes, his grave was marked by a neat white cross and a wreath of wild flowers. They had promised 'as long as we are in the neighbourhood we will keep his resting place worthy of him.'[38]

Freddie Smith and his comrades from the Huddersfield Territorials entered the trenches for the first time at Estaires, a few miles south of Ypres on 24 April. Bullets whistled overhead from the German line just 200 yards away, one whizzing between him and the next man. He was in the line for 24 hours and fired 15 rounds.

> Really I don't think I could kill one even if I had him at my mercy.[39]

In early May Freddie witnessed death for the first time. He was on guard outside his billet when a shell burst yards away, killing three and wounding another four: '... this catastrophe made us all miserable I can tell you.' Bravado helped to maintain their spirits, and at 'stand to' on 5 May the lads in their trench sang impolite songs about the Germans, including 'Has anyone see a German band?' The Germans responded with volleys of rifle fire into their sandbag parapet.

Mr Fritz has a very dirty habit of splitting the tops of our sandbags, when we are cooking, and dropping us a bit of "muck" in our edibles.

"There goes our blinkin' parapet again."

There was further points-scoring the following day when the Germans left a flag half way across No Man's Land. Corporal Harry Convoy from Huddersfield nipped across at twilight and captured it, 'much to the amusement and amazement of our men.' The flag had 'John Bull Kaput' written on one side and 'Mitt Gottfür Kaiser ü Reich' (God and right is with the Kaiser) on the other.[40]

By mid-May Freddie Smith was pre-occupied by hunger. He was extremely grateful for a food parcel from his parents and took issue with Private Bowell's assertion in the *HDE* that they were well fed.

> I don't like grousing but I must class him as an "awful liar" ... we are on short rations we have seen no bread yet ... I was thin to start with, but I am going thinner.

He added:

> ... if ever I do come back, which I hardly think I shall, the P.M. [Primitive Methodist] Chapel at Taylor Hill will have an enthusiastic member in me.

Freddie continued to find solace in Christianity, several of his letters commenting that in the growing sea of destruction, crucifixes were invariably undamaged, 'not a scratch', even when the buildings where they hung were destroyed. Similarly, churches seemed to suffer less damage than the surrounding structures.

Freddie took 16-year-old Sam Dyson under his wing, and began by persuading him to improve his language.

> I never heard a lad his age curse as much ... it is no place for a lad 16 years of age out here. I am too young myself.[41]

By the end of May the Germans were running low on supplies and manpower, and resorted to bombarding Ypres, blasting much of it to rubble. The strategy prolonged the 5th Dukes tour in the trenches as it was 'unsafe to traverse the communications trenches.'[42] During the Second Battle of Ypres the Germans had reduced the Allied salient to three miles across and five miles deep, inflicting 69,000 casualties whilst suffering 35,000, a difference mainly explained by chlorine gas.

The dispiriting British failures in the spring battles of 1915 were blamed on an embarrassing shortage of ammunition, some of which had been diverted to Gallipoli. A tirade by Lord Norcliffe's *Daily Mail* also cited 'the wrong type of shells.' In May 1915, Germany was producing 250,000 shells per day, one hundred times more than the 2,500 per day from British factories.[43] It was a scandal that saw Lloyd George instated as Minister of Munitions and hastened the demise of the Liberal government. The urgent need for armaments would have immense repercussions for Britain's iron and chemical industries and the role of women in the workplace, not least in Huddersfield.

The 5th Dukes: in the Trenches and Behind the Lines, Summer 1915

History records no major offensives during the summer of 1915, but the trenches had to be continuously manned. The British Army lost about 300 men per day to sniper and shell fire, and the *HDE* reported a steady stream of local injuries and fatalities.

Freddie Smith spent much of June out of the trenches. His platoon began the month on the much-dreaded night time ration-carrying duties, supplying the front line with food, ammunition and barbed wire. On 4 June, twelve of them were walking the mile back to headquarters to collect 20 coils of barbed wire when a non-exploding range-finder shell burst 20 yards in front of them. As they scrambled for cover in adjacent reserve trenches, three more shells whistled over, one of them landing on the roof of a farmhouse 100 yards away.

> It burst into flames and in less than half an hour a fine house ... belonging to an oldish lady (a poor one too) had been reduced to ashes. She salvaged a few things not worth many francs, crying quite hysterically.[44]

Shortly afterwards Freddie was 'on rest' – trench-digging, which was '50 times harder than being in the trenches.'[45] They were rarely out of range of the German artillery, and Freddie had several narrow escapes. He was washing when three shells burst 20 yards away. He and two comrades leapt for cover ...

> ... but I was all covered with soap so I turned back again and hastily swilled myself, put the soap in the towel, and crash the tin bowl I had been washing in was sent flying, smashed by shrapnel. A minute sooner and I should have been minus head.'[46]

Sketches of Tommy's life
Out on rest. — N° 3

Sometimes when you are « out on rest », you think you'd almost rather stop in the trenches.

It was vital to keep their behind the lines locations secret, as far as possible. In August Freddie's platoon was out of the trenches for six days in the grounds of a large chateau. The keeper and his wife were caught signalling to the enemy and 'signalled no more.' After two days with no signals, the Germans concluded their spies had been caught and shelled the chateau.[47]

Large isolated dwellings made comfortable billets, but were regularly targeted. In early June, Freddie's platoon was undergoing a rifle inspection in the garden of a large house, a quarter of a mile behind the lines when a shrapnel shell burst 50 yards to their left, followed by a second to their right. Lieutenant Leslie Crowther 'rushed us all into the cellar – just in time ... crash one came through the building and burst at the cellar head.'[48]

On 15 June, back in the trenches, they were alarmed at the construction of a machine-gun strong point in the German trenches, 170 yards away. At 11.15pm Lieutenant Crowther, Captain Stott, Lieutenant Liddal and Corporal Harry Convoy crept across to investigate. They reached the German barbed wire but a German patrol circled behind them. A hand grenade exploded, knocking Convoy's rifle from his hand and seriously wounding Crowther. Liddal 'emptied his revolver into the rotters' who ran towards their own trenches. The Huddersfield men began their own tortuous return journey, Stott, Liddal and Convoy taking turns at covering their retreat and at crawling with the unconscious Crowther on their backs, inching him back to the British trenches. Stretcher bearers came out 'under heavy rifle fire' to carry him the last few yards, but it was too late to save his life.

Lieutenant Leslie Crowther, a popular comrade – 'exceptionally sociable' and 'fond of a hearty sing song' – was laid to rest well behind the trenches 'amongst a cluster of well-tended "Heroes" graves.' The service was conducted by the Colonel, with his comrades as bearers.

When we pass his resting place practically every head is turned reverently towards his grave ... We are accustomed on leaving the trenches, to indulge in singing and mouth organ selections on reaching a certain point behind the lines ... But not a murmur passed from us as we marched quite solemnly to our billets. His familiar figure was not to be seen at the head of our Platoon, therefore the gloominess cast over us.[49]

The Huddersfield and Colne Valley Territorials endured a torrid 18-day tour in July, split evenly between third line, front line and ration-carrying duties. On the first morning Privates J Howson and Harry Brook of Marsden were scouting 800 yards from their battalion when Howson was struck by shrapnel. His leg was broken, and he recalled:

Harry tried to get me on his back to carry me out of the firing line, for the bullets were flying around us all the time, but ... I could not stand it being moved like that. So he ran for the stretcher-bearers. I think I am lucky to get away with a broken leg ... we had gone in for 18 days and there were eight more wounded before 10am on the first day.[50]

On 10 July, 20 men of the 7th Dukes were among the first to experience a new German weapon, gas shells. Sergeant W Warwick reported that they 'had not time to get our helmets on.'[51] Freddie Smith saw some of the victims reeling through the communication trenches, 'just like drunken men, eyes rolling, biting their tongues, and gasping for breath.' Anxious to allay his parents' fears that they were defenceless again the gas, he added, 'We have all got 2 respirators and a gas helmet. The helmet is made of thick flannelette with a celluloid eyepiece.'[52]

Three days later the 5th Dukes suffered a similar fate, a private confirming:

... large number of men ... gassed today by gas shells ... you must excuse my writing, as my eyes are still watering from the effects ... although we are in the support trenches we are shelled all day and all night. The noise is awful and makes our heads ache ...

Our men are to be admired. They are more than brave ... A shell has just come over and burst about twenty yards away, and the splinters have come into the dug-out. I am all right, unless a shell bursts over the top, and then it will be all up. If we had not been such a good regiment they would not have put us here. Huddersfield ought to feel very proud of her battalion.[53]

His constant fear was that 'it was our turn next.'[54] On 21 July it was the 'turn' of seven men of the 7th Dukes. Bandsman and stretcher bearer Robert H Watson wrote:

A trench mortar shell burst in the middle of seven of the Marsden Company and wounded them all. Sidney Uttley was amongst them, and I am afraid he will lose both his legs. They amputated one ten minutes after the affair happened.'[55]

'Shockingly wounded', 30-year-old Sidney Uttley died a week later.[56]

Relatives of the fallen received the dreadful news by telegram, often accompanied by a letter of sympathy and commendation from a commanding officer. The following letter was written by Captain Cecil Lockwood to the parents of another Colne Valley Territorial, 16-year-old Private Herbert Lionel 'Bertie' Broadbent, who was killed near Ypres on 31 July 1915.

Dear Mr and Mrs Broadbent,

It is with the greatest regret that I have to inform you of the death of your son, who was killed early this morning whilst on duty. He was shot through the head by a sniper and death was instantaneous. I wish to convey to you on behalf of the officers, NCOs, and men of the company our deepest sympathy on your loss. You son was an excellent and efficient bomber; he was one who will not be easily replaced. It will be some consolation to you when you remember that your son died doing his duty for his King and country. He is to be buried tonight by the side of some of his comrades.[57]

Private Walter Owen Davies of the 5th Dukes was luckier. He and three comrades were playing cards outside their dug-out but decided to go in as it was quite windy. Within seconds a shrapnel shell burst precisely where they had been playing.[58]

Amidst the hullabaloo, many yearned for the familiarity and security of home. Private Victor Mallinson of Golcar wrote to his father:

> I can just imagine the old valley now, and hear the old voices, and the noise of the traffic. It would feel grand to read the old books, and argue the old politics … some of the chaps are just singing "Jesu, lover of my soul," at a church meeting a few yards away, an aeroplane is supplying the tune up above, and shells are bursting just in front ... I don't know how it is, but I can pray better and feel God better when I am alone than at a church meeting. The shells are still bursting, the birds are still singing, the sun is still shining, and hell is still where we are … I wonder how long we shall walk in darkness, and how long we shall remain ignorant and selfish, and if we shall ever learn the true story of Christianity and the Sermon on the Mount.[59]

E Dixon, a Sapper with the Royal Engineers, expressed his longing for home in verse.

Oh Huddersfield!
by E. Dixon, Sapper, Royal Engineers

Oh Huddersfield!
Could I but see your spires and chimneys tall,
Could I but hear my footsteps fall
Upon your noble streets and roadways wide,
Then would I rest contented, satisfied.

Oh Huddersfield!
When on that day I left your precincts rare,
I thought that I should see towns just as fair.
But little did I know the grief and pain,
That I should feel e'er I returned again!

Oh Huddersfield!
I've seen St Paul's and viewed the Albert Hall,
Trafalgar Square with Nelson's Column tall.
But, pooh! These sights I find can ne'er compare
With Gledhill Chapel and St George's Square.

Oh Huddersfield!
One evening, feeling like a bloomin' hero,
I ordered dinner at the Trocadero,
And dined like any Lord; but without boast,
I much prefer a Whiteley's egg – on toast.

Oh Huddersfield!
I left old England's shores one summer night,
And saw our fairest isle – the Isle of Wight,
But I would give the island (if I could);
Just for one glimpse of Grimscar Wood.

Oh Huddersfield!
They talk about the "boulevards" in France,
And Rue de Whatnots, where they sing and dance;
But all those things would vanish in the dark
Could I but hear the band in Greenhead Park.

Oh Huddersfield!
I've seen the German "coal-boxes" come o'er
And smash perhaps a dozen chaps, or more;
But still for thrilling scenes this isn't in it
When Wagstaff gets the ball for half a minute!

Oh Huddersfield!
The "statesmen" say that if we only try
Berlin we shall all get to bye-and-bye.
I'll bet the first to tread the streets will be
A lad from Huddersfield. Just – "wait and see."[60]

Freddie Smith was also pining for home, dispirited by 'fleas, flies, mosquitoes and shells' and of conditions that left him 'clayed-up, unshaven, unwashed.' He 'thought nothing of catching 20 [fleas] at a time and they are as big as flies.'[61]

His platoon ended July with six nights of ration-carrying from 8.30pm each evening. Their journey began across fields which were open to rifle and shell fire 'in four directions.' On arriving at the many identical-looking support, communication and front line trenches, Freddie navigated by using the signposts that had been erected - 'Skipton Road, Huddersfield Road, Colne Valley and Argyle Street.' He was 'up Skipton Road' at 10pm one evening when a wave of homesickness struck him:

> … my working pal said where were you at this time last year ... of course that knocked the stuffing out of me, as I recalled Lockwood Cricket Club Gala.[62]

None were seriously wounded in the platoon's perilous nightly journeys, but Freddie confessed:

Sometimes you get so far in the rear, marching in, you are as good as lost
when you come to a spot where different trenches branch off.

… this last 6 days have knocked me out, my nerves are going, I am sure. The least noise or the sound of a shell makes me duck and get under … I shall be alright when we shift from here, but oh God if we stay here much longer it will wreck me and many more.[63]

Like thousands of others, he found that smoking helped him to cope.

I know you don't like me to smoke heavy dad, but believe me when I tell you, it has a nice soothing effect on the nerves.[64]

The unrelenting anxiety compounded the debilitating effects of poor diet on Freddie's physique and morale. By 7 August, towards the end of the tour, Freddie was 'not as well as I might be ... a bit upset in the nervous system.'[65]

We get solid food but hardly enough variation ... I am losing weight. I'll bet I don't weigh 7 stone… By gum I am hungry Dad. Half a loaf a day and a bit of boiled fatty bacon ...[66]

Freddie celebrated his 19th birthday on 18 August, and was overjoyed to receive a cake from his parents which, despite his hunger, he shared with his mates.[67] Freddie's letter of 5 September suggests that the extent of their food shortages may have been concealed from the bigwigs.

The last four days we have had in our tent (of 14 men) 4 loaves per day, but yesterday when we were inspected by General Plumer we had 7 loaves in our tent.[68]

General Plumer was not averse to belittling the troops at inspections. On learning that diminutive 18-year-old Willie Heywood from Todmorden was 'a weaver' he replied:

I know the type. Sleep four to a bed and go to the football on Saturdays.[69]

Freddie was becoming increasingly resentful.

We are overworked … They expect us to be just as if we were at Doncaster, but ... we don't get the like grub.[70]

In late July he was disciplined for smoking whilst coming out of the trenches and losing his gas helmet. After six days of extra fatigues he had to go sick with 'bad feet.'[71] He received a further hour of fatigues following a parade and inspection in early September.

I wanted a shave, the officer got hold of my few shagglers and was pulling them but I pulled away from him and stared him in the face.[72]

After an arduous summer, the local battalions spent the first half of September on rest, and Freddie decided to do something about his hunger. Employing his skills as an apprentice tailor, he patched up some of the officers' clothing, earning 5 francs (4s 2d), equivalent to over four days' pay. Then he set off with Charlie Bateman of Huddersfield 'to a neighbouring village and bought some eggs and bread, custard powders, and post cards, glass of lemonade, biscuits, buns, coffee, more biscuits … oh what a spread.'[73]

Sketches of Tommy's life
Out on rest. — N° 5   A regular carouse of coffee and fried eggs is one of the things we always have when we get to one of these villages.

They were in such a quiet part of the line that 'the lads have made improvised rafts and float up and down the (Yser) canal not a mile from Ypres.' Freddie paid a second visit to town to see the 6th Division's Concert Troupe, 'The Fancies'. Once again he 'ate and ate.'[74] By mid-September he reported that 'The food is better, though still not enough of it.'[75]

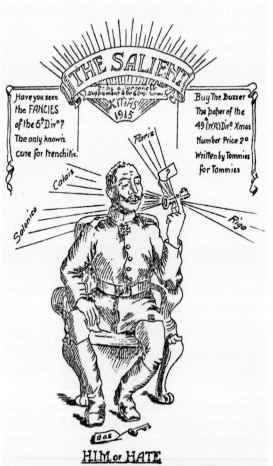

Left: Front cover of *The Salient* dated Christmas 1915, one of many satirical newspapers produced on the western front. Top left is an advertisement for the concerts of 'The Fancies.' Top right is an advertisement for *The Buzzer*, a similar publication produced by the 49th (West Riding) Division.

Above: Seven weeks after *The Salient* was published, the first issue of *The Wipers Times or Salient News*, the most famous of the western front newspapers, was published by the 12th Battalion Sherwood Foresters (Nottingham & Derbyshire Regiment).

The Battle of Loos

By August 1915 Great Britain and her Empire had 28 of the 132 Allied Divisions on the Western Front, France supplying 98 and Belgium 6. They were opposed by 102 German Divisions.

The British, as a minor partner, were cajoled by the French into supporting their large scale September attack in the area around Loos. British forces would advance between Loos and Givenchy over difficult terrain that hampered the speed of attack and the arrival of reinforcements. Little went right. Poor weather, well-positioned and fortified German trenches and machine gun positions, well-timed counter-attacks, mostly by troops kept out of range until artillery barrages had ended, and superior German weaponry, all conspired to frustrate the Allies.[76] Even the first use of chlorine gas by the British army, released on 25 September, had a mixed impact. Some of it blew back into the Allied trenches. In addition, some of the keys to release the gas did not fit the cylinders so that the still full cylinders released their deadly contents into the British trenches when pierced by fragments from German shells. The Germans suffered hundreds of gas casualties, but there were also over 2500 British casualties from their own gas, seven of whom died.[77]

Signaller Harry Clay of Huddersfield served at Loos with the 10th Battalion, York and Lancaster Regiment, part of the British Army's 21st Division. Landing in France in the first week of September, they joined the reserve lines at the battlefield, already exhausted from days of marching.[78] To compound their weariness, as Signaller CW Storin of Huddersfield recalled, 'On Saturday night [25 September] and Sunday we were without food and water, and wet to the skin.' At 9am on Sunday 26 September they were ordered into the second wave of an attack on a German stronghold at the summit of Hill 70, a strategic position key to controlling passage along the Lens-La Bassée Road east of Loos. By 10am the Allies were being driven back and the official order to retreat came at 11am. Signaller Storin continued:

> The fighting had been heavy … and we had suffered heavily and I had not gone far before I received a bullet wound in the left ankle … to come out alive I had to get away, as we were being shelled … and the fire from machine gun and rifle was awful … I could not walk, I crawled bit by bit till I saw Harry [Clay], and he asked me the trouble. I wanted him to leave me and get away, as gas shells and shrapnel burst all around us. But he would not. He threw away his kit and rifle, and carried me on his back. We went through barbed wire and captured trenches, resting in places that seemed sheltered from shells and bullets. It took him quite an hour to convey me to the field dressing-station, where he dressed my wound.[79]

Private H Kaye from Newsome also served at Loos, with the 5th London Field Ambulance which remained in the vicinity as minor skirmishes continued after the main offensive was abandoned on 14 October. Writing at the end of October, he had …

> … not had my boots off for over a week, and I see no prospect of having them off yet … we are in a lively corner indeed. We are shelled every day but always send plenty back. Passing through the village [Loos] every night we are fired at by scores of snipers. During the day we dare not get out of the trenches for a minute. The village is creepy by night; not a house has escaped bombardment, and as one passes through in black darkness great shell holes bar the whole road.
>
> There are some bodies out in the open before our dressing station. They have been there almost a month and no one dare bury them. It is a very civilised war is it not?

At the start of November he was shot in the chest, but regarded this as a blessing in disguise.

> Had it not come then it probably would have later that night, for I was going up the line as guide to a bearer party, and I must admit I was not looking forward to the journey. Stretchers were impossible in the trenches and we were going to go up the road. I had been along the same road the previous night and a dozen bullets or more had whistled close by … [being hit] saved me the trouble of going up the line.[80]

Autumn at Ypres

Freddie Smith had similar thoughts in early August when he suffered 'a graze with a bullet above the elbow ... I was mad it wasn't a bit worse, another half inch would have got me to Blighty.' Through the summer the Dukes had manned the trenches east of Ypres, close to the Yser Canal longer than any other regiment. By 18 September they were back in the front line at the head of the Ypres Salient, 'practically surrounded.' Freddie was on sentry duty, eight hours on, six hours off ... 'Then they are surprised when you are caught asleep on sentry.'[81] The trenches were 'so shallow' that they could not make 'a drop of tea' and had to be very careful when lighting a cigarette at night.[82] Any fallen comrade could not be rescued until it was dark, when the Germans would fire grenades, 'as they knew we should be attending to him.'

> You go down a trench on your knees of course and you find yourself creeping over dead bodies, partly buried men's feet sticking out of the parapet, and this lot coupled with plenty of sentry and little sleep, and any amount of work ... pick up a paper and read of shirking ... It is enough to knock a fellow daft. If some of them stayed in these trenches many days I guarantee they will not be far off Storthes Hall [psychiatric hospital].
>
> I could tell you lots of things ... but there is a man called the "Censor," who is liable to get you "First Field Punishment" ... strapped up to a tree so ... we are not allowed to speak our minds and we must bide time.[83]

A planned rest period for the 49th Division on the coast was postponed owing to renewed German activity. Somehow, the Germans had been informed of British plans and, having disrupted them, shouted across No Man's Land: 'We hope you enjoy yourself at Calais, you of the 49th Division.'[84] On 6 October, Freddie came out of the trenches so 'deadbeat' that he felt dizzy and collapsed.

Shortly afterwards, they learned that on their next tour in the front line they were to charge the enemy. In preparation, on 10 October Freddie's platoon was 'learning bomb-throwing' and 'practising the attack.' A German shell landed next to his dug out in the reserve trenches, making a crater 12 feet deep and 20 feet across, but Freddie was more concerned that ...

Next time it will be "over the top" and the best of luck to the 5th Dukes.[85]

Sensing that he had aged a great deal, Freddie had a photograph taken, and wrote to his friend, Frank Hirst:

> By gum, Frank, don't you think I have put 20 years on.

Sketches of Tommy's life

At the Base. — N° 9

You might one day put on all your stuff, and say to yourself " It is impossible to carry all this ". But all the time the Q. M. department is getting together a lot more to hand you as a parting gift !

By 14 October all was 'Bustle and Stir.'

> … we go into the trenches tonight ... As I look at my pack I wonder how I am going to carry it down to the trenches, a distance of 8 miles.[86]

Two days later, with the attack imminent, Freddie was 'on a digging party' close to the front line at Boesinghe, north of Ypres, when a shell burst among them. A large fragment struck Freddie. It was a fatal blow. His parents received the news in a letter from his pals:

> … he lived for about 15 minutes and kept cheerful all the time.[87]

Official notification came the following day from 2nd Lieutenant Gledhill, who attempted to sanitise Freddie's suffering:

> … his death was instantaneous.[88]

His pals paid him a glowing tribute:

> He was the life and soul of the Platoon and we shall miss his cheery face ... If at any time we felt a bit gloomy, he would have us altogether in his dug out, and give us a few selections on his mouth organ ... and we would sing with him and so pass the gloominess away ... it has been the severest blow ...
>
> He was laid to rest this afternoon, in a pretty little spot just behind the line amongst a cluster of well tended Heroes' graves. Nearly all our platoon was there and it could not have been possible to have a better service.[89]

The service was conducted by the Chaplain, Dr JMB Page who, at almost 70 years of age, regularly visited the trenches 'cheering the boys with comforts.'

Private Arthur Senior also wrote to Freddie's parents:

> I was there when he was put to rest. Never shall I forget the service. Oh it was beautiful.
>
> He often used to talk about you, and many a time the tears would roll down his cheeks, and he would say, "wait till I get back home, and I will do all I can to make up for what I have lost." He intended to do all in his power to help the work of the Chapel.[90]

Shortly before his death, Freddie had written to his parents:

> Yesterday in Arthur Senior's dug out we sat and sung "Jesus Lover of my soul" "I've found a friend" and other good hymns and I nearly cried, in fact I did do with joy. My voice was croaked and hoarse and his was flat, but I never enjoyed a sing better in all my life.
>
> I was happy as a King and as safe. Oh it's good to be a Christian, to acknowledge Christ as our Saviour and Keeper.[91]

Receiving and replying to letters from Freddie had become a way of life for his parents and sisters. There would be no more letters.

Year End: Stalemate on the Western Front

Despite the steady stream of casualties along the front line and heavy losses at the set piece battles – Loos alone cost 61,000 British casualties, including 7766 dead – there was stalemate on the western front. General French carried the can for the continued lack of progress and high casualty rate. Pilloried for delaying the mobilisation of reserve troops, he was replaced by General Haig as Commander-in-Chief.[92]

At the end of 1915 Germany's 'long game' strategy was on course. They had maintained a stalemate in the west and significantly eroded Russian manpower, resources, unity and resolve in the east. Emboldened by German successes and enticed by an offer of Serbian territory, Bulgaria had sided with the Central Powers in October. The Bulgarian army now prevented the Allies from assisting the Serbs from the south via Greece, leaving the Serbs beleaguered.

The Central Powers had, though, lost Italy which had switched sides in May, to the delight of Private Joseph Boetta, formerly a landscape gardener at Holmfirth, who wrote to the *HDE* from an army concentration camp in Bologna.

Really our officers are good to us, and all the soldiers are from a great family – the family of the new great Italy. Our king, our brave king, is always amongst his soldiers, encouraging, giving orders, and seeing that every soldier is well ... we have to fight against those terrible enemies – the cold, the Alps, and the Austrians. Yes, the Alps are a great obstacle and full of danger and the cold is great.[93]

The Italians would engage the armies of Austria-Hungary for the next three years, keeping them from other theatres of war. Most of the fighting was on a 400-mile front of the Isonzo River to the north of the Adriatic, now in Slovenia, but then just inside Austria. It was flanked by mountains on either side. There were 12 battles in total, four in 1915. Italy had the larger armies, but Austria-Hungary held the mountains, and the Italians suffered great losses attacking strongly fortified positions. By the end of the war there were 300,000 Italian and 200,000 Austrian and Hungarian casualties.[94]

On the western front the Huddersfield lads were more than doing their bit. JW Schofield, who had manned a Huddersfield-funded YMCA hut behind the lines, returned to Huddersfield and spoke with pride about the 49th Division. He told a packed Temperance Hall.

They held a record almost second to none of any men who had gone to France ... they held the hottest part of the line from July 20th to December 30th [1915], and in spite of one of the most terrible gas attacks had never lost a trench.[95]

Even allowing for bias and hyperbole, their record was distinguished. But for the troops and their families there were no more illusions about the nature of this war. The smiles of the departing battalions in August 1914 were a distant memory. By December 1915 many tears were shed by soldiers returning to the front after a period of leave.

On 1 December a reporter from the *HDE* interviewed Private JH Mulleague of the 2nd Dukes in his aunt's house at Nont Sarah. Private Mulleague had fought at the battles of Mons, the Marne, Aisne and Hill 60, and was on his last night of leave before returning to France.

To have come through most of the big battles in France and Belgium without so much as a scratch and to come home after serving for fifteen months at the front is unfortunately the lot of but few men.

In one of the spacious and airy tearooms was the gladdening sight of a well-built fire. The soft suffused light of an oil lamp revealed on the mantelpiece two of the long shell cases of the famous French "75" guns, nosecaps of various shells, and other war trophies – the outward evidence of the returned warrior.

... without an ounce of superfluous flesh, he looked remarkably fit and well. But there was that far away look about the eyes that one notices so often in the young soldier who has come back from "the jaws of hell".

Private Mulleague's older brother, Private Charles Harry Mulleague, had been killed at Neuve Chapelle, and he recalled several narrow escapes of his own when comrades had perished. At Arras a platoon of the 2nd Dukes was dug into a railway embankment when …

… a number of Germans advanced with their arms up in token of surrender. As soon as a number of our men went over the parapet to bring the prisoners in the Germans fell down flat onto the ground, revealing a large force behind them, who took a heavy toll of the Dukes.

At Hooge Wood in November 1914 Private Mulleague had been shot at, shelled, led a bayonet charge, and fought hand-to-hand. The German attack was repelled, but his battalion was reduced from 850 men to 107. Chillingly, he added that, to cope with the trauma of a bayonet charge …

… the men literally go mad and seem to remember little of it afterwards.

It was time to leave.

Private Mulleague got his great coat on and picked up his rifle ... After bidding farewell to his aunt and uncle he set out with one if his cousins and the "Examiner" representative for Outlane. As one trudged through the slush and met the driving snow one instinctively thought of the trenches on such a night, and of the noble self-sacrifice, the perpetual cheerfulness, and the never failing courage of the men who are face to face with death.[96]

TILL THE BOYS COME HOME (3).

Over seas there came a pleading, "Help a nation in distress!"
And we gave our glorious laddies: honour bade us do no less;
For no gallant son of Britain to a foreign yoke shall bend,
And no Englishman is silent to the sacred call of friend.

A postcard produced by
Bamforth and Co Ltd of
Holmfirth and New York

Blue Plaque on the Bamforth's factory in Holmfirth, part of Holme
Valley Civic Society's Blue Plaque Trail

Having said their goodbyes in Huddersfield, the local troops witnessed many more goodbyes on their journey south. Driver James McKenzie, a postman from Holmfirth serving with an Ammunition Supply Column, described the scene in London.

> On our arrival at Victoria, I almost thought I was in some barracks square – in fact, it could be called the khaki meeting place, as troops from every branch of the British Army were present, coming to catch the boat train for the last ride on English soil …
>
> My word, I don't think there is a writer in the world who could fruitfully describe the pathos of this parting place. Sweethearts, wives and mothers looked longingly at the train, as if they would have liked to have gone with those whom they are giving to England. You must not think that all the tears were on the women's side. They were on the cheeks of many a soldier – and who shall say it was any shame on their manhood? On the contrary, it rang out shame on those single young fellows who appear to think they have no right to do their turn.
>
> … the guard blew his whistle as a warning, and the bright chatter ceased as if by magic, and earnest hand grips were given with male friends, whilst husbands clasped wives in fervent embraces, and tried their best to comfort them with very shaky voices, and at the same time sweethearts were having a last lingering kiss.
>
> … a no doubt well-meaning friend with a cornet played "Homeland" and "Home Sweet Home"… pent-up feelings gave way. As the cry "All doors shut, please," sounded up the platform a rush was made for the carriages, and with the exception of a farewell salute from windows all goodbyes were over. As we steam out from the station a mighty shout goes up from hundreds of throats as if to remind each one that kindly hearts are ready to give us a hearty welcome on our return.[97]

A series of wartime advertisements for 'Perfection Soap' from the *HDE*. Ridiculing the leaders of the Central Powers, they double as propaganda.

Top left (15 November 1915): depicts the cleansing of Kaiser Wilhelm by Britannia and two servicemen. **Top right** (22 November 1915): Britannia extends the process to all the leaders, left to right, Kaiser Wilhelm; Mehmed V, leader of the Ottoman Empire; Francis Josef (Austria and Hungary); Tsar Ferdinand of Bulgaria (held by Britannia); and Crown Prince William, son of the Kaiser.

Bottom left (31 March 1916): Britannia mangles the leaders, left to right, Ferdinand; Crown Prince William; Francis Josef; Mehmed V; and the Kaiser (seated).

Bottom right (30 November 1916): Britannia, watched by an approving John Bull, hangs the leaders out to dry, left to right, Mehmed V; Ferdinand; Francis Josef; Crown Prince William; and Kaiser Wilhelm.

Chapter 7

1915-16: Gallipoli

The Strategy

In late 1914, Winston Churchill, First Lord of the Admiralty, devised plans to open up a war front to the east of the Central Powers. His target was the Gallipoli peninsula, 45 miles long and ten miles wide overlooking the narrow Dardanelles Strait which connected the Aegean Sea to the Black Sea, through Constantinople.

It made strategic sense. Control of the peninsula and the Dardanelles would provide a platform for an advance on Constantinople, the capture of which would secure a supply route to the Russians on the eastern front. The alternative supply routes west of Russia were blocked by the Central Powers and sea routes to the north were long and difficult. Protection of the Suez Canal would also be reinforced, and it might even be possible to progress westwards to open up further battle fronts that would stretch the armies of the Central Powers.

Opposing them were the Turks, whose leader, Enver Pasha, was a military officer and national hero. He had sided with the Central Powers with an eye to regaining territory from the Russians. Any qualms he had about opposing Britain, traditionally an ally of the Turks, dissipated when Britain commandeered all ships under construction in British shipyards, including two on Tyneside which had been paid for by the Turkish government through funds raised by public subscription. Germany exploited Britain's diplomatic blunder by giving two ships to the Turks, albeit ships that were effectively stranded at Constantinople for the duration of the war.

British forces first engaged the Turks in Mesopotamia, in protection of British oil wells in the Middle East. The first assaults on the Gallipoli peninsula were periodic naval bombardments between November 1914 and March 1915. Underestimating the strength and resolve of the Turks, and largely ignorant of the region's distinctive geography, Britain's naval assaults yielded no territory or control. Instead, they forewarned the Turks who strengthened their land fortifications and mined the Dardanelles. When the British stepped up the naval attacks in March they met unexpectedly stubborn resistance, and retreated when several ships struck mines.

The attempt to pave the way for an amphibious invasion had failed, but the strategic ends had such potential that the British War Council proceeded, unprepared for most of the practicalities.

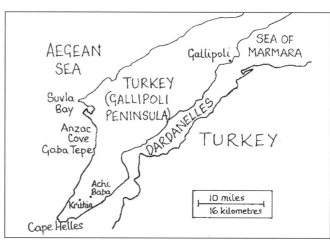

The Gallipoli Peninsula

April Landings

The Allies' Mediterranean Expeditionary Force which landed in April 1915 comprised the British 29th Division, which was an amalgamation of the last pre-war regulars, the Australian and New Zealand (Anzac) Corps, the Royal Marine Division and a French corps. Leading the force, Sir Ian Hamilton was unaware that the Turks were waiting in strongly fortified positions above the beaches, or that they had 84,000 troops, similar to his own numbers. He knew little about the inhospitable steep-sided, parched, rocky, scrub-covered hills and ravines, or about the paucity of fresh water.[1]

Serving in the Australian army were Lewis Dyson, a Netherton man who had emigrated to Sydney, and Private F Dent, formerly of Holmfirth. On 24 April 1915 they sailed from Egypt to Gallipoli aboard the dreadnought flagship HMS *Queen Elizabeth*. She was followed by destroyers, and 'the great bulk of the battleships.' Soon after midnight they approached their landing beach on the west coast of the peninsula at Gaba Tepe.[2] But the Turks were more prepared than the Allies had been led to expect. Lewis Dyson recalled:

> At 1am we filed into open boats, and towed by steam pinnaces, headed for the hostile shore … silence was maintained.
>
> I was in the first barge of the first tow – the first boat to reach the shore. We were loaded down with all our equipment, 200 rounds of ammunition and five days' supply of food. At dawn we approached ... with every sense alert. A dog barked, then a shot was fired, then two more, then a perfect fusillade, and the pinnace cast us off and shouted, "Pull for your lives, lads," and opened up with her machine guns. The boat grounded and out we jumped into the sea up to our armpits, with the shrapnel cracking overhead and machine guns knocking over our poor fellows.[3]

In a following barge, Private Dent described …

> … the enemy's shells and bullets … dropping all around us ... Our boat suffered no casualties, but most others did.

The immediate aim was to drive several miles inland and establish control of the high land. But a parallel Anzac force had drifted a mile off course, landed on the wrong beach at Ari Burnu and found their advance impeded by steep cliffs. There was greater initial success at Gaba Tepe. Lewis Dyson continued:

> There was a panting rush over 30 feet of beach and we fell under a ledge, threw off our packs, and fixed our bayonets as other boats landed. Then somebody said, "What are we here for? Come on the ninth," and up the hill we went in a mad rush for the Turkish trenches. The sight of cold steel and the thousands of the 3rd Brigade racing for them from the beach was too much for the enemy, and they fled – some too late got the bayonet – and we had the first ridge.

The Anzacs land at Gaba Tepe

Private Dent also pursued Turks who 'ran for their lives' at 'the least flash' of bayonet.

> We had to take a few hills in that way when we landed ... Fellows who have been at Mons say it was nothing to our work on the 25th, and an old Boer War man told me that he saw more fighting on that Sunday morning than he saw in six months in South Africa.
> It was a grim, desperate and successful struggle.

The attack was assisted from the sea.

> Our big battle squadron helped ... all around could be heard the awful crashing of the *Queen Elizabeth*'s 15 inch guns.
> Didn't we give a cheer every time she sent a shell. Otherwise we had only our own rifles against the enemy's ordinary artillery, howitzers, machine guns and rifles. We could not land our guns till we captured the hills overlooking the sea.
> We captured first one hill, and then the second and when we captured the third we came into contact with the main Turkish forces – with a lot of Germans amongst them.

The advance of the tiring Anzacs was losing momentum. The Turks and Germans held their line and the number of Anzac casualties escalated rapidly. The tide of the day's battle was turning, and Private Dent was shocked by the ferocity of the resistance.

> It was terrible! They simply rained shrapnel on us, also explosive bullets and dum-dums. I was wearing my C.E.M.S. (Church of England Men's Society) badge on a watch chain through the button hole of my left breast pocket and it was shot clean away ... [then] a bullet whizzed past my arm taking part of my tunic with it and scarring my arm.

Private Dent carried two wounded men through the deadly fire from the front line to the shelter of a gully. Then, at noon, he attempted a third such run.

> I had got about thirty yards off our firing line when a shrapnel shell burst, and I was hit. We knew well enough what the Turks would do if they caught us wounded, so I knew my best plan was to get back to the beach where the R.A.M.C. were, as quickly as I possibly could.

Sheltering where he could, it took Private Dent three hours to reach the beach. He had lost a lot of blood.

> No one can praise the R.A.M.C. too much. I reckon that every stretcher bearer there that Sunday won the V.C. if ever it was won.

He was ferried to a destroyer and shipped back to Alexandria. There were so many wounded aboard that there was insufficient food, and officers sacrificed their meals so that the injured could be fed. Hospitalised for several days, Private Dent reflected:

> War is a terrible thing, but it brings out in mankind all that is noblest, truest and best.

Meanwhile, Lewis Dyson was still on the peninsula as the battle raged on. Gradually beaten back, many Anzacs became trapped in valleys and gullies, vulnerable to fire from much of the surrounding land. Somehow, they consolidated on a narrow strip of high ground, the loss of which would doom them to annihilation on the beach.

On 3 May, nine days in, Lewis Dyson spotted a private who was badly wounded. Lewis started to help him back to the beach, but a bullet went through his left thigh. Requiring assistance himself, he made it to the beach under heavy shrapnel fire and was rowed out to a hospital ship. He had just boarded when an 11 inch shell burst alongside, sending up 'a column of water twice as high as the mast.' The ship retired out of range and Lewis was eventually hospitalised at Menoufia in Egypt.[4]

The battle was a catastrophe for the Anzacs. They lost 10,000 men on the first day alone. 25 April is still commemorated as Anzac Day. The extent of the disaster was concealed from the British public, and on 14 June 1915 the following poem, reprinted from the *Daily Chronicle*, appeared in the *HDE*.

'Scoring Well'
by
Special Correspondent of the *Daily Chronicle* in the Dardanelles

How often for the tented slopes
In summer, we've acclaimed
The stalwart drive that topped the ropes,
The wrist-stroke neatly aimed!
How long the bowlers strained each nerve
Before each wicket fell,
While waiting wires received the news,
"Australia scoring well."

How oft on winter days gone by
We've heard the crowds acclaim
The swift low pass, the brilliant try,
The hard but sporting game.
The while across the world there leaps
Brief messages to tell,
"Another triumph for All Blacks,
New Zealand scoring well."

And now, when greater games are played,
And greater deeds are done,
Where sing the bullet and the blade
Beneath an Eastern sun,
More welcome to the homeland flash
The messages that tell,
"Australians and New Zealanders
Continue scoring well."[5]

Simultaneously with the Anzac landings on 25 April, 35,000 British and French troops landed at five beaches around Cape Helles on the southern tip of the peninsula, with further French forces at Kum Kale across the inlet on the Turkish mainland. The main body was to push inland from Cape Helles and meet up with the Anzac forces, occupying the southern end of the peninsula.

British and French troops reached higher land unopposed from three of their five beaches but allowed the Turks time to regroup and were soon driven back by strong counter attacks. The Turks retained control of the tops and the Allies were soon entrenched on or close to the beaches in a stalemate that resembled the western front. Between 29 April and 8 May the British made two assaults on the village of Krithia, a target on Day 1 of the campaign. All the assaults failed, and Reverend Creighton of the British force commented:

The Turkish positions only get stronger every day. ... They are magnificently well-led, well-armed and very brave and numerous.

Entrance to Gully Ravine, Cape Helles

Trench Warfare

The pattern was set. The narrow peninsula enabled the Turks, supported by the Germans, to hold the line without becoming too stretched. It would be a war of attrition. In less than a month Hamilton had lost one third of his troops. The Turks had also suffered heavily and on 24 May a truce was declared to allow both sides to bury their dead.[6]

On 4 June the British forces attempted a third attack on Krithia and initially pushed through the Turkish lines. But the Turkish positions held and the British forces failed to press home their advantage. The battle cost 15,500 casualties – 4500 British, 2000 French and 9000 Turkish.[7]

The lack of success caused consternation among the top brass, but Churchill remained convinced that Gallipoli could provide 'some of the shortest paths to a triumphant peace.' The Dardanelles Committee met in London on 7 June and acceded to Hamilton's request for reinforcements and ammunition. These were reassigned from the western front, much to the dismay of the Allied generals there as it reduced their chances of success in forthcoming battles, notably the Battle of Loos.[8]

Despite the setbacks, the British progressed about half a mile inland, mainly by stealth during the night. Within range of the Turkish line they entrenched. Two lines of trenches now scarred the landscape and, as on the western front, soldiers in the front line were periodically ordered to charge the enemy, usually at great cost.

On 4 July Private Thomas Frederick Marsden of Holmfirth, serving with the 1/6th Battalion, Manchester Regiment was in the front line when the order came to charge. Nearby was Private Harold Jackson.

> Tom was only a few paces away from me in the trench. I lost sight of him in the rush forward. The next I saw of him, he was leaning over the parapet of a side trench.

Tom had helped to capture some Turks, who seemed happy to be out of it. Escorting them to the Allied lines, they were suddenly subjected to rapid fire from several Turkish machine guns, forcing them to take cover behind some gorse bushes. One of Tom's comrades was badly hit in the lungs and called to him 'to come and bind him up.'

> Tom, like the brick he was, without any hesitation, got up and started to crawl across the bullet-swept open ground. He had hardly left the shelter of the bush, when the 'messenger of death' struck him in the head. I could see that death was instantaneous, and that it was useless to stay with him, so I hurried over to my company … very shocked and sad at the horror of it all … [He] died, not only doing his duty – and doing it well, but braved an awful fire, to try and succour a comrade in distress. Of all the actions of gallantry and self-sacrifice I have seen during my month in 'Dante's Inferno' on the peninsula I have never seen one to beat Tom's action.
> We went into the charge with 670 men, but when we landed at the position we were to take there were only 107 of the good old battalion left.[9]

August Reinforcements at Suvla Bay

Hamilton's reinforcements arrived in August, landing at Suvla Bay, five miles north of Anzac Cove on the west coast. One of these was Gerald Parker, a teacher at Lepton Council School, who described his experiences in a letter to the school's headmaster Mr F Lodge, beginning with the journey from Alexandria:

> ... the time came when we had to pack up, board special cars, and take our joy ride through the town, singing "Tipperary" and the usual stuff ... we scaled the gangway of an Allen liner, dropped our kits ... [we] became ... black ... with the coal dust which was flying about during coaling operations.

He described a 'pleasant zig-zagging trip through the Aegean', standard practice to reduce the risk from U-boats, and a final 'four-hour trip by Isle of Man paddle steamer.' No vessel was too humble for war service. As the paddle steamer approached Suvla Bay in the early hours of 7 August, a combined land and sea offensive was already underway.

... we heard the general row long before we came in sight of anything ... reminded me very much of a firework display at a water carnival I had seen at Knaresborough some years ago. Around us were huge Union Castle liners – hospital ships one blaze of colour from hundreds of green and red lamps. These, with the brilliant stars and the lights of other shipping, were all reflected in the dead calm sea. On the hills were the flashes from the various batteries and the bursting of shrapnel shells.[10]

British horses on the shore at Suvla Bay

Already on the beach was Private Walter Hayward of Holmfirth. One of Walter's comrades wrote:

We ... had to start fighting as soon as we landed, and if ever a lad won distinction, Walter did that night. He carried a wounded captain of our regiment right out of the Turks' trenches to a place of safety, and the bullets were simply raining all around him. He then pulled back to his regiment, but it appears he got lost ... It is easy to get lost in a charge if you cannot see ten yards in front of you, for bushes and ravines all over the hillsides ...

Walter Hayward and his comrade, Lance-Corporal Wood, found themselves with Dutch Fusiliers. Three nights later they were involved in a bayonet charge. Once again they became detached from their Battalion and lost their bearings in the dark. Walter was wounded and the Lance-Corporal stayed with him until it became clear that he had to go for medical assistance. Having left Walter to find help, he could not find him again. Nobody did, and Walter was recorded as 'wounded, missing.' Lance-Corporal Wood was killed two days later.[11]

Also at Suvla Bay were Huddersfield brothers Horace and Edward Wintringham. Horace had the desperate duty of writing to inform their parents that Edward had been killed, and struggled to find the words:

I don't know how to put it together, as we had it very hard. There are not many of us left.

In a moment of crass insensitivity the censor wrote over the final sentence, 'Quite a lot, cheer up.'[12]

The waste of these lives becomes starker in light of the inept leadership of the Suvla Bay attack. Unwisely, the elderly, inexperienced General Sir Frederick Stopford was put in command. Failing to grasp the urgency required, he fell asleep on board ship during the night time landings, and was sacked just over a week later. By then, the element of surprise had been lost, relatively few Turkish snipers had inflicted many casualties, and the opportunity to push inland and capture Tekke Tebe, the large hill that dominated the Suvla Plain across the centre of the peninsula, had been squandered. Substantial Turkish reinforcements had arrived, turning Suvla Bay into another attritional front.[13]

Whilst leadership inertia allowed the Turks to gain a foothold, Lepton teacher Gerald Parker helped to establish a bridgehead on the beach.

For the next three weeks I experienced a period of heavy fatigue work which I shall never forget. We were continually on the go, having only a short time to snatch a little food and sleep ... everything had to be carried by hand.

Now you would be amazed at the change along the coast – small railways, hoists and landing stages have sprung into existence in a very short time. After the tiring work … we were glad of a week in rest trenches, followed by a day or two in the firing line ... I had to glue my eyes to the lower end of a periscope by day and gaze over our parapet at night, with a skyline of Turkish trenches. As we were facing due east I must admit my eyes strayed occasionally from the bushes and hollows to Orion and Jupiter. I remembered one or two lessons with Standard IV, as I had plenty of time to think of good old days – and they do seem a long way back now.[14]

Fatigue, Illness and Hypothermia

Suvla Bay was the Allies' last chance to make significant inroads to the peninsula. The essential link-up between the forces at Cape Helles, Anzac Cove and Suvla Bay was becoming increasingly unlikely and the weather and general living conditions deteriorated from inhospitable to inhumane.

A Huddersfield corporal explained how he coped with the trauma and stress.

Things all seem to move so quickly ... I suppose the horrors are crossed out by fresh ones which occur. New men fill up the vacant gaps, and we forget the many dear lads missing who went through that happy twelve months of training in the old country.

Humour and blithe repartee also helped. As he advanced during an attack, the Corporal passed his company quartermaster limping his way painfully to the rear with a bullet through his ankle.

... one of our fellows sang out, "What about our rations?" Well ... the language he got in return was not fit for publication.

The Corporal also enjoyed the narrow escape of Paddy, 'one of my lads' who 'had to swim out for an empty box to boil our tea with.'

He had just reached the box and was paddling it easily ashore when gurr, gurr, gurr, whop bang – and a great bomb dropped within a few yards of him and exploded. It was from a Taube [monoplane] and was aimed at a warship. There seemed to be a mountain of water for a minute, and a kind of paddle wheel going 500 revolutions a minute coming ashore. It was Paddy. I don't know what new strokes he invented, but we had to laugh, he was so comical.

He also found levity in their enforced righteousness.

How can we be otherwise? There is no drink here ... there are no bad women here ... There is no gambling because we have no money. As for smoking – well everybody smokes. We are always at it, for it seems to be our only pleasure. The only thing wrong for a man to do is to rob his fellow men, and as "nobody has nowt" we are baulked from even that little deviation from the right.

Above all, the Corporal believed in the cause.

Our confidence in Lord Kitchener is never shaken for a minute ... I find almost all men here ... are firmly convinced of our final victory ... every man has a kind of little pleasure of his own ... knowing that he is doing his little bit.

Such faith was severely tested as the beleaguered invaders faced adversaries more potent than their Turkish/German enemies. Flies, lice, mosquitoes and rats bred in millions, incubated and nourished by excrement, rotting food, unburied dead bodies, stagnant water and the intense summer heat. They were 'enough to keep the combative spirit alive without the Turks.' The stench was unbearable. Illnesses escalated to epidemics of dysentery, diarrhoea and enteric fever (typhoid), ravaging the exhausted troops on both sides.

In five months at Gallipoli, the Huddersfield Corporal never 'slept under a roof' nor had 'a change of clothes except for bathes in the sea.'[15]

Only twice during the whole campaign did the proportion of men being evacuated … with wounds – during May and the two weeks of the August offensive – exceed the proportion being taken off with some form of illness.[16]

By late summer, 'endless traffic of small boats and barges' ferried men to hospital ships waiting to transport them to base hospitals in Egypt, Malta, or on the Greek island of Lemnos.

As the scale of the losses at Gallipoli became apparent, increasing medical resources were deployed to the area. In July 1915, 44-year-old Huddersfield Staff Nurse, Ada Stanley, a member of the Territorial Force Nursing Service who had trained at Huddersfield Royal Infirmary, was posted to Gallipoli. She served aboard HMHS *Mauretania*, which had recently been converted from troopship to hospital ship. Tending the ill and the wounded on a return journey from the peninsula, Ada contracted dysentery. Staunchly, she 'refused to leave her post until every sick soldier had been taken ashore.' She then collapsed. Shipped back to England, Ada died at Netley Hospital, near Southampton, on 22 December 1915.

Her memorial service was held in a small wooden church in the grounds of the Third Northern General Hospital, Sheffield. The congregation of 'blue-garbed wounded soldiers and white capped nursing sisters' heard the Bishop of Sheffield commend …

> … the heroic devotion displayed by the women of the country … the beauty of faith was manifested in the deeds of heroic women such as Ada Stanley.

Ada was the only Huddersfield woman to die on active service during the war. She is buried in St Paul's churchyard, Armitage Bridge, and is commemorated on the plaque alongside the Five Sisters Window in the North Transept of York Minster.[17]

Whilst Ada Stanley was making her final voyage, a new terror struck the Gallipoli troops. In October, dressed in now battered uniforms which many had 'adapted' to the heat of the summer, they suffered the first of the peninsula's winter storms. At Suvla Bay Private D Shaw of Huddersfield was 'drenched for two days.' Their dug outs, constructed deep in the ground, flooded and collapsed leaving them with no shelter. The storms were followed by a severe frost.

> … our clothes froze on us as hard as a board. We got them dry by alternate freezing and thawing.

Many died and Private Shaw was transported to a Maltese hospital suffering from dysentery, frostbite and 'septic poisoning of the leg' – one of numerous conditions collectively known as trenchfoot.[18]

To arrest the deepening crisis, Hamilton requested a further 95,000 men. Informed that these could not be spared from the western front or from Salonika, where troops were supporting the Serbs against the Bulgarians, Hamilton asked for permission to evacuate, estimating a 50% casualty rate from the operation. Finding this unacceptable, the Dardanelles Committee replaced him with Sir Charles Munro. Assessing the situation quickly on his arrival, Munro agreed that evacuation was the only option. The Government prevaricated, reluctant to admit defeat.[19] Meanwhile, men huddled together for life-saving warmth and yet more froze to death. Perhaps sensing a weakening foe, the Turks attacked with renewed force. A Huddersfield Field Ambulance Medic serving with the RAMC wrote:

> We had a pretty warm time the last 3 or 4 weeks, as the Turks got up many new heavy guns … and shelled us throughout the day. Everyone says the shelling at Cape Helles, and I believe at Suvla, during our last month there was heavier than any that had been. The officers from

France who had been transferred to the Dardanelles all say it was much worse at Helles than in France, as we could not get away from them owing to confined space.[20]

In December a great blizzard followed by a spectacular thaw caused a further 15,000 British casualties. Eventually, on 7 December, the evacuation was ordered, and Churchill resigned.

Evacuation

A Holmfirth Police-Constable who was an army regular of the 29th Division assisted the evacuation of Suvla Bay. He found it surprisingly straightforward. 'Suvla Bay was not so bad, for the Turks hardly expected it.'[21] Anzac Cove was evacuated at the same time. Between 10 and 20 December 105,000 men and 300 guns were withdrawn from the two areas. Somehow, the Turks believed that these were troop movements and the shelling was no worse than usual.

The Constable was then re-assigned to Cape Helles to assist with the final evacuation of the peninsula, aware that this would be much more difficult as the Turks now knew all were to be evacuated.

From 28 to 30 December the shelling intensified and the Field Ambulance Medic, on duty as surgeon to the stretcher bearers in the trenches, treated many serious cases.

> They were carrying stretchers along the trenches ... in parts the mud reached to the middle of their thighs, and they took eleven hours to get one case the full two miles.

Numerous men gave up their dug-outs and food for the patients.

> They were just splendid, and I am proud to say ALL north countrymen – Yorkshire, Lancashire and Tynesiders – mostly miners.[22]

With almost 40,000 troops to evacuate, not all could leave at once. How could the Allies prevent the last left on the peninsula from being overwhelmed and annihilated? They had a front line three miles long to protect, and it was five miles from the three landing stages on the southern beaches. Much of this territory could be seen from the Turkish fortress at Achi Baba. Somehow, they had to prevent the Turks reaching the beaches until just about everyone was on board ship.

From 29 December, evacuation subterfuge began in earnest. Under cover of darkness, barbed wire entanglements were positioned to impede any Turkish advance. It was perilous work. Half a mile from the Turkish line, the Constable was shot through the heel. Two nights later, working in an eleven-strong party, he was half buried in dirt from a shell. Later that night another shell 'knocked seven of our men to pieces ... It was a living hell.'

Despite this Turkish aggression, after 2 January the British fired no shots after 10pm. Would the Turks notice when there was hardly anyone left to fire them? On 7 January accurate German gunners destroyed the British galley, signalling station, two dug outs and several trenches. The following day they pounded the same trenches, roads and beaches 'harder than they had ever done before.' The Field Ambulance Medic confessed that ...

> ...they were all, officers and men, including myself, a bit shaken ... they never expected to even leave Helles, and many did not unfortunately.

Cape Helles on 7 January 1916; in the distance a fountain of water erupts from a shell that has just missed a landing stage.

The evacuation was now gathering pace, but the Huddersfield Constable drew the shortest of straws. He was ordered to man the furthest point of the front line.

> On the last fearful night and morning … I had orders to go with a staff captain to far outpost duty. We had to be at our post at 6pm as soon as it became dark.
>
> Troops were evacuated from there until 10pm. All had to leave with bags on their feet for silence, carrying only their rifle and ammunition… it was great to see them leave … not a murmur, not a sound, not a light. They left like ghosts.

There were now only 200 men left to hold the front line right across the peninsula. At the far end, the Constable and Staff Captain were just 50 yards from the Turkish trenches. For forty minutes they waited.

> … just think of the staff officer and me, the fix we were in. If the Turks had only known! That forty minutes is like a month to us.

At 1am they were ordered to leave. The last to traverse the trenches, they began the long, silent, ponderous walk under the parapets, and out onto five miles of paths, roads and scrubland to the beach.[23] There, several Huddersfield men were boarding the last few rowing boats. These included, at 3am, the Field Ambulance Medic, and 20-year-old Private Oswald Fisher from Paddock.[24]

Second-Class Warrant Officer JH Crabtree, of Divisional Headquarters, Royal Naval Division, also from Huddersfield, was undertaking voluntary 'special duties.' It is likely that he was mining the dug-outs, and the paths and roads to the beach. He boarded the penultimate boat to leave the shore. Mentioned in despatches for 'excellent work and devotion to duty during the Gallipoli campaign', and twice more during the war, Crabtree was awarded the Meritorious Service Medal in 1918.[25]

Between 3 and 4am the Constable and Staff Captain, still with bags on their feet, completed the exodus to the beach. The Constable recalled:

> When we arrived ... all our troops were aboard a transport ready to move away.

Waiting for them was a naval officer. They had one last task to perform.

> We… set fire to the stores and other resources, to leave as little for the Turks as possible. Seeing the flames, the Turks knew they had been tricked and opened up with shells – but there were only three of us left to hit!
>
> We hid behind cliffs, got to the water and met a jack tar with a motor boat … we all joined hands and stepped into the boat together, so that none of us could say he was the last man to leave the peninsula.

By 4am the three of them were aboard a battleship.

> … both the naval officer and staff captain shook me by the hand, and complimented me on the way I had stuck through it all … The battleship fired at the stores and at the Turkish positions. To see the fires from the sea and to hear the row of the Turks, it was pure hell … I shall never forget my last night and morning on the peninsula.[26]

There were further shocks in store for the Turks:

> The traps laid for the Turks were fiendish … on opening doors of dug-outs to obtain food … contact was made and mines blew them sky high.

Similar devices wired in the trenches and along the roads were observed to go up on the following day by officers aboard observation ships.

But the escaping British were not out of the woods. Half an hour from Cape Helles on the 40-mile westerly voyage to Lemnos their overcrowded destroyers hit a storm. The Huddersfield Field Ambulance Medic attempted to treat the ill and injured, but the decks were …

> … crowded with 760 men and officers, absolutely awash … The men had a fearful time… Imagine putting a splint on a man's leg with heavy seas washing over one, and so many

The guns of HMS *Cornwallis* add to the destruction of British stores on the beaches of Cape Helles, begun by the Huddersfield Constable, the Staff Captain and the naval officer.

> people on the deck that we could not move the men to the sick bay … all of us soaked to the skin and no available means of getting dry for 24 hours.

The voyage took almost nine hours, but the island port of Mudros offered little sanctuary …

> … a fearful place. It has rained incessantly for 48 hours and is blowing a gale. Many tents have collapsed, and all the men are soaking wet.

Back home, friends and relatives feared the worst. News from Gallipoli had dried up. There could be no public announcement of the evacuation and mail from the peninsula ceased as all the ships were required for troop transport. Relatives were left to wonder and worry.[27]

For some of the local survivors, the evacuation was only a reprieve. Private Allen Cliffe, who landed at Suvla Bay in August and suffered frostbite in November, was killed by a shell on the Somme on 28 September 1916.[28] A month later Private Oswald Fisher was also killed on the Somme.[29] Sergeant Elton Clay, a teacher and secretary at Sheepridge Wesleyan Sunday School, and a soldier of 'marked ability' who earned 'rapid promotion' following the Suvla Bay landings, was fatally wounded at the Battle of Arras in the spring of 1917.[30]

The fall-out from Gallipoli was considerable. With so much confusion on the battlefield, there are various estimates of the numbers of casualties, roughly 250,000 Allied and 300,000 Turks, with over 60% of these incapacitated or dead through illness.[31]

The Government was firmly on the defensive, claiming that the campaign was carefully planned and agreed by the 'experts'. The positive spin was that it had saved the Russians from defeat in the Caucasus and had annihilated the flower of the Turkish army.[32] These were peripheral to the stated objectives. Equally unquantifiable was the cost of diverting troops, ammunition and supplies from the Battle of Loos to Gallipoli.[33]

The Gallipoli campaign failed in its objectives. The stalemate represented success for the Central Powers, if a costly one in Turkish lives. The Allies' only success on the Gallipoli peninsula was getting off it. Not one life was lost during the brilliant evacuation.

Chapter 8

A Khaki Economy

The Demand for Khaki

When war was declared, Huddersfield's woollen and worsted industry, the heartbeat of the local economy, was immediately in crisis. The upheaval in Europe severed many export markets and suppliers of raw materials. The lucrative German buyers were gone for the duration of the war. At home, the uncertainty made consumers nervous, many restricting their spending to essential goods. Some volunteers for the forces added to the confusion by leaving work without notice. On 11 August, one week into the war, the *HDE* reported that most mills were on half time.

This situation was not peculiar to Huddersfield. John Hargreaves in his book *Halifax*, notes:

> The outbreak of the First World War resulted in an immediate shortage of raw material which brought the Halifax textile industry to an abrupt halt.
>
> Moreover, since Germany had been one of the industry's most important overseas customers ... many exporters found themselves owed substantial debts by German customers.

The cotton towns to the west were similarly affected. In Todmorden some mills closed. Fielden's, the town's leading employer, promised to keep their mills running as far as possible but stressed that employees should not 'spend more than can be avoided until matters clear up.'[1]

Whilst the cotton industry continued to struggle, within weeks the woollen industry was booming. Government orders for khaki flooded into the district and, after a short downtime for the adjustment of machinery, the mills were in full-swing. For manufacturers who had routinely adapted to the fluctuations in the peacetime fashion market, concentration on standard military cloth was very efficient.[2] On 2 November, the *HDE* reported:

> ... army-work has transformed the trade into a veritable hive of industry ... so that it now throbs and pulsates with all the energy of full and vigorous life.
>
> Huddersfield and the surrounding districts have benefitted to quite a remarkable degree by the war which is now being waged ... it is certainly incongruous that we should be basking in prosperity when just across the narrow streak of water that separates this country from ... the continent of Europe the horrors and devastation of war are present in all their poignant forms. But the fact remains that ... trade in this locality has reached a state of unprecedented boom ... Never before has there been so great a demand for khaki for the British army.
>
> The spectacle which presents itself any night in the week of the brilliant illumination of mills on the bleak hillsides and in the populous valleys is one which will not soon be forgotten by the present generation.

The mills
of the
Colne Valley

A correspondent from *The Times* was in awe at the scene.

> While London sleeps under the dark veil which the war has drawn across its face, the Colne Valley flings to the night a radiant challenge. It is burning the candle at both ends to keep the troops supplied with khaki. It knows no rest or playtime, its nights are more brilliant and not less busy than its days. There are no scenes in industrial England today to be compared with the nightly spectacle of the woollen mills that stride down the valley from Marsden under the fells of Yorkshire and Lancashire borderland to the junction of the Colne and Calder below Huddersfield. There is little enough romance in the valley by day but night hides the thick smoke belched from lofty chimney stacks, the greasy effluent oozing into canal or dyke, the cold severity of grey stone, the monotony of mill design. There is nothing to be seen but lights, great square masses of lights, the length of a score of windows and the height of half a dozen storeys, tiny punctures of light marking the tiny track up bleak hillsides to the undiscovered country which goes by the expressive name of T' back o' t' Moors.[3]

Each British soldier's uniform required about 32lb of wool, compared to the average civilian's clothing consumption of about 13lb of wool per year.[4] Every woollen manufacturer in the district was working to full capacity, 5000 looms producing an estimated 250 miles of khaki per week. The average lifespan of a uniform on the western front was about six weeks and, although many were worn for longer, orders soon included material for replacements. Demand was further boosted by blue serges for recruits to Kitchener's army, light blue-grey cloth for the French troops and flannel for shirts.[5] The local mills where output was transformed included: Hirst and Mallinson, Bolton Hall Mills, Milnsbridge; Cliff End Mills, Longwood; and Charles Lockwood and Sons Ltd, Black Rock Mills, Linthwaite, where 'almost the entire plant was engaged in the making of khaki for the English Army, and blue-grey cloth for the French Army.'[6]

National Government Demand for Woollen Products

Product	Average Annual Demand March 1911 to March 1914	Actual Demand March 1918 to March 1919
Cloth	1,390,988 yards^2	95,000,000 yards^2
Flannel	1,083,767 yards^2	107,705,000 yards^2
Blankets	165,650 articles	17,370,000 articles

Pre-war, army consumption of cloth was less than 1% of total orders. Three months into the war, the War Office demands were up to 20% of total orders, totalling 10 million square yards of khaki by the end of 1914. Production expanded further to meet orders from the Belgian, Italian, Portuguese, Serb and American forces and by 1917 War Office demands equalled the total pre-war consumption of the UK. Although local firms were directed to concentrate on British uniforms later in the war, by 1918 80% of local output was for the military.[7] The value of woollen and worsted exports from the West Riding rose from £33 million in 1915 to £47 million in 1916.[8]

Alongside the Huddersfield textile trade's outstanding response to the enormous wartime increases in demand, related trades also prospered. Local clothiers stitched the khaki cloth into uniforms and great coats, and leather curriers made thousands of haversacks and ammunition pouches for the French army.[9]

In January 1917, Government inspectors praised Huddersfield's ...

> ... pre-eminence ... in the manufacture of British khaki goods ... in perhaps no other district ... is the industry so well-organised or to such a large extent self-contained. Almost the whole of the woollen manufacturers spin their own yarns, and many firms do their own dyeing and finishing. ... therefore little time is lost between one department and another, and by running spinning machinery all night as well as all day, if necessary, the looms can be kept running at a high pitch of pressure.[10]

Lord Islington, an experienced senior politician and at that time Under-Secretary of State for India, added his congratulations.

> ... Huddersfield had played probably as important a part in the war movement as any industrial centre in the country. From the factories in the town and immediate neighbourhood they have provided in great abundance and with admirable rapidity and punctuality many of the essentials for the successful and efficient conduct of the war.[11]

These compliments softened the blow of losing contracts for the Russian army to mills in Leeds, Batley, Morley and Dewsbury in January 1917. This released capacity for Huddersfield to concentrate on more British uniforms, which were of superior quality but yielded a much smaller profit margin. The *HDE* commented:

> The material insisted upon by the War Office for our troops is superior to the Russian cloth, and involves, besides higher quality wool, more care and a greater degree of skill. The Russian fabric is easier to make and the same high standard is not enforced ... the Colne Valley is left the task of meeting the very exacting requirements of the British War Office. It is one of the penalties of great efficiency - a pill, if you like, but a very nicely sugared one.[12]

Wartime opportunities for the textile industry were not universal. Such was the concentration on khaki production that worsted manufacturers suffered a shortage of wool, although when demand outstripped the capacity of the woollen mills they adapted to fill the breach.[13]

West Yorkshire's good fortune that khaki is a woollen product was illustrated by the continued calamitous impact of the war on the Lancashire cotton industry. In Burnley, for example, cotton mills which were the most prolific in the world as recently as 1910 were operating at 25% capacity. Such problems worked to Huddersfield's advantage as the shortage of male labour was partly made up by 'transference of cotton operatives from the depressed districts of Lancashire.'[14]

Women for the Workforce

A letter to the *HDE* of 13 November 1914 questioned the assertion that mills workers could not be spared for the forces, arguing that older men and women could replace them.

> I remember hearing grumbles that the women folk were spoiling the men's chances in the mills. What is the matter with the women now? Have they forgotten how to weave?

Five months later, Lloyd George, as the newly appointed Minister for Munitions, began to target the female workforce.[15] His initiative was publicised at a meeting in Huddersfield Town Hall on 19 April 1915, when women were urged to...

> ... show their patriotism in a more practical way by registering their names so that the employers could allow the men to render more useful service.[16]

The employment of an increasing number of women only partly alleviated the conflicting demands on manpower to prosecute the war. The introduction of conscription in January 1916 accelerated the loss of skilled operatives. By April 1916 an estimated 8000 local men were serving with the forces of whom about 5000 were from the woollen and worsted industries.

> Until recently, by resorting to various expedients, the depleted ranks were filled up, but the problem has become more acute, and it is no longer possible to carry on ... Important Government contracts ... are at present being seriously delayed by the lack of skilled labour. The revised list of certified occupations has not improved matters ... so many occupations in the textile industry are now unstarred that ... in the near future further large numbers of men engaged in the woollen and worsted mills will be called up for military service.

Among other industries affected by the 'withdrawal of large numbers ... for military service', the postal service was compelled to reduce deliveries, collections and the opening hours of the Head Post Office and the Cloth Hall Street Branch.[17]

There was additional competition for labour from other war industries. In June 1915 the Huddersfield Munitions Workers Bureau was established at the Town Hall. Within a month 181 volunteers had enrolled, many of them skilled turners and fitters.[18] The men were each given a certificate to prove they were engaged on munitions work, and to prevent them escaping their family duties by claiming that they had been posted away. There was to be 'no wife dodging.'[19] This nod to morality pleased the church which was perturbed by the extension of the working week to Sundays, in addition to overtime and nightshifts.

Whilst some accepted Sunday-working as a necessary evil in essential industries, particularly textiles and munitions, there was always likely to be hard bargaining about additional hours and overtime pay. In December 1914, weavers in Marsden demanded overtime pay of 1½d per hour. When this was refused they began an overtime ban that quickly spread along the Colne Valley to Huddersfield and lasted until April 1915.[20]

Socialist firebrand Mary MacArthur, in an article reprinted by the *HDE* from the *Daily Chronicle*, deplored the almost universal sidelining of working time regulations. Many men and women had been working seven days a week with one Sunday off a month. Twelve-hour shifts were the norm and some lasted 16 hours. At times the workers left one shift at 10.30pm and started the next at 6.30am the following morning. Discounting travel, eating, washing and dressing, they had less than four hours to sleep.[21]

"Breakfast was a bit short

the other morning—no eggs, no butter—and I could see Mother was rather worried. 'Never mind,' I said, 'as long as we've got Rowntree's Cocoa, it makes up for a lot and it keeps you going wonderfully while you're standing at the machine. But I tell you what, Mother, I'm going to have *two* cups this morning just to make up.' Mother smiled and brought out the biggest cup she could find. 'I shan't worry about you now, Nell,' she said, and I went off to the factory feeling as fit as could be."

a cup of

Rowntree's

Elect Cocoa

makes a biscuit into a meal

Advertisement from the *HDE*, 1 January 1919, one of a series for Rowntree's Cocoa that depicted women in a variety of war-related occupations.

One solution to the problem, suggested by the Home Secretary Herbert Samuel and President of the Board of Trade Walter Runcimann, was the importation of migrant women workers. Huddersfield's first 'batch' of migrant women arrived on 7 April 1916, from 'Harrogate, Scarborough, Bridlington, Goole, Grimsby, Hull, Mansfield and other towns.' Some would be employed in munitions but the majority of this first group were despatched to the spinning departments of the woollen mills to address the 'great shortage in yarn … which is responsible for keeping a large number of looms idle.' They replaced 600 men who were either called up or transferred to heavy manual labour which was unsuitable for women.

It was agreed from the outset that men at the front were 'entitled to be reinstated in their former employments if and when they return fit for resuming them.'[22] Many of them would not. With industry in such a state of flux, in July 1916 the Huddersfield branch of the General Union of Textile Workers appointed Mary Luty as their first full-time representative and organiser of women workers.[23] At the end of 1917 the Huddersfield branch of the National Union of Women Workers was formed. Its aims were to unite women for the 'social, civil, moral and religious welfare of the community' and to 'distribute information likely to be of service to women.'[24]

Working on Sundays

The thousands of migrant workers rocketed the numbers engaged in essential industries to unanticipated levels, but most of the workforce was still working on Sundays. Some service industries and shops followed suit, offering greater choice of when to shop for a workforce with little free time, whilst also profiting from the increased affluence in parts of the community. A steady decline in the numbers receiving poor relief from the Huddersfield Union, despite soaring price inflation, was further evidence of the amount of work available.[25]

The issue of Sunday-working came to a head in June 1917. At a quarterly meeting of Fartown Wesleyan Methodist Church, Mr HA Lodge decried 'the indifference to scriptures and the lessons in them by many people.' A sharp rise in the Fartown population, primarily migrant workers in the 'new industries' was not reflected in church congregations. But did they have the time or the energy?[26]

The following month the Council's Watch Committee provoked an outcry by banning Sunday trading. Writing to the *HDE*, 'ONE WHO KNOWS' was appalled that working people would be denied access to provisions on a working day. To be morally consistent, the Corporation would have to ban the sales of Sunday newspapers, of beer and tobacco in public houses, and 'cease running tramcars' on Sundays. The Town Council was split. Those wanting to retain Sunday as 'The Sabbath' were accused of espousing 'religious propaganda', but the decision to ban Sunday trading stood.[27] The Huddersfield Society of Small Shopkeepers, founded during this dispute, was disappointed by the outcome, but had been 'bound ... together for future battles.'[28]

It is doubtful that those who lost the Sunday trading battle used their additional time to swell the local congregation. Nor were speeches that belittled industrial and economic difficulties likely to attract the masses. One such was given by the Reverend AT Guttey at Northumberland Street Primitive Methodist Church on his return from the trenches in 1916:

> He had no sympathy with the man who complained of failing business, and of heightened prices. These were days of war, and if they had breakfast on the table at all on the morrow let them remember that they owed it to the boys in the trenches.[29]

Inflation and the Cost of Living

The discontent alluded to by Reverend Guttey had been growing. A shortage of labour and materials produced galloping inflation. In three years from January 1914 typical working class family expenditure increased by 60%, led by an 87% rise in retail food prices.[30]

Whilst the large war-related industries prospered, small businesses were vulnerable to the volatile economy. At the beginning of June 1916 the Huddersfield Bankruptcy Court heard several local traders attribute their difficulties to wartime prices. Fred Stott, a Linthwaite brewer, could no longer afford to purchase sugar and saccharine for his beer, or petrol for distribution. Shelley corset manufacturer Albert Fitton had problems accessing materials and paying the interest on loans. He had been working in munitions at night and at his own business by day to make ends meet. Thomas Londesborough, a wholesale and retail clothier and draper from Marsh, had promissory notes and bills of exchange for money that he was owed, but his debtors were from other struggling businesses.[31]

The loss of skilled employees to the forces also impacted heavily on small businesses. In April 1917, the business of Crosland Moor master painter and decorator Hubert Burgoine folded after his main assistant was called up.[32]

The soaring cost of newsprint contributed to the demise of the *Huddersfield Chronicle*, a rival to the *HDE*, which ceased publication at the end of April 1916.[33] During the rest of the war the *HDE* itself frequently advertised for old newsprint to recycle.

Wages also rose, but by much less than prices, as shown by the war bonuses agreement of the textile unions in Huddersfield in lieu of overtime in January 1916.[34] These bonuses were held over for the duration of the war and, for many, had accumulated 'to a tidy sum' by 1919.[35]

Category	Bonus per week
men and women earning 10s per week or less	1s 0d
women earning over 10s and men earning 10s to 20s per week	1s 6d
men earning over 20s	3s 0d

In July 1917 a Commission of Inquiry reported on the growing industrial unrest in 'many cities and towns' of Yorkshire and the East Midlands. Discontent was ...

> ... clearly associated not only with the industries ... but to ... wider social, domestic, or national questions affecting the homes and domestic concerns of the people ... high price of food and necessary commodities of life ...

Pay had decreased in real terms and there were many examples of ...

> ... the utter inadequacy of wages ... to secure the bare essentials for living at a much lower standard of comfort than was considered essential in their homes before the war.

A widespread conviction that excessive food prices were caused by 'profiteering' was eroding the acceptance of wartime sacrifice and discomforts.

> ... insufficient steps had been taken by the government departments to prevent profiteering, exploiting and plundering.

The Government was also at fault in issuing 'numerous and conflicting departmental regulations.' Pre-war problems were festering between employers and employed, providing opportunities for militants to inflame the workers, who had ...

> ... apparent universal distrust ... of the Trade Union executive and of the Government departments who act with, and through them.

This had led to ...

> ...the formation of a vigorous defensive organisation for the protection of the workmen inside their own separate workshops, known as the 'Shop Committee' or 'Rank and File' movement, with shop stewards elected from the workers in every shop.

The skilled workers' unions and their members were dismayed at the unskilled being employed alongside them, diminishing their status.

Inequalities and unfairness of pay were a major issue. Women workers were paid a minimum of 80% of the wage of the men they replaced. The principle of paying lower wages to women was based on traditional 'family' roles, in which the man provided the income whilst the woman looked after the home and the children. With no electronic labour-saving appliances, the woman's role was very physically demanding and time-consuming. It was assumed that women who worked either didn't have a family household to run, or were providing additional income. Either way, they needed less money than the main family breadwinner.

As women flooded into the workplace, there were fears that profiteering employers would use them to undercut men's wages in the long-term, jeopardising overall standards of living. The clamour for equal pay grew but it would be 1975 before this became law and, a century after the Great War, inequalities of pay in the workplace remained an issue.

There was even greater discontent in factories where established workers were still paid per week whilst new employees received 'piece work payment.' This was introduced so 'haphazardly' that some women and even children were earning more than the skilled workers who taught them.

The Commission's summary of recommendations was quite a list: cheaper food; control of essential supplies; limitation of profits; speedier industrial grievance procedures; clearer wartime aims; equality of piece and time workers' earnings; periodic holidays; reduced fares for migrant munition workers; and increased taxes on the rich.[36]

The financial problems of some manufacturers further complicated the picture. Increased taxes, generally regarded as necessary to help fund the war, adversely affected industry. Some had 'done very well' out of large contracts for military cloth, but others had made insufficient allowance for the rapid increase in costs of raw materials and labour. In addition, some had large debts owed by Continental companies that were unlikely to be paid.[37]

Addressing the Shortage of Wool

To reduce costs in the woollen industry, the Government established an Army Clothing Department in May 1916. Recycling military uniforms through a 'new khaki for old' scheme, it was 'one of the greatest industrial undertakings of the war.' It saved hundreds of thousands of pounds per year by eliminating the profiteering middle men who bought old uniforms cheaply and sold them on at vastly inflated prices.[38]

In January 1917 the Government added the supply wool to the increasing list of resources it tried to control. The following month, AJ Sherwell, Liberal MP for Huddersfield, complained in Parliament about...

> ... the principle of monopolist central control ... of the ... supply of raw materials. Under the mad project of an over-taxed department headed by amateurs regulating the distribution of wool, serious injury is being done to a great and important trade. Many hundreds of small firms are being ruined, and even large ones are being put out of commission ... nothing but harm could be done from great traders and manufacturers being harassed and bullied by amateur bureaucrats.

Leading woollen manufacturer Theodore Taylor concurred:

> ... the works of distribution would be done more efficiently, expeditiously, and economically by the old system of merchants than could possibly be done by Government officials.[39]

The Government was attempting to counter the German submarine blockade of the western approaches which impeded the Merchant Navy bringing supplies to Britain. But, in the case of wool, they failed to avert the impending shortage and realised just in time that they needed to listen.

In May 1917 they replaced authoritarian dictates with an 'Industrial Advisory Committee' comprising members from the War Office, woollen employers and trades union representatives. The Industrial Advisory Committee spawned a Board of Control of Wool Textile Production which met at the War Department Cloth Office in Bradford under the chairmanship of Huddersfield mill owner Charles Sykes.[40] Its duty was to secure maximum numbers of men for war service and simultaneously increase production in the woollen industry to meet the requirements of the British and Allied governments and the export trade.[41] Government priorities were to be adhered to in all woollen and worsted mills. Class A contracts, placed by the Admiralty, War Office, Ministry of Munitions or Allied Governments had to come first. They were followed by Class B contracts, exports certified by the Government. This left the home civilian market a poor third.[42]

In June 1917, the Government announced that civilian clothing was to be manufactured from a 'standard cloth' of 'a quality affordable to all.' In practice, this meant a thinner cloth. The new Board set up a 'Yarn Merchants' Rationing (Sub) Committee' with the production of thinner cloth top of the agenda.[43] Civil consumption needed to decrease by an estimated 30% by April 1918.[44]

Spinners and manufacturers were now working for the Government on a commission basis. The effect on cloth for civilian use was ...

> ... to cause a great shortage ... a deterioration in their quality, and a very large increase in price. The shelves of the world were cleared of wool textile goods and there was an absolute famine in cloth ... 1917 began with a modicum of control; it ended with a Board of Control.[45]

Military supplies were just about maintained to the end of the war, but products on the civilian market remained plain, sparse and distorted in price until many months after the armistice.

Woollen textiles was not the only major industry transformed by wartime demands. Schoolgirl Vivien Hirst described a Huddersfield that ...

> ...hummed with activity; dyes and chemicals, munitions and khaki cloth pouring out of the factories and mills.

There was accompanying guilt that, despite the volatility of the district's khaki-driven economy, local fortunes 'ran high' whilst 'men were enduring horror and suffering at great sacrifice.'[46]

Chapter 9

Munitions Factories

The Need for Munitions

The lack of firepower, blamed by Lord John French, Commander in Chief of the British Expeditionary Force, for the failures of the spring campaign in 1915, had major repercussions on the home front. The massive shortfall in weaponry, ammunition and explosives was potentially disastrous. Not only were shells in short supply, but the *Daily Mail* reported that they were the 'wrong kind of shells.' Besides the obvious handicap in battle, it reflected on the Government's competence. They had failed to anticipate the nature and longevity of the war, and could hardly demand loyalty and commitment from troops they failed to equip. The challenge was immense. The army had increased six-fold to one and a half million in nine months. The use of mops and brooms as improvised rifles in training camp drills was unsatisfactory enough, but to ration ammunition with the enemy in range undermined everything.[1]

The new Minister of Munitions, Lloyd George, sought to harness British industry more closely to the war effort. Production was urgently accelerated. In the twelve months from August 1915 the national output of high explosive shells, the most effective weapon in trench warfare, increased 94-fold, part of a programme that increased annual national shell production from 500,000 in 1914 to 76,000,000 in 1917.[2]

Ironworks Adapt

In Huddersfield, as elsewhere, many steelworks were wholly or partly converted to the manufacture of equipment and armaments, and chemical factories were rapidly adapted to produce explosives. Within a short time, the manufacture of munitions was second only to the woollen industry in providing Huddersfield's wartime employment. Such urgency, however, came at a price. Health and safety, often derided, but paramount in factories packed with explosives, was seriously and recklessly compromised.

In Huddersfield, several local factories were modified, including Thomas Broadbent and Sons Ltd (Central Ironworks), WC Holmes and Co Ltd, Calvert and Co Ltd, David Brown and Sons Ltd, William Whiteley and Sons Ltd, Sellers and Co, and Richard Carter Ltd.[3]

Richard Carter Ltd needed little modification. A hand tools manufacturer from Holmfirth, they despatched thousands of shovels per week from Kirkburton Railway Station to the front line. Many of the trenches were dug using Carter's shovels. Ernest Carter, one of the four brothers who ran the company, was married on his last day on British soil. He returned to his unit later that day and was killed at Gallipoli, aged 26.[4]

Kirkburton Station, from where Carters despatched thousands of shovels per week to the western front.

David Brown's was founded in 1860 as a pattern manufacturing company. By 1914 the company was manufacturing complete gear units, bearings and shafts, worm drive gears, and had helped to pioneer the development of turbine gears. Demand was stimulated by a massive wartime increase in vehicle production and shipbuilding, and in 1915 the Admiralty moved into Brown's Park Works site to oversee the manufacture of heavy gears that drove ships' propulsion units. Fulfilling extensive orders placed by the Canadian Maritime Board and leading companies such as JP Thorneycroft and John Samuel White, David Brown's equipped a range of ships, from tankers and oilers to destroyers, flotilla leaders and patrol boats.

David Brown's employees were exempted from military service and directed to work in this essential industry. This did not prevent 'the more adventurous spirits' from signing up, then being frog-marched back to Park Works on discovery. As in other industries, long hours and seven-day working weeks became the norm. Joint owners, Frank and Percy Brown, who inherited the works from their father, were sticklers for hard work. Frank in particular acquired a reputation for dismissing on the spot anyone he thought was slacking, on one occasion mistakenly sacking an employee of an external building contractor![5]

Another of Huddersfield's ironworks companies, Thomas Broadbent and Sons Ltd, contributed a variety of products to the war effort. After a brief suspension of operations in August 1914, they resumed work on their standard products, such as centrifugals used in the manufacture of explosives and chemicals, cranes and other heavy-lifting plant. Many of Britain's battleships at the Battle of Jutland, including HMS *Lion* and the Orion-class vessels HMS *Conqueror*, HMS *Monarch*, and HMS *Thunderer* were equipped with Broadbent's ammunition hoists.

Broadbent's also adapted to new demands, including the manufacture of an unusual electric travelling under-hung jib crane to handle three tons of molten metal in a foundry on the repair ship RFA *Reliance*. The Admiralty imposed severe tests to ensure that crane and load were safe whilst the vessel was at sea.

In 1916 Broadbents was awarded a large contract to build the casings for 112lb cast steel aerial bombs. This necessitated an extension. A new steel foundry was built adjacent to the main site and equipped with the latest electrical furnaces but, owing to a miscalculation, they remained idle during the daytime as there wasn't enough electrical power in Huddersfield to run them! They eventually operated through the night, but electricity costs were so expensive that the steel foundry was converted to an extension of the iron foundry immediately after the war.[6]

Sellers and Co, near Chapel Hill, was involved in similar work, making mine casings for the Admiralty.

112lb bomb casings in production at Thomas Broadbent and Sons Ltd

Dyeworks and Explosives

The most drastic changes were made at Read Holliday and Sons Ltd. Founded in 1830 at Tanfield and moving to Turnbridge in 1839, Read Holliday had established the development of dyestuffs and chemicals as one of Huddersfield's major industries, complementing the textile trade and exploiting the Yorkshire coalfield for both fuel and the coal tar from which the early dyes were distilled.

From 1884, handicapped by a heavy excise duty on alcohol – imposed at least in part to appease the temperance movement – and by import duties into foreign countries, Read Holliday Ltd declined along with the rest of the British dye industry. German dye companies flooded the wide-open British market and by 1900 had 90% of the world's chemical trade, compared to Britain's 3%. Although alcohol for industrial use was relieved from excise duty in 1906, the British chemical industry was still re-building in 1914. Two-thirds of British dyes were still imported from Germany and home production was mainly dependent on German raw materials. On the outbreak of war, supplies disappeared, prices rocketed and, overnight, the industry was in crisis.

Read Holliday Ltd had responded to wartime demands before. In the 1903-04 Russo-Japanese War they supplied the dyes – at 350% above their usual price – for Japanese Army blankets which were manufactured in the West Riding. At the outbreak of World War I, they responded again, making salicylic acid, a mordant yellow dye component for the British army's khaki uniforms.

In December 1914 Read Holliday learned that they were to become part of British Dyes, a new Government company formed by the Board of Trade to address the acute national shortage of aniline dyes and intermediates.[7] Increasingly, British Dyes and other dye-works were compelled to prioritise colours for khaki and by August 1915 Britain's fashion designers were anticipating an impending period of 'dreadful drab.'

> The country is beginning, in no uncertain way, to feel the pinch of the shortage of dyes. Not long after the war began ladies doing their shopping were rather taken aback when told that certain colours could not be "matched". Now they are rather amazed if their wants can be met in that respect once in a hundred times. "Can't get the German dyes" is the almost invariable reply.
>
> According to one expert "we shall almost be reduced to seeing nothing but monotonous sameness of hue in both women's and men's attire … black, white, grey, or "natural" colours.[8]

Designs became neat, quiet and plain. It was many months after the 1918 Armistice before there was any sign 'of a return to the pre-war variety of colour and pattern' for which Huddersfield had a fine reputation.[9]

Even before the amalgamation with British Dyes, Read Holliday had been commandeered by the Admiralty which had installed eight autoclaves for the manufacture of Tetranitroaniline, a volatile explosive compound used as a detonator for torpedoes. Again, the company was able to draw on previous wartime experience. In 1899, during the Boer War, it had received a lucrative contract to produce lyddite, also known as picric acid, a basic ingredient for dyes that was also used as a gunpowder substitute in high-explosive shells. The sheds erected for the purpose, in isolation from the rest of the plant across the River Colne, were still there, despite a large explosion in 1900 when a spark from a workman's chisel ignited a batch of lyddite, wrecking the Acid, Benzol and Aniline laboratories.

Major Holliday, son of the firm's founder and a director, was one of few people who understood how to manufacture picric acid. When the munitions crisis hit the British army in the spring of 1915, he was seconded from France where he was a Major in the Duke of Wellington's West Riding Regiment, to run a picric acid plant at Bradley.[10] In June 1915 the creation of the Huddersfield National Shell Factory, effectively a branch of British Dyes, was announced.[11]

Production of picric acid began in October 1915 and averaged 100 tons per week by the end of the year. Meanwhile British Dyes had added trinitrotoluene (TNT) to its output, and had bought Read Holliday and Sons Ltd for £422,000. Major Holliday used his share of the proceeds to buy a 60-acre site at Deighton from Sir John Ramsden's estates, to establish LB Holliday and Co Ltd for the manufacture of dyes and munitions. He also constructed a neighbouring wharf at Vernon Lock.[12]

A direct rival to British Dyes, he cashed in on the khaki dye market and, in February 1917, acquired 23 German patents 'covering the entire range of colours in the anthracine series for vat dyeing', the Board of Trade receiving 2.5% in royalties.[13] British Dyes also acquired a site close to Holliday's Deighton factory to increase their manufacture of explosives, employing 1960 construction workers and expanding the combined areas of their sites to 450 acres. Once all their plants were operational, they employed 4000 workers on the production-lines.[14]

Major Holliday was awarded the OBE in 1918. When he died in 1965 he had become Britain's biggest private racehorse owner, with 50 horses at the Lagrange Stables, Newmarket. His best horse, Hethersett, won the St Leger in 1962 and was 9-2 favourite for that year's Derby but was brought down in a mass pile-up. He also won the Oakes with Neasham Belle in 1951 and the One Thousand Guineas with Night Off in 1965. He was Britain's leading racehorse owner in 1956, 1961 and 1962.[15] British Dyes became part of ICI when it was founded in 1926.[16] In the 21st century ICI still occupies the same site.

Air Pollution

The key to British Dyes' manufacture of high explosives was sulphuric acid, 'the elixir of chemical life.' Vapour from boiling sulphuric acid was emitted 'day and night' as the Leeds Road factory at Dalton worked round the clock, risking public health and devastating local plant life.[17]

A letter from 'VIATOR', printed in the *HDE* on 1 June 1916, denigrated ...

> ... the filthy fumes and noxious gases with which our town is engulfed ... From Deighton to Castle Hill, from Castle Hill to Outlane, we all suffer in turn, according to the direction of the wind; no district escapes.
>
> This morning Deighton, Bradley and Kirkheaton were enveloped. One day last week the residents of Woodbank, Cowcliffe and district were very nearly poisoned ... On Monday last the fumes were so bad in John William Street and St George's Square that passengers emerging from the railway station were compelled to cover up their mouths with handkerchiefs.
>
> Strong men cannot stand these foul vapours, whilst delicate people and invalids suffer severely. The symptoms are violent pains in the chest, choking sensations in the throat and nausea.
>
> We have recently heard a good deal of claptrap as to the advantages to the town of having these establishments in Huddersfield. Personally I curse the day they were allowed to set foot in the district. Are we to stand by without protest whilst our beautiful town is being made into a second "Widnes"; our lovely outskirts, our pastures, corn fields, and gardens blasted and withered by these fearful gases, and the health of our loved ones jeopardised?
>
> ... In the present crisis one naturally does not wish to ... interfere with the production of munitions of war; but surely something can be done ... to mitigate this appalling state of things; if not, in the course of twelve months Huddersfield [will be] shrouded in gloom, its inhabitants unhealthy, and its atmosphere impregnated with foul acids.

'RICHARD THE THIRD' of Birkby was another sufferer:

> Some days ago I met the fumes in question as I was coming along St John's Road, and in consequence was seized with such violent pains in the chest and feeling of suffocation, that I was compelled to stop and rest ... Kilner Bank ... was not very long ago a beautifully wooded country, with cottage gardens full of flowers. Look at it now! ... we must take refuge in "gas masks," which I notice an enterprising chemist is putting on the market.[18]

A letter from 'HEALTH' on 30 June 1916 criticised the shortness of the Dalton work's chimneys, which released the gasses only just above house roof level.

The *HDE* editorial of 1 June 1916 reassured the public that a recovery plant to capture the sulphuric acid vapour and recycle it would be completed as quickly as possible. This invited the question duly asked by a 'Hillhouse resident.'

> Why wasn't the acid recovery plant … included in the first plan, instead of filling the town with these ghastly vapours, whilst we are being slowly asphixiated? ... We were so affected one morning we could not eat our breakfast and … felt ill all day through inhaling these ghastly fumes ... the town needs protection … from this impending calamity.[19]

The charitable answer was that in this unprecedented industrial war, the Government was constantly and hurriedly adapting to new circumstances – or, less charitably, they were making it up as they went along. The controversy came before the Town Council on 19 July, reported by the *HDE* under the provocative sub-heading 'LEEDS ROAD SMELLS.' Councillor Canby proposed formal action to address ...

> … the abominable state of things … Owing to the geographical position Leeds Road has always been a sort of dumping ground, and for that reason it is not a very salubrious neighbourhood …There were not only unpleasant smells, but the fumes were affecting the health of the people, who were depressed and could not eat their food properly.

He expressed particular concern for St Andrews schoolchildren, adding that ...

> … vegetation was being destroyed. He had seen samples from Councillor Thompson's rose garden which were enough to make any man weep.'[20]

For all the hot and poisoned air, there was little they could do except encourage the rapid construction of the recovery plant. It would be 1917 before it was operational. Meanwhile, the manufacture of explosives took priority over clean air. The noxious gasses were singled out for derision in a poetic eulogy about the new train journey to Kirkburton, printed in the *HDE* on 14 November 1916.

A Trip to Kirkburton

by a Kirkburton resident
(inspired by 'the new motor train service to that village')

If you're wanting a tip
For an afternoon trip;
When you've got a few hours to spare –
The motor express on the Kirkburton line
Reveals you a landscape exquisitely fine,
And scenery so rich and rare.

With a puff and a slide,
And a beautiful glide,
The train leaves Huddersfield station
Are a positive treat
For humorous and gay conversation.

Both Asquith and Law
With their wonderful "jaw"
Are eclipsed by these comical jokers
Whilst the King and the Kaiser
Would both be the wiser
If they travelled in Kirkburton smokers.

No fear of infection
On the Kirkburton section,
As you pass British Dyes on the way,
For as the train passes
It pours out its gasses,
And drives all the microbes away.

The canal with its fleet,
Bringing cargoes of wheat.
And of coals up to Popplewell Wharf,
Brings treasures untold,
And thousands in gold,
Enriching the merchants – "not arf."

When Deighton is passed –
If you've not then been gassed –
The aspect is wondrously fine;
And the view from Kirkheaton
Can only be beaten
The further you get up the line.

Some critics – not many
Declare that at Fenay
The loveliest view can be got;
But it's pretty well certain
The one at Kirkburton
For beauty surpasses the lot.

On the left and the right
A magnificent sight
Is presented for your admiration;
For the view superfine
Of the North Western line
Is the one from Kirkburton Station.[21]

TNT Poisoning

In addition to polluting the district, British Dyes had health issues inside the factory. Before the takeover, Hollidays had acknowledged the hazards of working with explosives by awarding a bonus of 2s 6d per week – the equivalent of 4½ hours' extra pay – for 'the men in the picric acid sheds.'[22] In November 1916 in the House of Commons, Edmund Harvey, Liberal MP for Leeds West, referring specifically to British Dyes, asked the Home Secretary if he knew whether the 'insanitary ... prevalence of chemical eczema amongst the workers had been the subject of inquiry by the factory inspectors.' It clearly hadn't. The generic reply from Mr Brace, Under Secretary to the Home Office, described arrangements as 'not insanitary; but owing largely to the rapid and continuous growth of the factory ... provisional and somewhat primitive', adding that the Corporation of Huddersfield would need 'to provide increased sewer facilities.' The prevalence of tub closets shared by several dwellings and used in some factories was a public health issue, but it was hardly specific to the outbreak of eczema and dermatitis. More helpful was an instruction from British Dyes' management that gloves would now be exclusive to each worker and no longer shared.[23]

British Dyes fell abruptly under the factory inspectors' scrutiny when Edith Stanley from Golcar, a labourer in the TNT department, became seriously ill at Christmas 1916. Employed by the factory since March that year, she had initially worked long shifts in the 'pit bottom', a small, very dusty, unventilated room not designed for the volume or type of munitions work located there. According to one employee, it was unpopular with the women as 'it made them cough' and caused 'irritation of the throat.' By June 1916 Edith had suffered two bouts of laryngitis. She was then moved to the benzol and tuluol department, where her health was better until 23 December when a two-and-a-half-pound spanner fell thirty feet and struck her on the head.

The factory doctor diagnosed shock and concussion but Edith's panel doctor and a senior physician from Huddersfield Infirmary observed a yellowing of her skin. On 11 January 1917 Edith lost consciousness and died. She was 27.

A three and a half hour inquest at Huddersfield Royal Infirmary heard evidence from, among others, Miss Adler (His Majesty's Senior Lady Inspector of Factories), Mr Peacock (the local factory inspector) and the three physicians. Edith had toxic jaundice. The verdict of deputy coroner EW Norris and the jury was 'Accidental Death from TNT poisoning, accelerated by the blow on the head from the spanner.' British Dyes was ordered to formalise an 'alternate system of employment' – a rotation system – to limit continuous time down the pit.[24]

Three weeks later, on 7 February 1917, the *HDE*, in an editorial praising Huddersfield Royal Infirmary as 'a haven of rest' for the overspill of wounded soldiers from the Royds Hall War Hospital, added:

> The many industries which have been established or extended in the neighbourhood for the provision of munitions have considerably increased the demands upon the Infirmary ... on behalf of those who have been wounded or broken in health ... in the munitions factory.

Edith Stanley's reaction to TNT was extreme, but others too were suffering. The skin of many employees had gradually turned yellow after over-exposure to explosives. Across the country women TNT workers became known as the 'Canary Girls.'[25] In Huddersfield it was not just the

Advertisement from the *HDE* of 15 October 1917, targeting munitions girls.

women. Schoolgirl Vivien Hirst observed men 'with yellow faces' walking about town, 'dyed from their work at British Dyes.'[26]

The *HDE* editorial about Edith Stanley's death obliquely acknowledged an unspoken policy; men at the front were risking their lives, so those at home should also accept risks to keep them supplied. Munitions factories had been allowed latitude in health and safety that would not have been countenanced in peacetime, but Edith and others across the country did not die in vain.

Two months after her inquest, on 13 March 1917, the Government published new rules to improve the health of the workers, most of them to reduce the risk of TNT poisoning. Tellingly, they had already 'been in force for some weeks.' There was to be:

- a canteen for workers
- a free half pint of milk per worker per day
- adequate washing accommodation
- dressing rooms for outdoor clothes
- close medical supervision
- precise methods for ventilating and cleaning the factory
- no food consumption in work clothes
- compulsory washing before leaving the premises, cleaning all the skin
- no food or tobacco in the TNT processing areas.[27]

Ironically, British Dyes was probably one of the more hygienic TNT manufacturers, having installed baths for the picric acid workers in the summer of 1915. The new rules, resembling those eventually applied to coal mines, made a difference. Among munitions workers nationally, Edith Stanley was one of 169 'serious illness cases' from TNT poisoning between October 1916 and March 1917, and one of 109 wartime deaths. There were just 42 'serious illness cases' from October 1917 to March 1918, and only five during April and May 1918.[28] As further protection, some munitions girls started to powder or varnish their faces, and to wear a thin gauze veil to protect their skin, eyes, nose and throat.[29] Others had to be educated about and prevented from using TNT, or its equivalent, tetryl, 'to give their hair an auburn tint.'[30] On 2 July 1918 the *HDE* reported that '... close medical supervision, improved methods, and the use of mechanical processes have resulted in a great diminution of danger.'

On the day of Edith Stanley's inquest, the Government announced that there were half a million munitions workers and that another half a million were needed. The Ministry of Munitions commended women's excellence in 'the precision work of wiring and assembling fuses, filling shells, stoking acid stills, acetylene welding, gauging, testing and inspecting.'[31]

Housing the Migrant Workforce

The many migrant workers introduced to British Dyes and to other munitions and textile manufacturers created a problem for the Huddersfield authorities.[32] Where were they to live? Huddersfield had a housing crisis that pre-dated the war. Much available accommodation had been taken by refugees, primarily from Belgium. A proposal that private homes could accommodate migrants in the rooms vacated by servicemen had limited potential as it did not account for men coming home on leave. The Women's Hostel at Belmont Street, opened in 1912, was 'full to overflowing.'

There was little manpower or material for building new houses, but the Town Council meeting of 17 March 1917 resolved that, with the migrant workforce expanding so rapidly, they were 'morally bound to erect workmen's houses at the earliest possible date.' One consequence was the conversion of the Albany Hall, which had 'rendered good service in the social and educational life of the borough,' into a hostel for women workers at British Dyes.[33] Looking further ahead, the *HDE* added:

> ... one significance of the new hostel seems to be that women workers are to take more than a merely temporary part in Huddersfield's bid to become the dye-producing centre of the country.[34]

Women had become integral to factory life, as reflected in the parody of a popular wartime music hall song, 'Where are the Lads of the Village Tonight?' sung by munitions workers watching women similarly engaged at a neighbouring works.

> Where are the girls of the village tonight?
> Where are the girls we know?
> On New Street or in St George's Square?
> No, not there; no not there.
> Taking a trip down to David Brown's
> With their mob-caps on they look so bright,
> Busy making petards* are the little sweethearts,
> That's where they are tonight.[35]

*small bombs used to blast down doors

By July 1917, in addition to the women at the Albany Hall, over 2000 working men were 'living at the Corporation Model and other lodging houses.'[36] Huddersfield's population, 107,825 in the 1911 census, was officially given as 116,632 in 1917, reflecting workforce increases of 3000 at British Dyes and a combined 5769 at ten other large firms.[37] The district's demographic make-up was also changing.

Cosmopolitan Huddersfield

Huddersfield appears to be becoming more cosmopolitan every day ... not very long ago there were comparatively few inhabitants who were not born in the neighbourhood, excluding the Scottish and Irish communities. War conditions have changed that state of affairs very rapidly. Most conspicuous ... are the numbers of young Irishmen, who are very easily recognised. So large has the influx of Irish become that a certain local works is losing its British appellation and gaining that of Irish Dyes. Contractors who are engaged in local works have brought with them a large number of Scotsmen, and the number of Jews in the town seems to be increasing. There is also a fair representation of the Welsh speaking immigrants, and a number of French women workers. The number of Negros in the town is also increasing.

Race Will Tell

The Scots "stick to business well." Younger Irishmen like a jaunt over to "the ould country." The Negros are said to be good time-keepers, and to stick well to their work during working hours, but they "down tools" immediately the whistle blows, and do not like to work overtime.[38]

Curbing the Demon Drink

Employed in an 'essential occupation' of 'national importance', most munitions workers were exempted from joining the forces. They were, nevertheless, subject to attempts at military-style discipline. Breaches of the 1915 *Munitions of War Act* warranted an appearance before the local Munitions Tribunal.

At one such hearing in July 1916, P McAtee and J Henry cited the gas as the cause of three hours' illegal absence from British Dyes. Returning from lunch late, 'the worse for drink and ... not fit for work', Henry claimed he had been 'gassed' and had gone to the Black Horse for two 'special whiskies.' 'Is that good for gas?' asked the Chairman. 'Yes. It is a remedy of 23 years standing', replied Henry. McAtee denied that he was 'gassed' but his 'head was very bad owing to the gas.' WA Ward, manager of the firm, gave evidence that the gas, 'the smell of burnt sulphur', was not dangerous, just an irritant.

> It would be necessary for a man to breathe a very considerable quantity of gas ... before it would put him into a comatose state ... it is recognised that the anti-dote is not whisky, but a peppermint lozenge.

He had gone too far. The exasperated Chairman would not allow the court's complicity in diminishing the impact of the gas, exclaiming:

> At all events, the remedy is not at the Black Horse!

The verdict was guilty but the fine – ten shillings, just one sixth of the maximum £3 tariff for the offence – was lenient, as 'all are aware of these fumes.' A sub-text of such leniency, consistent with other cases at the Munitions Tribunal, was that the country needed these workers. The primary purpose of the tribunals was not to punish or demoralise, and certainly not to induce resentment, but simply to keep the munitions workers in line.[39]

There was a growing problem across the country of itinerant workers with no ties to the local area and 'little to do with their wages and free time other than drink to excess.'[40] Absenteeism from drunkenness was impeding the war effort, and the temperance movement was keen to assert that 'there can never be complete patriotism without complete abstinence.'[41] A prohibition meeting at Huddersfield Town Hall on 27 April 1917, attended by representatives of the Church of England, the Free Churches, plus temperance and social workers, catalogued reasons why alcoholic drink should be banned. It delayed munitions and shipbuilding by keeping men from work, occupied valuable shipping space, congested the docks, wasted fertile land, delayed and consumed essential food supplies, and 'shattered our moral strength.' The meeting was chaired by Joseph Turner JP, Chairman of British Dyes.[42] A pillar of the Huddersfield community, he had joined Read Holliday in 1881 at the age of 12 and worked his way up from the shop floor to the Board of Directors. He was also Chairman of the Huddersfield Northern Union Rugby FC.[43]

The Government had acted on such concerns in January 1915, extending the 1914 *Defence of the Realm Act* to the watering down of beer and to a ban on the sale of alcohol on licensed premises after 9pm. This 'aroused ... strong resentment' in Huddersfield, causing 'inconvenience and annoyance without any corresponding good results.'[44] In March the King announced that no beer, wines or spirits would be consumed in the royal households[45] and the government considered prohibition, described in the *HDE* as 'one of the boldest steps ever taken by a government of this country.'[46] The Government thought so too, shying away from a complete ban, but implementing further restrictions.

GETTING STOUT AND BITTER, AS USUAL.

The first of these arose from drunkenness of epidemic proportions among munitions workers, mainly itinerant Irish, in Carlisle. To address the problem they were limited to buying one drink each, but it proved impossible to police when workers took to buying a round, including their one drink, then downing the lot. So in October 1915 the government introduced the 'No Treating Rule.' No one was allowed to buy an alcoholic drink for anyone else.[47]

Why do people stare aghast?
Why these long and gloomy faces
In the pubs and "public" places
After nine o'clock is passed?

Has some dreadful news come in?
Has the country been invaded,
Has some local works been raided
By a German Zeppelin?

Prithee, let this silence cease
Have the Germans captured Joffre?
Have the Russians made an offer
To accept a separate peace?

Why this reticence unkind?
Has the Navy, underrated,
Been at last annihilated?
Has the Government resigned?

No! Then what is there to fear?
Why so woebegone and sickly?
Why? – and echo answers thickly –
It's too late to order beer.[50]

In November 1915, more new regulations specifically applied to areas where 'war material is being made, loaded and unloaded, and dealt with in transit … and men belonging to His Majesty's naval and military forces are assembled therein.'[48] As a centre for munitions and khaki production, and two battalions of the Duke of Wellington's West Riding Regiment, this included Huddersfield. By December 1915 alcohol could not be consumed on licensed premises after 8.30pm and, in a new development, could not be drunk away from licensed premises after 8pm.[49]

Enforcement was far from easy, and local convictions were interspersed with acquittals, a number of prosecutions and police methods deemed unfair. Police Constables Chadwick and Marshall were responsible for one such case in December 1915. Acting on information received they called at the Royal Hotel, Birchencliffe, dressed in plain clothes, at 8.30pm. The upshot was that the landlord, Peter Rawnsley, was charged with serving after hours, and eight customers were charged with 'aiding and abetting.'

Two days later, before Huddersfield Magistrates, the prosecution claimed that drinking had continued until 9.30pm, when PC Chadwick produced his warrant card. As the officers began taking names the customers made 'quite a commotion' and 'rushed out of the house.' Chadwick had to admit that he left the premises 'with only four names … and three of those were wrong.' PC Marshall added that on leaving the hotel …

> There was a crowd round the corner of the house, and when we got fifty yards down the road stones started flying and a stone hit the tram standard close to us. We thought they were after us, and so we cut across some fields and came out at Lindley.

From there they caught the tram to town, returning the following day with Inspector Drinkwater to find several of the men who had been drinking the previous night.

Defending counsel Mr Willey suggested entrapment.

> The policemen commenced to play dominoes for beer shortly before 9 o'clock and treated others to drink in order to keep the … men there … in order to get the law broken.

He had a strong case. Just before 9pm a Mr Gledhill had got up to leave, but the constables then paid for another round, including a drink for Gledhill and for a woman selling lavender, whom the landlord had refused to serve because she was 'a bit fresh.' Of the drink sold after 9pm, three-quarters had been sold to the two policemen. Indeed, by 9.30pm Chadwick had drunk two bottles of beer and three shandies, and Marshall had downed four pints.

> Not a bad job, this special duty? Four pints in forty minutes. Not bad going? Were you quite sober?

Willey had the policemen's measure. Their methods ...

> ... were not "cricket" ... An officer who treated a woman who had been ordered out by the landlord was a disgrace to the uniform ... Before the police started there was no one playing dominoes for money or money's worth [of drink] ... any company of Yorkshiremen ... seeing the men flouting the landlord and flouting the law would be incensed when they found out that they were policemen.

The case was dismissed, bar a charge against the landlord and his family of obstructing the police. They were bound over for a sum of £5 to be of good behaviour for the next six months.[51]

The new drinking regulations made an initial impact. Convictions for drunkenness in Huddersfield fell from 210 in 1914 to 171 in 1915. The reduction was less than the national decrease of 50%, but there was satisfaction that Huddersfield retained second position of 20 large Northern towns and cities for sobriety per head of population.[52] It didn't last. In 1916 national convictions for drunkenness were the lowest for 50 years, but in Huddersfield they increased by 54%. Reduced to 16th of the 20 towns, the Chairman of the Huddersfield Licensing Sessions declared himself 'really ashamed of Huddersfield.' He attributed this 'collapse of morality' to ...

> ... the large influx of men in the labouring classes who were receiving abnormal wages who were not Huddersfield men and did not know how to spend their money.[53]

Further investigation was necessary to absolve Huddersfield. Within 24 hours the Chief Constable had the evidence. Of the 263 convictions, 148 were of men engaged at the munitions factories. It was the off-comers who had brought 'shame on the town.'[54]

And it wasn't just the men. 'Importations and war conditions' also explained a perceived increase in drinking 'amongst the female residents of Huddersfield', and elsewhere.[55] In January 1917 the military authorities instructed the police to report 'cases of drunkenness by soldiers' wives', threatening 'strong action' independent of any civil action.[56] This was, in part, motivated by an increase in sexually transmitted diseases. By June 1918, 4% of the army had venereal disease, and in industrial towns an estimated 10% of adults had syphilis and 14% had gonorrhoea.[57] The war had created a potent sexual mix of a large, mainly single, itinerant workforce, an unprecedented proportion of women workers, and soldiers, predominantly young and single, home on leave after months away and with a precarious life-expectancy. An increase in prostitution was another symptom, and it became an offence for a woman to transmit a sexual disease to a serviceman. This more permissive society was hindering the war effort. It would also be a legacy of the war.[58]

Disputes about Holidays

At Whitsuntide 1916, with the week-long bombardment that commenced the Battle of the Somme imminent, the need for ammunition, particularly shells, was urgent. The Brierley Wood Council Infants School Log Book of 9 June 1916 records:

> In compliance with a request from the Minister of Munitions, the Education Committee have decided to postpone the holidays for Whitsuntide, so that school will be open all next week.[59]

The week was 'tacked on to' the summer holiday, extending it to four weeks.

At short notice, local munitions workers were instructed to work at 'time and a quarter' over Whitsuntide. They demanded and were refused 'time and a half', so 280 of them took their holiday in breach of the *Munitions of War Act*. The Munitions Tribunal heard their case at a chaotic Huddersfield

Town Hall on 4 July, three days after the start of 'the Big Push.' Defendants thronged the corridors outside the courtroom, singing and attracting much attention 'by rather boisterous conduct and the occasional blowing of bugles.' The Chairman of the Tribunal implored the men to work for the 'well-being of the State and … of their fellow countrymen, who … were fighting for our liberties', and to 'trust those "in the know".' The law had been infringed but he did not want the 'penalties to be vindictive.' The fines imposed – graded according to wages and length of time off – were less than half of the maximum £3 available.[60]

" GIVE US SHELLS."

WHAT THE TROOPS SAY TO THE WORKERS.

THE ONLY GRUMBLE.

HIGH EXPLOSIVES SHOULD BE AS COMMON AS SEA SHELLS.

MUSIC OF THE SHELLS.

'Everywhere we had impressed upon us that the sweetest music they hear and the music they wanted to hear more of was the whistling of the shells overhead destined for the trenches opposite them.

Headline and paragraph from the *HDE*, 4 October 1915

When the Tribunal eventually delivered the maximum penalty it was headline news, even though serial offender RA Ackroyd had been fined on three previous occasions – 20s, 40s and 25s – for poor time-keeping. Described by the prosecution as 'afflicted with chronic laziness', Ackroyd's £3 fine was substantially more than his weekly wage of 45s.[61]

To appease the munitions workers, the Town Council, working closely with the military authorities, instructed all local workers to forgo their Whitsuntide holiday of 1916. As an attempt to show they were 'all in it together', it was clumsy, transparent and inflammatory.[62]

> It is childlike and idiotic to want people to work unnecessarily because a few others are required to work … this is a farce, not a necessity.[63]

The textile workers voted overwhelmingly to take their holiday, at which Mayor Blamires made a formal appeal in a letter to the *HDE* of 7 June, gilding the spur of patriotism with the assertion that men at the front were striving 'day and night' for the cause. This only widened the rift. He was not comparing like with like. Many textile workers had 'worked 100 hours per week in order that our army and those of our allies should be clothed.'[64] The vast majority of workers were committing and sacrificing a great deal, and needed time off to relax. The troops faced many dreadful ordeals, including, at times, protracted, exhausting, sleepless stints both in the front line and behind the lines. But even in the trenches there were long periods of inactivity and boredom between the fighting. They did not endure months of unrelenting working weeks of up to 100 hours.

The *HDE* acknowledged the workers' dilemma:

> Workers have felt that any relaxation they … needed for the purpose of toning up their jaded nerves could be obtained only at the risk of their country's welfare.[65]

Across different industries, many obeyed the call to work through the 1916 Whitsuntide holiday. Shortage of players caused the Huddersfield and District Cricket League to postpone its Whit Monday and Tuesday fixtures, 'except for clubs that can raise teams.' But along with the 280 munitions workers, many textile workers took their break.[66]

At the behest of the military authorities, the Mayor pressed on. Targeting all holidays for the foreseeable future, he convened a 'Conference of Employers of Labour' at the Town Hall on 27 July. The trades unions were not invited. The conference voted unanimously to postpone all holidays until the Government said they could be held. Representatives were to meet 'works people's representatives

... to ... arrange for holidays to be postponed.' With tensions still running high from Whitsuntide, this was not the way forward. Simultaneously with the Mayor's conference, a meeting of the Huddersfield and District Trades and Labour Council voted to organise their own conference to decide whether to take their holidays or not.[67]

The upshot was inconsistency and confusion. During August the Executive of the Huddersfield and District Woollen Manufacturers' and Spinners' Association recommended taking a week's holiday in September as usual.[68] Local shopkeepers decided to close for two days that week, but the Shop Assistants' Union voted to close for three.[69]

The increasing unrest in Huddersfield had been mirrored around the country. Some of it was motivated by perceived profiteering by employers on the backs of an underpaid workforce. Mainly, it was from sheer exhaustion. In the six months to July 1916, British Dyes' output of 18-pounder shells increased from 1200 to 4500 per week.[70] Many workers, particularly in munitions and textiles, could not sustain the pace and intensity demanded of them.

The turning point came in the last week of August. Under the stark headline 'HOLIDAY OR BREAKDOWN?' the *HDE* reported that, nationally, sick pay had increased by 20% owing to workers 'breaking down.' Most of the absentees worked in munitions factories.[71] This health crisis was a potential public and industrial relations disaster and the Ministry of Munitions relented on its dogma of 'no holidays' and 'continuous supply of munitions.' This was the key to more holidays for everyone.

Cutting its losses, the Ministry allowed four days' holiday for munitions workers, from Thursday 28 September to Sunday 1 October 1916, intending that it would benefit production as well as the workers' health. Factory and shipyard machinery had also been flogged into the ground. The holiday was an opportunity for much needed maintenance and repair. On their return, refreshed employees would work more efficiently on more efficient machines.[72]

Munition Worker's Holiday
by
Charles Lunn

The "shops" are silent for a spell,
The dynamo and lathe are still;
The furnace and the crucible
No more their molten metal spill.

A halt is called for those who strive
The nation, in its need, to serve –
A halt their vigour to revive,
To ease the strain of tortured nerve.

This but an all too brief respite,
But duty's call is loud and clear,
And naught must hinder those who fight,
For England, and for freedom clear.[73]

A number of local industries, including the textile trade, introduced staggered holidays, and on 4 September 1916 the HDE reported:

> Now ... it is possible to enjoy holidays in relays, and our readers can take their much needed rest with clear consciences.

In this way the wheels of most industries would keep turning.

The following August Bank Holiday, 1917 was 'probably ... more of a real holiday than any since the outbreak of the war.' Many migrant munitions workers returned home for a few days and 1200 travelled by train to an expensive break in Blackpool. There, motor buses and char-a-bancs topped by white balloons storing their coal-gas fuel reminded them of Huddersfield, not in appearance, but in exhaust emissions redolent of 'the atmosphere near the gasworks.'

Unnamed Poem

by

Charles Lunn

We sought the pure sea breeze to refresh our tired brains,
We sought to leave behind the fret and care,
We travelled in discomfort in oppressive crowded trains,
And we paid just half as much again for fare.

We spent our mornings walking on the prom, or on the pier,
Our afternoons in resting on the shore.
We bought our Sunday's joint and veg, and thought them very dear;
And at night we made our bed upon the floor.

The breezes from the sea our bodies brace and fortify,
But seaside prices send us home quite poor.
Next year we'll try the moorland up at "Nont's" or "Isle of Skye,"
Or we'll take a little cot on Honley Moor.[74]

Huddersfield Station, looking towards Manchester

Preferring to maintain Britain's Liberal tradition and to govern by consensus, the Government also throttled back a little on working hours after 1916. A '48 hour week' was the qualification for the munitions workers' war bonus of 16s per week in January 1918, although many were still working much longer hours.[75] By allowing more holidays and rest they elicited greater co-operation and energy during periods of urgent demand. There was, for example, no respite during the German's spring offensive of 1918, the Minister of Munitions, Winston Churchill, insisting that:

> A special effort must be made to replace promptly the serious losses in guns, machine-guns, and ammunition which are resulting from the great battle now in progress ... There should be no cessation of this [munitions] work during the Easter holidays.

These were the decisive days of the war, and the *HDE* reported on ...

> ... the unity of all classes in the face of a common danger ... there are signs that all differences are for the moment forgotten and the whole nation is ranging itself behind the courageous men at the front in their gigantic effort to stop the German advance ... it is gratifying ... to learn ... of the spontaneous assurances ... received from men in many districts that in spite of the Easter holidays there will be no loss of output. The whole nation is "up against" the greatest crisis in its history, and it is the supreme duty of all to ... help in the cause.[76]

This commitment was rewarded in July, when Churchill did not desire ...

> ... to interfere with such customary holidays as establishments engaged on munitions work think well to give to their employees during the summer and autumn of this year, subject to any special demands ... in order to maintain the supply of essential munitions to the front.[77]

Factory Explosions

Overtired staff posed an additional risk in TNT factories. An accident or worker error could ignite the explosives in the storage sheds. There was an early warning locally when picric acid exploded at White Lee Chemical Works in Heckmondwike on 2 December 1914. Ten munitions workers were killed and six were injured.

The remains of
White Lee Chemical
Works
in Heckmondwike
following the explosion
of picric acid on
2 December 1914

Seven months later a similar fate befell aniline dye and chemical company John W Leitch and Co Ltd of Milnsbridge. Leitch's had become the first UK company to manufacture industrial quantities of TNT in 1902. Output was increased enormously at the start of the war, but the equipment was old. At 8.30pm on 19 July 1915 a corroded steel coil of a six-year-old nitro-toluol still snapped. The still erupted in a huge explosion. One worker was blown from the roof and was fortunate to escape with minor injuries. The lighting system short-circuited, igniting other stocks of chemicals in a chain of detonations. Six of the seven sheds in that part of the factory were ablaze. As the smoke billowed skywards thousands came to watch the flames. There was great concern about the fire spreading to houses in the heavily populated neighbourhood. One child was so frightened that he fled to the railway station and boarded a train to Leeds. By extreme fortune, no one was killed, but the dangers of adapting factories to the mass manufacture of explosives were clear. Similar stills were subsequently fitted with a relief valve at Leitch's and elsewhere, but this did not prevent much worse disasters.[78]

On 2 April 1916, 200 tons of TNT exploded in a munitions factory at Faversham in Kent. It was the biggest explosion of the war. 115 employees were killed. The blast blew out windows in Southend and was heard over 120 miles away in Norwich. Fortunately, this factory was sited on remote marshland.[79]

Most explosives factories, such as British Dyes, were adapted chemical works, located in the vicinity of the terraced houses built for their workers. The Low Moor Chemical Company, near Bradford, was similarly situated.

Four months after the Faversham disaster, on 21 August 1916, the Low Moor company had 30,000lb of picric acid in its drying sheds awaiting sifting, packing and shipment. At 2.25pm two uncovered drums were pushed towards the sifting area when a fire started in one of them. Twenty minutes later a large explosion showered the area with wood, bricks and ironwork, one piece of metal being found a mile away. Half an hour after that, as the fire service fought the blaze, there was a second, much larger explosion. An entire building went up, killing six firemen and destroying their engine, fragments of which came to earth at Heckmondwike Railway Station, four miles away.

Among the many nearby buildings struck by the debris was a Corporation gasometer which fractured and also exploded. At 6pm the company's sifting and packing shed exploded. Detonations, large and small, continued for two days. A second gasometer was destroyed, numerous factories were severely damaged, and a variety of other properties, including several schools, required repairs. About 2000 houses were affected, 50 being demolished. Thirty nine people were killed and 60 were hospitalised. During the next few days Low Moor was the destination of choice for many of Huddersfield's cyclists, curious to see the devastation.

The investigation concluded that the picric acid had ignited either from friction caused by transportation between the sheds, or by reacting with iron in the barrel from which it should have been shielded. It was an accident but, with a little more care, an avoidable one. Safety had been compromised to hasten production.[80]

The steep escalation in 'heavy shell' production was achieved partly by bi-passing rigorous, standardised procedures. Experienced staff were diluted by the rapidly enlarged workforce, and no limit was set on the quantity of explosives that could be stockpiled. Men were risking their lives in battle. If arming them involved risking lives in Britain, those risks had to be taken. It was difficult to argue against it.

On the evening of Friday, 6 October 1916, seven weeks after the Bradford disaster, a large fire broke out at British Dyes in Huddersfield. Producing almost 5000 18lb shells per week, British Dyes packed far more explosives than either Low Moor, or indeed Read Hollidays at the time of the Boer War explosion on the site in 1899. As the smoke billowed skyward, visions of Low Moor loomed large. Panic spread through the densely populated neighbourhood. Hundreds of homes were evacuated and streets were thronged as residents moved to a safer distance from what was effectively the biggest bomb Huddersfield has ever seen. Inside the factory some employees remained to fight the blaze. John McMaddocks rushed to operate the fire extinguishers, then used his body as a draught excluder to prevent the flow of air from 'fanning the flames' into the explosives stores. His main assistance came from employees Ethel Brown and Private Charlie Shaw, before the fire brigade arrived. Thankfully, after several hours, and at considerable risk, they extinguished the blaze.

The *HDE* was only allowed to publish the story after 'Press Bureau consideration.' Realising that the incident could not be 'hushed-up', the censors permitted a short, low-key report that underplayed how grave the situation really was.[81]

In 1918, McMaddocks, who hailed from Sheepridge, Ethel Brown of Brighouse, and Private Charlie Shaw of Moldgreen were awarded the MBE 'for courage and resource in dealing with a fire at an explosives factory at great personal risk.' Private Shaw had been recalled from serving with the Duke of Wellington's West Riding Regiment in 1915 to utilise his expertise in chemicals and munitions at British Dyes.[82]

Disastrously, the war continued to take priority over the safety of workers and other citizens. In December 1916 an explosion in Leeds killed 35 women.[83] The following month 73 died and over 400 were injured when 50 tons of TNT exploded at Silvertown in East London. Most of the casualties were residents in three rows of adjacent cottages. Over 70,000 properties were damaged or destroyed, including a gasometer at Greenwich where burning debris ignited 200,000 cubic metres of gas in a fireball.[84] In June 1917 a further 43 died in an explosion at Ashton-Under-Lyne. Shortly afterwards the Government started to 'close all works of that type in populous centres.'[85] This did not prevent a further 137 deaths in an explosion at the National Shell Filling Factory at Chilwell near Nottingham in the spring of 1918.[86] Such disasters were not confined to Britain. In July 1917, 90 Germans lost their lives at a similar incident in Detmold.[87]

On 5 June 1918 there was a second explosion at a Huddersfield TNT factory when Standard Fireworks, based at Crosland Hill, suffering considerable damage but thankfully no fatalities. Working for the Admiralty during World War I, Standard Fireworks was an obvious supplier of explosives and had one of the safest munitions sites, in a stone quarry with purpose-built gunpowder stores from quarry-blasting.[88]

By 1918 Huddersfield was manufacturing 33% of Britain's high explosives, the majority at British Dyes. The catastrophes elsewhere suggest that, on 6 October 1916, British Dyes came perilously close to causing Huddersfield's greatest-ever disaster.

Chapter 10

Zeppelins and the Blackout

The Zeppelin's Fall:
or Lucifer Debased
by
'V' of Holmfirth

England lies asleep, the cool wind blowing o'er her;
The soft night wraps her round; the dark sea beats before her.
Brave English hearts are resting, while Heavenly devotion
Is breathed to all the Earth, by wind and sky and ocean.
Would all the world were peaceful! But no! An evil omen,
That whirring sound aloft! Here are the German foemen!

England starts awake! Silence no more enfolds her.
The sleeper springs to life; a fearful tumult holds her –
Sounds of millions sighing, through the darkness thrilling,
A thousand footsteps flying, a thousand whistles shrilling!
Searchlights far are flashing! Now the guns are booming,
Where afar, above, an evil shape is looming!

Swift the form makes answer! In her wake there follow
Cries of wounded children, and the echo hollow
Of their falling homes, groans of women dying,
Fathers at their guns hear, and, quick replying,
Reap fierce revenge. Sudden the tumult ceases,
The thunders die away, the breathless hush increases!

See! The enemy, like a meteor, dashes
Swiftly down, and falling, still more whitely flashes.
Then sinks, a quivering monster, mangled pieces, dying!
Silence reigns! But soon triumphant voices crying
Echo England's joy. Hers is the mission splendid,
To battle thus the foes of God till war on Earth is ended.[1]

Bombing of the East Coast

MEN OF BRITAIN! WILL YOU STAND THIS?

Nº 2 Wykeham Street, SCARBOROUGH after the German bombardment on Dec! 16th. It was the Home of a Working Man. Four People were killed in this House including the Wife aged 58, and Two Children, the youngest aged 5.

78 Women & Children were killed and 228 Women & Children were wounded by the German Raiders

ENLIST NOW

On 16 December 1914 the rules of warfare were re-written. The German navy bombarded Hartlepool, Whitby and Scarborough, killing 173 civilians, including a six-month old baby, and wounding almost 600. As an attempt to lure British warships from the security of Scapa Flow into open waters, it failed, but its psychological impact was immense. Admiral Beatty was pilloried for failing to engage the enemy, but the hesitancy of naval high command was secondary to confirmation of Germany's ruthless intentions. It was not just soldiers on the battlefield who were fair game for German guns.[2]

Invoking fear, disgust and anger, the attacks were consistent with atrocities against whole families in Belgium and became a propaganda weapon. Churchill labelled the Germans 'baby-killers', cartoonists emphasised the point and recruitment posters exploited the raw emotion.[3]

Scarborough, along with almost the entire east coast, was already a designated prohibited area for 'enemy aliens' from the Aliens Restrictions Act, emergency legislation passed three days into the war. The conditions were maintained well after the armistice, much to the misfortune of German-born violinist Paul Schaefer, who had resided in Huddersfield since the 1880s. On 30 March 1919, carrying a permit signed by the Chief Constable of Huddersfield, Paul Schaefer was 'charged with being an enemy alien', having entered 'the prohibited area of Scarborough without permission.'

The case illustrated Scarborough's psychological scars. Schaefer's defence, that he had 'lived the life of an Englishman for 30 years', and that it was his 'misfortune to be born in Germany', earned an acquittal, but only after an uncomfortable 24 hours.[4]

REMEMBER SCARBOROUGH!

ENLIST NOW

The Zeppelin Threat

On 19 January 1915, just over a month after the attacks on the north east coast, the threat to Britain's civilians was confirmed when Kings Lynn and Great Yarmouth were bombed by two German Zeppelins.[5] No one on the coast or inland was safe. Overnight, the war took on a new, sinister and terrifying face.

Huddersfield, as a centre of munitions and khaki production, and with a mainline railway station that was vital for transportation of war materials and troops, was a possible target. On 22 June 1915 official air raid advice appeared in the *HDE*. A siren or whistles would warn of an approaching airship. People should then '… stay indoors; keep doors and windows closed to protect against gas attack; have buckets of sand and water ready to fight fires; check the safety of chemical extinguishers; don't turn gas supplies off; use a respirator or a pad of cotton saturated in washing soda held in place by gauze.'

The number of Zeppelin attacks on Britain increased during 1915, particularly along the east coast, but local implementation of the blackout was tardy, even after a devastating attack on London on 8 September 1915 caused half a million pounds worth of damage.[6] By 1916 it was becoming clear that the blackout was effective against the Zeppelins' primitive navigation equipment.[7] Zeppelin navigators had great difficulty locating inland conurbations. The further they travelled, the greater their chances of becoming lost and of being shot down.[8] There were larger and closer targets than Huddersfield, which was not 'on the usual itinerary of the raiders.'[9] Even so, bright lights could serve as navigation beacons and could invite the much-feared attack.

Huddersfield got its blackout act together after a local man witnessed some of the carnage inflicted by half a dozen Zeppelins on 31 January 1916. Fifty nine civilians lost their lives in the south east and the Midlands.[10] His letter, signed 'PREVENTION', was printed in the *HDE* on 7 February 1916.

> ... it is time the inhabitants of Huddersfield and the Colne Valley, insisted on the Lighting Restrictions Order being carried to the letter ... In every town that suffered the lights were not obscured and the towns that escaped were those that were plunged into darkness ... After my experience of the recent raid I consider that everybody, whether manufacturer or householder, who fails to obscure all lights is a traitor to the community in which he lives. Mills in the Colne Valley are fully alight all night. I ask the authorities why?

He went on to question the Lighting Order itself which, bizarrely, applied to Huddersfield, Golcar and Linthwaite but not to Slaithwaite and Marsden.

> Travelling by tramcar to Marsden, a stranger might suppose that the upper part of the valley considered itself immune from danger ... On the Slaithwaite side of the boundary is a picture house with flaring lights, and within a stone's throw cottages are compelled to darken their windows.

Three days later Huddersfield's Chief Constable, Mr J Morton, announced that all lighting restrictions were to be strictly enforced. The Reverend AT Guttey certainly noticed the difference, complaining to a packed Northumberland Street Primitive Methodists' Church on 25 April 1916 that 'there is far more danger from lamp-posts than Zeppelins.'[11]

Motivated partly by the dangers of the blackout, but mainly as a means to alleviate coal shortages, daylight saving was introduced, the clocks going forward by an hour on 19 May 1916. The concept had been mooted by William Willetts and first rejected by Parliament in 1909. Germany and Austria altered their clocks three weeks before Britain and by the end of May 1916 a further ten European countries had followed suit, including major combatants Belgium, France, Italy and Turkey and neutral countries whose economies were impacted by the war, the Netherlands and Sweden.[12]

The main impact was in saving fuel. Any impact on road safety in the blackout was marginal, as the main dangers were in the darker winter months. In Huddersfield the move was extremely popular with sportsmen. Golfers could play a full round after work and bowls matches could be played late into the evenings. Daylight saving coincided with bowls becoming the first local sport to encroach onto the Sabbath. The dismayed Lord's Day Observance contingent argued that bowls on Sunday evenings in full view of people's houses was 'offensive to a large number of residents', and that the long summer evenings gave no excuse for this.[13]

In September 1916, as the nights closed in, there were complaints that there was no 'uniform standard' about shop lighting, with prosecution too dependent on the subjective judgement of officials.[14] It was a timely reminder. German Zeppelins were at that time targeting inland centres of armaments and munitions manufacture. On 24 September 1916 Nottingham was bombed.

Two nights later half a dozen Zeppelins left their base at Nordholz, north west of Hamburg. Two of them, L21 and L22 crossed the Lincolnshire coast at 9.45pm. L22 bombed Sheffield, killing 24 civilians. L21 was seeking Derby, but was hit by strong winds that blew it north westwards. Its commander, Oberleutnant Kurt Frankenburg was lost and looked for any sizeable conurbation that might be Derby. In fact, he was heading towards Huddersfield. Fortunately, as he passed close to Holmfirth and Meltham the 'country ... was mostly blacked out.' L21 then passed over Todmorden and Bacup, eventually dropping 22 bombs along the Irwell Valley from Rawtenstall to Ramsbottom. Drawn to the glow of Bolton's foundries, it dropped a further 23 bombs, killing 17 Bolton residents, before returning north east. It released its final bomb over Bolton Abbey north of Leeds and crossed the coast at Whitby at 3.05am.

Back in Germany, Oberleutnant Frankenburg reported that L21 had successfully bombed Derby. Two months later the L21, again commanded by Frankenburg, was shot down over Lowestoft while returning from a raid. All 17 men on board were killed.[15]

On 1 October 1916, five days after this near miss, a number of Huddersfield boys, excited by general expectation of an air raid, 'were seen playing at searchlights with flash lamps – a very dangerous practice.' The local authorities had seen enough and on 3 October a much stricter enforcement of 'lights out' was announced. The new regulations included stopping all tramcars after a second warning of aircraft in the vicinity.[16] From national level came a directive that all vehicles were to have two front lights, darkened by a cover with six holes. The 'small flashlights' that many people were carrying were to be 'directed as near to the user's feet as possible.'[17] No fireworks were to be allowed on 5 November.[18]

Such enforcement did not prevent lights at Meltham Hospital blazing away during an air raid warning. The lights were strangely unaffected when the gas supply was cut at the gasworks, and the staff remained oblivious to the warning.[19]

Danger in the Darkness

The blackout brought its own dangers on the roads. Francis H Knaggs, in a letter printed in the *HDE* on 4 August 1916, expressed concern about transporting injured soldiers from Huddersfield Railway Station to the War Hospital at Royds Hall 'through the absolute darkness of the route with its many awkward corners.' The validity of such concerns proved well-founded when, that evening, Tom Drake, a master-tailor from Moldgreen, was knocked down by a motor taxi-cab at a junction near to the top of Long Lane. Tom, who was blind, died five days later. Eye-witness Eliza Bates gave evidence that it was '… very dark and the lamp at the crossroads was not lighted.' The cab driver could not have seen him in time to stop and the jury recommended that, where four roads meet, street lamps should be left lit. Their verdict, 'accidental death', set a precedent for a catalogue of similar blackout tragedies.[20]

The absence on war service of several business drivers exacerbated the problem. A letter from 'STRESS' described their less experienced replacements as '… callow motormen … raw youths who are quite unfit for the job.' They presented 'a new and increasing danger in the streets of Huddersfield.'[21]

Wild driving was not an accusation levelled at Huddersfield's tramcars. In November 1916 a passenger, anxious to catch a morning train and exasperated by his tram's lack of speed asked the conductor: 'Can't you go faster than this?' The conductor replied: 'Yes, I can; but I've got to stay with the car.'[22]

Nevertheless, unable to change direction and with a greater stopping distance, trams were to prove far more lethal than motor cars in the blackout. It is questionable whether they should have been running in conditions so dark that passengers were 'unable to discover … whether the tram has arrived at their destination.'[23]

On the evening of 14 October 1916 Effie Firth of Berry Brow was struck by a tramcar in John William Street. Lucky to survive, she claimed £100 damages, alleging that negligent driving had caused her injuries and loss of earnings.

> Owing to the darkening of the tramcar windows there was very little to be seen of the tramcar even when it was close … The negligence alleged was that the driver did not give any warning – no gong or bell was sounded.

Eye witnesses suggested that the driver had little time to react. The judge's sympathies were with the defence.

> The darkening of the streets imposed a burden which the law had put upon the system, and from which the Corporation had no power to depart.

Effie Firth lost her case, but at least she was alive.[24] Others were less lucky. On 23 November 1916 36-year-old Lewis Dickinson, a tramcar driver from Moldgreen, was fatally injured when his tram hit a wagon of the Great Northern Railway Company on Manchester Road.[25] Three weeks later, Emily Waterhouse (45) of Outlane, who had poor eyesight, was struck by a tram at Swan Lane and killed instantly. In both cases 'the dimmed lights of the car made it difficult for the driver to see anything unless it was actually on the track.'[26]

19 January 1917 was another 'very dark' night. William Crabtree was driving the Deighton to

Huddersfield tram on Leeds Road opposite the Waggon and Horses at no more than five miles per hour when a silhouette appeared in the road two to three yards in front of the tram. The tram screeched to a halt within ten yards, but had hit Robert Crowther aged 65. He did not regain consciousness and died two hours later. Like Tom Drake and Emily Waterhouse, Robert Crowther was handicapped, being 'somewhat deaf' and having poor eyesight.[27]

LEEDS ROAD TRAMWAY FATALITY.

———— o :————

TRAMWAY MEN'S DIFFICULTIES OWING TO BAD LIGHTING.

HDE headline, reporting Robert Crowther's death

All these accidents would have been less likely 'in normal times with lighting'[28] and the verdicts were 'accidental death.' Tom Drake, Lewis Dickinson, Emily Waterhouse and Robert Crowther were, effectively, victims of war.

The local authorities were now questioning the necessity and wisdom of such all-enveloping blackness. Mr S Proctor, Deputy Town Clerk, representing the Huddersfield Corporation, informed Robert Crowther's inquest that:

> ... the drivers of the Corporation are experiencing exceptional difficulties, especially on such an evening as last Friday when there was no moon. The lighting regulations are the order of the Home Office and the Chief Constable has written to the competent military authority pointing out that there have been three deaths through the bad lighting in six weeks.[29]

The HDE took up the baton:

> Timely warnings of the approach of air raiders have always been given and ... the fact that light can be cut off at its source ... would seem to indicate the possibility of allowing more lights to be shown in the thoroughfares of the borough in the evenings.[30]

February and March 1917 brought a further seven serious tramcar accidents, including two fractured skulls and three fatalities. At the inquest into one of these the jury concluded:

> Owing to darkness and the fog the driver could not see more than a couple of yards in front of him ... if anything had been in the way he would have been bound to run into it.[31]

Was the blackout inflicting damage disproportionate to the Zeppelin threat? At the inquest of 54-year-old Mary Elizabeth Flood of Fartown, knocked down and killed 'at a very dark spot' by the Sheepridge tram on 17 February, the Chief Constable informed the court that in Sheffield trams were now allowed full headlights. Sheffield had endured 20 tram-related fatalities during the last six months, but the headlights were making little difference. He thought the solution was street lighting. The foreman of the jury agreed, describing Huddersfield as 'the worst lighted town in the district.' The Deputy Town Clerk, Mr Proctor lamented that the town's gas lamps would take too long to extinguish in an air raid. The solution was electric lamps, but it was 'impossible to get the material for electric lighting at the present time.'

The jury's inevitable verdict of 'accidental death' was accompanied by a recommendation that the Chief Constable should try to get more lighting at places known to be dangerous.[32]

By the following September 'Huddersfield was lighting its lamps' until 11pm, but the inconsistency across the district continued. Linthwaite Urban District Council refused to follow Huddersfield's example, rejecting a request to light alternate lamps in Milnsbridge, where 'people were running into each other.'[33] One disgruntled resident responded in rhyme.

Untitled Poem
by
Milnsbridge Resident

Normal time now is here, and the long winter nights
Will be with us in darkness intense,
When we grope our way homewards without any lights,
Longing for an additional "sense".

When we bump up against every man that we meet,
And we can't find the garden gate wide;
When we bash our poor shins on the old garden seat,
For there's never a glimmer to guide.

How we long for the well-lighted streets once again,
How we long for the nights as of yore.
But mostly we long for the happy day when
Normal times shall return to our shore.[34]

The *HDE* of 28 March 1917 compared pre-war accident statistics with those of the previous 12 months. There were 142 street accidents to the year ending March 1914, compared to 97 in the year ending March 1917, the difference reflecting the much quieter streets of wartime. Of the pre-war accidents, 14 (10%) were tram-related, one of them fatal. Of the wartime accidents, 20 (21%) were tram-related, six of them fatal.

Permitting street lighting in Huddersfield until 11pm had the desired effect. Tram-related accidents were significantly reduced, with just one fatality in the year from March 1917, 60-year-old Emma Jubb who was struck by a tram in St John's Road on 19 February 1918.[35] The more relaxed regulations coincided with more effective anti-airship defence measures – better early-warning communications, more searchlights and guns, and fighter aircraft igniting the Zeppelins' hydrogen balloons with explosive shells, all contributed to significant inroads to the Zeppelin fleet. Of 115 Zeppelins, 77 were shot down or disabled. There were only eight raids over Britain in 1917 and three in 1918.[36]

The Huddersfield constabulary, assisted by the Motor Volunteers, continued to enforce the regulations. No one was above the law. At 12.20am on Saturday 9 March 1918 PC Preston saw an external light at Clevelands, Marsh and, finding no one home, extinguished it. Three days later the former Mayor, Alderman Joseph Blamires, who continued to promote local support for the war and still chaired Local Military Tribunals, was somewhat embarrassed to be fined £1 by local magistrates for breach of the Lighting Order.[37]

A Close Encounter

Huddersfield's closest encounter came in the last major Zeppelin attack of the war, on the evening of 12 April 1918 when five Zeppelins targeted Lincolnshire, Yorkshire and the Midlands. One of these, the L61, was believed to be seeking Sheffield but, blown miles off course, bombed Wigan, killing seven civilians.[38] It returned almost due east and sometime after 3am the residents of Lockwood and Paddock were rudely awakened by the deep hum of the Zeppelin's motors. The *HWE* commented:

> It was felt that one night justified all the excellent blackout arrangements undertaken during the war. The fact that the shops and the public houses closed early, and the street lamps were extinguished at 11pm no doubt contributed to this.

No bombs were dropped on Huddersfield.

Post-war, opinion was divided about the blackout. It had proved effective in protecting the district and, 'on the whole … the public bore the inconvenience and danger with very commendable equanimity.'[39] But the fact remained that the only air-raid related deaths in Huddersfield were caused by the blackout, not by Zeppelin attack, leaving families of the bereaved to wonder whether, even at the height of Zeppelin activity, precautions needed to be quite so stringent. No one will ever know.

Chapter 11

War Hospitals

There's a Hospital in Yorkshire,
Royds Hall it is by name;
No matter what the regiment
The welcome's just the same.[1]

The First Wounded Tommies Arrive

During the first months of World War I, the British Red Cross began to work in partnership with the Order of St John of Jerusalem. Both organisations were tasked with recruiting Voluntary Aid Detachments (VADs) to help with the care of the returning wounded Tommies. To aid efficiency, the two organisations merged to form the Joint War Committee (JWC), operating under the authority of the Red Cross name and emblem. The JWC was run most efficiently from Devonshire House in Piccadilly, London, loaned for war use by the Duke and Duchess of Devonshire. Surprisingly for the time, much of the JWC's high level administration was undertaken by educated women who had been involved with the VAD scheme since its inception in 1909. In response to the flow of wounded troops returning from the continent in the autumn of 1914, the British Red Cross began to set up auxiliary war hospitals in most British towns, often commandeering church halls and public buildings, and gratefully accepting many offers of accommodation in private houses.[2]

In Huddersfield, the four auxiliary care locations that accommodated the first convoy of wounded soldiers in October 1914 had doubled to eight for the arrival of a convoy of 90 troops on 3 February 1915. They were distributed as follows:

Huddersfield Royal Infirmary	30+
Holmfirth	5
Durker Roods, Meltham (home of Col Charles Brookes)	30
Lightridge House (provided by Charles Sykes)	8
Trinity St Nursing Home	3
Bradley Lane	2
Caresbrook House	10
Howley	2

The platforms at the railway station were cleared and outside, spaces for ambulances and cars were cordoned off from the 'large crowd eager to cheer the fighting men.'[3] Huddersfield's warm yet business-like welcome for such convoys was sustained throughout the war. Volunteers and boy scouts would cordon off areas around St George's Square to allow ambulances and transport volunteers to gain access with their vehicles.

Huddersfield
Royal Infirmary,
Portland Street

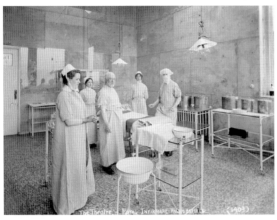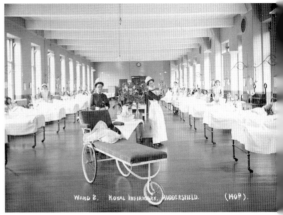

The Operating Theatre (left) and Ward 2 (right) at Huddersfield Royal Infirmary during World War I

Admiration and sympathy for the wounded Tommies was unabated and there was a strong consensus that everyone should do their bit to help them. On 4 May 1915 the poignant and distressing sight of convoys from the battlefields of Hill 60 and Neuve Chapelle emerged from Huddersfield Railway Station, 400 troops who had fought alongside Huddersfield men of the Duke of Wellington's West Riding Regiment.[4]

Within days, headlines began reporting that some of these warriors had died. On 11 May hundreds attended Edgerton Cemetery for the funeral of Richard Wright of Liverpool.[5] The following week 20 year-old Private Harold Bradley of Scarborough died from a gunshot wound to the thigh at Bradley Lane Surgical Home, the fourth fatality from the latest convoys.[6]

The National Motor Volunteers

The town continued to respond to the growing demands, and when the fifth convoy of one hundred wounded men arrived in Huddersfield on 20 May, public ambulances were supported by the newly formed ambulance section of the Huddersfield Automobile Club, its members selflessly volunteering their private vehicles and paying for their own petrol.[7]

After working for two months alongside the Huddersfield Corps of the St John Ambulance Brigade, the Automobile Club's efforts were formalised as part of the West Riding Royal Army Service Corps Motor Transport (Volunteers) in July 1915.[8] In November 1916, Boer War veteran W Norman, the trainer of Huddersfield Town FC and formerly trainer of Barnsley's 1912 FA Cup-winning team, was promoted to Sergeant-Major and drill instructor of the corps.[9] Part of a fledgling national initiative, the National Motor Volunteers [NMVs] were to use their private transport to link the counties of England, to assist in maintaining lines of communication and, in their spare time, to transport wounded soldiers and aid recruitment initiatives. In Huddersfield their primary function was to provide transport to and between the war hospitals in the local area, effectively running the service as they had many more vehicles than St John Ambulance. On 28 July 1915, the Huddersfield Number 1 Platoon of the NMV was inspected on the recreation ground at Greenhead Park. Its 40 members had in total 25 cars and a motor bike.[10]

At New Year 1917 the NMV innovated a free 'night cars for soldiers' scheme, transporting servicemen who returned on leave by late night trains from the railway station to their homes.[11] This demanded careful and skilful driving in the blackout and over bleak moorland,[12] the volunteers driving as far as Wakefield, Barnsley, Penistone, Hebden Bridge and Denholme on poorly maintained roads. After surviving the front lines, soldiers had still to survive the dangers of darkened British highways![13]

Such journeys necessitated frequent cleaning of the cars, outside and inside. Troops often arrived infested with fleas and coated in mud. In January 1917 a 'Fenay Bridge Highlander' was driven home along with 'a good portion of France on his boots, puttees, and kilt.'

Pride in the commitment of the NMV was evident in the regular and comprehensive reports of their activities by the *HDE*'s anonymous weekly contributor, 'OLD VOLUNTEER'. In February 1917 he detailed their work. Every night, three cars with eight men and an officer were on duty at Huddersfield station from 10.30pm to 2am (10 till 2 on Sundays). If the trains were late, it was sometimes 4am before they could retire. They provided a rest room with a fire and refreshments for soldiers waiting to be transported who, on any night, could number as few as ten or as many as 40.

> ... though some of them may not thank me for mentioning the fact – lest their better halves should insist upon having a practical demonstration in the home circle – they wash and dry the crockery ready for the next relay of guests with the greatest celerity.[14]

By September 1917 similar schemes were running in Birmingham and London, and the *HDE* was affronted that 'Birmingham, which started after Huddersfield is claiming to be the pioneers.'[15] The *HDE* reinforced this claim in its 1919 summary of the war.

> The ... Motor Transport (Volunteers) ... set a fine example to other motor corps, as a result of which the work was extended to various parts of the country.[16]

The Huddersfield NMV was also the only such group which continued to fund its own fuel without Government assistance. This generosity never wavered, despite spiralling costs caused by the increasing numbers of wounded men, and diminishing petrol supplies that triggered price rises in the already inflationary economy. To cut costs, the NMV developed a motor cycle section which, in September 1917, adapted a motor bike and sidecar as an ambulance to 'move single patients at lower cost than conventional motor ambulances.'[17]

As unrestricted German U-boat attacks in the Atlantic further impeded fuel supplies, the use of motor vehicles was limited by law in 1917 and further curtailed to essential and military business by the Motor Spirit and Gas Restrictions Order in January 1918.[18]

The upshot was a resurgence in cycling, replacing motor cars and for some, trams, which were making fewer stops to save the additional fuel used in stopping and starting, particularly on the many uphill routes out of Huddersfield.[19]

The NMVs were vital to the functioning of all the local war hospitals. During the war Huddersfield received 119 convoys, totalling 20,000 wounded soldiers, 'at all hours of day and night', and the NMVs were unfailing in their duties.[20] In 1917 alone they met 35 convoys, comprising 5678 soldiers, of whom 3855 stretcher cases were transported by ambulance and 1823 walking wounded were transported by car. During 1917 the three ambulances travelled 13,440 miles.[21]

The wives of the NMVs were also proactive. Acquiring the use of a Lloyds Bank-owned building between the bottom of St George's Square and Railway Street, they equipped and staffed it for the comfort, rest and recreation of wounded soldiers. Open from 10am until 2am daily, the facility had easy chairs, a writing room, piano, gramophone, newspapers and magazines, draughts, dominoes and chess, cigarettes, biscuits and an oven for tea and coffee. The refreshments were free as soldiers did not receive army pay whilst in hospital, but as back-pay 'in the future.'[22]

The impact of these NMV initiatives can be gleaned from the first week of August 1917, a typical week, when 1123 wounded troops were entertained in the recreation building and 232 local troops were met from late night trains and taken home, the volunteers driving a total of 900 miles.[23]

The gratitude and general good cheer of most troops helped to make all these efforts worthwhile. In May 1915, a convoy of 100 soldiers, 60 of them 'stretcher cases', arrived singing popular songs and each cheerfully and gratefully received a gift of cigarettes from Sir William Raynor. In March 1918, a convoy arrived 'straight from the fighting ... uniforms ...still thickly coated with mud from the battlefield ... a proportion of them ... suffering from the effects of gas', but they were 'one of the cheeriest convoys ... yet.'[24]

Inevitably, there was also misery among the injured. Perhaps it was well-hidden, perhaps the *HDE* was less inclined to report it, but it didn't go unnoticed by schoolgirl Vivien Hirst, who visited the war hospital at Royds Hall with her mother to help comfort the soldiers.

I only remember the one visit, mainly, I think because I still recall the lonely soldier, so far from home and family, and still feel a little regretful that my shyness did nothing to cheer him.

She also recalled the crowds that greeted a new convoy of soldiers as they arrived at the hospital.

I waved and cheered with the rest, but after a while I grew silent, for the pale, haggard faces of the men sitting in the doorway staring at this enthusiastic throng with empty expressions, made me ashamed. I felt as though I were looking on a scene which should have been quietly hidden from sight. It was suddenly an indignity to be there.[25]

Royds Hall War Hospital

By 1918, hospital provision in Huddersfield had increased beyond recognition. During 1915 local facilities had struggled to cope with the increasing numbers of injured. That summer, whilst awaiting a convoy of wounded soldiers at Huddersfield Railway Station, the RAMC's supervisor of the local war hospitals, Lieutenant-Colonel William Marshall, approached Lieutenant-Colonel Coward, secretary of the district's VAD, suggesting that it was his duty to ensure that a military hospital was built in the district. The Mayor Alderman Joseph Blamires, and Sir William Raynor were also present, Raynor 'making the characteristic reply that if any other town could do so Huddersfield could build a war hospital.'

Shortly afterwards, Joseph Blamires hosted a meeting in the Mayor's Parlour where a committee was formed to organise the scheme. It comprised himself as Chairman, Alderman Jessop as Vice-chairman, Sir William Raynor, Charles Sykes and Julius Hirst, who was vice-president of the VAD.[26] Sykes had seen first-hand 'the disadvantages of the small hospital' for wounded soldiers, having accommodated eight of them at Lightridge House in recent months.[27] As he did so often, Sykes set the financial ball rolling and by the end of the meeting the committee had pledged a combined £12,000 towards erecting and equipping the hospital. Within a fortnight a public appeal had increased this to £30,121.

Huddersfield's War Hospital was built on land lent by the council 'on the estate at Royds Wood, Paddock', previously used as emergency accommodation for Huddersfield's first Belgian refugees in October 1914. Royds Hall was the only war hospital in the entire country to be built and fully equipped from local public subscriptions without Government support.

Royds Hall

On the suggestion of Blamires and Sykes, Royds Hall adopted the 'open air' design. Patients were kept dry and, as far as possible away from drafts, but one wall of the wards was open to the elements so that air could circulate freely. Evidence from military field hospitals during the 19th century, and the lower death rates of infants at coastal resorts compared to industrial centres, suggested that fresh air was healthy. Whilst patients benefited from blankets and hot water bottles, the medical staff were not so lucky, and working conditions could be arduous in the winter.[28]

Using their personal contacts, Blamires and Sykes had seen such wards 'pioneered at Cambridge' where they were designed and innovated by Brevet-Colonel German Sims Woodhead of the RAMC. Born in Huddersfield in 1855, German was the son of Joseph Woodhead, who was Mayor of Huddersfield in 1876-1877, MP for Spen Valley 1885-1892 and one of a group of liberals who founded the *Huddersfield Examiner* in 1851, and the *Dewsbury Reporter* in 1858. German's brother, Ernest, became proprietor of the *Examiner* in the 1880s and remained so beyond World War I.

German was educated at Huddersfield College and studied medicine at Edinburgh. There, he became an expert in tuberculosis and founded and supervised the Royal College of Physicians

Laboratory, the first pathology laboratory in Britain. In 1890 he moved to London to become Director of the Laboratories of the Conjoint Board of the Royal College of Physicians (London) and Royal College of Surgeons (England). German founded the *Journal of Pathology and Bacteriology* in 1893 and edited it until 1920. The publication continues in the 21st century as the *Journal of Pathology*. Since 2006 the Sims Woodhead Medal has been awarded to individuals in recognition of distinguished service to the Journal.

In 1899 German became Professor of Pathology at Cambridge University and was still there in World War I when his vision of open-air hospital wards became a reality, both at home and behind the lines at various theatres of war. German Sims Woodhead was awarded the OBE for his pioneering work in pathology in the New Year's Honour's List of 1918. He died in 1921.[29]

Whilst Royds Hall was one of many war hospitals built to the Sims Woodhead 'Cambridge' design, open air wards were also added to existing hospitals as the country responded to the growing numbers of wounded.

The conversion work on Royds Hall's brick foundations, timber frame and asbestos walls began in early August. The hospital was opened by the Mayoress Mrs Blamires on 4 October 1915. Its ten wards could accommodate 500 patients, 60 medics and 45 nurses. It also had 'blocks' for administration, kitchen, operations, RAMC, recreation, hospital supplies and 'disinfecting', plus a mortuary and a boiler house. The whole conversion and construction work cost £22,500.[30]

NEW WAR HOSPITAL OPENED AT HUDDERSFIELD.

---:0:---

LARGE BUILDING EQUIPPED BY PUBLIC SUBSCRIPTION.

MAYORESS'S TRIBUTE TO THE WORK OF THE WOMEN'S COMMITTEE.

The Huddersfield War Hospital, built by public subscription at Royds Hall, was opened this afternoon by the Mayoress (Mrs. Blamires), in the presence of a large and representative company. Among those present in addition to the Mayor and Mayoress (Alderman and Mrs. Blamires) and Surgeon-General and Mrs. Kenny were Sir Wm. and Lady Raynor, Col. Land (in command of the Flying Column), and Col. Mosse of the 25th Battalion, West Riding Regiment)

(Left) The *HDE* reports the opening of the Royds Hall War Hospital, 4 October 1915;
Allotments (top right), and lunch in an open air ward (bottom right) at Royds Hall.
The loose screens of the 'open' wall are on the right hand side of both pictures.

The tranquil settings of Royds Hall were ideal for convalescing and the surrounding Paddock area was alive with military 'hospital blues' uniforms. Soldiers tended nearby allotments as a means of relaxation. Local allotment owners still find buttons and other military paraphernalia in their patches. Local families welcomed visiting relatives and convalescing soldiers into their homes, the local community helping to heal the physical and mental scars of war, and to restore the morale of the soldiers.[31]

Volunteers' Medical Training

The need to develop local medical services was met by classes in first aid and home nursing which trained over 500 volunteers in the early months of the war. A further 600 gained certificates after training classes were centralised at Primrose Hill in April 1915. Run by Mrs Porteous under the auspices of the British Red Cross Society, these classes later moved to the Temperance Hall.

Two hundred of these volunteer medical trainees enrolled to run additional nursing divisions of the St John Ambulance in Huddersfield, and four additional divisions in outlying districts – Dearne Valley (Denby Dale) Men's, Dearne Valley Women's, Lepton Men's and Honley Women's – increased the number of local divisions to eight.

The volunteer trainees also supplied VAD nurses and male staff for the RAMC at home and abroad. Several male members joined the 1/5th Duke of Wellington's West Riding Regiment, serving in France and Belgium as stretcher bearers. Others joined: the RAMC of Southern Command; the Navy as sick berth attendants; the staffs of hospitals in Malta and Greece; or were attached to other units. Nine of their number, primarily stretcher bearers, lost their lives serving abroad. Two of these, Privates John Marriot and WH Pearson, won the Military Medal for bravery, Pearson 'for carrying live bombs and rendering them innocuous.'

Many of the trainee volunteers staffed Royds Hall and the local auxiliary war hospitals, each of which was run with military discipline.[32] VADs were issued with a British Red Cross Society (BRCS) Regulation Uniform, trained to a very high standard and required to carry a code of conduct booklet upon their person at all times. This national publication included guidelines for care of equipment, a comprehensive list of 'Don'ts for VADs', and extensive advice about personal hygiene, for example:

> It is advisable to gargle morning and evening, but especially evening. Carbolic 1 in 60; Listerine, 1 teaspoonful to 5oz. Water; Glyco-Thymoline and water, ½ and ½ to be used.[33]

Although highly trained in first aid and nursing, the VADs' daily tasks could include cooking, cleaning and driving the ambulances. The detachments were split up by gender and given a Warrant Officer Number. Male detachments were the odd numbers and the female detachments the even numbers. Each detachment included a Commandant, Medical Officer and Quartermaster. Female detachments had 22 women, two of whom were trained nurses, and the male detachments had 48 men, four section leaders and a pharmacist. All were required to meet for training at least once a month but they often met weekly. The unqualified women had a year to complete their training and gain their certificates in Home Nursing and First Aid.[34]

On 9 October 1915, a week after it opened, Royds Hall's first convoy of 100 wounded soldiers, including 50 on stretchers, arrived from Southampton. It took from 6.00pm until 7.10pm to transport them in the usual assortment of ambulances and motor cars, whilst the Huddersfield and District Volunteer Corps kept St George's Square clear of traffic and pedestrians. At the hospital a cordon of fifty boy scouts prevented the crowds pressing too closely. The men were provided with a pint of hot soup, a pint of hot milk and as many cigarettes as they liked to smoke. Many of them were Scottish troops of the Black Watch, Cameron Highlanders, Kings Own Scottish Borders, the Seaforths and the Argyls, and had been injured in the first attacks on Loos and on Hill 70.[35]

The first death at Royds Hall was reported only a week later, Gunner John L Watson of the RFA succumbing to a perforated gastric ulcer, probably caused by gas poisoning. His mother travelled from Leith (Edinburgh) and was with him when he died.[36]

The relatives of wounded servicemen who were visiting their loved ones were often indebted to the Motor Volunteers' willingness to go above and beyond the call of duty. In August 1917 a mother who had travelled from Cardiff to visit Royds Hall was 'plonked down' at Huddersfield station at 2.40am:

> There was nowhere to go, and no place to get food. So she waited down the platform till morning, went to see her boy at the hospital, and returned to the station in the forenoon ready for her return journey only to find that there was no train until 11.19pm. A kindly porter suggested that she go across to the N.M.V. rest room. There she found food and a warm welcome. Arrangements were made for her to spend the afternoon and evening with her boy and she was ultimately "seen off" by the kindly motorists. She remarked … that she had no idea there was so much goodness in the world. She said she arrived in Huddersfield dispirited and lonely, and went away after spending one of the happiest days of her life.

The NMV also came to the aid of parents who had journeyed from Coventry to see their son who was seriously ill at Denby Dale Auxiliary Hospital. The NMV telephoned, thankfully learning that the boy was improving, then drove his parents over to visit him.[37]

Funding the War Hospitals

The funding of Royds Hall and partial funding of surrounding auxiliary hospitals was of the highest importance to Huddersfield's prominent community leaders. A wide variety of fund raising events, and subscriptions to the *Huddersfield War Hospital Magazine* ensured a steady income. This was supplemented by occasional big events, the most appropriate and lucrative of which was the exhibition of the Lancashire and Yorkshire Railway Company's ambulance train at Huddersfield Station on Saturday 12 February 1916. Constructed for the use of British Soldiers in France, its 16 khaki-coloured coaches, each emblazoned with a red cross, spanned 313 yards and could accommodate over 400 patients. Six thousand visitors paid 1s each, raising £300 as queues snaked across St George's Square to the George Hotel.[38]

The Lancashire and Yorkshire Railway Company's Ambulance Train

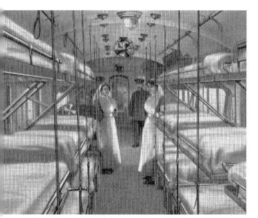

A Ward Car inside an ambulance train.

Mayoral party, with Mayor William Jessop in the centre, board the ambulance train at Huddersfield Station, 17 November 1917.

The queue to view the ambulance train snakes round St. George's Square, 17 November 1917.

Most fund-raising events were more intimate. Members of the RAMC gave several impromptu concerts to patients at Royds Hall. The tenacious organisers of the War Hospital Egg Fund raised £8000 by selling over 750,000 eggs.[39] The hospitals also benefited from numerous large donations, notably £3000 from Mrs Hurst of Kirkburton towards the building of the Royal Infirmary's 'Reginald Hurst Ward' in memory of her late husband.[40] A regular calendar of events was punctuated by subscription funds for specific causes and, as ever, lists of subscribers were published in the *HDE*. Invariably headed by large sums from the town's wealthy and generous philanthropists, these lists repeatedly showed immense generosity from across the community, and provided their own incentive to contribute.

The 'Big Push' offensive of 1916 sparked a further increase in wounded Tommies. Travelling throughout the night, Number 1 ambulance train arrived from Southampton at 6.40am on 7 July, six days almost to the hour after the start of the Battle of the Somme. The convoy comprised 215 wounded, more than double the usual number, but the local volunteers' tried and tested procedures saw all patients admitted to a hospital by 8.00am. Some had been in the trenches just forty-eight hours earlier. Their injuries were 'chiefly from shrapnel and high explosive shells and machine gun bullets.' One man had 17 machine gun bullet wounds … 'dressing his wounds each day was no small undertaking.'[41]

The Allies suffered 600,000 casualties in five months on the Somme. Throughout the country even further beds were needed and the auxiliary hospitals around the district were expanded. All were administered from Royds Hall, which assumed this responsibility from medical authorities in Leeds.

Auxiliary War Hospitals

Holmfirth Hospital had humble beginnings from a St John Ambulance Association course, 'First Aid to the Injured', delivered by local GP Dr Williams. Shortly after the outbreak of war two members of the course, Mrs AH Roberts and her sister-in-law Mrs J Roberts, initiated Holmfirth Auxiliary Hospital which opened on 12 November 1914 in a house in Landsdowne Terrace, loaned by Mssrs T and J Timber of Bottoms Mill. Its initial capacity of six beds was expanded to meet the demands of 1916 by the erection of prefabricated huts in adjacent fields. The first of these was opened by Sir Berkeley Moynihan on 16 September 1916. By 1918 the Holmfirth Auxiliary War Hospital was treating 76 patients. The war office furnished and equipped the hospital and contributed 2s per day towards running costs, supplemented by extensive local fund raising schemes.

As at Royds Hall, Holmfirth Auxiliary Hospital was run with military precision and order. Founder and Matron, Mrs AH Roberts, 'would not tolerate slackness, indiscipline or excuses from any of her staff or the patients.' Subsequently she won the silver medal of the Royal Red Cross Second Class which was presented to her by King George V at Buckingham Palace on Armistice Day.[43]

Staff and patients at Holmfirth Auxiliary Hospital (left) and their Matron, Mrs AH Roberts (right)

Honley Auxiliary Hospital had similar humble beginnings. During November 1914 Mrs Oswald Sykes and Mrs Smales established a small convalescent home for soldiers at Far End House. It was maintained by local subscriptions and in two years to November 1916 cared for 153 soldiers. To fund much-needed expansion, house-to-house collections began on 13 October 1916 and in less than three weeks raised £1200 – worth almost £70,000 in 2014. This funded the conversion of the Congregational School into a larger hospital which was formally opened on 1 November 1916 by Colonel Marshall, who praised Honley as 'one of the pioneers of these auxiliary hospitals.' He added that, in the year since the Huddersfield War Hospital opened, the number of beds for wounded soldiers in the district had increased from 500 to 1060. Two days later, a convoy of patients filled all 26 of Honley's new beds.[44] The additional staff were provided by volunteer trainees of the Honley Nursing Division, with the Honley Men's Division acting as orderlies.[45]

Wounded soldiers enjoy an afternoon at Huddersfield Golf Club, Fixby, 10 August 1916

In January 1916 Meltham Mills Convalescent Home was selected as a soldiers' convalescent home, not least because of 'the fine fresh air of the district.' Initially 20 beds were occupied, but by the following December all of the home's 64 beds were taken over by the military authorities. In May 1917 the number of beds was increased to 100. Entertainments such as dances, whist drives and concerts were organised on five days each week. When the home reverted to its former purpose in March 1919, 1,334 soldiers had recuperated there.[46]

A further much-needed auxiliary hospital was established at Bradley Gate, Marsden. Situated on a 14-acre site, the hospital was adapted from a tuberculosis sanatorium gifted to the Corporation by the late Mr John Sykes of Acre House, Lindley. £2,043 was raised by public subscription to equip the hospital, and it was officially opened by the Mayoress, Miss Jessop, on 1 March 1917. Subsequently a replacement children's tuberculosis pavilion was erected funded by Mr Sykes. The Corporation added an adults' pavilion and administration block, and the YMCA erected one of their £600 huts. In total, Mr Sykes' capital covered 30% of the administrative costs.[47]

By the end of the war there were 21 local auxiliary hospitals with a total of 2,247 beds. They treated over 15,000 patients of whom only 114 died. The generosity of the Paddock householders who opened their homes for the recuperation of patients at Royds Hall was replicated in the vicinity of the auxiliary hospitals. In addition, 22,000 patients were treated at Royds Hall which had the lowest death rate of any war hospital in the country.

The greatest challenge faced at Royds Hall came during the German's spring offensive of 1918 when, expecting a convoy of 217 soldiers, they were asked by General Bedford, the Deputy Director of Medical Services, Northern Command, to treat

Open Air Concert at Royds Hall, autumn 1915

War Hospital
Sports at
Fartown, 1918

a further 300. The staff 'rose to the occasion', accommodating over 500 new patients in one day. Sir John Maxwell, General Officer Commanding-in-Chief of Northern Command, said 'it was exactly what they expected from Huddersfield!'[48]

The ad-hoc 'needs must' commitment of resources to developing all these medical facilities was another facet of a district adapting to total war. Alongside the commitment, bloodshed and tears, a semblance of ordinary life went on. Notorious schoolboys in Fartown aimed fireworks at pedestrians, and there was romance and fun at Royds Hall.

One Royds Hall nurse, who had lost her sweetheart on the frontline, treated and fell in love with a local Tommy. After the war they got married and spent much of their lives living happily abroad.[49] Another nurse, completing the card of a newly admitted patient, asked him his religion. He replied 'Sheffield United!'[50] Recovering troops enjoyed regular visits to Huddersfield's theatres and cinemas, and concerts by local musicians and schoolchildren at the hospital. They enjoyed trips to countryside beauty spots organised by the NMV, and sports and refreshments afternoons at the Huddersfield and Outlane Golf Clubs and at Milnsbridge Bowling Club. In July 1917 and July 1918, crowds of 6000, including large numbers of wounded soldiers, attended memorable War Hospital Sports afternoons at Fartown. The latter event raised £661, described by the Reverend Herbert Gwyer, as 'beyond the most sanguine hopes of the promoters.'[51]

Amidst the heart-rending grief and suffering, the professionalism and care of the district's war hospital staff shone. The NMV were a 'God-send' to many thousands of soldiers at the end of a weary journey. Their selfless efforts epitomised the warmth and kindness that made Huddersfield a welcome haven from the traumas of the front line. Royds Hall, 'erected on such a grand scale by the generosity of Huddersfield's people' remains an abiding memorial of Huddersfield's compassion for the wounded. The soldiers who were treated there were unanimous in their gratitude.

An Appreciation of Royds Hall
by
'a private without any pretensions to being a poet'
(who wishes to remain anonymous)

If ever I go to the front again,
And get wounded by bullet or ball,
The only wish that ever I'd wish
Is to be conveyed back to Royds Hall.

For there the nurses are simply great,
They work hard night and day,
And they gratify your every need,
In even the smallest way.

And also the good folk of Huddersfield,
Whose kindness I will ever recall,
They opened their purses and gave us the nurses
Who minister at Royds Hall.[52]

Chapter 12

Recruitment and Conscription

On 4 February 1915, precisely six months into the war, Sir William Raynor, Chairman of the local Civilian Recruiting Committee, declared his pride in Huddersfield's recruitment record. He announced that the locality now had 4000 men serving in the army and navy, and 4000 territorials in training, increased from their respective pre-war numbers of 1200 and 1800. Huddersfield was doing its bit. He attributed this success to Huddersfield's prompt response in August 1914, 'almost three weeks in advance of almost every other town in the North of England.'[1]

Support from the Suffragettes

Sir William's announcement was made at a prestigious recruitment rally, organised by the local branch of the Women's Social and Political Union at Huddersfield Town Hall, where he shared the stage with high-profile militant suffragettes Annie Kenney and Flora 'General' Drummond. They were an unlikely trio. Sir William was President of the Huddersfield Liberal Association, whilst the women had a history of arrest and imprisonment for disruptive protests against, amongst others, the country's leading Liberal politicians.[2] The war, however, trumped their political differences. As Mrs Drummond told the meeting:

9 March 1906; Flora Drummond and Annie Kenney are arrested in Downing Street for repeatedly knocking on the door of Number 10, where Liberal Prime Minister Henry Campbell-Bannerman was in residence.

> The Kaiser is responsible for many things, but one of the greatest things he is responsible for is that of bringing Sir William Raynor and myself side-by-side on one platform … our differences are not to be thought of while this great enemy is knocking at our door.

The Suffragettes had aligned their cause with patriotic duty, reasoning with accurate foresight that women would successfully undertake traditional men's roles in the workplace and make an irrefutable case for equality. Both women said that, given the chance, thousands of women would 'flood to the colours' and make 'fine soldiers.' Meanwhile, 'men fight and women work.' All parties were fulsome in praise of the first wave of women in the workplace who had freed men for the front, whilst Sir William proffered the now familiar rhetoric that those who did not volunteer were 'slackers and weaklings.'[3]

Fluctuating Recruitment Numbers

Sir William's pride in local recruitment looked a little premature when volunteer numbers for that week slumped to 58, including just 12 from the Colne Valley.[4] There was little improvement over the next few weeks. The willing idealists and those naively swept away by the excitement of escape and adventure had already gone, and many of those left were unwilling to volunteer. Descriptions of life at the front, both in letters to the *HDE* and first-hand accounts from soldiers on leave, were far from enticing, and Huddersfield offered an increasing amount of war-related work, with overtime. Many had family or business commitments, and others refused to fight through strong religious, pacifist or political convictions.

Several factors influenced a temporary upturn in recruitment during the spring of 1915. There was a push from Northern Command to replace the locality's 'significant losses' at the Second Battle of Ypres and, in addition, Huddersfield was 'expected to raise one or two brigades for the Royal Field Artillery.'

A meeting at the Town Hall on 20 April to register local women for war work proved most timely. On 6 May, a recruitment parade of 6000 men, 'the greatest military display that has been seen in this district' marched from Marsden, Elland, Brighouse and Mirfield.

People in the scattered hamlets walked miles to the moor edges to see the troops, and thousands lined the routes in the town …

Anger at the sinking of the *Lusitania* the following day brought more recruits. On 1 June 1087 men, 170 horses and four guns of the new 168th Brigade, Royal Field Artillery (RFA) were paraded in Greenhead Park. When the Brigade left for the front, in record time, on Boxing Day 1915, there were still enough men left to supply most of another Brigade in the Staffordshire Regiment.[5]

The Greenhead Park spectacle did not include an applicant who was rejected by the Huddersfield Recruitment Office for being over the age limit of 40. When he emerged with the news, his mate asked: "How old did you say you are?"

"Forty-six," was the reply.

"Oh, but go back in and tell them you are thirty-eight, and that you made a mistake."

The man agreed and, re-entered the Recruitment Office, confident of success. Recognising him, the officer in charge asked him his business.

"Oh," said the would-be recruit. "I towed you I were forty-six, but I made a mistake. I'm only thirty-eight. It's mi mother that's forty-six!"[6]

In June the Town Council ordered a census of local men who were eligible for military service. The information was collected via house-to-house calls by the Territorials, but there was no legal compulsion to cooperate and the results were not published.[7]

Despite the spring spike in recruitment figures, the numbers quickly fell away again. In August the Mayor wrote to employers imploring them to replace eligible men with women workers.[8] On 21 September, the *HDE* reprinted a letter from 'City Press' contrasting Huddersfield unfavourably with London. The writer had …

> … just returned from a visit to the West Riding of Yorkshire, which I left in disgust, although a native of the shire. In all the towns and villages the outstanding feature is the hordes of young men walking about. When questioned, the reply is that these young men are engaged on munitions, but that is untrue, for they are at work on the tramcars, as postmen, in the shops and banks, indeed everywhere. It seemed as if London was sending out its men to fight for the purpose of allowing the men in Yorkshire to have a comfortable time and make money.

A 'workers own' recruiting demonstration on 25 September was 'half empty' and in early October Huddersfield's 2nd battalion, the 2/5th Dukes, was still 300 men under strength.[9] Local soldiers at the front were dismayed, Huddersfield Privates I Dean and C Smith writing …

To the Boys at Home
by
Privates I Dean and C Smith

I am writing from the trenches	The 3rd 5th is now in training
To the boys who stay at home,	So go and take your chance
To ask a little favour	You'll have a pleasant holiday
From the boys across the foam.	And perhaps a trip to France
You know your country wants you;	And then you've got to trust to luck
Then why not come and join.	And do your level best;
You're disgracing good old Huddersfield;	And if a bullet finds its billet
It's not yourself alone.	There's glory "going West"[10]

Conscription was in the air. A Government poster released in July was ominously headlined 'PUSH AND GO: It is better to go than be pushed.'[11] In the same week, medical re-examinations were ordered for those previously refused because of 'weak eyesight, defective teeth, or slight physical defects ... in future no man who is organically sound is to be refused.'[12]

UNDER
LORD DERBY'S SCHEME
A MERE
PROMISE TO ENLIST
IS OF NO VALUE.

If a man wishes to be placed in a Group he
MUST BE ATTESTED
BY
DECEMBER 11th

In October Lord Derby, the Government's Director of Recruiting, introduced his 'Derby Scheme', enabling men to attest their willingness to fight when called upon. A moratorium until Saturday 11 December, during which married men who attested were promised that all the single men would be called up before them, attracted a last minute rush of 1500 'recruits' in Huddersfield. The Recruitment Office was so overrun that the doctors deferred most medical examinations until the men were called-up. As news of the deferred examinations spread, it was alleged that men who knew they would fail the medical went along to collect their two and ninepence pay and their armlet – at least until 1pm on Saturday when the Office ran out of armlets. There was similar chaos across the country and at Saturday teatime the Government issued a telegram extending the moratorium until midnight on Sunday. This news was distributed to Huddersfield's 'various picture houses and put up on the screen.'

The number of recruits was deceptive. Anticipating conscription, the majority were married men hoping to delay their call-up, or men in 'starred' (essential) trades advised by their employers to attest so that they could 'be placed among the indispensable' by the local Military Service Tribunal (MST), almost 2000 of which were established under the Derby Scheme.[13]

Although it further prepared public opinion for conscription, the Derby Scheme was abandoned as a failure in December 1915. Only about 60% of single men had attested, and calling up married men first was unthinkable.

Conscription

Conscription duly arrived with the Military Service Act (No. 2) on 27 January 1916. It came into operation on 10 February and applied to single men aged 18 to 40, who could only avoid military service if they were medically unfit, in a 'starred' occupation or by exemption on appeal to their MST.[14]

Recruits enlisting before 2 March could state their preferred arm of the forces and how they wished to serve. After that, all would be automatically taken into the army reserve. This produced such a rush that the Huddersfield Recruitment Office again ran out of armlets and resorted to handing recruits 'a hastily written "scrap of paper" to show that they were soldiers of the King.'[15]

Military Service Tribunals

On Monday 21 February the Huddersfield MST sat in the Town Hall to consider its first batch of appeals – cases that the local Military Advisory Committee had refused, or had sent for more detailed consideration. A film producer with a firm that would lose £5000 in capital if he was conscripted was granted a month's exemption for the company to 'make other arrangements.' A toffee manufacturer applied for the exemption of one of their chocolatiers on the grounds that 'ten girls on the same production line would also lose their jobs.' Their application was refused. Chocolate was not essential and the girls could do other work that might release men for the front.[16]

Many manufacturers, trying to retain valued employees, would be similarly disappointed. Allowances were made for some skilled workers, but the influx of women to the workplace made it harder to argue that men were irreplaceable. A Huddersfield dentist's appeal for his apprentice was refused after the tribunal asked 'could not girls do the work of drawing teeth? They are doing all sorts of things now.'[17]

In addition to the Huddersfield MST, there were District Tribunals at Golcar, Holmfirth, Honley,

Linthwaite, Marsden, Newmill, Shepley and Slaithwaite. MSTs comprised three, four or five local worthies, mainly from similar backgrounds. Nearly all were middle class, middle aged or elderly men, predominantly with experience of white collar occupations. In Huddersfield, the councillors among them were selected in proportion to seats on the Liberal and Conservative-dominated council. Barely diluted by a token Labour/working class representative, nearly all were pro-war.[18]

Huddersfield Town Hall

Each Tribunal also had a Military Representative. As cases had already appeared before the Military Advisory Committee, he had either first-hand knowledge of them, or had been briefed about them. During the early weeks of the MSTs, whilst other members were still finding their feet, proceedings were often dominated by the Military Representative's absolutist militaristic convictions. Arthur P Crosland and FW Hirst fulfilled this role on the Huddersfield MST. The *HDE* found Crosland's often intimidating, aggressive and bullying tone particularly quotable. When Crosland sat appellants effectively began their hearings 1-0 down, needing to sway the other members. Hirst was more tolerant and, as his daughter Vivien recalled, felt the heavy responsibility of these duties:

> Daddy grieved bitterly that he was too old to become a soldier and as he could not go to the front he gave up his business and devoted himself to war work.

Hirst became Assistant Adjutant of the Volunteer Defence Force, but it was his work on the Military Tribunal, that 'proved to be … most responsible and harassing.'

> … With Daddy's sensitive nature it was, to him, a terrible thing to have the power to order a man to go, of course paying regard to real hardship, such as three sons already serving, or a son running a business for his widowed mother, entirely dependent upon him …

> … I remember Daddy, all this time, working at very high pressure for the casualty lists grew longer and longer and it was urgent that reinforcements should be sent for training in a steady stream. He would rush in for a quick dinner, eat it at speed, and always run down the road, his coat flying, to catch the tram. It became a great strain, and most certainly aged Daddy considerably.

On one occasion a man with a revolver threatened to shoot her father and the rest of the tribunal 'rather than be sent', but eventually allowed himself to be disarmed by the police.[19]

There was little apparent respect for tribunal members, or awareness of the stress they might feel. When a local schoolteacher asked his class to 'name some recreations of today', the children's first three suggestions were 'walking', 'running' and 'sitting on tribunals.'[20]

FW Hirst was an exception among the hard line local Military Representatives. Cyril Pearce, in his acclaimed *Comrades in Conscience* states that their presence …

> … helped to characterise the Tribunals as extensions of the war machine and not impartial judicial bodies ... there is broad agreement that the Tribunals were muddled, inconsistent, prejudiced and unjust.

As Tribunals were improvised bodies of local amateurs, under pressure of time, making many, often marginal, decisions that were crucial to men's lives and livelihoods, inconsistencies and dissatisfaction was inevitable.

Appearing before the MST was a considerable ordeal for men unaccustomed to public speaking and fearing the public notoriety reserved for 'shirkers.' Charlie Hirst, a 24-year-old Meltham farmer, was found hanged on the day of his hearing. At the inquest, his brother Edmund attributed his suicide to fear 'of going before the Tribunal.'[21]

"And what work are you doing of National Importance?"
"Why, I'm rearin' eight children an' helping to make airyplanes!"

Between February and December 1916 the Huddersfield MST considered 18,704 applications, one third of which were second applications.[22] As Vivien Hirst indicates, in the vast majority of cases, the criteria they were asked to consider related to the appellant's family and/or workplace.

The Tribunals were generally sympathetic to men who had a large number of dependent children, though not entirely for family reasons, as the Government paid a support allowance per child. On 20 March 1916 a cashier who had six children was granted three months' exemption to support his family on the rationale that 'This man will make a very expensive soldier.'[23] There was more genuine sympathy for sole carers of ill or disabled relatives.

The MSTs found work-related appeals more taxing as there were more factors to consider. How essential was the appellant to the continuation of the business? Could he be replaced? What impact would losing him have on other employees, on the community and, not least, on the war effort?

An application that ticked every box came from a firm of spinners on behalf of their foreman dyer whom they had tried and failed to replace. The foreman was in charge of 18 men, they had already lost 40 to 50 employees to the army, and he was the chief support for his mother and family of four girls, two of whom were ill. The tribunal granted him exemption providing that he remained in a certified trade.[24]

A compromise was reached in the appeal of two brothers, partners in a shipping company, who had lost goods worth hundreds of pounds through the sinking of several vessels, including the *Baralong* and the *Appam*. They were allowed to choose which one of them would be exempted to run the business, and which one of them would go to war.[25] One of them immediately withdrew his appeal.

Betrayal of Attested Married Men

Eligible single men received their call-up papers in March 1916. When the married men who had attested learned that they would be called up in May they felt betrayed and misled by the promises that all the single men would be called up first. Now 'all the advantages lay with the unattested men', married or not. A mass meeting of Attested Married Men attracted over 500 to the Town Hall on Sunday 2 April. A letter was read from Councillor Harry Dawson, who could not be present.

> The inequality of sacrifice between those who go and those who stay at home is the most glaring anomaly of the war. We expect our best to go on fourteen pence per day with bully beef and biscuits and without the comforts of home, while those who stay at home are earning bigger wages and spending more than ever before.

A resolution protesting 'against the utterly inadequate allowances and grants recently suggested by the Government' was passed unanimously. They feared that their paltry army pay and separation allowance would see their wives and children on the breadline and unable to pay the rent or mortage.[26] Such fears were compounded by reports of under-payment, late payment and sometimes no payment at all as the army of volunteer clerks struggled with an ever-increasing workload. The otherwise forbearing author of *The West Riding Territorials in the Great War*, Laurie Magnus, is scathing of the over-bureaucratic, penny-pinching separation allowance system. Remuneration was dependent on:

> the number, sex and age of his children [and] the paraphernalia of coupons, postal draft-books and money orders, in the calculation and readjustment of rates owing to information advised from the soldier's unit or to domestic changes reported or detected, in the grading of 'unofficial wives' and other official relationships, and, summarily … a system which seems expressly designed to squeeze out of the officers administering it the last drop of the milk of human kindness without any compensating gain in the civil virtues of economy and efficiency

Moratorium
(to "Keep the Home Fires Burning")
by
Touchstone

They were summoned up in classes,
By the flourish of a pen;
For they wore the khaki armlet,
That denoted they were MEN.
They had thought it would be later,
But they happened to be wrong;
And as Britain claims her fathers,
You may hear them sing this song:-

Chorus:
Keep the landlord waiting,
Since we're dedicating
Life and limb to Britain's cause across the foam
Make no single payment
Save for food and raiment;
Turn the tax-collector out till Papa comes home!

They were told the young and single
Would be quite the first to go
But the rule has "some" exceptions,
And it isn't always so.
But they think of wife and children
If the bailiff claim their "sticks"
And there rings this mighty chorus
For the fathers in a fix:-

Chorus:
Keep the landlord waiting, etc.[27]

Conscientious Appeals to the MST

A small minority of cases were from moral, religious or political appellants, collectively called Conscientious Objectors (COs) who were forced into the open by conscription. This further complicated matters for the over-burdened tribunals. Still getting to grips with the practicalities of family and work-based criteria, their members had neither the time nor, in some cases, the patience, to consider the complexities of abstract ideologies, and they received little help from the Military Service Act's ambiguous 'conscience clause.'[28]

A poem printed in the *HDE* on 28 March 1916 presented the popular, simplistic view of COs, and indicates the degree of pressure they were under.

The Conscientious Objector

An Office Boy's Opinion

March 2nd had passed, and armlet had he none,
To a reserved occupation neither had he gone;
But as the time was drawing near for khaki to be worn,
How to escape this entangling net alarmed him night and morn.

He scanned the paper every night to see
If the Military Tribunal were exempting such as he.
Unfortunately for him most applications were refused
As appeals put forth by conscientious he eagerly perused.

On domestic grounds an appeal was quite absurd,
Not having a dependant, and bachelors were preferred,
His employment as a clerk didn't justify appeal,
And the medical examiner no unfitness could reveal.

As none of these could help him, whatever could he do?
An appeal on conscientious grounds he thought he might pull through;
His conscience would not let him fight or take a life, he said,
And probably his conscience would refuse him sleep in bed.

For behind his stale objection was a slacker's device,
To let some war-torn Tommy do "his little bit" twice.
If by the Allies, this war of justice must be won,
Each man must do his duty, leaving double share to none.

Postcards depicting stereotypical disdain for conscientious objectors.

With his call-up imminent, Meltham CO Ernest Victor Quarmby made his position clear in the press. Sapper JE Preston denounced him as a traitor and Ernest defended his religious beliefs in a second letter:

… the views I hold are truly honest and in accordance with my highest conception of right and liberty … I have no desire for my action to be looked upon as heroic … but I do claim an individual interpretation of what is right.[29]

A subsequent letter from J Egdol accused Ernest of hiding behind *The Bible*, arguing that British servicemen across the world were 'doing God's work.'[30] Herbert Weed of Huddersfield interpreted Ernest's stance as not only anti-war, but anti-British, and asked 'must I believe that all the devil's men are warfaring and all God's men are at home?'[31] Emotions were running high.

At the MSTs, adding a conscientious objection to family or work reasons could be counter-productive. A 39-year-old French polisher claimed his business of 18 years would be terminated by his call-up, adding that *The Bible* says: 'Thou shalt not kill.' Military Representative Arthur Crosland was quick to exploit contradictions in *The Bible*, responding, 'David did not take much notice of that.' This proved to be the decisive argument, and the appellant was ordered into a non-combatant section of the army.[32]

Some of the first local CO appeals were heard by the Honley MST on Saturday 4 March 1916. It was immediately clear that, in addition to their pacifist convictions, such applicants needed the composure and intelligence to articulate their case under hostile questioning. The appeal of four 'bobbin turners', who were manufacturing 15,000 wooden shell cap cases per week, floundered because one of them was also a CO. Military Representative, Captain Bradbury, was quick to highlight the hypocrisy: 'He will make shell caps with which to kill Germans, but he won't kill them.' Bradbury had greater difficulty breaching the defences of a 27-year-old pattern weaver.

Applicant:	On religious and moral grounds I cannot assume the responsibility of taking the life of any man – the life that came to him from the source of all life – nor can I decide for another the issues of life and death, and since the military machine involves the wholesale slaughter of mankind, I cannot assist its function in any way.
Cpt Bradbury:	Your principal ground is a conscientious objector to taking life?
Applicant:	Yes.
Cpt Bradbury:	How long have you held these views?
Applicant:	For a great many years.
Cpt Bradbury:	You are opposed to non-combatant service?
Applicant:	I am opposed to anything that involves the taking of life.
Cpt Bradbury:	What about service in the R.A.M.C? That involves the saving of life?
Applicant:	If you save a man to go and kill again; if he has to go back into war I cannot help him.
Cpt Bradbury:	What would you do if a man came to you with a gun and threatened to shoot you?
Applicant:	I should try to disarm him; but under no circumstances would I take a life to save life.
Cpt Bradbury:	If you see a man shooting someone, and you were in a position to kill him first; if you saw a German actually dropping a bomb, and you could kill him and save a life, you wouldn't do it?
Applicant:	This is only a matter of numbers.
Mr Jagger:	Would you object to weave any patterns for khaki cloth?
Applicant:	I object to anything that is involved in the military machine.

The applicant was granted exemption from combatant, but not from non-combatant service. Another appellant seeking exemption admitted that his occupation involved handling the yarn of any cloth.

Applicant:	I had no other way of existence.
Cpt Bradbury:	Therefore if it is a question of your existence or your conscience your conscience has to go?
Applicant:	Not as regards the military machine.
Cpt Bradbury:	Suppose you had no other means of existence than that of joining the Army.
Applicant:	I should die a pauper.

Again, the applicant was directed into non-combatant service.

Whilst the Tribunal was deliberating these cases, Captain Bradbury commented that COs 'were a great evil, and would hinder recruiting if they were left.' The verdicts created a further dilemma for the appellants.[33] If they refused war-related work they were likely to be imprisoned or sent to the army and subjected to military justice. If they undertook such work, they were transgressing their own beliefs, and there was no guarantee that this would not be held against them at a future hearing.

Even more controversial were those who refused war service on political grounds. Huddersfield's long tradition of dissidence was alive and kicking in the district's working class institutions, influenced to varying degrees by Quakerism, Owenism, Marxism, and late nineteenth century Socialism. At Huddersfield's Socialist Sunday School children were taught a different set of commandments including:

> 6. Do not be cowardly, be a friend to the weak, and love justice.

> 9. Do not think that he who loves his own country must hate other nations, or wish for war, which is a remnant of barbarism.[34]

The influence of these doctrines for local Socialists and their supporters is evident in their eagerness to question and defy the authorities at their MST hearings. The most spectacular exchanges occurred in Huddersfield Town Hall on 20 March 1916, before a Tribunal that included its ex-officio Chairman Mayor Joseph Blamires, Military Representative Arthur Crosland, hard line Conservative WH Armitage, and Joseph Pickles, the only Labour member of the council to appear on the Huddersfield MSTs.

> The public attended the Huddersfield Military Service Tribunal yesterday afternoon in larger numbers than on any previous occasion. Packed in the Reception Room at the Town Hall were between 300 and 400 persons. Lively scenes were created when a prominent Socialist Mr. Arthur Gardiner, came forward in support of his claim to be exempted on conscientious grounds.

The Huddersfield Branch of the British Socialist Party;
Arthur Gardiner is second from the left on the front row.

As soon as Mr Gardiner stepped forward he was cheered ...

The Mayor: After that demonstration I shall clear this court. We shall hear the case in private.
Voices: Stand together, chaps.
A Voice: The Act says plainly enough he can have it in public if he wants.
               (There followed a discussion among the Tribunal members.)
The Mayor: The feeling of the Tribunal is that we shall take this case in private. We shall have the Press present, but we shall not have any audience (To the audience): I must ask you to leave the room, please.
               (The audience showed no signs of leaving.)
A Woman: He doesn't want it in private.
               (Mr Gardiner said he was prepared to have the case taken in private if his witnesses stayed behind.)
The Mayor: We don't require witnesses.
Mr Gardiner: I require witnesses.
The Mayor: We will meet that when we come to it.
               (A member of the audience stepped forward and clutched Mr. Gardiner's shoulder)
Audience Member:
               Come on, Gardiner! They are all a lot of rogues.
               (The Reverend EE Lark, Minister of Paddock United Methodist Church and official 'watcher' at the hearing for the 'No Conscription Council', said there was no pre-arrangement to applaud Gardiner. He was a 'very popular name in the Socialist movement' and he 'hoped the Tribunal would reverse their decision.' Mr Gardiner added that he too was surprised. His only explanation was that he was known to have held anti-war convictions before 1914. The Mayor again asked the public to retire.)
A Voice: It is not a case of misbehaviour, but of very strong feeling, which I think will not occur again.
The Mayor: It is an unfortunate expression of feeling. (Hear, hear.) We are in a difficult position, and we are trying to do that which is best and that which is right.
               (Mr Tom Beaumont (a leading activist in numerous local socialist organisations) said they were not taking up a position of antagonism to the Mayor or the Tribunal, but as citizens they had the right to stay.)
The Mayor: I will not have any further discussion.
A Voice: It isn't a fair trial if it is in private, you know.
Mr Armitage: It is your own fault, you know.
               (Cries of 'Free Speech' and 'Can you throw us out without any help?' For several minutes there was deadlock.)
A Voice: I understand this is a court of justice, and not an autocratic assembly. ('hear, hear' and cheers) If you boast so much about liberty give him fair play, and stand up for the liberty you are supposed to believe in.
The Mayor: I wanted to give this man fair play, and I couldn't have.

HUDDERSFIELD TRIBUNAL SCENES.

:o:

SOCIALIST CHEERED AND PUBLIC ORDERED TO LEAVE.

The public attended the Huddersfield Military Service Tribunal yesterday afternoon in larger numbers than on any previous occasion. Packed in the Reception Room at the Town Hall were between 300 and 400 persons. Lively scenes were created when a prominent Socialist, Mr. Arthur Gardiner, came forward in support of his claim to be exempted on conscientious grounds.

As soon as Mr. Gardiner stepped forward he was cheered. The cheers were unmistakably enthusiastic.

The Mayor (who presided): After that demonstration I shall clear the court. We shall hear this case in private.

Voices: Stand together, chaps.

A Voice: The Act says plainly enough he can have it in public if he wants.

Mr. J. Pickles (the Labour member of the Tribunal) said they were trying the case of Arthur Gardiner, who perhaps had no part or parcel in the demonstration. They should try the case as they had tried others, and it ought to be a warning to the demonstrators in future.

Mr. A. P. Crosland (military representative): I should clear the room.

The Mayor: The feeling of the Tribunal is that we shall take this case in private. We shall have the Press present, but we shall not have any audience. (To the audience): I must ask you to leave the room, please.

The audience showed no signs of leaving, and a woman was heard to say: He doesn't want it in private.

Mr. Gardiner said he was prepared to have the case taken in private if his witnesses could stay behind.

The Mayor: We don't require witnesses.

Mr. Gardiner: I require witnesses.

The Mayor: We will meet that when we come to it.

A Voice:	Let us have a fresh chairman.
The Mayor:	I don't think you are acting fair at all … This is not a public Tribunal.
A Voice:	Prejudice.

(Mr Gardiner said that if he appealed to the audience to be silent he believed they would be.)

A Voice:	We think more of Gardiner than the Tribunal
The Mayor:	You think a great deal of Gardiner.
A Voice:	More than we do of you.

(Uproar, and cries of 'Order'. Mr Gardiner eventually appealed to the public to be quiet whilst he was 'on his trial.')

The Mayor:	You are not here on trial.
Mr Gardiner:	I think I am.

(The application proceeded, Mr Gardiner confirming that he was a dyer, 26 years of age. He would undertake neither combatant nor non-combatant service. For a number of years he had advocated the economic and moral uplifting of humanity. He was opposed to all forms of militarism.)

Mr Crosland:	I am as much against militarism as the applicant, but that is no reason why he should not fight for his country.
Mr Gardiner:	I have no country.
Mr Crosland:	What are you doing here if you have no country? Why are you receiving all the benefits of citizenship when you have no country?
Mr Gardiner:	Whatever benefits I may be receiving I have only got by the organisation of the workers. I am quite prepared to leave the country if you will allow me to do so.
Mr Crosland:	I think the country will be very glad to be rid of you.
The Mayor:	Which country would you claim as being the best?
Mr Gardiner:	It is immaterial which country I go to.
The Mayor:	Germany?
Mr Gardiner:	Perhaps so; I might not be worse off there than I am here.
The Mayor:	I think you are talking out of your hat.
Mr Gardiner:	That is a matter of opinion.

(Gardiner then said he wished to go into the highways and byways to get people converted to his opinion. That was the way to settle wars.)

The Mayor:	You can convince the people in time of peace, but when there is a war going on it is a different matter.
Mr Gardiner:	If it were left to the people to settle the war it would have been settled long ago.
The Mayor:	The country is acting through its Government, which is constitutionally elected and representative of the people.
Mr Gardiner:	If the Germans lick us do you think the militarists of this country will be content?
The Mayor:	You won't do non-combatant service?
Mr Gardiner:	Certainly not.
The Mayor:	The workers of Germany are fighting against you?
Mr Gardiner:	They are not fighting against me.
The Mayor:	Well, you are a unit of this Empire.
Mr Gardiner:	No, I don't think my name has been brought up at all in the German Reichstag.
The Mayor:	It would be absurd to say so. You are in this country?
Mr Gardiner:	It is not my fault I was born here.

(Asked what religious sect he belonged to, Gardiner replied 'I am an atheist.')

Tribunal member:	Have atheist's consciences then?
Mr Gardiner:	Yes.
Mr Crosland:	I should refuse it. If you grant exemption I shall oppose it.

Arthur Gardiner's argument that his loyalties were defined by social class, not national boundaries was new to the Tribunal which, by a majority, decided that he was 'entitled to call himself a conscientious objector.' They regretted that a man of his 'attainments and ability' could not see that this was not in the interests of the country at the present time. Gardiner was granted temporary exemption for two months, 'which would carry four months.' Gardiner said he could not accept the decision and would appeal, to which the Mayor replied, 'That is just what we want you to do.'[35]

Possibly anticipating a flood of similar applications, the Tribunal wanted a ruling from the East Central Division, West Riding Appeals Tribunal, based at the West Riding Court House in Huddersfield. Arthur Gardiner was a test case. Eventually offered non-combatant service, Arthur refused and went on the run with fellow CO Percy Ellis. From May to October 1916 they cycled around Yorkshire and Lancashire as fugitives. The pair eventually gave themselves up and were dispatched to Rugeley for court martial, departing Huddersfield Station to wild cheering and a resounding rendition of *The Red Flag* from their supporters. Both were imprisoned until the spring of 1919. Ellis refused to cooperate with the Home Office 'Brace' Scheme to employ COs in useful work under guard, and endured harsh conditions at Winchester. Subjected to dark, solitary confinement at Wormwood Scrubs, Gardiner had a breakdown and undertook forestry work in East Anglia and textiles-related work at the Wakefield Prison Work Centre, returning to Huddersfield after the war.[36]

There were many reported renderings of *The Red Flag*, the Labour party anthem, in Huddersfield during this period. The lyrics had particular resonance with COs owing to their portrayal in some quarters as traitorous cowards.

The people's flag is deepest red,
It shrouded oft our martyr'd dead
And 'ere their limbs grew stiff and cold,
Their hearts' blood dyed its ev'ry fold.

Chorus:
Then raise the scarlet standard high,
Within its shade we'll live and die,
Though cowards flinch and traitors sneer,
We'll keep the red flag flying here.

On 23 March 1916, three days after Arthur Gardiner's appearance before the Huddersfield MST, there were further 'wild scenes' as the Huddersfield MST heard the appeals of more COs. WH Armitage had devised a 'Catch 22' question that he fired at successive applicants:

> Suppose you had been in a position to have shot the men who fired the torpedo which sank the *Lusitania*, would you have done so?

Armitage had preordained that if the applicant answered 'yes' he wasn't a genuine pacifist and if he answered 'no' he must be lying! The first recipient of Armitage's question was a pulley-maker who was a member of the Socialist Sunday School.

Pulley-maker: No, because I realise it is wrong to take human life.
Mr Armitage: And you would let those persons drown?
Pulley-maker: That would not be my fault.
Mr Armitage: It would be your fault if you did not shoot the man.

On these hypothetical grounds, the application was refused. The next CO would also not pull the trigger.

Mr Armitage: I do not believe you. What are the Belgians to do?
CO: They never declared war.
Mr Armitage: The Germans would overrun this country as they overran Belgium.

> (There were loud cries of 'Question! Question!', followed by considerable uproar. Mr Armitage rose to address the public.)

| Mr Armitage: | We had quite enough of you on Monday, and we want none of your nonsense today. We have the right of proper respect, and I'll have you removed when the Mayor will take my advice. |

Again, the application was refused. The next applicant worked for a cycle accessory company.

CO:	I would refuse to obey any military orders, whatever the result might be … I want to know, Mr Armitage, what would you do if you see an English submarine attacking a German vessel? (Loud applause) That question I consider hypothetical.
Mr Armitage:	I have the right to ask you questions so that I can form an opinion as to whether you are a conscientious objector or not. It doesn't help you to behave like that.
The Mayor:	I really shall have to take measures to clear this room if there is another demonstration.

(Mr Armitage again put the question about the *Lusitania*.)

CO:	I have not been in that position and I don't think I ever shall be, so I can't tell you.
Mr Crosland:	(reading one of the CO's letters of support) It says you have been working for international peace. So have I.
CO:	Of course your international peace goes with a revolver. Mine doesn't.

This third application was also refused. Amidst increasing unrest another CO repeated Arthur Gardiner's claim that 'if the working classes were all united they could stop this war.' At this the Mayor announced an adjournment until the room was cleared.

As the Tribunal members filed out into a side committee room, three policemen shepherded the public peacefully into the corridor, where they immediately sang *The Red Flag*. It was followed by an impromptu meeting which passed a resolution 'condemning the actions of the Tribunal.'[37] The resolution was proposed by Archibald Key, and seconded by Tom Beaumont. Archibald Key went on to refuse non-combatant service at his own hearing on 17 April, evade the authorities as a fugitive and emigrate to the USA, eventually settling in Canada.[38]

The cases proceeded with only the Press present, but the calling of Arthur Dawson 'was the signal for another outburst of cheering.' A textile worker, Dawson was a 'firm believer in the solidarity of the workers.' His requests for a public hearing and for three witnesses were refused by the Town Clerk. Dawson in turn refused the offer of non-combatant service, or to respond to his call-up papers. Hauled before the Magistrates on 29 January 1917, he was fined, handed over to the military, court martialled and imprisoned first at Rugeley, then at Ripon, until April 1919.[39]

The fervour of the hundreds who supported Arthur Gardiner and the other CO applicants is testament to Cyril Pearce's belief that Huddersfield's resistance to conscription, and tolerance of anti-war sentiment could be unique.[40]

On the day of Arthur Dawson's hearing, 23 March 1916, Mr Justice Darling of the King's Bench Division, ruling in *R. v Central Tribunal ex parte Parton* 'brusquely declared that absolute exemption was available only in cases of essential employment, financial hardship or ill-health … it is common sense that the Military Service Act did not allow a conscientious objector to avoid military service entirely.' This was contrary to Government directives that 'expressly instructed … that absolute exemption was an option.' Darling's independent judicial interpretation was widely adopted by MSTs.[41] Thomas Norton, Chairman of the West Riding Appeals Tribunal, decided that they 'had been asked not to let anyone off.' That is, their power of exemption was limited to combatant service, and COs of all hues should be directed to non-combatant service as a minimum. There was widespread local condemnation from the socialist, pacifist and religious fraternities, but it was academic for many local COs. Of the 111 CO appeals heard by the Huddersfield MST in 1916, 80 were in March and most of these were before Mr Justice Darling's summing up.[42]

Thomas Norton was true to his hard line views at the West Riding Appeals Tribunal the following week, when a firm of film producers appealed the decision of the Huddersfield MST to send their manager to war. It was unfortunate timing for the appellant, as two of Huddersfield's picture houses had recently fallen foul of the local Watch Committee's moral paternalism. The Committee had refused to allow a Sunday screening at the Empire, and refused to renew the Olympia's licence after a showing of *Five Nights*, a 'romance' that it – and numerous other authorities – had banned for immoral sexual content likely to corrupt the young.[43]

The Tribunal happily aligned scorn for the cinema with a pro-war outcome to the hearing. Even socialist Ben Turner, a founder member of the Independent Labour Party and a Trade Unionist, went native. Mr Ward, the appellant's solicitor, opened proceedings by citing Mayor Blamires' prejudice against films at his client's MST hearing.

Mr Ward:	The Mayor at the sitting said we can do without films.
Mr Norton:	I agree with him. (Laughter)
Mr Turner:	Well, we can do without some of them. (Hear, hear)
Mr Ward:	That is another story. They are very important at the present time.
Mr Turner:	Many of them do a lot of harm.
Mr Ward:	Many working people are working long hours and the cinematograph is a cheap relaxation for them. If they went to one of those picture houses …
Mr Norton:	I'm afraid we can't allow you to make a speech on this question.

Mr Ward would surely have referred to the showing of propaganda-laden war films which were appearing more frequently, and to the cinemas' fund-raising events. He was cut off before he ever got that far and the appeal was dismissed, as were all appeals at the West Riding Appeals Tribunal that morning.[44]

Meanwhile, Huddersfield witnessed further passionate anti-conscription demonstrations. On Sunday 30 April 1916 there were 'lively scenes … in St George's Square at a meeting of the Huddersfield and District No-Conscription Council.' At the heart of the speakers' arguments was a deep mistrust of the ruling classes. The Chairman believed that conscription had a sinister motive – not just to get more men, but to 'militarise' the working classes so that 'stripped of their freedom, they could be sent to wars abroad, and used in strikes at home'.

Mr Ben Riley, who moved the motion opposing conscription, decried the conscription of 18-year-olds as 'trying to meet military requirements without authority and without a mandate … To take youths … who had no voice in the policy of the country … was an outrage upon our common humanity.' He blamed the 'abominable campaign' of the pro-war Northcliffe Press, giving voice to 'unscrupulous men in the political associations clamouring for more men ... This wicked gang of unscrupulous adventurers pushed one door after another trying to get access to the portals of conscription ... while they were ostensibly fighting to destroy Prussian militarism it was their deviant wish to establish Prussian militarism in this country.'

As the meeting closed, JA Flanders mounted the platform and announced that he …

> consientiously objected to military service … In proof of his sincerity he would publically burn the papers he had received from the military authorities.

NO CONSCRIPTION.

NECESSARY MEN FROM THE VOLUNTARY SYSTEM.

LABOUR LEADERS' VIEWS.

"WE ARE AT WAR TO KILL IT NOT TO SET IT UP."

Headline from the *HDE*, 27 August 1915, reflecting the fear that conscription would establish German-type militarism in Britain.

When the breeze repeatedly blew out his matches, a voice exclaimed: 'They won't burn; they are too rotten to burn.' Eventually the papers were alight, Flanders announcing: 'The flames express my contempt for the Government.' The audience sang *The Red Flag*, and gave three cheers 'for a man who has the courage of his convictions.'

The meeting had been interrupted by frequent 'disturbances' from pro-war soldiers and civilians.

There was further heckling as the meeting dispersed, at which a CO called Williams shouted:

> We who hold conscientious scruples will face death even as you military gentlemen have to face death by the character of your military oath.[45]

There were very few such distrubances at Huddersfield's anti-war meetings. The most notorious came on 3 February 1917 when Labour MP for Blackburn, Philip Snowden addressed a Socialist meeting at a packed Victoria Hall. A group of about 20 servicemen wearing Royal Flying Corps uniforms infiltrated the Hall via a side entrance, six of them reaching the platform where their leader rushed forward flourishing his cane', shouting, 'Where's Snowden? Let's get at him! Rip him!' They attacked Snowden and the other dignitaries. Three of them, including two women, were hurled or fell off the stage. One of the invaders also found himself at the front of the audience.

> ... several members of the audience, roused to fury by the outrage of the invasion, belaboured the soldier with walking sticks, and he was soon bleeding from the head and otherwise damaged. Another soldier who had got a short way along the floor of the hall was drastically dealt with, one woman breaking her umbrella over his head, and he and his comrade were removed helpless by the police. A third man in uniform came hurtling down the steps from the platform and was taken out by the scruff of the neck.[46]

The remainder were 'unceremoniously driven back' through the side entrance, to loud cheers. Resuming his address, Snowden commented that 'the unpleasant little incident ... showed that there was just as much need to crush militarism at home.'

A cogent argument against COs was made by Driver James McKenzie, the Holmfirth postman.

> Self preservation being the first law of everyone ... I wonder what the result would be if Huddersfield had been Lille or any of the other cities of France, in the early parts of the war, when the Germans were driving everything and everybody, soldiers and civilians alike, before them. Would they have claimed the right to do as they wished ... they would have been called upon to perform the natural duty of man, i.e. guard and protect the women and children?
>
> I consider any ideas that may have been formed in the security of debating centres such as Huddersfield and district, are beside the mark, when comparing them with actual conditions in France and Belgium. Will ever the French or Belgians forgive the inhumanity of Germany? Talk about the solidarity of workers, it is a myth.[47]

Right or wrong, in the face of widespread disapproval, the willingness of the absolutist COs to accept court martial showed a different kind of wartime courage. In the spring of 1916 they could not be sure what their sentence would be. The military shipped 50 COs to France where 35 of them were court martialled and sentenced to death for refusing to obey orders in a theatre of war. Uproar in Parliament saw the sentences commuted to ten years' penal servitude and they were returned to British prisons.[48]

Nationally, ten COs died after suffering horrendous conditions in jail and about 70 died elsewhere. The number of these who took their own life is not recorded. One such was 37-year-old Fred Turner from Longwood. He received his call-up papers in August 1916. Shortly afterwards he was found hanged at Park Valley Mills, South Crosland.[49]

Harold Wagstaff's Military Service Tribunal Hearing

After a contentious, fractious three months, the Huddersfield MST became more conciliatory. Several factors influenced this change of tone: locally and nationally, married men had made a strong, dignified and influential case that single men should be called up first; there were far fewer CO cases coming before them; and on 15 May 1916 the Government issued clarification about the claims of small traders. A small trader could be exempted provided:

1. That he is the sole head of the business.
2. That there is no other person available who would carry on the business on his behalf with reasonable efficiency.
3. That ... there is a reasonable likelihood of the business being closed down.
4. That such a man has a wife and children dependent on the business.[50]

This directive was particularly valuable to the Huddersfield MST where 'about 90% of local industries were involved in war work of some kind.' The Huddersfield MST began to offer more exemptions, many of them temporary as a compromise to allow businessmen time to make arrangements for their absence.[51]

Their first reported appeal after receiving the new guidance was from a firm of wholesale fruit and vegetable merchants for two 24-year-old married employees. The first to be considered was the firm's salesman and head bookkeeper. Notorious Military Representative, Arthur Crosland, suggested 'I should give him the concession we are giving to all the married men.' This was the first indication that married men were, for now, to be granted 'at least two months'' exemption, with further leave to appeal.

The second employee, the firm's only motor driver, was Harold Wagstaff, captain of the Huddersfield and Great Britain Northern Union rugby teams. The greatest player of his time, 'Ahr Waggy' was a revered sporting icon far beyond Huddersfield. He had learned to drive during the autumn of 1915, probably to boost his income after the Northern Rugby Football Union banned all payments to players until the end of the war. Crosland, himself a prominent amateur sportsman and administrator, was suddenly, uncharacteristically friendly. He found …

> … it was a strongpoint in favour of Wagstaff that he had qualified himself in motor driving in order to get in the motor transport section.

Wagstaff denied that this was why he had learned to drive. He did, however, quickly point out that he had attested under the Derby Scheme, did not know that he was in a certified trade, and that it was his employer and not he who had appealed. Wagstaff was nobody's fool. In 1914 he became the first working class man to lead an official British overseas party – from sport or any other sphere – when he captained the Northern Union rugby tour of Australasia. He did so with diplomatic aplomb. These skills were very much in evidence at the MST, as both he and Crosland shadow-boxed around their personal reputations, Crosland anxious not to be outcast as the ogre who sent Wagstaff to war, and Wagstaff anxious to avoid the suggestion that he was a 'shirker' or a coward. The result was a unique hearing, the Military Representative presenting the case for the appellant and the appellant suggesting that he had no objection to fighting for his country.

Like his company colleague, Wagstaff was granted two months' exemption with leave to appeal. Later in the summer he joined the Army Service Corps Motor Transport Unit and in 1917 was posted to the Middle East, far from ideal as Wagstaff's lifelong vulnerability to illness saw him unwell for part of his wartime service.[52] As a local trooper explained, life was far from easy in Mesopotamia …

> … or 'Mess Up' as it is known to the troops. There is no canteen and the nearest shop is in Baghdad over 100 miles away. There are only two seasons, 'Dust and dysentery' and 'Mud and malaria.'[53]

Harold Wagstaff

Conscription Criteria Tightened

Following the initial furore over conscription, and the heavy press coverage of COs, recruitment entered a new stage. By the summer of 1916 the supply of fit and eligible men was drying up.

In June 1916 a new phrase, 'combing out', entered the national consciousness. Its first appearance in the *HDE* was a quote from the Shepley MST's Military Representative Mrs C Tinker, who referred to 'single men ... being gradually combed out of the industries.'[54] This unfortunate expression, which implied that the military authorities were cleansing the nation of a pestilence, would be used for the rest of the war. Later that month the Shepley MST was criticised for 'combing out' the village barber

> … the smart young men of the village will regard the decision as an unkind cut. A stranger visiting the village a few weeks hence may conclude from the uncut locks that the residents are a race of poets.[55]

The absence of the huge numbers who had gone to war was being felt across the district. The importation of migrant workers ensured that the munitions and woollen factories worked to capacity, but in other industries an increasing amount of machinery was going unused. John Whiteley, Chairman of the Golcar MST, stated that 'we cannot take more men away without handicapping industry.'[56]

The familiar cry of 'tickets please' was now an infrequent feature of tram journeys as most of the inspectors were at the front. Despite the Colne Valley's acute shortage of doctors, one of the remaining medics, Dr Edlington, was called up in February 1917.[57] From July 1917 to the end of the war there were just five dentists in Huddersfield and its surrounding areas to serve 250,000 people.[58] The Huddersfield and District Head Teachers' Association took future Mayor, Alderman Jessop, to task for claiming that the loss of 30 local teachers to the forces would 'not significantly affect the efficiency of schools.'

> The whole trend of education in recent years has been in the direction of giving to the child more individual attention … very necessary in the case of one who leaves school at the age of 13 … justice cannot be done to a child when a class is large and unwieldy … we appeal to those who have the love of education at heart not to sacrifice the children of the nation on the altar of a false economy.[59]

By May 1918, 22,000 (30%) of the nation's teachers had joined the forces, 1600 of whom had been killed.[60]

Despite the increasing strain on local businesses and services, the forces still needed more. Losses on the Somme increased the pressure on recruitment and the final months of 1916 saw a renewed nationwide 'search for shirkers.' In September, at the start of the football season, the police camped outside the Fartown and Leeds Road stadiums on match days, and raided music halls and tea rooms, arresting men who could not produce their exemption cards.

Whilst such tactics yielded 250 'shirkers' from one match at Hull Kingston Rovers, very few were discovered in Huddersfield, at least in part reflecting the town's great many war-related industries.[61]

In October, as recruitment slowed and fatalities continued unabated, the Military Service Act was extended to include all men up to the age of 41. In January 1917 the age limit was raised to 42. On 9 February conscription was brought in for all men aged 18-22 except for those in the now diminishing list of starred occupations. On 13 February the *HDE* reported that 'large numbers of young men in munitions factories and Government Departments were now being released for the army.'[62] In late March 1917 a revised Military Service Act called for the re-examination of practically all who had previously received exemption, including those on medical grounds, with the

This Certificate must be signed by the holder in the space provided below and must be carefully preserved by him. It must be returned to the Local Tribunal when it ceases to be in force. If the Certificate is conditional and if the conditions are no longer satisfied, notice must be given to the Local Tribunal. The man who fails to do this is liable to a penalty.

Signature of holder of Certificate. (The Certificate should be signed as soon as it is received.)

(a 689") Wt.   150M 2/16 H & S

R. 39.

MILITARY SERVICE ACT, 1916.

CERTIFICATE OF EXEMPTION.

expectation that one million men would be seen and that 100,000 of them could be raised for the forces.[63] This provoked a protest meeting of discharged soldiers in St George's Square on 5 May, one speaker proclaiming this…

> … re-examination of discharged soldiers a piece of Prussianism … it was … very unfair and cruel that a man who had volunteered at the beginning and who had been sent home knocked up should be called up for the army again.[64]

Simultaneously, advertisements appeared in the *HDE* for boys under military age to enrol for a Volunteer Battalion, so they could be trained prior to reaching the military age of 18 although it was promised that they would not see the front until they were 19.[65] Three months later there were still 250 places available for 16 to 17 year olds, and 'Old Volunteer' in his weekly column was at pains to quell scepticism and rumour that such youths would be sent to the front earlier than promised.[66]

In January 1918 the Government announced that all exemptions on occupational grounds could be re-examined and quashed, and that where exemptions were withdrawn the standard two months grace was abolished. In April 1918 the age limits were extended from 18-42 to 17-51. This pattern of attempting to grub more men out of the dwindling healthy male population, and of fast-tracking the training of new recruits, would continue until the end of the war.[67]

In addition to servicemen for the regular forces, recruitment was stepped up for the Local Defence Volunteers. In February 1917, voluntary enrolment was introduced for 'essential traders' aged 17 to 61.[68] Leading by example, the Mayor, 56 year-old William Jessop, enrolled and issued 28,000 letters appealing for others to follow his lead.[69]

As regular, incremental extensions to the Military Service Acts eroded the right to exemption by age, work and medical criteria, the MSTs were required to make increasingly unpopular decisions. On 22 April 1918, in perhaps its harshest judgment of the war, the Huddersfield MST withdrew the exemption of a married man with four children who had a medical certificate confirming that he could neither drill nor even walk properly. Tribunal Chairman Alderman Blamires commented wearily that 'the army .. would make him better of his varicose veins.'[70] Although the Military Representatives demanded just about everybody, the saving grace for the MSTs and numerous appellants was the growing food crisis. In 1918 they often directed married men who had several children into agricultural work.

Recruitment in Huddersfield broadly reflected the national picture. The initial rush of adventurous spirits was followed by an increasing grind to encourage volunteers. Many were dissuaded or prevented from enlisting by family, vocational and financial responsibilities until, from 1916, the MSTs were required to implement national conscription criteria.

Between 14,000 and 15,000 men joined the forces from the borough of Huddersfield alone, approximately 12% of the 120,000 population, with a similar percentage estimated from the outer districts.[71] National statistics suggest that just under half of these were conscripted.[72] Criticism of Huddersfield's overall recruitment rates proved to be largely unfair, and probably underestimated the high number of exempted occupations in the district. This was one of two main aspects that characterised local recruitment.

The other was the passion of those who refused to serve, along with the support for and tolerance of their dissidence. Far from everybody agreed with the religious, pacifist and socialist COs, and some expressed open contempt for them, but the COs had strong roots and support in the churches, Sunday Schools, workplaces and clubs of the district. Huddersfield's longstanding socialist culture was integral to community life, its views espoused and reaffirmed in the local socialist newspaper *The Worker*. Politically separate sections of society worked and played together, and whilst the war polarised views along political fault lines, they largely continued to live and let live.

No record has been found of white feathers being delivered in the district as a symbol of cowardice. Huddersfield's eloquent absolutist anti-war protesters were courageous in resisting great pressure to conform. But, perhaps uniquely, they also had solid backing from a substantial section of the community that ensured they were not isolated and ostracized.

Arthur Gardiner, Huddersfield's socialist anti-war figurehead of World War I, remained a staunch left-winger for the rest of his days. In 1941 he was elected Mayor of Huddersfield, serving for two years when World War II was at its height. In 1960 he was made a Freeman of the Borough.[73]

Chapter 13

1916: The Somme

The Chantilly Agreement

In December 1915 the Allied leaders signed the Chantilly Agreement, committing Britain, France, Italy and Russia to simultaneous attacks in the summer of 1916. Their strategy, to stretch the armies of the Central Powers to breaking point, was disrupted when Germany committed one million troops to a massive attack at Verdun on 22 February, promising 'to bleed France white.'

On a potentially vulnerable salient towards the southern end of the French lines, but heavily fortified, Verdun was seen as the prestigious key to French morale. Both sides poured troops into the area, and the prospect of France playing a major role in the planned summer attacks receded.[1]

Local Troops in the Trenches and Behind the Lines, Spring 1916

For the local troops in the 5th Dukes, the first six months of 1916 were relatively quiet, partly because they received no reinforcements until June 'owing to the difficulty of recruiting in England.'[2] They took their turn in manning the trenches, where conditions seemed to deteriorate with each tour of duty.

> We … occupy huts made from wood, corrugated iron, felt etc. They are rather too well ventilated and in a sea of mud. There are rats galore … one man had his nose dressed after an early-morning bite … They are big, cunning and daring.
>
> In the trenches there is a device to remove water which is an exact copy of the stone and bucket balance in use on the Nile in Biblical times …[3]

There were, however, no major attacks and few casualties. The first reported local fatality of the year was from the Royal Flying Corps. Lieutenant John Reed, 'a skilful airman' who had flown at 3000 feet over German lines, suffered mechanical failure and crash landed at Aldershot. His experienced pilot suffered a broken arm but John had a fractured skull and never regained consciousness.[4]

The first two infantry fatalities came in the first week of March. On 5 March, Lance Corporal B Hanson of the 5th Dukes was in a deep dug out at Authuile, north of Albert, when a trench mortar exploded on top of it. His comrade, Corporal Hoskins, was dug out, but Hanson was 'struck by falling timber and must have been killed instantly.' In the same week Corporal CW Crosland of the 9th Dukes was killed whilst leading a bombing party.[5] Both were from Honley, one of the few local villages hitherto unscathed, a remarkable survival rate as their young men had signed up in droves. Indeed, Honley Cricket Club had abandoned cricket for 1916 as practically all of their 60 playing members had joined the Army or Navy.[6]

The death in April of 23-year-old Private Ernest Bailey from Longwood, shot by a sniper, was reported to his mother in a typical, compassionate letter from his commanding officer, Sergeant AB Fleming.

> He fell into my arms … and I did all that I possibly could for him, but it was of no avail … He lived only two minutes. He did not suffer much, and died in my arms. I know it is hard indeed for you to hear such a great loss, but keep up your heart, and rest content, for he died a hero's death, doing his duty. He was liked by all who knew him, and you have the sympathy of all the N.C.O.s and men.[7]

The local men in the 168th Brigade RFA saw more action than the infantry during this period. Recalled early from Christmas at home to relieve a Brigade that had proved ineffective, the artillerymen enhanced their reputation for fast, sustained and accurate firing in support of infantry divisions at Meulte in January. They suffered casualties in a retaliatory action by the Germans close to Albert in March, the heavy fighting leaving them short of ammunition for a period, but in late April they successfully covered a raid by the Highland Light Infantry.[8]

During this period, the *HDE* carried a preponderance of reports and musings about life behind the lines. Fundraising in Huddersfield had recently financed two of the fifty or so YMCA huts for the troops. Within sight of the flashes of British guns and enemy shells, each hut was comprised of one large hall, 100 feet by 25 feet, and three smaller rooms – one for the officers, a kitchen, and a staff mess room with shelves and rudimentary mattresses to serve as bunks. One of the Huddersfield huts was inspected by Sir Douglas Haig who 'expressed his delight and deep gratitude for the provision of such magnificent centres of rest and recreation.'[9]

JW Schofield of the Huddersfield YMCA manned it and witnessed its immense value to the men.

> Men come in to the hut from the trenches weary and tired at all hours of the day and night … hot coffee, cakes, chocolate and cigarettes are available for them at practically cost price … After having their coffee etc. they fall asleep on the floor, and only wake up in time to go back to their duty in the firing line. Sometimes their clothes are frozen stiff, so you will be able to imagine with what joy they welcome the YMCA Hut, with its warm and comfortable room.

The YMCA provided daily activities and entertainments. In the week beginning Sunday 20 February 1916 staff at one of the Huddersfield huts organised:

Sunday:	Divine Service
Monday:	Singing competition for the troops
Tuesday:	Lantern lecture 'of a popular subject … of an interesting and educational nature'
Wednesday:	Conjuring entertainment by YMCA staff
Thursday:	Pathescope with assorted films, e.g. Charlie Chaplin
Friday:	Military band concert
Saturday:	Brigade sing-song

Every night ended with a hymn, a prayer and the National Anthem.[10] In May 1916 JW Schofield spoke to a packed Temperance Hall in Huddersfield about his experiences, revealing the ...

> … emotion of the Sunday evening services, and the indescribable feeling that overcame him as he saw the lads going out to face perhaps heaven and eternity without hearing the message again … going, not because they wanted to go, but because they were there to fight our battles, to win through …

During a gale, he had worked two days and nights to keep the hut standing because he 'knew what it meant to the men.'[11] The soldiers certainly appreciated the entertainments, one writing:

> Besides the YMCA hut we now have a Crystal Palace Picture Show run by a neighbouring division. The fine old barn is neither crystal nor palatial, but for 2½d one may see fairly good pictures, and the soldiers get the benefits of the profits. There is also a variety show run by 'The Mudlarks'. This is also a success.[12]

As preparations for the summer offensive gathered pace, the town of Albert and its surrounds, four miles behind the lines, was transformed into a British transit camp, almost a miniature city. Stretcher bearer Stanhope Firth and his colleagues of the RAMC even cultivated their own allotment.

> I am getting a good deal of lettuce from "our garden" just now, and the other day, when it was my turn to cook, I made a three course dinner. I have made porridge, soup, bread pudding, and blanc-mange lately, so we have not been badly off for grub, and have not touched "bully" [beef] or biscuits for quite a while now.[13]

Fare from the allotment contrasted with rations on the front line.

An Outlane Lad's Bit

by

(No 21,504, Private JA Whitwam, BEF, France)

We gets our rum and lime juice,
We gets our bully beef,
With half a dozen biscuits
That break our bally teeth.

We gets no eggs for breakfast,
But they send us over shells;
And you dive into your dug-out,
And get laughed at by your pals.

We gets a bit of bacon;
Just for fun we call it ham;
And for four fighting soldiers
There's a one-pound tin of jam.

Sometimes we get some rooty,
(The civvies call it bread);
It ain't as light as feathers
And it ain't exactly lead.

But we manage to digest it,
And never send it back,
Though it's smothered up with whiskers
Which get rubbed off in the sack.

The dust blows in our dixies,
And there's dust upon our mit,
So can you really wonder
Why the Pals are full of grit?

But still we mustn't grumble,
For we're feeling well and fit,
And our greatest consolation is
We are to Do Our Bit.[14]

In January 1916 troops from the 5th Dukes spent a convivial evening with Huddersfield's Great Britain international northern union rugby half back, Jim Davies, who was passing through with his regiment.

> I met Jim Davies, the idol of the Fartown crowd yesterday. He is in the C Company, 10th Rifle Brigade, and I was pleased to see he has been promoted to sergeant.
> Davies was delighted to see the Huddersfield boys again, and we had a good chat about old times and bygone matches. We talked quite a long time about that memorable Wigan match which resulted in a draw of 10 points each. Jim, who stayed the night with us, said, "I have enjoyed myself so much that it has been as good as a leave to me. It has taken me back to the happy years I spent in Huddersfield. Nothing would give me greater pleasure than to step on to the Fartown field again wearing the claret and gold."
> In one accord we burst into singing the old club song, "Hurrah for the Claret and Gold", and he was delighted. He was just like a youngster on his holidays.[15]

An abiding memory of Ada Ward, a lecturer and performer from Huddersfield who toured the British and Commonwealth camps in 1916, was of 'The English soldier … constantly talking and singing of home.'[16] The Reverend George Evans, Pastor of Golcar Baptist Church, who spent five months with the YMCA in France, concurred:

> They dream of home … to them it is the most beautiful thing in the world.[17]

In Good Old Huddersfield
by
Driver P Haigh MT, ASC, BEF

I have wandered in far countries, I have sail'd across the seas,
I have heard the sounds that ravish, I have seen the sights that please;
But my heart it still goes homing,
And I ever would be roaming
To my little home in good old Huddersfield.

O, the grey smoke's rolling o'er the ghastly battlefield,
And we're hunting back the foe, for they know we'll never yield.
But I never have forgot
In the crushing hail of shot,
My little home in good old Huddersfield.

O, the pale moon's shining on the wounded and the dead,
And some lad lies a-sleeping in his narrow earthen bed.
But his brave heart has gone homing,
And perhaps his spirit's roaming
n his little home in good old Huddersfield.[18]

For many young troops it was their first time away from home. They had no choice but to grow up very quickly in this baptism of fire.

The Dude
by
Kingussie, May 1916

1914
He lounged upon the Monkey-rack
And on John William Street,
A "three-five" suit upon his back,
Bright "patents" on his feet.
With "trews" turned up and waist so slim
And socks as bright as flame,
He challenged e'en the seraphim,
And thought sensation fame.
He wore his hair turned back and long,
To win each maiden's heart,
And passed, this hero of my song,
The smartest of the smart.

1916
He crouches in the muddy trench,
Where fly the shot and shell,
Nor heeds discomfort, wet, and stench,
Nor battle's shrieking hell.
His puttees are caked up with clay,
His chin shows rough and blue;
His khaki tunic's foul and grey,
His hair's all tumbled, too.
Mid wounds and death, to right a wrong –
A threatened world to save –
He fights, this hero of my song,
The bravest of the brave.[19]

The Battle of the Somme

The ultimate test of that bravery loomed large. Suffering heavy losses at Verdun, the French insisted that the Allies accelerated their summertime attack plans to relieve the pressure on them.

On 4 June the Russian army embarked on the Brusilov Offensive in Ukraine. It cost many lives and eventually petered out with no major territorial gains, but also diverted 15 German divisions from Verdun, relieved the Italians from an Austro-Hungarian assault at Trentino, and broke the back of the Austro-Hungarian army.

Field-Marshall Haig brought forward the attack on the western front by one month to 1 July. Twenty-two Divisions of Britain and her Allies from the Empire would be supported by five French divisions, not 40 as originally planned, but they still outnumbered the 16 divisions of the German 2nd Army that opposed them. The battleground would be the rolling hills around the valley of the River Somme, although Haig would have preferred Flanders. The plan was simple enough on paper. The British 4th Army would advance 1.5 miles on a 14-mile front. The 5th Army would march through the gap, capture the town of Bapaume, then swing north to Arras.[20]

Preparations for the 'Big Push' gathered pace in June. The local battalions dug trenches and marked out cross-country routes at Aveloy Wood, north of Albert. Towards the end of the month, the local RFA of the 168th Brigade moved to advanced positions in Authuille Wood near Albert, where they distinguished themselves in 'wire cutting and in generally preparing the ground for an attack.'[21]

Incongruously, 25 miles behind the lines, Ada Ward watched doctors and men of the RAMC in final rehearsals for *The Mikado* at a YMCA hut. In the last week of June, dress rehearsals were performed against an almost constant 'vibration of the earth … something terrible was going on somewhere.' This was the precursor to the 'Big Push', a seven day barrage of 1.7 million shells fired at the German lines. With scenery painted and costumes acquired from London, *The Mikado* was ready for its 1 July opening 'when news came that the theatre was required as a hospital. The "Push" had begun. Without a murmur of disappointment the opera was abandoned.'[22]

Just before 7.30am on 1 July the ground shook as never before. For many months, 50,000 men had silently and secretly dug mines leading to ten chambers under the German trenches. Packed with amatol, the chambers were now exploded, throwing debris 4000 feet into the air. The largest crater was 80 feet deep and 300 yards across. Fragments of bone are still found there.

At 7.30am the whistles blew and troops from the first line trenches, many of them territorials going into battle for the first time, emerged over the parapet, assured by their commanders that victory was theirs. Their confidence was based on a catalogue of catastrophic false assumptions:

- the bombardment of the previous week had surely obliterated most of the German dug outs and troops. (It hadn't. The Germans were protected by 30 feet deep bunkers, dug into the strong, chalky terrain, almost subterranean forts. The bunkers were undamaged. Many of their troops had retreated just beyond the range of the British artillery for the duration of the bombardment. The British did not have enough long range, heavy artillery, to reach them, and 30% of the hastily manufactured British shells failed to explode.)
- the Germans would be in disarray from the mine explosions. (In the main, they weren't.)
- German machine gun posts would not be manned. (They were. The week-long bombardment was a trade-off against the element of surprise, and Hawthorn Mine, towards the northern end of this battlefront near Beaumont Hamel, exploded ten minutes early, giving the Germans advanced warning that the attack was imminent and vital time to prepare. Their machine guns covered every angle of attack with overlapping zones of fire, each gun with a range of 200 yards unleashing 500 rounds per minute.)
- the shelling would have left gaping holes in the German barbed wire. (In many places it hadn't.)
- the remaining wire would be easily snipped with cutters attached to British rifles. (It wasn't. The Germans had thicker barbed wire than the British. The troops who got that far were

forced to pass through small areas where the wire was breached, areas on which German machine gunners could concentrate their fire.)

- Germany's significant territorial advantage on the higher ground would be negated. (It wasn't.)
- advancing by walking straight lines was the best tactic, particularly with inexperienced troops, as it would enable officers to more easily direct them. (It wasn't. Zigzagging darts of 5 to 10 yards by small groups, each covering the others, known as 'fire and movement', was much more effective.)
- it would save time if troops carried heavy supplies to set up camp in the German trenches. (It didn't. It slowed them down, many leaving the trenches slowly, intent on conserving their energy for the final dash for the German trenches. The final dash itself was impeded as the bombardment had churned up the ground they had to traverse.)[23]

The trenches remained much easier to defend than to attack, and British tactics made their own troops easier to hit.

They fell 'like sickled grain.' Among them were local lads from various regiments. Eighteen-year-old Private Frank Fielding of Marsden 'died instantly … at the beginning of the great advance.'[24] Twenty-year-old George Stanley Guse, also of Marsden, was shot in his left lung and leg and never recovered.[25] Dead and injured bodies began to present further obstacles, blocking the first few yards of No Man's Land, then backing up into the communication trenches. Forced to raise their heads above the parapets to clamber over them, many men were cut down before they even reached the front line.[26]

Private N Wilkinson made it into No Man's Land, but was carried from the battlefield with 'a piece of shrapnel in his head.' Relieved to be alive, he wrote from London's Camberwell Hospital:

> I don't know whether they are going to take it out … and more, I don't care either.[27]

He was safer where he was. Rifleman Robert Preston of Honley, serving with the King's Royal Rifles, was another No Man's Land casualty.

> … the enemy blew a mine, and as I was a bomber I went to defend the crater. When I got there, there was nobody to help me. I threw three bombs at the enemy, and then I got about thirty wounds in my left side from one of their grenades. Needless to say, I was helpless, and when three men surrounded me it was an easy matter for them to drag me fifty yards to their trench. I was taken into a dug-out, thirty yards underground, and immediately dressed and put to bed. I had about six drinks of cognac or brandy and plenty of coffee. An officer came to me and said I was all right and would soon be happy in Germany. Altogether I have been treated very well, but of course, I am still in hospital.

Robert was moved around different German hospitals in France, and it was September before his parents learned that he was convalescing in a prison camp in southern Germany. They had been in mourning for two months, assuming that he had been killed on the first day of the Somme.[28]

Of about 100,000 men sent into battle on 1 July 1916, there were 57,470 casualties, including 20,000 fatalities. It remains the worst day in British military history. The few pockets of success were towards the southern end of the line, where the French bombarded the enemy with greater accuracy and left their own routes of attack undamaged.[29]

Relying on official reports, the *HDE* Editorial of 3 July portrayed a controlled operation and sanitised the reality:

> AFTER months of patient waiting, "the big push" has begun … This is no sudden attempt to "break through," as was the case at Neuve Chappelle, and Loos. It is the beginning of a slow, continuous, and methodical push, sparing in lives, until the day when the enemy's resistance, incessantly hammered at, will crumple up at some point.
> We have no parallel by which to judge these operations … in the method … scale, and objective, they are without precedent.

We shall keep pounding away, now here, now there, until he [the enemy] reaches a point of exhaustion. The victory, first won in the workshops of Britain, is now being pushed home on the fields of France. The munition workers at home know now why they were asked to postpone their Whitsun holiday. The news which electrified the whole country during this weekend would have been far different had the factories failed in their duty to the man at the front.[30]

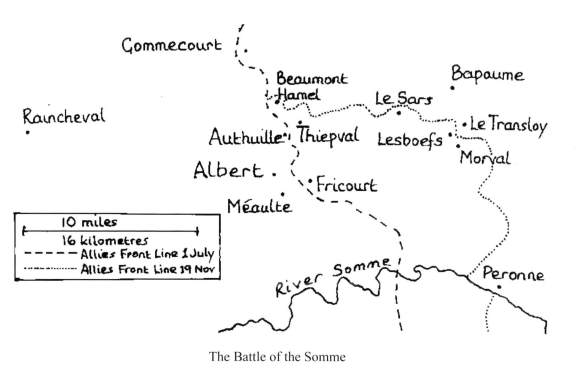

The Battle of the Somme

As the casualty lists grew, the *HDE* temporarily sidelined the 'sparing in lives' propaganda, but continued to promote the unquestionable heroism, courage and sacrifice of the troops. This from an 'Embarkation Officer':

> … never in my life have I seen anything finer than the way our successive waves of men marched singing and cheering into the bath of lead. The more casualties they saw in front of them the louder they cheered and sang, the harder they pressed forward into it … if Mister Bosche had had no machine guns, he would have stood no chance at all … our chaps … went into it as though it were a football scrum.[31]

Lance-Corporal AC Thompson, Northumberland Fusiliers, wrote from the Lord Derby War Hospital, Warrington of the Northern Division's successful attack on Fricourt Wood and, beyond it, Fricourt village on 2 July:

> To see our brave lads going into action, smiling, singing or smoking cigarettes – many, alas, for the last time! – was the sight of a lifetime … Our battalion went over the top … to take the Fricourt Wood. Away we raced under a hail of bullets and shell fire for perhaps thirty or forty yards. 'Down, down!' goes the cry, and we flung ourselves to the ground in shell-holes – anywhere to escape for a moment that awful storm of lead. A few moments pass: 'Ready boys? Come on then!' and away we race again for another 30 or 40 yards. We are near the German trench by now, but sadly we realise that our forces are far weaker than when we started. Here we lie for perhaps ten minutes, during which time we get our machine guns into position and at work! Our bombers get busy bombing the enemy out of the trench. Off again and this time we reach the trench to find it clear … 'Down again,' and as we go down I hear a voice cry, 'Oh!' – that's all, but another soul has crossed the bar. Another lad on my right

is in the act of flinging himself down – but before he reaches the earth a bullet catches him in the stomach … and makes an awful wound … Away again, sadder, but still determined forgetting, temporarily, the comrades we have left behind … Another 'breather' and we are in the wood itself. 'Hurrah; they're on the run!' and the wood is ours … A few yards more and I shall be safely through the wood, when, bang! I'm hit in the leg from behind. Two other lads are also hit … the fight is over for us, so we sit down to bandage our wounds.

Lying wounded we are fired upon by snipers, but as the fighting moves on, at length are taken to hospital, and how kindly we are treated there.[32]

Local casualties from 1 July would have been much higher had the 49th Division gone over the top. They were in reserve to the 32nd and 36th Divisions between Thiepval and Albert, where the front line advanced at first but, by the end of the day, remained substantially the same. The surviving troops were so 'utterly worn out' that the local lads would soon be required.

The local men in the 168th Brigade RFA covered several waves of these attacks, identifying distant troops by the tin triangle that each wore on his back as a precaution against friendly fire. At 3.45pm on 1 July the artillerymen trained an intense barrage on Thiepval, but the follow-up infantry attack failed to materialise. They were then subjected to retaliatory night-long bombing. The ground assault on Thiepval finally began on 3 July, but was soon abandoned. On the evening of 3 July further lack of infantry support compelled them to withdraw after three days defending the line, their potential as one of the crack artillery brigades wasted, but fortunately with few casualties.[33]

Behind the lines, Amy Ward was …

… in suspense as to whether things went well or badly for the Allies, when two despatch riders … arrived with the news that we were progressing. But the toll came … that long line of hospital trains bringing their loads of wounded … German wounded brought to hospital also and they were just as well cared for as the British.

She read a letter found on a dead German from his sweetheart: 'The Germans were in anguish as well as the British.' She also attended a funeral in a beautiful French churchyard but …

… did not feel despondent. She felt that the man had died for something which was worth dying for – the world's honour.[34]

The 5th Dukes entered the front line in Thiepval Wood on the evening of 2 July. The Allies' trenches there were 'battered fragments', affording little cover and overlooked by Thiepval Ridge from where the Germans frequently unleashed formidable barrages of high explosive shells, shrapnel shells and gas shells. The 5th Dukes suffered an immediate blow when Major AN Wheatley, a 'fearless and intrepid officer', was carried from the trenches severely wounded. Later, news arrived later that he had died.[35] Their situation was so vulnerable that the order to go over the top was cancelled at the last minute. Although occasional charges would be necessary to unsettle the enemy, holding this part of the line would be success in itself, at least for now.[36]

Thiepval was pivotal to the fighting in the northern part of the Somme. The local Battalion spent the next seven, exhausting weeks in the front line there, sustaining almost 300 casualties, mainly from shells into their trenches. Brothers Arthur and George Dawson of Hinchcliffe Mill, Holmfirth, were killed on 6 and 10 July respectively. Arthur (26) was struck by a bursting shell and George was shot whilst going over the top on a charge.[37]

Second-Lieutenant Henry Greenhow of Birkby saw his commanding officer, Lieutenant-Colonel FHS Rendall, shot through the right lung during a perilous raid on the German trenches. Greenhow and Major Shaw carried Rendall into a German dug-out. Whilst Greenhow stayed to look after him, the Major rejoined the fray, but was killed as the Germans re-took the trench. Following their standard practice, the Germans threw bombs into the dug-outs to flush out any remaining resistance, one bomb hitting Henry on the back of the head, but failing to explode. Stunned, Henry was taken prisoner, along with the Lieutenant-Colonel and three other men, but their senior officer, Rendall, died of his wounds.[38]

Twenty-year-old Private Fred Shackleton of Delph was one of 21 men who attempted to cross No Man's Land to raid a German trench, but was not one of the three who returned. For six months he was among the missing, then in January 1917 his parents were informed of a grave at the spot, inscribed: In memory of eighteen English soldiers.' There was no remaining doubt that their son was 'one of these nameless heroes.'[39]

Elsewhere on the battlefield, Private William Speight, a stretcher bearer with the Royal Welsh Fusiliers, was killed by a shell whilst standing at the entrance to his regimental aid post. Pre-war he had been assistant master in the School of Art at Huddersfield Technical College.[40] On the same day, one of William's former students, Alfred Priestley, a courageous and resourceful signaller with the 16th Royal Welsh Fusiliers, died instantly when a shell exploded over him and his companions, killing four and wounding eight.[41]

The Signaller
by
Signaller FW Beaumont, Wood St, Longwood
(with the Tyneside Scottish Regiment)

Who is it humps the biggest pack,
Not just valise and haversack,
But phone and wires and other tack?
Why, the Signaller.

Who was it on July the first
Midst shot and shell and shrapnel burst,
Laid wires when hell was at its worst?
Why, the Signaller.

Then lads, give credit where it's due.
Although you think we've "nowt" to do,
You always find him staunch and true –
The Signaller.[42]

By 11 July, many first line German trenches had been taken, but to repel the British threat a substantial number of German troops had arrived from Verdun, virtually doubling their numbers. The first phase of the Battle of the Somme, the Battle of Albert, ended on 13 July, but whilst many other divisions moved on, the local troops in the 49th (West Riding) Division remained in the most static part of the line at Thiepval. Sustained periods of shelling each day stretched nerves to breaking point and on 23 July Lance-Corporal WD Siddle of Sheepridge was invalided back to Birkenhead Military Hospital with shell shock.[43]

The number of bereaved and mourning families continued to increase across Huddersfield, as it did across all the combatant nations. Private John Roberts of Longwood was buried by a shell and died before he could be dug out.[44] Private Fred Wood of Honley was killed by a piece of shell whilst carrying a bag of bombs to the front line.[45] The luck of Sergeant Joseph William Ettenfield of Lockwood finally ran out. In 1915 he had been gassed at Hill 60 and invalided home. Returning to his Battalion in February 1916, he narrowly survived Easter Monday when shrapnel pierced his cigarette case over his heart, but on 3 August he was killed instantly by a sniper's bullet.[46]

A loss most 'keenly felt' in the 5th Dukes was Acting Sergeant-Major Charlie Cox, a most respected officer who had just received the Military Medal for repeatedly rescuing wounded men from No Man's Land.[47] On 19 August the Battalion was finally relieved from the front line and went into billets at Raincheval. One territorial wrote:

> We have not had our clothes off for six weeks … so you can guess how we shall appreciate a good bath when we get the chance.

This was somewhat at odds with his observation that:

… we have to wash and shave every 24 hours so that, although we are in the trenches, we take pride in our appearance.[48]

The 5th Dukes had accounted for numerous Germans and taken several prisoners, but the loss of almost 300 of their own was a high price to pay. 'Old Volunteer', in his weekly column for the *HDE* paid a heartfelt tribute. It had been a …

> … terrible ordeal [but] they bore themselves like the seasoned soldiers they have become … "People can get used to anything" we are sometimes told, and after our experiences of the horrors of the most brutal war in history I believe they can. The lads who were brought up in the workshops, mills, warehouses, and business establishments of this district, without any thought of war or warfare, are now defending the cause not only of the Empire but of civilisation against a ruthless foe with a courage and devotion that fills us with admiration.[49]

The following week, Bombardier E Atkinson, RGA, of Birkby forwarded the following poem.

Lines Written in a Dug-Out
by
The Wanderer

Land of war – and little sleep;
Land of "Whizz-bang" and "Pip-squeak";
Land of poison gas and shell;
Land of fury worse than hell;
Land of bully-beef and mud;
Land of the anti-aircraft "dud";
Land of ruined homes and churches,
Where the "caterpillar" lurches;
Land of weary Tommies "fed",
Where much is done and little said;
Where soft beds would a hardship be;
Land of Blood, I speak of Thee!

Land of Blood, wherein do meet,
Experiences both sore and sweet,
Where lads write home "I'm in the pink"
While from fatigue and pain they sink;
Boys not yet at manhood's stage
Facing still the battle's rage;
Land where Maxims rip and rattle,
And Huns come up like driven cattle!
Surely ne'er was flesh and blood
Baptised in such a gory flood!
None of us the end may see;
We leave that for posterity.[50]

Meanwhile, the *HDE* Editorial interpreted a lull in local casualty numbers with particularly insensitive patriotic hyperbole.

> … the British High Command in France has now attained an extraordinary high standard of efficiency in the matter of flesh and blood economy.[51]

Behind the lines, the local territorials were given ten days of intensive attack training and some recreation, their numbers restored by 'Northumberland Fusilier Territorials and recent 'Derby' recruits from all parts of Yorkshire.' They had anticipated a lengthy rest but on Sunday 3 September they began the march back to the front line at Thiepval Wood, accompanied by lively tunes played by the divisional band.

When they left us about four miles away from the trenches, they began to play "Michael Cassidy," and the boys of 'A' Company did not half give it 'gip'.

… We got to the trenches about 3.30 on the [Sunday] morning, and found the artillery bombarding the German front line …[52]

The bombardment had begun almost a week earlier, and a general attack right across the front line was imminent. At 5.10am, in semi-darkness, the 5th Dukes went over the top, with the 4th (Halifax) Dukes on their right and the West Yorkshire Brigade on their left. Twenty-year-old Private W Hawksworth of Milnsbridge got no further.

… a high explosive shell burst on the top of the trenches and blew me up in the air. I thought my number was up, I can tell you. I had to lie there ten hours before they could get me out.

Private Hawksworth had three operations before, invalided to Reading War Hospital, his right leg was amputated above the knee.[53]

As the attack continued …

… The Germans spotted us about twenty yards from their wire, and the machine gun and rifle fire was terrible. It's a wonder how we came through it alive ... When we got to the German barbed wire we were stopped until the artillery raised their guns so as to reach the German second line …

It was anticipated that the bombardment had cut the German wire. As on 1 July, it hadn't. Repetition of this mistake across the battlefield cost many lives and remains a serious indictment against Britain's military leadership. Whilst the Germans organised, took aim and unleashed their weaponry, the 4th and 5th Dukes 'fought like demons' and, at great cost, reached the German lines. Of the 5th Dukes' four companies, C Company was in reserve whilst …

… good old 'A' Company went into the German first line trenches, 'B' Company had to take the second line, and … 'D' company another bit of ground.

They now occupied an area called the 'Pope's Nose' between Thiepval and St Pierre Divion, but unfortunately the support on their left flank lagged behind and had not reached the German trenches.

The Germans started to work round us with their bombs and it became so hot that we had to retire to our advanced trenches.

Driven back to their own lines, the Huddersfield and Halifax Battalions had neither lost nor gained any ground. After just eleven hours in the line, the 5th Dukes were withdrawn for reorganisation and reinforcements. Their casualties were 12 officers and 355 men, with 11 taken prisoner. A German report of the day's events suggested that the Germans suffered at least as many casualties. There was little solace that …

... the effect is not felt in Huddersfield as severely as would have been the case in the early days of the war, when all the men in the battalion were raised in this district … As it is, there are many sad hearts among us.

Corporal H Brook of Marsden wrote:

I am out of the trenches now … after the worst twenty-four hours we ever had.[54]

The injured were taken to war hospitals across the country, but for the first time in the war, the exhausted, bedraggled, mutilated convoy that emerged from Huddersfield Railway Station included many local men. 'Old Volunteer' observed:

… some of those who came back wounded were so absolutely tired out that it would have been better if they had been taken to hospitals so far away from Huddersfield that fewer of their friends would have been able to visit them. They would then have been able to obtain the rest of which some of them were so greatly in need.[55]

In Huddersfield, the events of 3 September were known as 'The Great Battle for Thiepval' and, for several months, simply as 'the attack.'[56] In the *HDE* the long lists of killed, wounded and missing included a high proportion of amateur sportsmen, particularly cricketers, association footballers and rugby footballers.

Lieutenant AN Sharpe, 'reported wounded and missing', played for Huddersfield Cricket Club and captained the YMCA Football Club.[57] Also missing was Private GW Beaumont, whose cricket skill made him an 'exceedingly good bomb thrower.' In the chaos, his commanding officer confessed that it was 'quite possible for him to have been wounded and gone to hospital without our knowledge, or he may be a prisoner of war.'[58]

Such hope usually proved false, but some of the missing turned up. On 30 September the grieving parents of Private Allen Cowgill received a postcard from him. He was a prisoner of war in Germany and asked for 'a parcel as soon as you can. You must keep your spirits up, and let me have a letter with all the news from home.' The *HDE* concluded: 'This should give encouragement to many local parents whose sons have been missing since the same engagement.'[59]

The carnage on the Somme in the region of Picardy inspired one of the famous songs of the war *Roses of Picardy*. The romantic lyrics, sung by a soldier on the Somme to his beloved, were written by Frederick Weatherley, who also wrote the lyrics to *Danny Boy*. The melody was composed by Haydn Wood of Slaithwaite. During the war the sheet music sold at 50,000 copies per month. One of songs repeatedly sung in the trenches, it also helped soldiers being treated for shell shock to regain their powers of speech.

Roses of Picardy
lyrics by Frederick Weatherly, music by Haydn Wood

Verse 1
She is watching by the poplars, Colinette with the sea-blue eyes,
She is watching and longing and waiting, Where the long white roadway lies.
And a song stirs in the silence, As the wind in the boughs above,
She listens and starts and trembles, 'Tis the first little song of love:

Refrain
Roses are shining in Picardy, in the hush of the silver dew,
Roses are flowering in Picardy, but there's never a rose like you!
And the roses will die with the summertime, and our roads may be far apart,
But there's one rose that dies not in Picardy!
'Tis the rose that I keep in my heart!

Verse 2
And the years fly on forever, Till the shadows veil their skies,
But he loves to hold her little hands, And look in her sea-blue eyes.
And she sees the road by the poplars, Where they met in the bygone years,
For the first little song of the roses, Is the last little song she hears:[60]

There were many vacancies in the 5th Dukes, and Corporal Charles Edward Mills of Huddersfield was promoted to Sergeant, reward for 'distinguishing himself' in the battle.[61] Numerous new conscripts were absorbed into the ranks over the next ten days, and on 14 September the 5th Dukes returned to the front line in the Leipzig Salient, south of Thiepval. Their main duties were bombing raids on the German lines 'which severely tested the grit and endurance of the new drafts.'[62]

On 17 September 26-year-old Corporal GH Eastwood of Newsome led his platoon in one such raid when …

> … A shell burst and severed one of his legs from his body; not withstanding his agony he called to his men to proceed. Before he could be properly attended to he passed away with "a bright smile on his face".[63]

During the following week, 19-year-old Private M Fahy from Primrose Hill was reported missing

A few days later Corporal Shearon (KOYLI) was out 'between the lines.' Checking identification disks, he found Private Fahy among a number of bodies cut down by a shell. The Corporal returned his belongings to his parents. They included two photographs 'cut at the edge … apparently bloodstained' from where the shrapnel had struck him.[64]

The local troops were relieved on 29 September, and Gunner GA Charlesworth of Kirkburton reflected on his experiences of the summer.

Keep Up Your Courage
By
Gunner GA Charlesworth, Kirkburton

I sit in my lonely dug-out,
And think of the time gone by,
When peace around reigned supernal;
What joy there would be if 'twas nigh.

I think of my distant homeland,
The anguish and suffering there;
And wonder will the strife soon be o'er,
Or is there yet longer to bear.

There are tears when we get downhearted;
But this soon passes away
When you think of the chaps singlehanded,
Dashing their way through the fray.

You sit there in wonderful silence,
Not a sound is there to be heard;
When, all of a sudden, with violence,
Shells roar and burst very hard.

You pick up your papers and ponder,
How the battle was fought and won;
But you cannot imagine the valour,
And the spirit our soldiers have shown.

The roars of the guns is like thunder,
And deafens you there as you sit.
But you think of the battle, and wonder,
How soon you'll be doing your bit.

Your excitement carries you onward,
You are anxious to reach your goal;
The danger you face does not matter,
You long for success in your soul.

And seldom are we disappointed,
For all we take from them we hold.
But what a great price it has cost us;
All that remains to be told.

Cheer up, all you British people;
The Germans have now had their day.
The time will soon come for England,
To name the big price they must pay.[65]

Horrors similar to those suffered by the local battalion emerged from Huddersfield troops in other parts of the line. Thirty-year-old Private C Gash of Moldgreen, serving with the King's Own Royal Lancaster Regiment was 'wounded by shrapnel in the face and both hands, and his left leg has been amputated.' He had a wife and five children, and was employed as a 'concreter' before the war.[66]

On 24 September, Private Fred Riches of Crosland Moor, serving with the Durham Light Infantry was shot through the chest and, as he lay on the ground, was struck by shrapnel. Crawling into the cover of a shell hole, he heard voices nearby and called out. Fortunately they were stretcher bearers who carried him to safety.[67]

New to all of this was Private Wilfred Greenfield from Birkby, a 19-year-old grocer's assistant with the Hillhouse Co-operative Society. He enlisted in April 1916 and by August was serving with D Company in the 2nd Dukes.

As for Private Freddie Smith a year earlier, letters from home were Wilfred's lifeline '… we value them as much as anything you can mention.' In his own frequent letters he shows great appreciation of the correspondence and parcels sent to him. He received cigarettes and toffee, and his requests included the weekly edition of the *Examiner*, pencils and paper. He also requested 'refills' for a small stove sent by his friend Clarence, as the nights were 'very cold … winter is coming on and we cannot expect anything else.' Most poignant was his letter of 14 September, his second letter in three days.

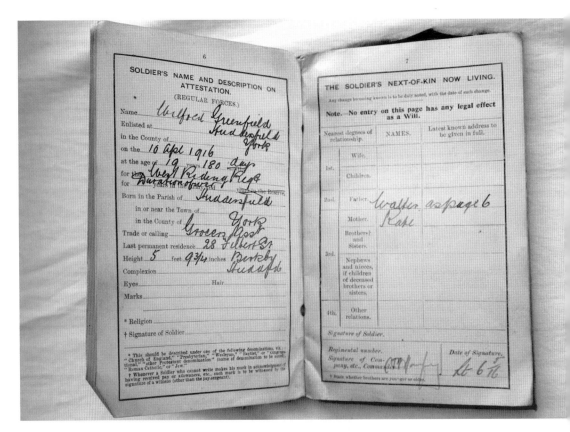

You will wonder why I have wrote so soon but to tell you the truth I am spent up. We are expecting some pay before long but if you can spare a little I shall be greatly releaved [sic] as I cannot live on nothing at all.

Wilfred was careful not to reveal any military information, but on 21 September warned his parents that it could be 'a few days before you receive this letter as we are on the move again.'[68]

The Allies were beginning to gain territory. Tanks had been used for the first time, hastening the capture of Flers on 15 September, although their psychological impact as yet exceeded their reliability. They would also assist the capture of Thiepval on 27 September. By contrast, on the British eastern flank progress was frustrated by a strong and rapidly developing German trench network around the villages of Le Transloy, Beaulencourt and the town of Baupame. This was the destination of the British 4th Army, including Wilfred in the 2nd Dukes. The rain to which Wilfred had referred in all his letters intensified, conspiring against them. Battlefields, bombarded to dust in the summer, became quagmires, and Sir Douglas Haig's official despatch from the Somme admitted:

Two of Wilfred Greenfield's letters home, dated 14 and 21 September 1916

… constant rain turned the mass of hastily dug trenches for which we were fighting into channels of deep mud. The country roads, broken by countless shell craters, that cross the deep stretch of ground we had lately won, rapidly became almost impassable, making the supply of food, stores and ammunition a serious problem.[69]

During the early hours of 11 October, the 2nd Dukes relieved a battalion from the 41st Division in the front line. Wilfred Greenwood's Battalion was joined by about 600 men of the 2nd Battalion Lancashire Fusiliers. At 6.30am the following day an eight-hour barrage of the German trenches began along the whole 4th Army front on the Le Transloy Ridges, from Morval to Le Sars.[70]

Wilfred, just past his 20th birthday, was in a section of the line assigned to capture 'Spectrum Trench', a little north of Lesboefs, where the Germans had three lines of trenches ahead of three further partially constructed lines, all joined by a network of communication trenches. The combined eight companies of the two battalions were to attack the enemy's position, 1400 yards away, in eight waves. The first four waves of Lancashire Fusiliers were to take the first line trench, push forward and dig in. The 2nd Dukes were to follow in support.

Poor visibility on 12 October denied them any aerial intelligence about German troop numbers or movements, but at 2.25pm infantry right along the front line of the 4th Army went over the top. Everywhere troops floundered in 'thick glutinous mud-clogged boots the size of footballs.' Forewarned by the barrage and a repeated pattern of afternoon attacks, the Germans were ready. A and B companies of the 2nd Lancashire Fusiliers wallowed into a hail of bullets fired by two machine guns from a small, undetected German trench, well ahead of the others, that had escaped the barrage. Lieutenant VFS Hawkins of B Company described the unfolding catastrophe.

> 2-30pm Fifty per cent of Company already down. Whole Brigade appears to be held up. Lance Corporal Fenton, one of my Lewis gunners, has got his gun going in a shell hole on my left. Awful din ... Yelled at Sgt Manin to take the first wave on. He's lying just behind me. Hodgkinson says he is dead. Sgt Mann on my right, of 7 Platoon, also dead. Most of the men appear to be dead. Shout at the rest and get up to take them on. Find myself sitting on the ground facing our own line with a great hole in my thigh … Hodgkinson also hit in the wrist. Most of the Company now out … I put my tie round my leg as a tourniquet. Fortesque about five yards on my right still alive … yell at him to come over to me. Show him my leg and tell him to carry on. He gets into a shell hole to listen while I tell him what to do. Shot through the heart while I'm talking to him. Addison also wounded and crawling back to our lines. That's all the officers and most of the N.C.Os.

What must Wilfred and others waiting their turn have thought and felt? Through the carnage, sheer weight of numbers enabled isolated parties from the Lancashire's B and C companies to reach and capture part of the first line German trenches. The 2nd Dukes, including Wilfred in D Company, followed behind in support and also suffered heavy casualties. Wilfred made it to the German lines, and his Company tried to push past the first line as planned. The odds were heavily against them. Too few of them had got through and they had a high percentage of inexperienced troops, Wilfred among them. When the counter-attack came they would be outnumbered. In these circumstances, the multiple lines of trenches, connected by a maze of communications trenches, were a death-trap. Of the few who made it to the German lines, all of the Lancashire's B and C companies, and most of the West Ridings were either killed or captured as the Germans re-took their lost trenches.

During the evening further attacks were abandoned. Instead, 130 wounded survivors were rescued from No Man's Land. Of the 1000 or so involved in the attack, a roll call revealed 66 dead, 168 wounded and 101 missing.[71] Wilfred was reported 'missing' for the next four months. Then, in February 1917, his mother received the following letter.

BRITISH RED CROSS
—AND—
ORDER OF ST. JOHN.

ENQUIRY DEPARTMENT
FOR
WOUNDED AND MISSING.

February 26th 1917.

18, Carlton House Terrace, S.W.

Pte. W. Greenfield, 20009, D Coy. XIV Pl. 2nd West Riding Regt.

Dear Madam,

We regret to say that we have received a very sad report about your son from Pte. J. Castle, 12336, D Coy, 2nd West Riding Regt. (now in Hospital in France.) Our informant states as follows:—

"I saw Greenfield lying dead in a communication trench near Le Transloy on the date mentioned. It was a trench we had just captured. There was another man killed at the same time but I did not know him. I identified Greenfield by a large white "C" for Carrier which he had on his arm."

We are continuing our enquiries in order to obtain further details for you, and will let you know immediately if we are successful.

We hope you will accept our very sincere sympathy in your sad loss.

Yours faithfully,

K Robson.

for THE EARL OF LUCAN.

Mrs. Greenfield,
28, Filbert St,
Birkby,
Huddersfield.

GV RI

HE whom this scroll commemorates was numbered among those who, at the call of King and Country, left all that was dear to them, endured hardness, faced danger, and finally passed out of the sight of men by the path of duty and self-sacrifice, giving up their own lives that others might live in freedom. Let those who come after see to it that his name be not forgotten.

Pte. Wilfred Greenfield
W. Riding Regiment

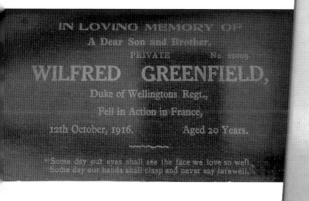

IN LOVING MEMORY OF
A Dear Son and Brother,
PRIVATE   No. 20009,
WILFRED GREENFIELD,
Duke of Wellingtons Regt.,
Fell in Action in France,
12th October, 1916.   Aged 20 Years.

"Some day our eyes shall see the face we love so well,
Some day our hands shall clasp and never say farewell."

Wilfred's artefacts include the scroll and 'death penny', presented to the next of kin of all the fallen, and his two medals, the silver British War Medal awarded to all who served overseas in the war, and the Allied Victory Medal. His family also had a plaster tablet moulded with the plaque (bottom) inset.
Wilfred is buried at Lesboeufs Guards' Cemetery, Grave 10, Row W, Plot 5.

I met him in the train one day,
A rough clad man, with hair turned grey,
A cattle drover kind of man,
Whose years had passed the three-score span.

His honest eyes were filled with woe,
He moved his trembling lips, as though
Repeating to himself a name,
The movements ever were the same.

I longed to show I understand,
And fain would help, if help I could,
I gently spoke to him, "My friend,
Time heals the wounds that sorrows send."

He turned his head with wistful look.
And from an inner pocket took,
A portrait of a soldier lad.
"He's dead - and he was all we had."[72]

Elsewhere in the line, the 7th (Colne Valley) Dukes overcame the treacherous conditions and a strong German position that had resisted all attacks for nearly a month 'to advance beyond the objective ordered.' Inevitably, they suffered many casualties. It was one of few British gains in the Battle of Le Transloy which was abandoned on 18 October.[73]

Similarly lauded were the local lads in the 168th Brigade RFA, operating towards the northern end of the British front line. In August they led a successful month-long 'pounding of the enemy at Bethune. They then played a key role in the Battle of Ancre Heights. From 10 to 12 October they unleashed a fierce bombardment and one of the first creeping barrages – lines of shelling moving steadily forwards with the infantry following closely behind – to support the advance of 'the famous 5th Division' as they attacked Stuff Redoubt, north of Thiepval.

In the same area on 23 October they were instructed to rescue a party marooned in Frankfurt Trench. They failed to find them, but progressed to Munich Trench where they captured an 18-strong German decoy party, and helped to seize the trench. Strategically valuable, Munich Trench overlooked the Beaumont Hamel Road, along which all supplies and troops moved up the valley. Beaumont Hamel itself was now within reach. Further bombardments and covering fire from the 168th RFA supported heavy fighting until the village fell into British hands on 15 November. A touchstone for British over-confidence, Beaumont Hamel had been an objective for Day 1 of the Battle of the Somme, 1 July.[74]

By 17 November the 2nd Dukes' communication trenches were impassable, clogged up with mud. Ordered to advance, they were forced into the open to reach their own front line, and came under immediate fire. Many fell, and as the rest sought shelter the cry went out for stretcher bearers. Lance-Corporal Leslie Sheard entered the storm of bullets, found a wounded comrade and dragged him 'inch by inch to the parapet.' He called for help. A soldier jumped out of the trench and was instantly shot dead. Seconds later the wounded man in Corporal Sheard's arms was shot through the head. Shaken, the Corporal leapt down into the trench. His valour was rewarded with the DCM, presented on 17 August 1917 at a garden fête in Mirfield.[75]

The 5th Dukes were in an equally boggy, but quieter part of the line, close to Gommecourt, which had been captured by the British in September. Kitted out with thigh-length boots to counter the now knee-deep mud, and fur capes to withstand the freezing nights, they drained and improved a succession of swampy trenches.[76] On 20 November Captain JB Cockhill led A Company on a raid, killing numerous Germans, even though Sir Douglas Haig had closed down the Somme offensive the previous day. On 4 December the 5th Dukes were moved to billets at Halloy, where they enjoyed a restful Christmas.[77]

Huddersfield's final fatalities of the Battle of the Somme were Private JH O'Brien, and Private Henry Thewlis, both killed in action on 13 November, and Corporal Charles Royle of Lindley, killed in a 'patrol encounter' in No Man's Land on 15 November. Prior to the war, 25-year-old O'Brien had graduated from the Royal College of Art as the outstanding scholar of his year, and was a teacher at Holmfirth Art School and Hillhouse United Methodist Church. Twenty-year-old Thewlis had been, potentially, the latest in a famous Lascelles Hall family cricketing dynasty.[78]

Reflections on The Battle of the Somme

Since 1 July the Allies had gained six miles on a twenty-mile front, including some strategically valuable ridges, but nothing decisive. They had also suffered 600,000 casualties and the Germans 500,000. The Battle of the Somme diverted many German divisions from Verdun, helping to keep France in the war, and preventing these divisions from transferring to other theatres of war. During the autumn the French re-captured lost ground and forts. The Battle of Verdun ended on 15 December, almost ten months after it began, the longest battle of the war. Both armies were irrevocably wounded – 550,000 French casualties, 434,000 German casualties, half of them fatalities. No land had been lost or gained, but the Germans could not endure further losses on this scale.

The military leaders, particularly Falkenhayn at Verdun and General Haig on the Somme, were responsible for prolonging the slaughter long after the decisive breakthrough failed to materialise. Lloyd George, who became Prime Minister of a coalition government in December 1916, and his French counterpart Raymond Poincaré, were determined that they would not risk so many lives again, their resolve strengthened by growing unrest on the home front. General Robert Nivelle, a successful veteran of the Marne and Verdun, replaced Joffre as Commander-in-Chief of the French Army. The Germans too changed their military leader. Their strategies of attack at Verdun and counter-attack on the Somme had both been too costly in lives and Erich von Falkenhayn was replaced by Field-Marshal Paul von Hindenberg and his deputy General Erich Ludendorf. By the autumn of 1918 Ludendorf would effectively be Germany's political and military leader.

Despite the continuing carnage, the strategy of charging the enemy, whilst more selectively implemented, remained largely the same for the duration of the Somme. Why was this? Honouring the Chantilly Agreement, and under pressure to relieve Verdun, the Allies were committed to attack. The scale of the June bombardment, and the months of mining and subsequent explosions brought pressures of their own to follow through, regardless of how successful they had been.

The technology of communication, like the technology of self defence, lagged behind the technology of killing. The commanders, who in previous wars had led from the front, were inexperienced at leading from behind the lines. They relied on hundreds of miles of telephone wire – laid above ground and frequently in need of repair – to learn about progress and to relay instructions to the front line. Adapting quickly to changing circumstances was well-nigh impossible. At times, orders remained orders long after they ceased to make sense.

Saddest of all, after the magnificent logistical achievement of shipping a million men and 400,000 mules and horses across the channel, along with the resources to feed, house, clothe, equip, train, deploy and treat them, they did not know how else to fight. They were learning as they went along – and not very quickly. The Somme was both a killing ground and a training ground.

Despite some questionable orders, military discipline was strong and the consensus that the cause was just remained resilient.[79] As Private Smith of Crosland Moor, serving with the Worcester Regiment wrote:

> Unfortunately the conditions of modern trench warfare make it impossible to make any progress without great loss of life. Looking over a battlefield, with dead bodies scattered

Pyramids of army food stores at Boulogne

about, one cannot help thinking … It is the sin of men has brought this about, and the greed for power … The just have often to suffer for the unjust, and some are called to be martyrs in the cause of liberty, and that is the light I look upon a fallen comrade. We are fighting that the strong shall not be allowed to crush the weak.[80]

Several strategies adopted during the year had proved instructive. At Verdun the Germans had advanced quickly in clusters, using zigzagging, fire and movement. On the Somme, the French had targeted their bombardment much more precisely, hitting some specific German targets and avoiding the land they needed to traverse to attack. The British found that creeping barrages had facilitated forward infantry momentum. Where tanks had been used, the British had gained twice the territory in half the time for half the usual number of casualties.

The military leaders were learning. Industrial warfare required speed of attack, denying time for the enemy to re-group, and forward momentum with close support to press home any advantage. Several stratagems had shown potential in isolation. Ultimate success would require co-ordination of these, using infantry, cavalry, artillery, tank and aircraft. Which side would master this, how long would it take, and how many more lives would be lost before the end?[81]

Chapter 14

1916: Jutland

U-Boats and Diplomatic Pressure from the U.S.

At the beginning of 1916, Germany's naval strategy was beset by the conflicting priorities of defeating the British without further provoking the United States. In February Germany admitted the illegality of U20's attack on the *Lusitania* nine months earlier and committed to paying an indemnity. Simultaneously, frustrated by the stranglehold of the British blockade of the North Sea, German High Command declared:

> Germany feels it will be impossible for her in future to consent to accept the regulations regarding submarine warfare as long as England continues to intercept goods coming to Germany via Holland.[1]

Whilst Britain continued to intercept German imports, Germany would retaliate with renewed unrestricted submarine attacks on neutral and British ships, including U.S. merchant ships. Britain relied much more on imports, particularly imported food, than Germany. Starving Britain of imports was a means to defeat her. By April, the indignant New York press was carrying daily condemnation of Germany's 'continued submarine recklessness … strongly advocating definite action against Germany.' The *Journal of Commerce* reflected the tone:

> Suppose it to be proved beyond all reasonable doubt that the German Government is determined to keep up the submarine attacks upon unarmed merchant vessels without warning, without examination, and without any attempt at saving lives or giving them a chance to escape, what are the neutral nations going to do about it?[2]

On 20 April, U.S. intervention moved a step closer, President Woodrow Wilson warning that unless Germany 'desists from carrying on submarine warfare as at present diplomatic relations will be severed.'[3]

The pressure was mounting on Germany to challenge the British blockade of the North Sea. The German High Seas Fleet had little to gain by running the narrow gauntlet of the English Channel, risking isolation in the Atlantic. This left the North Sea as the battleground where there was a major attempt by both sides to break the stalemate in 1916.

How could it be achieved? Britain had the greater numbers, but not by much. Both sides were wary of the other's mighty dreadnought class battleships, developed in 1906. These giants had reduced battle cruisers, and occasionally even destroyers, to screening and reconnaissance duties. Neither side would commit to a major attack unless it had a decisive strategic advantage, and its leaders were confident of victory.

The Run to the South

In the spring of 1916 the German Navy resumed sorties on Britain's east coast, seeking an opportunity to lure the British fleet, or at least part of it, from the security of its harbours at Rosyth and Scapa Flow. The British, however, had been supplied with the German naval code book, pilfered by the Russians from the captured warship *Magdeburg*. In late May the Germans laid a trap for the British Navy, but the British were one step ahead with a counter-lure of their own. For the only time in the war, the commanders of both navies felt confident to attack.

At 2.20pm on 31 May 1916, a relatively small British battle cruiser force left Rosyth under Admiral Beatty in his flagship HMS *Lion*. Aboard the *Lion* were stoker Maurice Booth of Marsden and seaman-gunner Harry Senior of Huddersfield.[4] Further north, the Grand Fleet, with its dreadnoughts, left Scapa Flow under Admiral Jellicoe, on course to meet Beatty's force.

Beatty sailed south and, as expected, encountered the German battle cruiser equivalent, commanded by Admiral Hipper. Apparently playing into German hands, Beatty chased Hipper's flotilla south, keeping a sharp look-out for the dreadnoughts and destroyers of the German High Seas Fleet, which he knew were waiting for him.

The first shots on this 'Run to the South' were fired shortly before 4pm. In the ensuing skirmishes, HMS *Indefatigable* was quickly sunk. The *Lion* too suffered several hits and caught fire, but was protected by rapid salvoes from the battle cruiser HMS *Queen Mary*. Then one of many shells from SMS *Derfflinger* struck the *Queen Mary*'s turret, causing a massive explosion which split her in two. Within 90 seconds she had sunk, leaving just a cloud of smoke. Only 18 out of 1284 officers and men survived.[5] Among the fatalities was Ship's Boy, 16-year-old Thomas Quarmby from Golcar.[6]

HMS *Queen Mary* (centre) explodes during the Battle of Jutland

Two German destroyers were also sunk. Then, at 4.40pm the German High Seas Fleet was sighted. Beatty immediately turned to head north, luring the main German fleet into a pursuit in open waters. Its commander, Admiral Scheer, expected to destroy the apparently isolated British battle cruiser fleet.

The German battle cruisers led the chase, engaging the *Lion* and the three remaining British battle cruisers for much of the way. Sandwiched between the German battle cruisers and the German High Seas Fleet was the British 5th Battle Squadron, which had delayed its turn to the north and was now engaging the van of the main German fleet, but exposed to heavy fire.

Among the British 5th Battle Squadron was the super-dreadnought HMS *Warspite*,

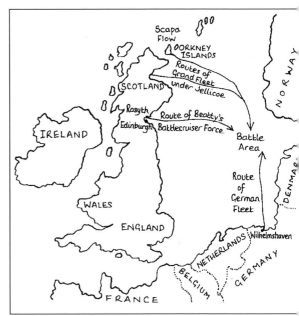

The Battle of Jutland

whose crew included Seaman Harold Scholefield from Lockwood, Seaman Hilton Beaumont of Fartown and Officer Steward Carter from Huddersfield. As the *Warspite* turned north, her engine room was struck by a shell, causing the steering to jam. Her Captain, Edward Phillpotts, decided to circle rather than come to a halt, as at least he could present a moving target. The *Warspite* was nevertheless, holed 150 times by the closing German fleet. Most of the *Warspite*'s crew was unaware of their predicament and saw little of the action, as Harold Scholefield revealed:

> ... we were piped down to our action quarters about 3.30pm on the Wednesday afternoon, and we had nothing but ship's biscuit until it was all over.

> We don't know much about it, only we kept smiling ... we saw the smoke from the German ships ... I was in the shell-room and saw nothing of the fight. Down below we could hear our own guns firing, and the sound of the enemy shells was like the sound of the big drum ... when the kettledrum is on a noisy crescendo.

Only the gun-layers, navigators and those directing the firing were aware that the end was nigh for the *Warspite*. Fortunately, after two full circles, intermittent helm control was restored and the *Warspite* limped northwards ahead of the closing German dreadnoughts.

Then, to Captain Phillpott's delight, Jellicoe's Grand Fleet crossed ahead of them and opened fire. As the Germans retreated, the *Warspite* slipped away in the fading evening light. Ordered back to Rosyth, she survived some wayward torpedoes, fired by waiting U-boats hoping to bag a crippled warship.

Damage to the *Warspite*

Despite the *Warspite*'s battering and 14 fatalities, Harold Scholefield claimed that 'everyone was supremely confident.' Three shell fragment souvenirs were reminders of their extreme jeopardy, and he added, 'I am not so silly as to want to go into action again, but when it does come I shall go in again.'[7]

By early evening most of the British fleet was in position, facing south, ready to pursue and attack. But with the trap primed to be sprung, Admiral Jellicoe hesitated, possibly on hearing rumours of U-boats in the area. The retreating Germans did a sudden and surprising about-turn, running broadside past Jellicoe, apparently trying to escape to the Baltic. In the next ten minutes they suffering 27 'heavy hits' whilst inflicting just two. But Jellicoe lost further time as the Germans turned again to retreat south, and the advantage dissipated as darkness and mist closed in.[8]

Far astern of the British fleet, 19-year-old Seaman William Stewart, a former pupil at Hillhouse School and 'a splendid footballer' saw none of this action.[9] He was serving on the battle cruiser HMS *Black Prince* which had become detached from the main fleet. Sometime during the misty evening, the *Black Prince* sighted a line of battleships ahead and sailed towards them, assuming them to be British. They weren't.

Painting by Irwin Bevan of HMS *Warspite* during the Battle of Jutland

Brilliantly lit by half-a-dozen searchlights, the *Black Prince* was raked from stern to stem by a tornado of shells and lay a helpless wreck before she could even fire a shot in reply. As she drifted down the German line, ship after ship opened up on her ... the *Black Prince* ... blowing up with a tremendous explosion, vanishing with all hands.[10]

Meanwhile, zigzagging south, the German High Seas Fleet attempted to escape across the rear of the British Grand Fleet, which was screened by the British 4th Destroyer Flotilla. Leading the Flotilla was HMS *Tipperary*, captained by 44-year-old Charles John Wintour of Clayton West, son of a former vicar of that parish. He had an unenviable task as poor visibility favoured opportunist counter-punches by the fleeing Germans over co-ordinated British attacks.

At about 11.20pm, the *Tipperary* spotted the shadowy outlines of three four-funnelled vessels to starboard. From the bridge, Captain Wintour made the challenge, but the *Tipperary* was instantly floodlit by searchlights from all three ships. They were German dreadnoughts, among

The *Warspite*, holed by an exploding shell

them SMS *Westfalen*. A blizzard of shellfire flashed into the *Tipperary*, the first salvo sweeping away the bridge and Captain Wintour with it. The *Tipperary* fired both her torpedoes, but she was a flaming wreck within minutes. The lifeboats were smashed and a few of her crew took to the life-rafts. They could only accommodate a handful and most had to take their chance in the sea. From her crew of 197 almost 180 were eventually lost. [11]

On the west wall of Clayton West Parish Church is a memorial to Captain Charles John Wintour, under a window dedicated to his father, a former vicar of the parish.
The memorial depicts HMS *Tipperary* and the text commemorates Captain Wintour's courage at the Battle of Jutland. It was unveiled on 19 May 1919 by Admiral Tyrwhitt, himself a distinguished naval veteran and future Admiral of the Fleet.

The remaining ships of the 4th Destroyer Flotilla, now led by Commander Walter Allen of HMS *Broke*, attacked at short range, sinking the light cruiser SMS *Frauenlob* and inflicting severe damage and casualties on several German dreadnoughts, but also suffering heavy losses in return.

At 11.40pm a shell strike to the *Broke* killed 50 of her crew including the helmsman whose body fell on the wheel, turning the ship hard to port on a collision course with HMS *Sparrowhawk*.

Seaman gunner on the *Sparrowhawk* was Norman Medley, who lived at the Waggoners Arms on Manchester Road in Huddersfield. At that moment, unaware of the impending disaster, he was gazing in awe at the last rites of the *Tipperary*, remarking to his mate that the starlight, searchlights, gun flashes and flames, punctuated by her exploding ammunition, were '... just like being in Greenhead Park on Whit Tuesday. Then', recalled Norman, 'the crash came.'

HMS *Broke* rammed into the side of the *Sparrowhawk* at 28 knots, wedging the ships together. A third destroyer, HMS *Contest* then ploughed into the *Sparrowhawk* sheering off her stern and jamming her rudder. The *Contest* steamed way, but it was half an hour before, amidst straining engines and crunching steel plates, the *Broke* and *Sparrowhawk* were separated, the *Broke* taking 30 of the *Sparrowhawk*'s crew with her.

Norman Medley remained aboard the *Sparrowhawk* which, with its rudder inoperative, was restricted to circling. The burning beacon of the *Tipperary* continued to attract dangerous attention to the vicinity until it sank shortly after 2am. Around 4am the shape of a German ship was sighted.

HMS *Broke*, the Destroyer Leader that collided with HMS *Sparrowhawk* at Jutland

Assuming that they were about to be sunk, Norman and the remaining crew gathered to say their prayers, and even discussed 'what it must be like to be dead.' To their great joy, the enemy vessel did not appear to see them and sailed on. As dawn approached, the sound of gunfire became less frequent and more distant as the two fleets disengaged, but the *Sparrowhawk* was gradually sinking.

At 6.10am the strains of *It's a long way to Tipperary* were heard drifting across the ocean. It was a raft of 26 men from the *Tipperary*. Five were already dead, and the rest were almost comatose from exposure. They clambered aboard the *Sparrowhawk* where three more passed away. For the rest it appeared to be merely a stay of execution. Then, shortly before 7am, another ship approached.[12]

It was HMS *Marksman*. The survivors transferred ships and the *Marksman* attempted to tow the *Sparrowhawk* to safety, but the ropes broke in the growing swell and with German submarines in the vicinity it was safer to abandon her. The *Marksman* fired 18 shells into the *Sparrowhawk* and she disappeared beneath the waves.

Of the previous seven hours, Norman Medley commented: '... it was pretty good sport until we got sunk.' It was less fun for his parents and wife who endured six days of 'dreadful anxiety' before hearing any news about him.[13] The report of Norman's experience, printed in the *HDE* a week after the battle, inaccurately stated that the *Sparrowhawk* was 'rammed ... by an enemy ship', the full truth a casualty of the propaganda war.[14]

The battle was less eventful for Edward Brook of Huddersfield, Lieutenant-Commander of the destroyer HMS *Lizard*. Part of the ten-strong First Destroyer Flotilla, the *Lizard* had helped to screen the 5th Battle Squadron on its perilous run to the south and then to screen the First Battle Cruiser Squadron, including Beatty's flagship, HMS *Lion*, as they turned and headed north. Lieutenant-Commander Brook was mentioned in dispatches for the excellence of his command and for the *Lizard*'s part in the battle.[15]

Return to Port

After over 40 hours at sea, Huddersfield's Maurice Booth and Harry Senior returned to Rosyth with the *Lion* and the remaining battle cruisers on the morning of 2 June. Repairs to the *Lion* took until 19 July. She had been hit fourteen times, made five hits on German ships and suffered 99 dead and 51 wounded during the battle.

Miraculously after its collision with the *Sparrowhawk*, HMS *Broke* made it home. The last British ship to return to harbour, it docked on the Tyne at 8am on Saturday 3 June. In total, Britain lost three battle cruisers, four armoured cruisers and eight destroyers, whilst Germany lost one battle cruiser one dreadnought, four light cruisers and five destroyers.[16]

Both sides claimed victory from the inconclusive outcome. The *HDE* reported that Britain had lost 14 vessels, not 15 and increased German losses from 11 to 18.[17] Of the surviving ships, Germany's had suffered much greater damage. In the short term, the battle had consolidated Britain's dominance of the sea and of the North Sea in particular. The blockade was secure, and that was valuable enough for now. But Jutland was also a blow to Britain's naval self-assurance in the longer term. This was not the anticipated rout – another Trafalgar – to boost morale. The Royal Navy was undefeated, but not undefeatable.

There was a further blow to national morale in the North Sea the following Monday, 5 June 1916. HMS *Hampshire*, a Devonshire armoured class cruiser that had served at Jutland, was en route for Russia when it struck a mine west of the Orkneys. It sank with no survivors. On board was the Secretary of State for War, Lord Kitchener.[18]

Chapter 15

Sport and Leisure

Theatres and Cinemas

In 1914, Huddersfield, in common with most Edwardian towns and cities, had an extensive entertainment industry. Its well-appointed theatres staged plays, pantomimes, musicals and music hall variety shows, its picture houses screened the latest silent movies and newsreels, and it had numerous music societies, orchestras and brass bands.

Huddersfield had four main theatres. The Hippodrome on Queensgate was originally The Riding School. Built in 1846, it was converted into a theatre with a capacity of 2000 in 1905. The Palace Theatre on Kirkgate opened in 1909 and had a capacity of 1614. The Theatre Royal on Ramsden Street was adapted from a Lecture Hall in 1859. Photographs suggest a capacity of about 850. The Victoria Hall on Buxton Road was formerly a Temperance Hall.

Of the town's several picture houses, The Cinema, between Longroyd Bridge and Lockwood, and the Olympia in Fitzwilliam Street, both opened in 1912. The Olympia re-opened as The Star in 1916. The Empire, situated on John William Street, and the Lockwood Picture Palace both opened in 1915. They were among the few leisure venues to open during World War I, indicative of the growing popularity of moving pictures. The Picturedrome in Buxton Road was another popular venue. All the theatres and cinemas ran weekly programmes of entertainment, providing an abundance of choices that only dwindled after the advent of television. All would contribute to and be affected by the war in a variety of ways.[1]

The Hippodrome Theatre (left and centre) and Palace Theatre (right)

The Empire Cinema on John William Street (left) and
entrance to the Picturedrome on Buxton Road (right)

The theatres' first contribution to the war effort came on 13 August 1914 when the Hippodrome Theatre offered free admission to the wives of regular and territorial troops to see the popular play *The Pride of Byzantia*.[2] Such treats became a feature of the war. On Friday nights wounded soldiers from local war hospitals attended the Hippodrome, each receiving a box of matches, a packet of cigarettes and chocolate during the interval. Along with the cars and ambulances that transported them, their evenings were paid for by collections at other performances.[3]

Theatrical producers were quick to mine the rich and emotive seam of wartime subjects, and a fortnight after war was declared, the Hippodrome staged the new play, *Devil-May-Care*, 'a stirring military drama.' The *HDE*, which routinely reviewed and publicised the week's entertainments, commented …

> It is only to be expected that there should be a great demand for all plays dealing with military life and historical subjects during the present war. JA Campbell's 'Devil-May-Care' will quite rightly appeal to a large section of the public, for it presents the noblest side of character, grit, and determination in the face of great dangers.

That week's competition for *Devil-May-Care* from the Picturedrome included …

> … an excellent series of war pictures which everyone should see … scenes of enthusiasm in England, France, Belgium and Russia as men leave for the front and not even our enemies are neglected, though naturally, they are by the audiences in the matter of applause, which so far as the displays of the allies were concerned, was very vigorous.[4]

Theatres and cinemas were ideal for dissemination of wartime propaganda and appeals for recruits were commonplace. In April 1915, for example, such appeals were interspersed with the music of Harry Lauder's Pipe Band at the Victoria Hall. Sometimes the propaganda was integral to the performance, none more so than *Remember Belgium* in July 1915, when the Hippodrome was transformed into a contemporary battlefield …

> … during one scene there is a tremendous "bombardment," and such a lavish expenditure of gunpowder … that the whole theatre smells of it.

The villain was a German spy, played so convincingly by Mr Percy Brown that he was subjected to the audible condemnation of the audience.' The heroine was a Belgian Red Cross nurse, and the hero, a colonel in the British army, made 'several patriotic appeals for recruits.'[5]

In Time of War by C Watson Mill, performed at the Hippodrome in March 1916, was similarly patriotic. Germans spies tried to purloin confidential documents entrusted to the British captain of a wireless station, endangering the garrison, until 'British pluck' triumphed over 'German cunning' and the garrison was saved.[6]

By July 1915 the *HDE* reviewer was finding the surfeit of touring patriotic dramas wearisome.

> Mr Willard has gone for the South African war for his action, but nevertheless he has been able to introduce the ubiquitous German spy, without whose presence no military drama apparently would at present be complete.[7]

In January 1916, the reviewer was delighted that the Hippodrome's Christmas pantomime *Beauty and the Beast* avoided 'those now tiring jokes about the Kaiser and his huns.'[8]

It was a temporary lull. The Hippodrome's second pantomime of the season, *Little Red Riding Hood*, featured Miss Florence Eden as Robin Hood singing a patriotic song 'in the uniform of a British officer', with her chorus bedecked in the flags of the Allies.[9] The flags were unfurled again for 1917's reprise of *Beauty and the Beast*. They featured in the tableau finale alongside 'a parade of women workers' and 'a fine patriotic display in military uniforms' as the ensemble and audience sang *Land of Hope and Glory*. The propaganda was mixed with some pertinent satire.

> There is a food queue, and as the Food Controller has not had time to provide a remedy this ends disastrously for the shopkeeper.[10]

Across town at the Palace Theatre, *Dick Whittington* included a 'naval song on the deck of H.M.S. Iron Duke', the dreadnought battleship and flagship of the British Grand Fleet.[11] In the Hippodrome's

second offering of the season, Cinderella's journey to the Ball – by motor coach – was delayed whils
the Fairy Godmother inveigled some coupons out of the Petrol Controller and recycled the 'necessar
material from among the vegetables and rodents.'[12]

The most overt propaganda in the theatres came on the second anniversary of the war, 4 Augus
1916. A resolution was submitted to both of the large Friday night houses at the Palace Theatre …

> … of the inflexible determination to continue the war to a victorious end, as approved by th
> Government … a solemn declaration of the unity of the nation.[13]

Music Hall variety shows were popular antidotes to wartime burdens. Their flexible forma
provided multiple opportunities for satire and propaganda, and they raised a great deal of mone
for war charities. There was a rare treat when 69-year-old comedian JW Rowley appeared at th
Hippodrome in a charity matinee in May 1916. Rowley had performed at Huddersfield's first theatre
the Cambridge Music Hall in Upperhead Row, in the 1860s, and progressed to a successful professiona
career that included a season at the Middlesex Music Hall, Drury Lane. In the 1880s he returned to
Huddersfield to manage his own theatre, Rowley's Empire in St Peter's Street which opened in 188(
and, from 1896 until it was demolished in 1904, offered both stage and screen entertainment. Rowle
remained 'the people's idol.'

> … it is no exaggeration to say that many of those present, especially the older members of th
> audience, went with the primary object of hearing once again the artist who delighted them
> thirty, forty, or even fifty years ago. The prolonged ovation which greeted his entrance upon
> the stage visibly affected artist and audience alike.

Rowley's performances of 1860s favourites *Stay High* and *The Huddersfield Alphabet* showed that 't
… a remarkable degree he retains those powers which have won fame for him in the past.'[14]

Pre-war, travelling circuses had been in decline, supplanted by the popularity of music hall. A rar
exception was *Broncho Bill's Wild West Show* which attracted large crowds to the Great Norther
Street Fairground in April 1918. They were treated to Japanese jugglers, bare-back riders, horse
dancing waltzes and polkas, tumblers, a high-wire act and a clown, although the finale, an 'attack b
Indians on a stage coach', lacked impact owing to a shortage of 'natives', as several of the 'tribe' wer
serving at the front.[15]

Whilst live entertainment had the flexibility to reference the war, attendances at the picture house
were boosted by regular newsreels from the front line. A typical programme was shown at Lockwoo
Picture Palace in May 1916, when a Sexton Blake detective adventure, *The Great Cheque Fraud* wa
supported by Keystone Kops romp, *Her Winning Punch*, and an official war film, *The Destruction o
a German Blockhouse*.[16]

The censored war films concentrated on Allied successes but left local people under no illusion
about conditions in the front line. Two of the earliest were *Fruits of Victory on the Somme*, show
in August 1916, and *The Battle of the Somme*, shown the following month at the Empire and at th
Birkby Palladium.

> The pictures give a vivid impression of the terrible five days' bombardment of the Germa
> lines previous to the advance itself. Then come the fruits of victory – prisoners, still dazed b
> the heavy bombardment, contrasting with the happier faces of their captors. But the patho
> of victory is only too evident as we see the wounded – pathetic bandaged bits of humanity –
> brought down from the front line trenches … this part of the film shows with what wonderfu
> promptitude our wounded soldiers are treated.

After watching *The Battle of the Somme* Lloyd George commented:

> If the exhibition of this film all over the world does not end war God help civilisation.[17]

In February 1918 the film *Battle of the Ancre* gave locals a sight of tanks 'clambering over Germar
trenches … one could not get a better impression of their power.'[18] By then several multi-part wa
serials were doing the rounds, including *The Secret of the Submarine* which ran to 15 parts over 1
weeks, and the *Pathé History of the War* which ran for over 20 weeks.

Huddersfield's classical music organisations struggled on through the war, handicapped by the loss of members to the forces, reduced opportunities to rehearse owing to long working hours in the war-related industries, and additional home and family responsibilities, particularly among the female members. By October 1917, 17 members of the Philharmonic Society were serving abroad. The remainder performed strongly but the 'many vacant seats' at their Town Hall concert of that autumn were part of a wider trend.[19] Dr Bairstow, adjudicator of the 'Mrs Sunderland' singing competitions, where attendances were also 'sparse', offered an explanation:

> People nowadays want some form of relaxation that calls for no mental effort; they like to go where they could smoke and not have to think. A picture house, a music hall, or light opera was quite good enough for them. In this town, above all others that state of things ought not to be.

Most music festivals were mothballed during the war, but Huddersfield's annual 'Mrs Sunderland' competitions continued. First held in 1889, when they were funded by proceeds from the concert to celebrate the Golden Wedding of esteemed Brighouse soprano, Susannah Sunderland, the 30th annual competition was held in 1918. There were understandably fewer entrants compared to pre-war contests, including just two male voice choirs – Brighouse and Holme Valley – and six bass soloists, but the drop in choir boy entrants to eight was 'not so readily explained.'[20]

The Huddersfield Amateur Operatic Society was sustained partly through its commitment to donate a percentage of its profits to the War Relief Fund. In April 1916 the society was able to donate £105.[21] The Huddersfield Choral Society, founded in 1836 and reputedly one of the best in the country, followed the Operatic Society's example. Jolted by a loss of £39 in the season of 1916-17, the Choral Society promised that future profits would be divided between various war charities. They also adopted a more populist programme in 1917-18, highlighted by the visit of Sir Edward Elgar to conduct them in singing his most challenging work, *Dream of Gerontius*. Elgar was following a line of famous composers – Ebenezer Prout, Coleridge Taylor, Dr Wilfred Davies and Sir Hubert Parry – in conducting the Choral Society, and was extremely impressed by them. This momentous occasion was celebrated when the Society performed *Dream of Gerontius* for their 175th Anniversary concert in 2011.[22]

The Huddersfield Glee and Madrigal Society was another to adapt to wartime challenges. They lost many 'old subscribers' early in the war, but fears about their future were allayed when their programme for 1915-16 restored their subscription numbers.[23] A succession of superb performances persuaded their well-connected President, Charles Sykes, to arrange a London tour of prestigious war-charity concerts. After an extremely successful visit in November 1916, they were invited back in 1917 to perform a series of pre-Christmas concerts, primarily for wounded soldiers, by Prime Minister, Lloyd George.[24] They sang in Westminster Central Hall, accompanied by the London Symphony Orchestra, and became the first provincial choir to sing oratorio in Westminster Abbey, making an 'impressive impact' with Handel's *Messiah*, which was 'not so well known in the south.' A collection in the Abbey raised £54 for the Westminster Hospital, and in total the trip raised £550 for war hospitals, comforts for troops and post-war funds, taking the total raised by the Society to over £3000 since 1914.[25]

Both tours included invitations to 10 Downing Street, where they sang several glees and party songs for Mr and Mrs Lloyd George and 20 guests. They were 'most hospitably entertained', and in 1917 the Prime Minister 'so enjoyed' the *Holmfirth Anthem* that it was reprised at his request.[26] Permitted a 'peep' in the Cabinet Room, one of the singers commented that there were 'many Sunday school classrooms in Huddersfield better fitted up.'[27]

A leading figure in local classical music was Dr Arthur Eaglefield Hull, the organist at Huddersfield Parish Church and the Principal of the Huddersfield College of Music. He arranged and gave numerous lectures and concerts in support of war charities and, in 1918, founded the Huddersfield Music Society. The society's first concert featured Russian tenor Vladimir Rosing, who was described by George Bernard Shaw as one of 'the most extraordinary singers of the 20th Century.' Dr Hull later founded the British Music Society of which the Huddersfield Music Society was an original member, and the

School of Music in Huddersfield, the forerunner to the University of Huddersfield's music department. He wrote several books on music, including *Music: Classical, Romantic and Modern* (1927) some of which was found to be plagiarised, probably through careless omission of source citations. In 1928 humiliated by the criticism, Dr Hull threw himself under a train at Huddersfield Station and died from his injuries.[28]

In October 1917, as a wartime economy, Huddersfield Town Council decided to discontinue band performances in Greenhead Park. The town's many music-lovers were appalled, Mr VH Goldthorpe of Lockwood writing:

> ... there can be no doubt that we need more music, not less, during these stressful times. In this great test of national endurance, when so much depends on the maintenance of a steady, cheerful spirit in the civilian masses, any form of harmless diversion is worthy of encouragement ... Good music is not only a refuge from war worry, it is also to many people a unique solace in sorrow, and a most valuable source of spiritual stimulus and re-invigoration ... foremost among those amenities that refresh and re-equip the civilian in war-time.[29]

The Council relented 'as a tonic for war-weariness.' In 1918, addressing the shortage of musicians, several local brass bands amalgamated 'to make up one really good one' and performed some extremely popular promenade concerts in the Park.[30]

The Council had come under fire in 1915 from Irving Lee, local Branch Secretary of the Musicians Union, who cited hypocrisy and unfairness in the authorities' approach to musical performances.

> I notice the council have engaged Army bands as usual. It is rather surprising after seeing all the hoardings and every available space covered with appeals for every fit man wanted, etc. to find that the Guards, Marines, and others are allowed to travel about the country playing in parks, on piers and at exhibitions, and so displacing civilian musicians who are suffering from the present conditions enough, without being further subjected to army band competition. If it is true that men are wanted so very badly, why are the above bands not doing the work they are paid for, seeing they qualify for a pension, and are clothed, fed, and their instruments found by the State ... Most of our members (A.M.U.) have had to leave their work in theatres, music halls, and other places of amusement to serve in the trenches. On coming home wounded they found army bands playing in parks, exhibitions, and even filling in at theatre work which they have had to leave. Many theatres are closing for the summer months and many seaside resorts are, through the war, dispensing with musicians this time.[31]

Fund-Raising

Crowds and audiences provided fund-raising opportunities for Huddersfield's many war charities. The town's entertainment industry contributed a steady stream of donations, often splitting the proceeds between worthy wartime funds which routinely included the town's prolific Women's Committee, led by the tireless Mayoress, Mrs Mary Blamires. In August 1915 she booked three patriotic films for the Picturedrome, raising £68. 9 November 1915 was 'Cinema Ambulance Day', with proceeds to the Red Cross Fund.[32] 'Patriotic Concerts' across much of the local musical and theatrical range became a feature of the social calendar. Famous contralto Dame Clara Butt, whose concerts for service charities earned her the DBE, performed a couple of times.[33] Other visiting performers included the Royal Marines (Portsmouth Division) Band which played in Greenhead Park on 22 July 1916, raising £300 despite the hostility cited by Irving Lee.[34] Traditional events, such as the annual 'sings' at Golcar and Longwood contributed similarly, the 19th Longwood Sing helping the 1915 Longwood Festival to raise £376.[35]

Occasionally, local performers raised funds for non-local organisations. As part of 'Blinded Heroes Day' on 3 June 1916, a Variety Show at the Palace Theatre contributed to the town's total of £1187 for the national 'Blinded Soldiers and Sailors Hostel Fund.'[36] In April 1918 Josiah Lockwood of Linthwaite took a Huddersfield Concert Party to Kirkbymoorside where they performed five concerts in three days including one at the local Welburn Hall War Hospital, to raise funds for the North Yorkshire town.[37]

The emphasis of local sport also shifted significantly towards fund-raising. The Huddersfield, Meltham and Outlane golf clubs all held several members' fund-raising competitions[38] and on 29 July 1915 the *HDE*'s golf correspondent lamented:

> Golf for charity seems to be the only justifiable form of golf these days. The financial result is more important than the golf itself.

Huddersfield Golf Club at Fixby viewed from the 10th tee.

There were several charity bowls matches on Huddersfield greens which helped to pay for two £500 motor ambulances donated by the Yorkshire Amateur Bowling Association to the French Red Cross Society.[39] Most notable were professionals v amateurs events at Taylor Hill WMC, Berry Brow and the King's Arms, Moldgreen on successive evenings in September 1917.[40]

The grouse shooting seasons went ahead as usual, but from the 'Glorious 12th' August 1915, many moors were shot … solely to supply homes for wounded soldiers.'[41] Local cyclists attended National Cycle Union meetings which raised £700 for prisoner-of-war funds in 1917.[42]

With cricket's County Championship suspended from 1915 to 1918, Huddersfield's outstanding international cricketers, Wilfred Rhodes, George Hirst, Percy Holmes, Schofield Haigh and Alonzo Drake played as weekend league professionals and were in popular demand for a proliferation of midweek charity matches. All five played at Lascelles Hall in September 1917 when GH Hirst's XI played W Rhodes' XI for the benefit of Lepton War Hospital.[43] Similar matches were played at Fartown, and the local stars also travelled to play charity matches on numerous club grounds across industrial Yorkshire and Lancashire.[44] In August 1915, Batley Cricket Club hosted a match between the a Local Tradesmen's XI and GH Hirst's XI which featured the usual array of professional cricketers, plus Huddersfield's international northern rugby union stars, Harold Wagstaff and Johnny Rogers.[45] The local cricket stars featured in one of the biggest charity cricket events of the war, a 'carnival of cricket' at Bradford Park Avenue in August 1918, which opened with a match between Yorkshire and 'An England XI.'

Regular wartime collections were made during matches at Huddersfield's Fartown rugby ground, until the club suspended operations for two years in the spring of 1917, and at Leeds Road, home of Huddersfield Town. In September 1916 Leeds Road hosted the 'Huddersfield Military Police Sports' which attracted a crowd of 4000 and raised several hundred pounds for local war relief funds. Participation was restricted to soldiers and munitions workers, but there were 480 entries from as far afield as Derby County Athletics Club and Lincoln.[46] Cricket and football matches were also routinely used to disseminate propaganda and to appeal for recruits.

For all their fundraising, most local sports and entertainment organisations led a hand-to-mouth existence during the war, and were further encumbered by the much-loathed Entertainment Tax introduced by the Government as a 'temporary' wartime measure in 1916 but not repealed until 1960. Known locally as the 'killjoy tax', it took a percentage of the entrance money from all leisure venues, eroding finances and goodwill, and reducing attendances, particularly in cinemas. The district bowls committee responded by abandoning all entrance fees to cup matches until the semi-finals stage, whilst some cricket clubs circumnavigated the tax by replacing their entrance charge with voluntary collections round the ground.[47]

Sport
Huddersfield Northern Union Rugby Football Club (NURFC)

At the outbreak of war, British sport was enjoying a golden summer. Locally, large crowds basked in the sun at cricket and bowls matches, and the captain of Huddersfield's northern union rugby football club, Harold Wagstaff, was a national sporting hero.

Captaining the Great Britain team on their tour of Australasia, Wagstaff was the toast of the game after spearheading a remarkable 14-6 triumph in the third and deciding Ashes Test Match at the Sydney Cricket Ground. Injury-hit Britain were reduced to eleven men for much of the second half and at one point just nine. Known as the Rorke's Drift Test Match, it remains the game's most famous victory.[48]

The tourists were in New Zealand when war was declared, unaware of the furore in Britain about whether any form of football should continue. On 10 August 1914 the *Athletic News* presented the view that, after much soul-searching, prevailed in the professional association and northern union codes:

> Our games may only be 'trinkets' but they will tend to keep the life of the nation on old lines and they will assist to keep the body fit and the mind calm until such as right is vindicated. Courage, determination and patience are demanded of non-combatants, and sport tends to the development of these virtues. Let us not hastily give up that which has served a free people so well.

The amateur Rugby Football Union took the opposite view. RFU secretary Rowland Hill disparaged the professional codes as 'entirely governed by commercial principles.' Leading Yorkshire RFU official James Millar felt that 'playing fields were being desecrated at the present time.'

Players from all codes of football who volunteered to join the forces received universal acclaim but the northern union season proceeded with a majority of clubs close to full strength.[49]

Huddersfield's internationals arrived home on 26 September 1914 to rejoin a team that had made an inconsistent start to the season.[50] They galvanised the team, and from mid-October Huddersfield embarked on an excellent run, laying down a marker with a Yorkshire Cup Final victory over Hull at Headingley in November. It was, however, a muted occasion, the public pre-occupied by the growing magnitude of the war.

> Few favours were worn, there were no freak costumes; bugles, rattles, and other adjuncts of a crowd at a final were all conspicuous by their absence.[51]

The matches were, nevertheless, competitive, as demonstrated by the Fartowners' long-running feud with Bramley which resurfaced in February 1915:

> … after Huddersfield's meeting with the men from the Barley Mow the only feeling is one … of disgust. When Huddersfield went to Bramley in the earlier part of the season we had a really sporting game in which the players all tried to play football and it was hoped that the bad old days were over … however … Anderson twice tackled Wagstaff when the Huddersfield captain did not have the ball, and one time hit Wagstaff with his fist and the other time used his boot.

Later in the game, Anderson was 'heavily tackled.'

> … this so annoyed him that he rained blows on Longstaff, who … replied in kind. Huddersfield have an excellent record in the matter of reported players, a record that would have been practically untarnished in recent years but for the provoking nature of Bramley.[52]

Huddersfield won the match 79-0, part of a 37 match unbeaten run. The Yorkshire League title was secured and the next obstacle was Leeds in the Championship Final.

On 23 April 1915, the evening before the game, Wagstaff and Fred Longstaff were walking along New Street when a local tailor approached them. He offered Wagstaff the best suit in his shop if Huddersfield beat Leeds the following day. Longstaff complained: 'You fellows always think about the backs, never about the forwards. What do I get if we win?' The tailor promised Longstaff that if he scored a try he could also have a suit. During the game Wagstaff was through with only the full back to beat, when he heard a voice at his shoulder shouting 'Suit! Suit! Suit!' Wagstaff turned to see Longstaff charging alongside in support, committed the full back, fed the perfect pass and Longstaff duly planted the ball down between the posts. They both had a suit, Huddersfield winning 35-2.

The following Saturday the Fartowners beat St Helens 37-3 in the Challenge Cup Final to become only the second team to win all four available trophies in the same season. Huddersfield's 'Team of All Talents' had guaranteed their place in the game's history.[53]

Douglas Clark's Championship Winners Medal 1914-15

The club's unprecedented success was a fillip for anyone who was …

> … proud to see Huddersfield stand high, whether it be in athletics, in music and in song, or in the weightier matters of manufacture, education, and intellectual, moral and political import.
>
> What a glorious coping-stone … would be the enlistment of the men who have brought honour to Huddersfield … to set the example to large numbers of footballers … and of football followers, also, by offering their strength and courage to help to defeat the Huns![54]

Even the most vocal critics of wartime sport could see the impact on the morale of the town, but it was the last season of professional football for five seasons. During the summer of 1915, the northern union and association football authorities banned payments to players until the war was over. There was to be no formal northern union competition. The Football League also adapted, reorganising into regional leagues, with Huddersfield Town playing in the Midland Section. Following Football League rules, Town's players were only allowed expenses amounting to 3rd class rail fares and, to avoid accusations that players were 'war shirkers' living off 'back-handers', they had to have employment outside the game.[55]

With no supplementary income, most professional players of both codes found alternative sources of income. Some of Huddersfield's rugby stars picked up occasional funds from other sports. Quicksilver half back Johnny Rogers won £15 prize money in a 70 yards handicap at Salford Football Ground.[56] In July 1918 forward Arthur Swinden used his power to knock out Oxford boxer Chris Lake at an evening of bouts in a club on Colne Road.[57]

Most players found more regular income. Others had already signed up for the forces, including Fred Longstaff who joined the 16th Battalion of the West Yorkshire Regiment – the Pals Battalion from his native Bradford. This was one of many such battalions formed on the idea that lads who were friends were more likely to support and fight for one another. It was not anticipated that they might also die together, leaving whole communities bereft.[58]

With no players to pay, and only friendly matches to attract the crowds, the Fartown club slashed admission prices by 50% for the 1915-16 season.[59] The available players gave their services for expenses only, which sustained the club for fans and players alike. The team changed week-on-week, determined partly by who was home on leave. An unofficial 'War Emergency League' table was published, in which Huddersfield finished 6th out of 24 clubs, and victories still carried a degree of kudos, notably Huddersfield's win at bogey ground Salford – as rare as 'successful offences by the Hun Kiel Canal Fleet.'[60] But competitive rugby was now reserved for the encouragement of schoolboy and junior teams which were more vital than ever to the game's future. The *HDE* was incredulous that the Northern Union had grasped this particular nettle.

> Whatever other faults the Northern Union big-wigs may possess, too precipitate action has never been one of their pet sins [under] President "Wait and See" ... The aim is to construct a "pathway" for the schoolboy player which will extend right along to the entrance to senior league football ... thoroughly reviving the village club and junior clubs in every town's suburb.[61]

Meanwhile, 'friendly' wartime rugby did not prevent Huddersfield's November visit to Bramley descending into its traditional brutality.

> ... each of the Huddersfield players in turn became something worse than the savages who wrecked Louvain.
> How it was Ward [the Bramley half back] survived to finish the match was a surprise to some. The man who takes a running kick at an opponent just in front of the referee must consider himself fortunate to be allowed to continue.
> ... the suburban Leeds club [should] ... enforce upon its playing members the necessity of playing football as a sport.[62]

Huddersfield Town's matches also degenerated into occasional violence, most notably a mass brawl which saw two players sent off against Bradford City in 1917, but this was an isolated example.

In December 1915 the *Athletic News* noted that 786 northern union professionals had enlisted for the forces, along with thousands of spectators. In September 1916 the *HDE* listed 17 Huddersfield first team players who had joined the forces. In addition, 'practically every reserve team player' had gone. Of the 1914-15 Team of all Talents, full backs Major Holland and Illingworth were in reserved occupations and Arthur Swinden remained from the forwards, but Huddersfield made up the rest with 'any Northern Union or Rugby Union player ... who has ability and is living in the district and wanting a game.' These included guest players and local amateurs, although as the local amateur leagues were in abeyance even these players were short of form and fitness. Meanwhile, some of Huddersfield's stars guested for other clubs, depending on the locations of their military training camps, or where they lived.[63] Association football operated on similar lines, and Huddersfield Town benefited when Chelsea full back F Tye offered his services as he was working in Huddersfield.[64]

By the summer of 1916 Huddersfield's northern union rugby club was struggling financially, a loss of £455 partly explained by a fall in membership from 1295 to 788. By comparison, Huddersfield Town, despite an inevitable drop in receipts – from £3325 to £1288 – broke even, benefiting from the context of playing in a recognised league, and by their success in finishing third in the 14-club Midland Section.[65] Town's playing record reflected the increasing problem of player availability for away matches. They won 11 of their 13 home matches, but won just two and lost nine away, including a 5-1 defeat against runners-up Sheffield United, when Town played the first half hour with nine men after which they were 3-0 down.[66]

Huddersfield NURFC limped on into 1916-17. There were now fewer fixtures requiring long railway journeys, but fulfilling them became an increasing struggle. On 23 September they were still looking for players ten minutes before kick-off at Batley and predictably lost, 16-7. The *HDE* asked supporters to ...

... charitably remember that a full hard week's work – in some cases long hours of exhausting overtime – does not conduce to fast movements on a football field ... when personal inclination must often turn to rest rather than vigorous football. The pace of football today is a war-time pace, and, in justice to our munition players everywhere, don't let us overlook this fact.[67]

Seeking further solace after a fifth straight defeat, the *HDE* commented:

We have seen the days when Huddersfield could win, like sportsmen, and it was even more pleasing to see that they could take their gruel, and it was a stiff dose, with a smiling face and unflagging spirit.

... I am sure every Huddersfield man on the ground would be delighted with the way the wearers of the claret and gold accepted such an unprecedented situation.[68]

Reinforced by a few rugby-playing guards stationed on the east coast, they finally won at the sixth time of asking, 28-2 at York.[69] November's match at Bramley started late owing to delays on the railway,[70] and the 'Northern Union fiasco' of 25 November 1916 showed a game on its knees.

The players were "all mixed up" so that many clubs had foreign help, three games were abandoned because of the weather, in one match only fifty three minutes' play took place, in another the players "went in" because of the rain – an unheard of thing in serious football – and refused to come out again; whilst still another match [Bramley v Hunslet] ended in a free fight.

Huddersfield's match at Hull KR started 15 minutes late and ended 22 minutes early as it was 'too dark to continue.'[71] Seven days later Huddersfield's return match against York kicked off with only 19 of the requisite 26 players on the park, of whom York had eight.[72]

The Football League, also suffering escalating problems of player shortages and late kick-offs, reduced all matches from 45 to 40 minutes each half.[73] This did not prevent the abandonment of Huddersfield Town's Boxing Day fixture in 1917 when Lincoln City's train arrived too late to even start the match.

Compounding the problems, Christmas 1916 brought a 50% increase in passenger rail fares and, to prioritise fuel for transportation of troops, horses, munitions and other supplies for the front, a reduced service.

As the players are scattered all over the country in ... munitions, mining, engineering, and other work, heavy travelling expenses are entailed every week.[75]

The final straw for Huddersfield came at Wigan in April 1917. The team's 17-0 defeat was secondary to the presence of seven guest players from Leigh and only three Huddersfield players in 'the most strangely constituted ... ever ... Huddersfield team.'[76]

Huddersfield finished 23rd out of 26 teams in the unofficial War Emergency League table. Interest and crowd numbers had dwindled, and Harry Lodge, the club's representative on the Yorkshire NRU, could not 'see any possibility of fielding a team such as would satisfy our members and supporters.' In addition, the financial losses endangered the club's future; it would be safer to suspend operations. The Fartown committee reluctantly announced that Huddersfield had played its last match of the war. Keighley and Wakefield Trinity did likewise. The Northern Union ...

... regretted Huddersfield's decision and they would gladly welcome the club back into the ranks when normal times returned.[77]

During the summer of 1917 the Northern Union agreed that matches would be 12-a-side for the rest of the war, and set up a relief fund to tide clubs over.[78]

Meanwhile, leading Northern Union players who had enlisted into the army reserve were invited to play for military teams in prestigious rugby union charity matches. The highest profile of these was between a North of England Military XV and an Australian and New Zealand representative side at Headingley in April 1916. The North team included Huddersfield's Harold Wagstaff, Ben Gronow and Douglas Clark, plus Willie Davies, the captain of Leeds, whilst Huddersfield's Tommy Gleeson, best man at Wagstaff's wedding in January 1915, played for the Antipodeans. Harold Wagstaff had previously only seen one rugby union match, but by half time had adapted and in the second half ran half the length of the pitch to score what proved to be the match-winning try.[79]

The war has wrought many changes in our national life, but probably none more striking than the bringing together of Rugby Union and Northern Union football players on common ground.[80]

On 20 May 1916, the North of England Military XV now boasting seven Northern Union players including Fartowners Wagstaff, Gronow and Johnny Rogers, defeated a Welsh side before a crowd of over 15,000 at Goodison Park, home of Everton FC.

Bowing to the inevitable, on 4 October 1916 the RFU reluctantly passed a resolution that:

> Northern Union players can only play with Rugby Union players in bona-fide naval and military teams. Rugby Union teams can play against naval and military teams in which there are Northern Union players ... These rulings only obtain during the war.

The cream of the Huddersfield team was head-hunted by Major Stanley, the Oxford University representative on the RFU committee, and commanding officer of the Army Service Corps (Motor Transport) Unit at Grove Park, near Bromley in south London. Wagstaff and his Huddersfield team mates Albert Rosenfeld, Ben Gronow and Douglas Clark were drafted into the Unit and, during 1916-17 formed the backbone of their rugby union XV. Winning 25 of their 26 matches, and scoring 1110 points whilst conceding just 41, they were not only the best rugby union team in the forces, but probably in the entire country.

Army Service Corps at Grove Park, including Douglas Clark (back right), Ben Gronow (third from right, middle row), Harold Wagstaff (second right, front row) and Major Stanley (front centre)

Albert Rosenfeld

In 1917 the ASC team was posted to various theatres of war – Clark and Gronow went to the western front, Wagstaff to Egypt, and Australian Rosenfeld to serve with the Australian army in Mesopotamia (Iraq), his papers calling him Rosenfield to conceal his Jewish heritage and faith protecting him from victimisation should he be captured. Rosenfeld was to win a silver cup for the 110 yards dash in the 'Convoy Staff Company Sports' in 1917. Of these four great players, only Ben Gronow would come through the war without illness or injury.[81]

Their Huddersfield colleague, Fred Longstaff, served on the western front a year earlier. He was among the 2000 Bradford Pals who went over the top to attack the village of Serre at zero hour on the dreadful first day of the Battle of the Somme. Within an hour 1770 of them had been injured or killed. Fred survived, and on 9 July his battalion took over part of the front on the Leipzig Salient which was 'to be held at all costs.' On 15 July the Germans charged, led by bombers and a new weapon, liquid flame throwers. Fred climbed onto his fire step just as searing flame shot across the ground and over the parapet. Seriously wounded, he was transferred to a nearby field hospital. He died from his wounds on 22 July 1916 and is buried at Blighty Valley Cemetery, Authile Wood.[82]

Fred Longstaff was one of two Huddersfield players to perish.

Fred Longstaff

19-year-old Edward Haigh, a clerk at Huddersfield Railway Station and a forward in the second team was killed in Flanders on 1 June 1915. He is one of 55,000 soldiers whose bodies were never recovered and are commemorated on the Menin Gate at Ypres.[83] Former second team player John Hirst who had emigrated to Canada and was serving in a Canadian battalion, was killed in January 1918. He had also played amateur rugby for Underbank Rangers and cricket for Scholes.

Huddersfield Town Football Club

Huddersfield Town also suffered. Lance-Corporal Larrett Roebuck, a full back signed from the Silverwood colliery team near Rotherham, went to France as part of the 2nd Battalion York and Lancaster Regiment with the BEF in 1914. On 18 October, on the eve of the First Battle of Ypres, his battalion attacked an enemy position near Beaucamps-Ligny. After the attack he was among the 35 men reported killed or missing, one of the first professional footballers to die in action.

Huddersfield Town had been sending Larrett's wife £1 per week since his call-up, but on hearing of his death Arthur Fairclough, the club's secretary-manager, wrote her an apologetic letter explaining that the club could not afford to continue the payments. Indeed, the club was losing money and having to go cap-in-hand to the Football League to ask them for funds to tide them over. To cushion the blow, Town's directors sent her 10s per week out of their own pockets for the next month. A collection among the players of £2 5s, intended as a gift for Larrett when he was next home on leave, was also sent to her.[84]

Larrett Roebuck

Three other Huddersfield Town players were injured on the Somme in 1916. Left back Fred Bullock and centre forward Jack Cock had both joined the Footballers' Battalion. Bullock was struck in the back by shrapnel during fighting at Delville Wood in August, and Cock was injured in October. A letter from Jack Cock, printed in the HDE on 3 November 1916, highlighted the misinformation that could emerge from the chaos and confusion on the battlefields:

I see that it has been in the papers that I have been killed, but, thank goodness, I am quite well and kicking.

Jack had recovered and had been playing football behind the lines in France. He and Fred Bullock survived the war and resumed their careers, although in 1918 Bullock, by then promoted to Corporal, was wounded for a second time.[85]

Sidney James, who played both centre-forward and centre-half for Town in 1915-16, went out to France with the 9th Battalion, KOYLI in 1916 was also injured on the Somme. He too recovered, but perished on 9 April 1917, the first day of the Second Battle of Arras.[86]

Huddersfield Town footballers Jack Cock, Sidney James and Fred Bullock.
Cock and Bullock were both injured on the Somme in 1916. James was killed at Arras in 1917.

Town also mourned the loss of three former players, Privates Jack Cameron, Charles Randall and Leigh Roose. Cameron, who played briefly in 1911, served with the Cameron Highlanders and was killed early in 1916. Randall, who played for the club from 1908-10, served with the Coldstream Guards and Roose, a goalkeeper, played in 1910-11 and served with the Royal Fusiliers. Both were killed on the Somme, Randall on 27 September 1916 and Roose a fortnight later on 7 October.[87]

Despite the losses, injuries and irregular availability of players, and uncertainties about transport and finances, Huddersfield Town fulfilled all their wartime fixtures. They followed their 3rd place finish in the Midland Section of 1915-16 with three more top half finishes – 4th, 8th and 6th in the three subsequent wartime seasons. They were equally competitive in the end-of-season subsidiary competitions against Leeds City, Bradford City and Bradford Park Avenue. Over these four seasons Town played 142 matches, winning 64, drawing 29 and losing 49. The war had confirmed that association football was embedded in Huddersfield's, and indeed Britain's, culture.[88]

Among the many professional and amateur sporting careers prematurely terminated by dreadful injuries was that of promising Wakefield Trinity forward, Ben Johnson, who was remarkably sanguine after being crippled in an explosion.

> It took my foot straight off … It flew up into the air, and I caught it coming down! I never felt it at all, and I have not felt it much up to now. I expect I shall be getting a wooden foot now.[8]

In March 1916 the *HDE* reported a particular interest in footballers and cricketers from the Royal Naval Air Service.

> The reason is simple. The authorities have found that men who have excelled in those games have developed a keener eye and are more competent in the gentle art of bomb-dropping.[90]

In 1917 prominent amateur sportsman, Jack Haigh, son of the Yorkshire and England cricket all-rounder Schofield Haigh, was accepted into the air service, by then known as the Royal Flying Corps. Jack, who played cricket for Armitage Bridge and football for the YMCA, was inducted to the first Royal Flying Corps unit established as a pure fighter squadron. He was killed when his single-seat aircraft crashed on a training flight in the south of England on 15 August 1918. He was 19 years old.[9]

Local sports grounds were used in various ways to assist the military and the war effort in general. Fartown and Leeds Road were used as shooting ranges for the RFA, for drill practice and hosted sports afternoons for recuperating soldiers. From September 1915, Huddersfield Golf Club was also turned over to the local territorials for rifle shooting practice on two afternoons per week.[92]

Shooting skills had improved nationally as the result of sustained initiatives by Lord Roberts to address the problem of abysmal shooting by the British Army in the Boer War. These included development of the miniature rifle, formation of the National Society of Miniature Rifles in 1901, distribution of three million rounds of ammunition to miniature rifle clubs in 1906, a termination of the licence duty for guns used on the premises of affiliated clubs, and a national competition inaugurated in 1908. This was entered by the Huddersfield territorial volunteers.[93]

Crown Green Bowling

Although the less vigorous sports such as golf and bowls also suffered from the loss of young players, they were …

> … not handicapped so severely as the majority of outdoor pastimes … age is no bar, and … the veteran may excel. There are sufficient "non-eligibles" left with us to keep the game alive.[94]

Bowls largely continued as normal, with matches arranged to minimise journey times. Keen interest was sustained, as demonstrated by a controversial Drayton Cup match at Dalton Liberal Club between B Eastwood of Crosland Moor BC and H Lodge of Skelmanthorpe Central BC in June 1916. During the match two spectators bet 50s on the outcome. The gambler who had backed Lodge then called Eastwood to the side of the green for a chat. Subsequently Eastwood bowled so poorly that the scorer, Mr Firth, refused to mark the scores and told the gambler who had supported Eastwood to demand his money back. All bets were declared off and Eastwood suddenly improved and proceeded to win. At the enquiry, the Crosland Moor club distanced itself from the conduct of Eastwood, who was expelled from the competition and suspended from local bowls sine die.[95]

Owing to lack of manpower and resources, the condition and quality of the bowling greens deteriorated along with those at most other sports grounds. In 1917 the Whitsuntide Individual Merit Bowls Competition at Paddock was abandoned as the club was without a groundsman and would be unable to provide food and refreshments.[96] Huddersfield Golf Club experienced similar problems. In the summer of 1915 their greens 'had never been so slow', and the grass around the course was allowed to grow far longer than usual before being cut. Later in the war, as food shortages became acute, parts of a fairway at the club were dug up to make allotments.[97] Scores in the local cricket leagues were lower than usual as bowlers exploited under-prepared pitches and long grass on the outfields reduced the value of batsmen's strokes.

Cricket

With the exception of the Bradford Cricket League, which became a 'wartime sanctuary' for professionals, most cricket leagues across the industrial north were suspended. In the circumstances, Huddersfield's cricket leagues were admirably resilient, surviving the temporary loss of some major clubs to sustain their competitions. In 1915 the Huddersfield Cricket League introduced a play-off system which successfully kept clubs and spectators interested to the end of the season, a gate of 4500 watching an enthralling final tie in which Lockwood (167 all out) beat Slaithwaite (163 all out) by four runs.[98]

In 1916, whilst most clubs no longer employed a professional, there were still 32 active cricket clubs in the district – 12 in the Huddersfield League, 10 in the Huddersfield Central League, six in the Huddersfield Association and four playing friendly matches.[99] Twenty eight of these clubs survived into 1918, but were increasingly reliant on 'young members under military age ... "crocks" [and] munition workers.' Lack of depth in the ranks provided some easy lower-order pickings for the regular bowlers. At Fartown in July 1916 Kirkburton were bowled out for 16 against Huddersfield.[100] Four weeks later Huddersfield, spearheaded by England all-rounder Schofield Haigh, demolished a Lascelles Hall team comprised of 'three of their usual players, four or five lads under military age, and ... novices picked from spectators.' A letter to the *HDE* requested that the League should allocate experienced players evenly among the clubs to make the games more competitive and interesting.[101]

In September 1916 Primrose Hill Cricket Club capitalised on the proliferation of war workers to organise one of the town's first workshop competitions, the club's own team beating the munitions workers of Thomas Broadbent and Sons Ltd in the final.[102]

During the last two summers of the war, local league cricket was continued primarily to provide summertime activity for war workers and to ensure its own survival, as it was felt that 'many clubs would be lost permanently ... were cricket to be dropped altogether.'[103] In 1918, a letter from the front line, asking the *HDE* to publish the full scorecards of local matches, provided a third reason to continue.

> The boys who are far away ... are always anxious to see how their old clubs are faring ... anything we can do for the boys at the front should receive first consideration.[104]

Sports that did not rely on specific team numbers such as cycling, hunting, cross-country running and swimming continued through the war with reduced numbers, although the national Lawn Tennis Association suspended all activities in September 1915.[105]

There was a resurgence in cycling for essential and recreational purposes, in response to the fuel shortage which reduced transport by motor car, tram and train, although a local landlord noted of his cycling clientele that the war had 'cleared the young 'uns off the road.' Countryside pursuits were also sustained, including the weekly runs of the Longwood, Marsh United and Moldgreen United Methodists cross-country clubs, and the Colne Valley, Honley and Holmfirth hunts.[106]

Very few additional leisure opportunities were initiated during the war but, alongside the couple of new cinemas, Huddersfield Chess Club was a rare exception. Re-formed in September 1915, its club rooms at Robinson's Café on John William Street were well attended by members old and new.[107]

Swimming

There was controversy about expensive indoor sporting facilities, although the Huddersfield Rink won the Ice Palace Shield Curling title at Manchester Ice Rink in March 1915.[108] Later in the year the erection of new swimming baths was postponed until after the war, even though the baths at Lockwood and Ramsden Street were well-attended.[109] When Ramsden Street was closed for part of 1917 it was suggested that it should be run by volunteers with unheated water.[110] Despite the promise of a new filtration plant,[111] many locals were far from happy that the town's swimming facilities were …

> … behind the times. For the past twenty years or more swimming has been mostly dormant due mainly to unsympathetic and soulless management.

Swimming baths were about 'health, fitness and well-being' and not built 'solely with the view of paying in a monetary sense.'[112] On Saturdays, Ramsden Street Baths also offered youngsters under 12 the opportunity for a wash 'they did not otherwise get.'[113] There were also compelling counter arguments about prioritising increasingly scarce resources.

> We are urged to avoid spending on what can be done without … When the swimming bath was heated with coal in November I know persons who were shivering before fireless grates unable to obtain delivery of coal.[114]

In May 1918 the Corporation responded to the criticism by giving free passes to junior swimmers who reach 'a certain standard of efficiency.'[115] A good number of these were girls who, along with numerous women, had taken additional opportunities afforded by the absence of men to improve their swimming. In October 1916 the eight races at the Annual Slaithwaite Amateur Swimming Club Gala were exclusively for women and girls. Over the next twelve months the club doubled its membership to 216 and the 1917 event, advertised as a 'Ladies Swimming Gala', left no doubt about the 'great improvement … made by the ladies in the art of swimming.'[116]

It was a similar story at Brighouse where the swimming club 'could not have continued to prosper if it had not been for a strong and enthusiastic ladies' section.' As in so many other walks of life the women had filled the breach and proved to be excellent organisers, not least as 'expert gala promoters.'[117]

By 1918 the acrimony about leisure time activities, particularly rugby and football in the autumn of 1914, was a distant memory. The sports clubs, theatres, cinemas and societies had operated within wartime constraints, withstanding loss of personnel, financial hardship and scarce resources to more than justify the continuation of their activities. Fulfilling their primary recreational functions, they had engaged, entertained and rewarded war-workers and servicemen home on leave. They had provided havens of escape from unrelenting anxieties, and venues for fund-raising, recruitment and the dissemination of propaganda. Reports of their affairs had been eagerly anticipated and discussed by troops at the front.

Perhaps most importantly, they had sustained themselves. With the unavoidable exception of some decimated amateur sports' clubs, facilities had been preserved, resources husbanded, committees maintained, youngsters enthused and developed, and shared interests nourished. All could have withered. The surviving servicemen would return to a community with its sport and leisure infrastructure largely intact.

Chapter 16

Women: Vindication for Emancipation

Women in the Workplace

By February 1918 an estimated 1,400,000 British women were working in jobs that would previously have been done by men, of whom about half were working in munitions.[1] With its influx of local and migrant women workers to the woollen and munitions industries and, later in the war, to the crop-growing 'Land Army', Huddersfield was fully engaged in this social and vocational change.

The Government's first request for women 'to do the work of men who are of military age' was made on 19 March 1915 with the full and vocal backing of the suffragette movement. It elicited an instant' response in many places, 7500 women volunteering across the country.[2] Huddersfield's first recruitment and registration meeting, organised at the Town Hall by the Mayoress Mrs Blamires on 19 April, was a great success. The women were primarily allocated to meet the enormous demand in the woollen and munitions industries, but many were also appointed to a range of unfamiliar roles.[3]

Among the more conspicuous were lady booking clerks who began to work at Huddersfield Railway Station in May 1915, replacing station staff, many of whom had volunteered for the forces. The remaining men chivalrously worked the early and late shifts, whilst the women staffed the kiosks during the day. Later in the year the first women porters were employed at the station. Nationally, the number of women porters increased from three in 1915 to 10,000 in 1918.[4]

Two months later Huddersfield Corporation appointed its first women tram conductors.

> Something of the nature of a mild sensation was caused among passengers travelling on the Lockwood and Fartown cars yesterday afternoon, for they discovered four attractive young ladies learning the duty of tram conducting. The ladies seemed very businesslike, for they each wore the customary cross-over belts, with bell-punch and cash-bag. As for their enthusiasm and zeal it was obvious to anyone who watched them quickly learning their duties. The old adage of "None but the brave deserve the fare," will have to be altered to "None but the fair deserve the fare." This does not mean that passengers are to try and "do" the Corporation by seeking to escape the attention of the male conductors.

Whilst grateful for their assistance, tramway manager RH Williamson left the women in no doubt about their stopgap status.

> … the ladies are acting as "emergency conductors" in consequence of the difficulty … in obtaining sufficient suitable men who are not fit for military service … and will be dispensed with at the conclusion of the war or the return of our own employees, or immediately sufficient male labour can be obtained.[5]

Respect would have to be earned the hard way and the *HDE* did little to dispel prejudice and stereotyping in a feature on 27 August 1915.

> Quite a flutter of excitement is apparent among the half dozen women tramway conductors of Huddersfield just now. Some of them have already received their uniforms, and others are in the delirium of trying on what will be a really smart outfit ... Of course on such a vital matter the women themselves had to be consulted ...

> The uniform is of navy blue serge, with red pipings, and gilt buttons on the coat. The hat is also of navy blue serge, also with red pipings, and a red badge on the front being the Corporation monogram. In all the glory of navy blue serge and red pipings the women will be quite "dressed for the part." One of the chief attractions of the uniform apparently is that it resembles the usual tramworkers' dress as far as possible.

One woman conductor described the job as 'all rush and excitement' but she was 'getting her sea legs', which earned a mild reprimand as 'anyone knows that the Huddersfield Corporation tramcars do not roll from side to side like an "old tub" on the ocean.'

In the main, the public were kind to the women. Children would 'stand at street corners and affectionately wave their hands to the new conductors as they pass along.' Others tried to be supportive, a male passenger gently chiding one of the conductors for her politeness in requesting 'Fares please!'"

> Ax 'im straight aat. Tell 'im tha wants it.
> Doant be freetened on 'im.

One 'gruff male passenger' was less friendly, suggesting that the women conductors …

> … were only out looking for husbands. The ready wit of the woman conductor quickly silenced him. With a winning smile she suggested that all the decent men had gone to the front.

A little self-conscious of their novelty value when passengers impolitely nudged one another and whispered 'Woman tram conductor', the first four recruits quickly impressed Mr Williamson with their pluck and ability, and the tramway manager soon had a long list of further applicants.[6]

The Tramcar Girl
by
A.W.K. (reprinted from the *Daily Chronicle*)

The day is still young when she trips to her post,
It has waned ere she trails to her rest,
And through the long hours of physical strain
She conjures a smile at each jest.
And if you should ask her in puzzling tones,
Why she of such ills bears the brunt,
She softly makes answer, a light in her eyes,
"It releases a man for the front."[7]

The women tram conductors became an accepted part of everyday life, treated much the same as male conductors by passengers, whether polite, friendly, mischievous or malicious. In July 1916, several fines were imposed on passengers for ringing the bell to start their cars. In September 1917 the *HDE* reported that tramcar girls on the Leeds Road route were 'insulted almost every day.' One had been assaulted, invoking a 40s fine with 10s costs.[8] The tramcar girls required courage, resilience and character.

THE GIRL TRAM GUARD

DELIGHTS OF WEARING THE NEW UNIFORM.

NOT HUSBAND HUNTING

BUT GETTING HER "SEA LEGS" AS QUICKLY AS POSSIBLE.

Quite a flutter of excitement is apparent amongst the half dozen women tramway conductors of Huddersfield just now. Some of them have already received their uniforms, and others are in the delirium of trying on what will be a really smart outfit. There have been many informal consultations and discussions before the final choice of style was made. Of course on such a vital matter the women themselves had to be consulted. The sub-committee of the Tramways Committee who had to deal with the subject called in the help of their wives, and one of the conductors was asked to consult her colleagues. After much weighty deliberation the all-important point was settled.

The uniform is of navy blue serge, with red pipings, and gilt buttons on the coat. The hat is also of navy blue serge, also with red pipings, and a red badge on the front bearing the Corporation monogram. In all the glory of navy blue serge and red pipings the women will be quite "dressed for the part." One of the chief attractions of the uniform apparently is that it resembles the usual tram workers' dress as far as possible.

SEA LEGS.

During the intervals of winding up a wrist watch by means of which she "sets the tram off," the woman conductor gave a few interesting details of her work to an "Examiner" representative. She said that she liked the work, and was getting on very nicely with it, although it was all rush and excitement. The sensation of becoming accustomed to the running of the cars she likened in the nautical phrase to "getting her sea legs." The description was perhaps just a little exaggerated, as everyone knows that the Huddersfield Corporation tramcars do not roll from side to side like an "old tub" on the ocean. Anyone who has travelled on the Outlane section, for instance, realises that such a statement is a libel on the service.

The woman conductor may be forgiven for her use of the term. The fact remains, however, that actually three hours were once occupied in having her tea. Of course, she did her work also during those three hours, and she accepted the conditions as incidental to those of "life on the rolling stock."

Very pleasant relationships have on the whole existed between the women conductors and the public. "People have been very nice towards us" is the general opinion. The introduction of the women was at first a nine days' wonder, but it has died a natural death, and the only persons who still realise the novelty of the situation are the children, who stand at the street corners and affec-

The *HDE* of 27 August 1915 reports the novelty of the Tram Car Girls

The Lady Car-Conductor

by

Charles Lunn

She's up in the morning before the sun peeps;
She's trudging to work while yet all the world sleeps.
Her fingers are blue with the cold so intense;
She can scarce punch the tickets or count out the pence.
But it's "Longroyd Bridge" and "Paddock Bar,"
Or "Cropper's Arms" and "Spotted Cow."
She calls the stages as we pass,
The sprightly car conductor lass.

When she calls, "All fares please," you are ready to frown,
And without e'en a look you reply, curtly, "Town."
But you soon understand what a blessing she is
When the lines are snow blocked and you're walking to "biz."
Oh, it's "Full inside," "Step forward, please,"
"Now don't sit on the lady's knees;"
Or "What's that? Don't you know where you are?
Well, we have just passed Fartown Bar."

Does it hail, does it snow, she is there just the same;
Like the boys at the front she is playing the game.
She is taking the place of a man who is fit,
And helping her country by doing "her bit."
From Palace Theatre, Hippodrome,
She takes each one of you safe home;
But when you are all snug in bed
The cars don't run – she walks instead.[9]

In August 1915, 18-year-old Miss Mary Mitchell provided the strongest evidence yet of women's growing confidence, independence and versatility when she was employed to drive the van of Market Walk pork butcher, Frank Cooper. Huddersfield's first woman motor driver, she released the butcher's regular driver for service in the Army Service Corp's Motor Transport Unit.[10] The National Transport Workers' Federation was less enlightened. They drew the line at women mail van drivers and threatened strike action if men were replaced in this work of 'real national importance', although the post office employed women in a variety of other roles.[11]

Women ambulance drivers and mechanics, mainly supplied by the First Aid Nursing Yeomanry were an accepted part of life behind the lines on the western front, where motor ambulances replaced horse drawn wagons in the first months of the war.[12]

In 1916 Huddersfield Technical College began classes to train women in traditional male roles in industry and bureaucracy.' At Sheffield University, where 50 women were trained as 'steel chemists', the metallurgical department concluded …

… experiments have shown women to be as fitted for positions as men.[13]

As women emerged from decades – arguably centuries – of suppression their 'choices were no longer limited to being wives, nurses or servants.'[14] Indeed, a shortage of reliable servant girls was …

… driving many people … to distraction. Many girls do not desire to enter service while there is such remunerative work at the munition factories and at certain main occupations. Apart from the wages, the girls are attracted by the comparative liberty and every night off. Some ladies have brought girls from other towns and from country districts where lucrative positions are not so abundant; but … Girls have been known to come – their railway fare paid – and then to give notice without a blush, and "go on munitions." Even the casual door-step cleaner and the washer-women have assumed an independence that indicates that they can almost dictate their own terms.[15]

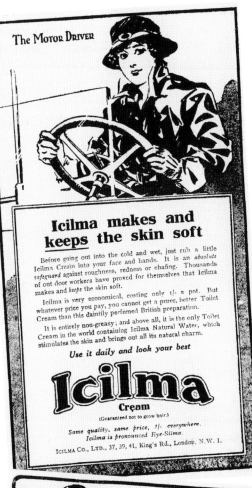

The Motor Driver

Icilma makes and keeps the skin soft

Before going out into the cold and wet, just rub a little Icilma Cream into your face and hands. It is an *absolute safeguard* against roughness, redness or chafing. Thousands of out door workers have proved for themselves that Icilma makes and *keeps* the skin soft.

Icilma is very economical, costing only 1/- a pot. But whatever price you pay, you cannot get a purer, better Toilet Cream than this daintily perfumed British preparation.

It is entirely non-greasy; and above all, it is the only Toilet Cream in the world containing Icilma Natural Water, which stimulates the skin and brings out all its natural charm.

Use it daily and look your best

Icilma
Cream
(Guaranteed not to grow hair.)

Same quality, same price, 1/- everywhere.
Icilma is pronounced Eye-Slima.

ICILMA CO., LTD., 37, 39, 41, King's Rd., London, N.W. 1.

Women Workers' Series. No. 2

When I went to stay with Jane

I took a tin of Elect Cocoa in my bag. Of course I offered her some, but Jane is a bit old-fashioned. "I never drink cocoa," she said. She could see how much I was enjoying it, but she said nothing all that breakfast time. Next day she said, a little shyly, "I think I'd like to try just one cup of your Elect Cocoa." She tasted it, and I could see by her face how pleased she was. "I never knew," she said, "that cocoa could be so delicious." She was as brisk as could be at work that morning, and she never starts out on the van nowadays without having had her cup of Elect Cocoa.

a cup of
Rowntree's
Elect Cocoa
makes a biscuit into a meal

BLACK CAT CIGARETTES

POSTWOMAN

THE LADY CONDUCTOR
prizes Ven-Yusa.

NONE of the war occupations of women call for so much exposure to the weather as does that of the lady conductor on tram or 'bus. Wet, wind and sun play havoc with the complexion, and unless the proper measures are promptly taken, a painful roughness of the skin and spoiling of the complexion are bound to result.

For this particular trouble, Ven-Yusa is the favourite application. It is most soothing and comforting to use.

The best method is, on the first sign of soreness, to rub a little Ven-Yusa in with the tips of the fingers and then go over the face with a soft handkerchief.

Properly looking after the skin in this way means giving it a regular "oxygen bath."

Therefore, let a jar of this exquisite toilet cream be your boon companion.

VEN-YUSA
The Oxygen Face Cream

Above: Black Cat Cigarettes produced a series of collectable cards 'Women on War Work.'

Advertisers quickly exploited, targeted and affirmed the new roles of women. These advertisements are from the *HDE* of 15 June 1917 (Conductor), 17 October 1916 (Horse Cab Driver) and 30 November 1917 (Motor Driver).

Suffragettes

Women's effectiveness in a wide range of occupations was compelling proof in the suffragettes' drive for equality. In July 1916 Lord Derby described women as 'part and parcel of our great army', at which the Huddersfield branch of the National Union of Women's Suffrage Societies asserted:

> the enfranchisement of the army must of necessity carry with it the enfranchisement of women.[16]

Even Prime Minister Asquith had changed his tune from pre-war discord with the suffragette movement.[17] By June 1917 enfranchisement seemed inevitable.

When Women Get the Vote
by
Charles Lunn

A revolution will take place
When women get the vote,
And sad will be the poor man's case
When women get the vote.
For ages man has ruled the earth,
But now new forces will have birth
Which will appraise his real worth
When women get the vote.

Man's ancient prestige soon will go
When women get the vote:
He'll very quickly be 'de trop'
When women get the vote.
His old clothes he will have to wear,
Such things as clubs he must foreswear –
To stay out late he will not dare
When women get the vote.

For he will have no cash to clink
When women get the vote,
And would he purchase smoke or drink
When women get the vote?
For avarice he must appease
Down he must go upon his knees
And say most humbly, "If you please,"
When women get the vote.

But compensation there will be
When women get the vote –
From suffragettes we shall be free
When women get the vote.
That noble band will cease to shriek,
And smite policemen on the cheek,
And hunger strike just out of pique,
When women get the vote.[18]

On 19 June 1917, a fortnight after this poem appeared in the *HDE*, the Representation of the People Bill was presented to Parliament. Receiving Royal assent on 6 February 1918, it granted the vote to women over 30 who were owners of property, and extended the vote to men aged over 21.[19] There were inevitable calls for equal voting rights with men, not least from the Huddersfield Women's Suffrage Society. In addition, Mrs Ogilvie Gordon, President of the Huddersfield branch of National Union of Women Workers, began the clamour for representation in local government, asking:

Why hadn't they women councillors in Huddersfield?[20]

Female candidates had been allowed to stand in district, town and county elections since the Qualification of Women Act (1907). The first woman on the Huddersfield Council was probably Mrs Mary Blamires, who was elected as a Liberal in 1923.[21]

Mrs Blamires had lead by example for many years, demonstrating tremendous organisational skills in voluntary fund-raising and providing all manner of resources to support the troops. On 9 May 1916 praised by the President of the Young Men's Christian Association (YMCA) for organising a Flag Day which raised £1560, she responded:

> ... the women have shown a deep practical sympathy with the YMCA ... mothers, wives sisters and sweethearts have helped heart and soul in the work ... the time was coming when the women would ask the men to back ... the provision of a YWCA institution.[22]

Nine days later Mrs Blamires called a meeting at the Town Hall at which the Huddersfield YWCA was formed. The main purpose was to build on the success of Huddersfield's first 'Girls' Social Rooms', opened in Market Walk in 1915. Over 500 working girls relaxed and socialised there in the evenings, but its rooms were too small to cope with the growing influx of migrant women workers. In July 1916 the YWCA opened a similar but larger facility in the YMCA building at 3 New North Road. Of £656 raised towards costs, £500 was donated by the family of Mr Charles Sykes.[23] The wholesome activities provided for young women at the YWCA were designed 'to make them good citizens and good wives', and to divert the working girls from frittering away their new found affluence in the pubs, a source of increasing moral outrage. By 1918, many of the town's 4000 girls aged 14 to 18 were using the facilities.[24]

Childcare

Simultaneously with the formation of the YWCA, the Citizens Guild of Help approached the Mayor Alderman Joseph Blamires, proposing a day nursery for Huddersfield. At that time there were about 150 day nurseries around the country of which 80 had been set up with the help of Government grants in the previous twelve months.

A nursery would not only release more young women from their household and family duties but also help family finances. An increasing number of women had been compelled to earn a livelihood because their husbands had been killed, wounded or were earning less at the front than they had in civilian life. Financial problems were often compounded by irregular or incorrect payments from the over-burdened regimental clerks attempting to implement complicated scales of pay and separation allowances.[25] In addition to pay determined by military rank, new monthly rates of separation allowances were announced by the Government on 18 January 1917.

ALLOWANCES

	NEW	OLD
No children	12s 6d	12s 6d
1 child	19s 6d	17s 6d
2 children	24s 6d	21s 0d
3 children	28s 0d	23s 0d
4 children	31s 0d	25s 0d

(Thereafter adding 3s per child – the old scale added 2s per child).[26]

A day nursery would also improve child safety. It was common for young mothers to ask a neighbour ɔ 'keep an eye on' their children, but a young boy in the town had recently slipped a neighbour's attention, set fire to himself and burned to death.[27]

The nursery needed £300 of local funds, which was raised almost immediately, enabling it to open n the first week of June 1916. In its first year it cared for 49 infants under the age of five, all of them vith working mothers.

By February 1917, aware that in some districts 'practically all the women' except the mothers ɔf young children were 'in the engineering shops', the Ministry of Munitions started to give further substantial support' to day nurseries. The nurturing of infants was becoming a priority for the Ɉovernment.

> It is obvious that this great war with its terrible loss of life makes it more imperative than ever that the nurture of child-life should be specially safeguarded.[28]

Alarmed at the birth rate, which fell by 25% between 1913 and 1917, and by the death rate among ne troops, the Government encouraged local authorities to further improve the infant mortality rate, vhich, nationally, had fallen from 108 per thousand in 1913 to 91 per thousand in 1916, roughly in ne with other countries. Sir Bernard Mallet, the Registrar-General of Births and Deaths for England nd Wales, attributed this fall to alcohol restrictions.

> … before the war one of the regular and … ugliest features of our social life was the number of deaths of infants … due to suffocation. They had been over-laid by their parents in bed. The number recorded on Sundays was always very much higher than on any other day in the week, the inference being that Saturday night's drinking meant the suffocation of the baby in bed before Sunday morning. Since the sale of alcoholic liquors was restricted there has been an appreciable decline in the infantile mortality attributed to this cause, and especially in the number of infant deaths recorded on Sundays.[29]

More, however, could be done. National figures revealed the startling fact that:

> It is more dangerous to be a baby in England than a soldier in France.[30]

A letter to the *HDE* from 'INTERESTED' on 9 July 1917 blamed the poor rates of soldiers' pay nd allowances, and advised natural selection by income:

> Can a family be brought up, clothed, and fed as they should be on 30s a week?
> … the better class [should] set the working mother a better example, and try and increase the population themselves (the only people who really can afford to at the present time).[31]

Huddersfield's Public Health Union renewed its efforts to great effect. In twelve months to June 918 Huddersfield's infant mortality rate was the second lowest among the industrial centres of the orth and Midlands.

Death Rates of Infants per Thousand

1. Coventry	77
2. Huddersfield	79

Selected Others:

Wolverhampton	81
Dewsbury	95
Halifax	114
Wakefield	118
Bradford	131
Leeds	131

The *HDE* proudly declared that, without the advantage of fresh sea air, Huddersfield's infant mortality ate was comparable to 'health' resorts such as Hastings (78), Southport (80) and Bournemouth (86).[32] Ɉenjamin Broadbent, President of the Huddersfield Public Health Union, disagreed that location was he cause of the improvement.

It is not climate; it is not industrial conditions; it is not general sanitation; it is not superior housing conditions. It is … steady, continuous, devoted, well-directed effort on the part of the combined official and voluntary workers.

… the local Public Health Union, has nearly 100 leading helpers and super-intendants, and by them a very large proportion of the babies in Huddersfield are regularly visited in their home and the mothers are helped in many ways.[33]

With so many absent fathers, there was also concern about the moral welfare of older children particularly the boys of the district. The number of cases coming before the Juvenile Court increased from 31 in 1914, to 64 in 1915 and 169 in 1916. The local Education Committee set up a sub-committee to decide 'what could be done.' 'Akela' advised that the scouts had previously 'done splendid work … in reclaiming juvenile offenders' but that local scout troops needed help. Scout numbers in Huddersfield had fallen from 800 to 500 in twelve months owing to 'the call up of volunteers who ran local groups.'[34]

Advertisements for children from the *HDE*; there was no escape from the war, *Puck* comic offering free gifts of a fort, tank and cannon on 31 October 1918, and local firm Rushworths choosing a battleship to promote their Meccano range on 22 February 1915.

The Education Committee decided to support all groups working for young people. These included the longstanding Cinderella Society, which organised holidays for children from poorer families. In June 1917 the Committee supplied five tents for a week's camp at Helme enjoyed by 25 boys.

The holiday had a wholesome effect upon the boys' health. They have been taught the value of cleanliness, order, and good conduct, and have learned to appreciate the beauties of the countryside ... it is all to the good that their activities should be diverted from mischief into channels of usefulness by giving them an interest in physical exercise, healthy outdoor sports and a study of nature.[35]

Notwithstanding this rose-tinted assessment, it had been another worthwhile enterprise by the Cinderella Society.

The dubious morality of popular films at the town's cinemas, 'the poor man's theatres', was attacked by some establishment figures for corrupting the young, but the consensus was that parents at the Juvenile Court were using films 'to cover … the obvious lack of parental discipline and control.'[36]

The absence of so many men was also felt by single girls. At the Holme School annual feast in June 1916, of over 30 dancers only two were male.

When the band left the field at 9 o'clock, instead of the kissing rings which used to be the vogue in other days, the maidens had to walk off in groups all on their "lonesome" – the youths are all away.[37]

Some boyfriends and husbands would never return. For some women, the role of single parent would become permanent.

The Widow
by
'V', Holmfirth

A shadow has fallen before the sun,
A cloud across my sky!
But peacefully sleeps my little one –
No tears bedim his eye.

Thou dost not share my grief, my son,
So I lament alone.
How can he grieve, my little one,
For one he has never known?

Thy day of childish care is done –
Thy father, too, has sleep,
Rest on, beloved, and little one,
While I keep watch – and weep.

And when my long day, too, is run,
This thought shall be my pride –
That I leave thee, my little one,
Worthy of him who died.[38]

For many women, the proliferation of wartime opportunities added to their many responsibilities. Managing home, work, finances, rationed resources and childcare, drained by constant, debilitating anguish about loved ones serving in the forces, demanded special courage and resilience. Even with the assistance of extended family and neighbours for which many women were grateful, the combination of practical and emotional burdens was unprecedented.

Overheard
by
Charles Lunn

In train or tramcar, road or street,
From those we pass, or those we meet,
A scrap of conversation tells
The thought that ever with them dwells.

"She's gone to see her husband; he
Is wounded, shrapnel in the knee."
Or, "He may never see again –
His eyes still give him cruel pain."

There's scarce a woman in the land
Who does not know and understand
The hidden hope, the hidden fear,
That lies beneath chance words we hear.[39]

Chapter 17

Appeals and Alleviating Distress

The myriad of wartime charities in Huddersfield and the torrent of money and goods that flooded into them were staggering, and only partly explained by the district's relative affluence as a centre of khaki and munitions production. Community leaders played a huge role, promoting and coordinating fundraising events, and kick-starting kitties with donations proportionate to their wealth. The *HDE* frequently printed lists of subscribers, headed by three, sometimes four figure sums from philanthropic individuals and businesses.

Support for Britain's Beleaguered Allies

The first major causes were galvanized by the plight of Britain's violated Allies. The local Belgian Famine Relief Fund attracted hundreds of donations and within a year had topped £10,000, in addition to £2500 raised to support the 540 Belgian refugees housed in the district. It was recognised by a letter of congratulation from the Lord Mayor of London, Chairman of the National Committee for Relief in Belgium, but this was only the start.[1]

On 10 July 1915 a 'France's Day' appeal raised over £1000, assisted by a procession and by the Huddersfield Automobile Club distributing badges and collection boxes around the district.[2] A week later Sydney Arnold of Holmfirth initiated a fundraising committee for the War Hospital at Yvetot near Rouen which he had recently visited. Managed by a mainly British committee, the hospital treated French soldiers, and Sydney Arnold was deeply concerned about the plight of their country.

> The toll paid by our noble ally has probably been nearly ten times as heavy as that paid by ourselves … The whole able-bodied manhood of France has been hauled into the fight. The richest industrial provinces are in the hands of the invader, and have been systematically bled of both treasures and supplies. Business throughout the Republic is largely paralysed.[3]

It was the first of many successful appeals for medical purposes. The Red Cross Society also made regular requests for finance and various initiatives on their behalf had raised over £6000 by the end of the war.[4]

By February 1916 the increase in the number of worthy causes was spreading the fundraising more thinly and the Belgian funds were consolidated into a more general 'War Sufferers' Fund.' The intention was to divide the moneys, 50% for Belgian relief, 25% for Serbian relief, and 25% for the Red Cross

BELGIAN FAMINE FUND
£711,000 SUBSCRIBED.

The total subscriptions to the National Committee for Relief in Belgium now amount to over £711,000. Among the donations received on Friday were £5,000, a further contribution from the South Australian Belgian Relief Fund, through Mr. F. W. Young, Agent-General for South Australia, £251 9s. 3d. from the Holmfirth and Newmill Belgian Famine Fund, and £250 through the Belgian Consul at Leeds.

If famine is to be averted among the 1,500,000 who are destitute in Belgium the monthly revenue of the National Committee must be considerably increased.

	£	s.	d.
Amount acknowledged on Saturday ...10,609		8	6½
GENERAL.			
J. C.	0	10	0
J. H.	1	0	0
Prise winners at College Municipal Secondary School for Boys (in lieu of prizes)	9	5	0
Boys' Staff at ditto	3	12	4
WORKPEOPLE'S SUBSCRIPTIONS.			
Corporation Sanitary Department, per Mr. W. J. Downey (17th)	1	16	6
Read Holliday & Sons, Ltd., Grove Colliery, per Mr. M. Riding (19th)	0	10	0
Wm. Thomson & Sons, Ltd., per Mr. W. Schofield (28th)	1	1	8
Benj. Crosland & Sons, Ltd., per Mr. J. J. Barnes (25th)	1	16	6
Britannia Mills Co., Ltd. (11th)	1	5	0
J. Hopkinson & Co., Ltd. (30th)	19	15	3
John Haigh & Sons, Ltd. (10th)	1	15	11
Meltham Spinning Co., Ltd., per Mr. C. A. Berry (12th)	0	19	0
Tom Liversidge & Sons, Ltd., per Mr. Lewis Linaker (11th)	4	0	0
Benj. Armitage & Sons, Ltd., per Mr. John Mosley (5th)	1	0	0
John Crowther & Sons, Queen's Mill, per Mr H. Dransfield (25th)	0	12	6
Longwood Finishing Co., Ltd., per Mr. A. Tweed (20th)	1	3	3
James Sykes & Son (10th)	2	12	0
Albany Mills Co., Ltd., per Mr. H. Castle (10th)	3	7	4
David France & Co., per Mr. F. Esmond (7th)	1	4	6
Netherwood, Dalton, & Co., binding department (12th)	0	5	7
Corporation Waterworks, per Mr. Kaye (27th)	1	16	9
Shaw Bros., Ltd. (14th)	1	14	0
Sykes & Wood (employees and firm), per Miss Brunton (22nd)	0	8	9
C. Greenwood & Co., per Mr. G. Crow (13th)	0	12	5
T. W. Thorpe, Ltd. (employees and firm) (7th)	2	9	0
Chas. Lockwood & Sons, Ltd., Priestroyd Mills, per Mr. Jas. Dyson (24th)	0	11	7
Pearson Bros., Ltd., per Mr. G. E. Taylor (23rd)	0	11	1
E. Wood & Sons, per Mr. J. W. H. Wood (6th)	0	10	0
Copley, Marshall & Co., Ltd., per Mr. W. Hirst (7th)	1	3	0
J. Holmes & Son, per Miss M. Clarke (18th)	0	5	2
Jos. Beaumont, jun., per Mr. A. Kippax (19th)	0	8	1
Firth Bros., per Mr. J. A. Pearson (5th)	2	2	8
G. W. Oldham, per Mr. Oldham (14th)	0	11	6
Globe Worsted Co., Ltd., per Mr. J. W. Hirst (14th)	3	9	0
Singleton & Co., Ltd., per Mr. W. Singleton (5th)	1	3	0
W. & E. Crowther, Ltd., per Mr. Irvin Chappell (25th)	5	7	4

Subscription list from the *HDE*, 3 August 1915. Scores of subscription lists were published by the *HDE* during the Great War. Such lists not only acknowledged donations, but were also an incentive to donate.

Society.[5] Donations from this fund to Belgian famine relief continued until May 1917 when the U.S.A. joined the war and 'generously assumed all financial responsibility for the work of the Commission for Relief in Belgium.' The £20,779 raised in Huddersfield and district for Belgian relief contributed to a national total of £2,400,000 and, locally, relied more on unsolicited donations than any other wartime fund.[6] After the U.S.A.'s intervention, a greater percentage of the local fund was directed towards the increasingly needy Poles and Russians. With justifiable pride, the *HDE* pronounced:

> Whatever may be said against the people of Huddersfield after the war … one thing is certain … our Allies will always remember the generous response that was made to the various appeals on their behalf.[7]

War Horse Day

The public's sympathy was also captured by a 'Fund for Sick and Wounded Horses', opened by the Duke of Portland on 1 January 1915 at the request of the RSPCA.[8] The Huddersfield branch played their part, equipping War Horse Hospitals on the Western Front with parcels that included 300 swabs and 200 home-made woollen pads to place under saddles as protection against sore backs.[9] Their greatest contribution came on 24 July 1915, War Horse Day, which they organised with the Town Council along the lines of other fundraising events. The procession was …

> … in some ways the best … that has taken place in Huddersfield [featuring] horses in slings and bandages, showing how … animals at the front suffer and the manner in which they are treated … two Shetland ponies and a zebra from Halifax Zoo. Thousands of people came by tram and train … all roads seemed to lead to St George's Square … and they gave liberally.

The event raised over £1200. It also raised awareness of the considerable suffering of horses on war service, and of the humane work of the RSPCA and the Blue Cross Society on their behalf.[10]

The Huddersfield and District Women's Committee for Wounded Soldiers and Sailors

The most durable and far-reaching of the local war-support organisations was the 'Huddersfield and District Women's Committee for Wounded Soldiers and Sailors.' Superbly led by Mrs Kilner Clark, Miss Emily Frances Siddons and the Mayoress, Mrs Mary Blamires, they collected, assembled and distributed thousands of goods parcels to scores of hospitals in this country and abroad, including all the local war hospitals. In addition, they supplied Belgian refugees, the British Red Cross, St John Ambulance, naval ships and all theatres of the land war. An army of women from every walk of life in Huddersfield and its outlying districts contributed a 'never-ending supply' to the Central Depot. Some women worked individually and many communally through the various churches, chapels, schools and societies.[11]

> No duty has been too humble, no sphere of activity, however onerous, has been left unfilled.[12]

At the Huddersfield Blind Society, for example, six blind girls knitted 23 balaclavas, 63 pairs of mittens, 34 pairs of gloves, 2 scarves and 1334 pairs of socks in the first year of the war.[13] In November 1916 local schools were circularised to request that pupils should knit 'as many woollen articles as possible for the troops.' Over the next few months there was a regular flow knitted predominantly by girls.[14] Schoolgirl Vivien Hirst was instructed by her father, FW Hirst, the military representative on the Huddersfield Military Tribunals, to …

> … take your mitten to chapel and during the sermon you must knit for the whole length of time … I protested vigorously. 'I can't do that, Daddy, everyone will look at me and people won't like it.' 'Never mind what people like. Think of all the garments that could be knitted, Sunday by Sunday, whilst they are sitting idly listening. They might just as well be doing something useful and greatly needed, and they can listen perfectly well at the same time.'

He was hoping to start a fashion, using 'all the hours throughout the year when hands were lying idle' as people sat listening to 'long-winded' sermons.[15] The Women's Committee meetings were also characterised by the clicking of knitting needles as they planned their next initiatives and the distribution of goods from recent ones.

In the autumn of 1914 the women quickly established a Belgian Refugees Clothing Sub-Committee which sent 16,000 garments overseas and distributed 10,000 in Huddersfield. When the static nature of the war became apparent, they made 23,000 sandbags. These were with the troops by February 1915. In April 1915, following the first chlorine gas attacks, they made 1300 respirators in a week. Over 24,000 items were donated to equip the Royds Hall War Hospital for its opening in October 1915. Twelve months later they provided much of the bed linen to support the opening of Honley War Hospital. To assist the heavy casualties of spring 1918, they sent thousands of swabs, bandages and anaesthetic pads to hospitals at home and behind the lines. This extraordinary catalogue was in addition to the regular supplies sent to the front which, by the end of the war amounted to almost 400,000 items, mainly garments, facilitated in part by generous donations of wool from local manufacturers and the most prolific Needlework Guild outside London.[16]

Parcels for Prisoners-of-War

Of all the women's initiatives, the one which 'appealed to the imagination and sympathy more, perhaps, than any other' was 'The Prisoners of War Help Committee', formed in June 1915. Numerous women adopted a prisoner and became known as 'Fairy Godmothers', sending out parcels once a fortnight, without which many prisoners would not have survived.

By December 1916 the women had 56 prisoners 'on the books.' There were only eight further additions until the 2/5th Dukes' 'fateful day' at Bullecourt in May 1917, after which a further 159 were added.[17] One of these grateful troops was Private Albert Bedford, who was wounded in the side and captured on 3 May 1917. After some rough and ready treatment in hospital, he was put to work in a sugar factory at Lubeck, lifting industrial-sized bags of sugar on a diet of potatoes, cabbage water, barley soup, and rotten vegetables. This combination of heavy work and poor diet caused his wound to rupture and he was assigned 'lighter' work on a farm in Mecklenburg. There he survived an outbreak of Spanish Flu which killed off one of his fellow prisoners. Albert was convinced that his constitution would not have survived injury and virus without the aid of food parcels.[18]

Report from the HDE of 4 November 1915 of the latest meeting of the Huddersfield and District Women's Committee for Wounded Soldiers and Sailors

Greenhead High School for Girls followed the women's example and from 1917 also prepared and posted parcels to prisoners of war in Germany. One beneficiary was Seaman Oswald Beaumont, captured at Antwerp in 1914 and imprisoned at Döberitz, a large camp eight miles from Berlin, where his daily diet was two slices of black bread made from potato peelings and sawdust, and occasionally oats, tea, acorn soup or coffee made from chestnuts. His health was also endangered by damp, cold accommodation and by rough treatment from the German officers, who scarred him with four bayonet wounds for trivial 'offences.' Conditions at Döberitz only improved after Mr Gerard, the American ambassador, visited their camp and made strong, formal recommendations. Released in an exchange of prisoners in April 1918, Seaman Beaumont …

> … expressed his deep gratitude for the kindness of the High School girls … But for the parcels from home, we couldn't keep going.

Recreation equipment was also highly valued in the parcels. Seaman Beaumont had befriended Everton footballer Tommy Lewis at Döberitz, and requested that a football be sent out to him. Leather was so short in Germany that they had played football with screwed up brown paper.[19]

The much-anticipated parcels were often delayed by the Germans' insistence on 'strict censorship, because of acts of sabotage practised through the parcel post.' Increasingly, parcels arrived raided and empty as the blockade by the British fleet left German civilians short of food. Seaman Beaumont had seen several German women shot by sentries as they tried to raid the parcels wagon. Private Knott of Lockwood, working on a prison farm in Magdeburg, saw numerous comrades die owing to 'lack of medical attention', which the Germans attributed to shortages caused by the blockade. He did, though, notice an improvement in their treatment when it became clear that Germany was going to lose the war.[20]

In 1916, complaints about the treatment of prisoners began to generate a degree of cooperation between the opposing powers. Private Harry Day of the Seaforth Highlanders was one of the first beneficiaries. Captured in 1914, his health had deteriorated sharply through the usual combination of poor food, undelivered food parcels, tough work and harsh discipline. In the autumn of 1916 his knee was crushed by a wagon on a work party and he was one of several prisoners transferred from Germany to recuperate in Switzerland. He was kept, by agreement, in a hotel at Chateau d'Oex, where his wife spent a fortnight with him, paid for by the Red Cross.[21]

In the summer of 1917, the British and German governments reached agreement at the Hague about the exchange, repatriation and rights of prisoners of war. British prisoners undergoing 'excessive punishment' were prioritised, and further such treatment was to stop.[22] The first batch of 405 repatriated prisoners of war arrived in London on 11 September 1917.[23]

The new agreement brought more local prisoners to the attention of the Huddersfield Women's Committee. Shortly afterwards, several local families were overjoyed to receive 'unexpected' letters from relatives previously reported 'missing, believed killed.' Some families had been mourning for several months, including that of Private Cyril Wilkinson whose sister Constance, an 'accomplished soprano', committed her talents to entertaining troops in the local war hospitals and on the western front with the Huddersfield Concert Party.[24] The Women's Committee made immediate arrangements to include these prisoners in the rounds of parcels. In November 1917 their load increased by a further 32 men, captured during the heroic efforts of the 2/5th Dukes at Cambrai, and 377 more were taken during the German offensive in March 1918.

After the Armistice, 70 more local prisoners materialised, bringing the total of local men who were prisoners of war to 739, 43 of whom died. Of these, the Women's Committee helped 669, 238 through 'Fairy Godmothers.'[25]

Funding of such a quantity of parcels was a huge challenge, exacerbated by rampant inflation which saw the cost per parcel rise from 12s to £3 7s 6d during the war, although prisoners' families made a contribution. The women's fundraising events were invariably well organised and lucrative. Prior to the opening of Royds Hall, for example, their Flag Day to provide beds and ambulances for wounded soldiers raised £2557 from collections, concerts and donations. These included the combined annual prize money of £26 donated by the leading scholars at Almondbury Grammar School. All who contributed were treated to a variety show at the Palace Theatre at the Mayoress's expense, showing appreciation for their efforts and fostering goodwill. In July 1916 the Women's Committee raised a further £2000 on 'Soldiers and Sailors Day', when a procession through the streets was followed by entertainments in Greenhead Park. A 'Sale and Exhibition' at the Town Hall in December 1916 raised £2600, including £515 from a grocery stall.[26]

With prisoner numbers rising rapidly, the women set and achieved a fundraising target of £5000 during the winter of 1917-18, starting with 'Prisoner of War Day' on 6 October 1917 which raised £350 from the sale of emblems. In total, the Women's Committee raised and spent over £20,000 on parcels for prisoners of war, and over £14,000 on other causes, in addition to the thousands of garments and other items made and donated.[27] A typical parcel might contain cigarettes, tobacco, chocolate, tins of sweets, small items of clothing, dice and small games, tinned food and local newspaper cuttings.

The outlying districts contributed much to the Women's Committee's Central Depot, whilst also sending additional support to their own troops. In the Colne Valley it seemed almost everybody 'was engaged in sending out comforts to the troops', and in 'serving on a Relief Committee.' In July 1915 Marsden newsagent Frederick Russell established a committee to send parcels to the front which raised £1186 9s 1d to pay the postage for 17,015 parcels to sailors and soldiers.

> ... all that local folk had to do was to take their parcels to the [newsagent's] shop, where they were weighed and stamped ready for post free of cost to the sender. The scheme grew to a remarkable degree and Mr Russell was besieged almost all day long by people passing in and out of the shop, and then taking parcels forward to the post office.[28]

The 'energy and devotion of the Marsden people' was again evident in 1917 when they raised £600 to purchase a YMCA Hut for their local Auxiliary War Hospital.[29]

Longwood was a similarly proactive community, founding the Longwood Aid Society in April 1915 which funded a monthly five-shilling parcel to each of the Longwood servicemen. When the number of Longwood men at the front leapt from 170 to 568 in the twelve months to July 1917, the Society held a large fundraising Demonstration and Gala. A spectacular procession from Botham Hall via Milnsbridge to Longwood featured three bands, including star attraction Lindley Brass Band, and mock-ups of a tank and a submarine. Entertainments in a nearby field followed, and the event was a huge success, if a little more decorative than intended.

> The local authority chose an unfortunate time for painting the lampposts in the Longwood District, for the paint was wet when crowds lined the streets ... and some of the spectators made an unwelcome acquaintance with it.[30]

The troops also received independent support from philanthropic individuals such as Mr T Brook of Huddersfield, who sent a 'beautiful gramophone and a few records' to the Huddersfield Battalion. This was, according to Lance-Corporal A Crossland ...

> ... appreciated by all and has been the means of many pleasant hours being spent by the men of 'A' Company whilst out of the trenches at rest ... Only tonight we had the gramophone going, but how much more pleased we should have been if only we had more records and I feel sure that many of the friends we have in Huddersfield would be only too pleased to forward a few records of the latest selections.[31]

Cinderella Society

The deluge of wartime funds left some old established charities gasping for air. The 'Cinderella Fund' acknowledged the competition, its appeal of June 1917 pronouncing that 'the hapless slum child ought not to be forgotten.' In 1917, 15d would pay for 'a day in the country with good food', 15s 'a glorious fortnight by the sea or in the country', and £13 'a party of 200 for a day.' The target, to beat the £137 raised in 1916, which had financed a day out for 1000 children and a fortnight's holiday for 20 of them, was exceeded.[32]

One of the less subtle advertisements for War Bonds and War Savings Certificates, from the *HDE* 6 February 1918

War Loans

The greatest threat to wartime charity funds came from the National Savings Movement, launched by the Government in March 1916. This was the latest initiative in the Government's 'War Loans' schemes. There was no pretence. People were being asked to loan money to hore up the ravaged national finances and pay for the war. The first Government War Loan Bonds were issued in November 1914 at an interest rate of 3.5%, followed by a second issue in June 1915 at 4.5%, less than the rate of inflation but better than the rates offered by the banks. These issues raised ˋ1.2 billion, but the Government needed much more.[33]

Increasing the armed forces through conscription and the huge expansion in munitions production at a time of rampant inflation threatened to bankrupt the country. In addition, the commitment of servicemen was threatened by growing discontent about unpaid wages, as reflected by Private JH Southward in the *HDE* of 1 February 1916.

> I wonder how many more men who served their country are experiencing the same difficulty as I am in obtaining their arrears of pay?

Tommy's "Grouse"
by
Private JH Southward (40 Springwood Street)

Am I just a "grousing Tommy"?
Not for Joe!
But I've stuck my blooming corner
'Gainst the foe;
I've for months, 'mid shrapnel shell,
Bursting bombs, and poison smell,
Bullet souvenirs as well,
Had a go.

'Twas a giddy life of pleasure,
And the pay
Worked out handsome, one and six
Ev'ry day.
Course I didn't draw full "brass"
Proving me a silly ass.
Thought I'd take it in the mass
Like a jay!

Now I'm home again and sick,
Rather bad;
And the country makes me feel
Sort of "had,"
Waiting weeks for well-earned pay.
"Hope deferred." What's that you say?
"Makes the heart sink?" Every day.
Makes me mad!

When you've done your country's work,
Seems to me,
You're not wanted; you can scoot;
You can "gee,"
On your "benders" pray "Kind sir,
Do have pity, send my share,"
But the cash stops in the air,
Up a tree.

The National Savings Movement of spring 1916 promoted the purchase of War Savings Certificate costing 15s each, still at an interest rate of 4.5%.[34] This time the Government mobilised the loca expertise that had so successfully raised patriotic funds for the war charities.

The Huddersfield War Savings Committee, one of hundreds across the country, was appointed by the Council's General Purposes Committee and led by the Mayor. It would evolve into an executive committee and six sub-committees comprising a total of 70 members. Within a fortnight of their firs public meeting on 16 May 1916, ten local war savings associations had been formed and over 1000 certificates had been sold.[35] Coinciding with the 'big push' on the Somme, the third week of July was designated 'National War Savings Week', and was promoted on posters around the town and on the tramcars.[36] A letter to all newspapers from Chancellor of the Exchequer, Reginald McKenna demanded support for 'the greatest military offensive in the history of our country' with the 'greates financial effort in our history.'[37]

Certificates were available at post offices and banks, but the local War Savings Committee spen the 'first few months ... organising meetings at mills, factories, workshops and schools, at which the Government scheme was explained.'[38] Workplaces were encouraged to form savings groups where 'a collector did the rounds each week to collect the savings and issue certificates', adding convenience and peer pressure to the mantra of frugality and patriotism.[39] Various schools formed War Savings Associations for staff and parents. On 13 December 1918 schools of the West Riding closed for the day to celebrate their combined contribution of £250,000 to the War Savings movement.[40] By the end of 1917 there were over 250 local war savings associations, including four in Marsh, five in Lindley eight in Birkby and 13 in Almondbury.[41]

Following the replacement of Asquith's Liberal Government with a Liberal/Conservative coalition in December 1916, the new Chancellor, Bonar Law, introduced a 'Victory War Loan' scheme, paying 5% interest. Holders of existing War Savings Certificates and Treasury Bills could convert them to the new higher rate, and many did. Boosted by £100,000 from the Town Council and several large sums from private companies, Huddersfield and district contributed £4.75 million to the new issue in its first seven weeks, the *HDE* enthusiastically announcing the headline figure without acknowledging that a relatively small percentage of this was new money.[42]

In 1918, Government-driven propaganda applied competitive psychology to the purchase of war bonds. For years the *HDE*, like other local newspapers, had fuelled inter-town rivalries, most obviously in sport, but also in such diverse facets of local life as music, industrial output and infant mortality rates. On 7 February 1918 the *HDE* compared the district's overall war loans total favourably with other places, but expressed dismay at sales of £9905 for the previous week which 'fell very much below' the target of £53,900, 'the proportiona amount on a population basis that should be subscribed ... every week ... to give the desired figure for the entire country.'

Tank Week

This was preparing the ground for 'Tank Week' which, in Huddersfield, began on Monday 18 February 1918. It was a shrewd idea, given the impact of British tanks at the Battle of Cambrai the previous autumn, and had particular resonance in Huddersfield as Cambrai had been the finest hour of the war for the local battalions.

The poster campaign for Tank Week challenged Huddersfield to beat West Hartlepool's record of £35 10s per person, and, with combative reference to Halifax, 'give the sister town something to beat. The tank bank *Nelson* was duly positioned in St George's Square, emblazoned with the imposing

England expects every man to do his duty.' Invoking the glories of Trafalgar, it carried a little more gravitas than the motto on the tank outside Marsden's Mechanics Hall.

> What Ho! The Marsden Tank!
> Invest your "brass" in the Marsden Tank,
> It pays more "divi" than the bank.
> You'll help the State to win the war,
> And help yourselves – so there you are![43]

Tanks save Brave Lives and Tanks cost money —about £5,000 each

The more Tanks we have the more brave lives will be saved—the sooner will the fighters return to "Blighty" and you.

Buy £1,000 worth of National War Bonds and you will have provided one-fifth of the money necessary to purchase a Tank. If you have less than a £1,000—even if it is only £5 — you can still buy National War Bonds.

Then you may consider yourself the part owner of a Tank, and the British Government will pay you 5 per cent. interest on your money and a few years hence will repay it, with a premium added.

Your idle bank balance can be turned into fighting money if you will use it to

BUY NATIONAL WAR BONDS at the HUDDERSFIELD TANK

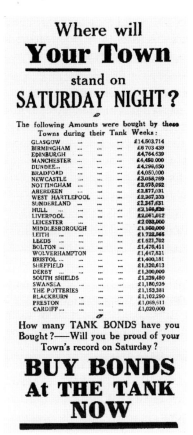

Where will Your Town stand on SATURDAY NIGHT?

The following Amounts were bought by these Towns during their Tank Weeks:

GLASGOW	...	...	£14,503,714
BIRMINGHAM	...	...	£6,703,439
EDINBURGH	...	...	£4,764,639
MANCHESTER	...	...	£4,450,000
DUNDEE	...	...	£4,296,650
BRADFORD	...	...	£4,050,000
NEWCASTLE	...	...	£3,058,769
NOTTINGHAM	...	...	£2,678,052
ABERDEEN	...	...	£2,877,031
WEST HARTLEPOOL	...	...	£2,367,333
SUNDERLAND	...	...	£2,347,531
HULL	...	...	£2,166,620
LIVERPOOL	...	...	£2,061,012
LEICESTER	...	...	£2,033,000
MIDDLESBOROUGH	...	...	£1,950,000
LEITH	...	...	£1,722,565
LEEDS	...	...	£1,521,702
BOLTON	...	...	£1,476,411
WOLVERHAMPTON	...	...	£1,447,831
BRISTOL	...	...	£1,400,181
SHEFFIELD	...	...	£1,320,613
DERBY	...	...	£1,300,000
SOUTH SHIELDS	...	...	£1,239,480
SWANSEA	...	...	£1,180,939
THE POTTERIES	...	...	£1,153,381
BLACKBURN	...	...	£1,102,290
PRESTON	...	...	£1,069,611
CARDIFF	...	...	£1,020,000

How many TANK BONDS have you Bought?——Will you be proud of your Town's record on Saturday?

BUY BONDS At THE TANK NOW

Advertisements from the *HDE*, 18 February 1918 (left) and 20 February 1918 (right), attempting to invoke the competitive spirit of the town

ST GEORGES SQUARE, HUDDERSFIELD.

St George's Square, where the tank *Nelson* was positioned just to the right of the railway station entrance.

The opening ceremony of Huddersfield's Tank Week was a triumph. Monday at noon, a procession left the Town Hall led by West Riding Volunteers and including some of their walking wounded. The streets were lined with people and 'thousands' awaited them in St George's Square, where the Mayor, Alderman WH Jessop, and his party, 'ascended to the top of the Tank' to a great cheer.

The Mayor fuelled the patriotic fervour by

introducing two war heroes. Private S Nelson of Longwood and the 7th Dukes, twice wounded at Ypres and once at Nieuport, was presented with the Military Medal for 'most excellent work on a wiring party ... under heavy shell fire.' Golcar's Bombardier Cranshaw of the RGA was presented with the French Medaille Militaire for 'conspicuous bravery ... in extinguishing a fire which had broken out in the battery ammunition dump.'

Two aircraft from Lincoln then treated the crowd to an aerobatic display, including loop-the-loop before dropping propaganda leaflets onto the town.[44] Children at Crow Lane School went into the playground to watch them fly overhead as they prepared to land at Botham Hall Farm, Golcar. The planes and the tank were a great attraction over the next few days. School attendances plummeted amidst all the excitement, and Brierley Wood Infants School compromised by granting a half day holiday on Thursday 21 February 'in honour of the visit of the tank.'[45]

Sir William Raynor, Chairman of the local Recruitment Committee, declared Tank Week open and announced that, for every £500,000 accrued, two rounds of blank ammunition would be fired from the anti-aircraft gun in Dalton Street. By 4pm it had fired twice. The following day's *Yorkshire Observer* commented:

> Huddersfield has long earned a somewhat enviable notoriety for the ease with which it appears to be able to raise money for worthy objects. The town surpassed itself yesterday when the magnificent sum of £1,079,952 0s 6d was invested with the tank bank "Nelson" between the hours of noon and 4pm. Only Glasgow of over 20 other towns and cities has passed 1 million and only West Hartlepool has more per head of population. By comparison, Manchester raised £292,124 and Leeds £269,337. On amount per head, West Hartlepool raised £12 9s 5d Huddersfield £10 0s 3d and third is Middlesbrough £7 3s 2d.[46]

The investments included £100,000 each from Huddersfield Corporation, Huddersfield Building Society and an anonymous 'friend of Huddersfield', £40,395 from the Marsden Tank Day and other sizeable contributions, mainly from businesses, though some came from private individuals.

By Wednesday, the Tank Week advertisement in the *HDE* included a league table of towns and cities, asking 'Where will your town stand on Saturday night?' It also published a letter from Sir David Beatty, commander of the fleet:

A MESSAGE FROM THE NORTH SEA

To the Mayor of Huddersfield.
Heartiest congratulations to Huddersfield on the fine achievement of their first Tank Day. It is a record of which the town may well be proud.
DAVID BEATTY[47]

The George Hotel, birthplace of rugby league in 1895 and used as an
emergency bank during Tank Week.

There are Two Sides to the Tank

THE NATIONAL AND THE INDIVIDUAL

This is Tank Week——

Advertisement from the *HDE*, 20 February 1918.
The left hand caterpillar track lists how the Government
will spend the savings. The right hand track lists the
future benefits of saving for the individual.

Alongside the tank bank were daily entertainments on a concert platform, briefly interrupted when a storm blew down the awning on Thursday afternoon. The climax on Saturday included performances from a military bugle band, Lindley Brass Band, Golcar Harmonic Quartet, Professor Land (ventriloquist), Master Arthur Barrow (boy soprano), Mr Claud Burt (conjuror) and 'a boxing exhibition by Mr Fred Hill's two champion midgets (aged 10 and 18).'[48] There were 'long queues' to invest throughout the ten hours of trading and to cope with demand additional bank staff were hastily deployed to run a second office in the stockroom of the George Hotel.

The final total, a staggering £2,680,899, bore testimony to the enthusiasm, organisation and rigour of the local campaign. The Halifax authorities immediately retreated to the moral high ground, pronouncing that, unlike Huddersfield and Bradford, they would not offer the enticement of a free War Savings Certificate for every tenth investor as 'the practice savours of gambling.' The *HDE*, meanwhile, delighted in publishing the league table of northern towns and cities, ordered by the criteria that placed Huddersfield in second position. Only the people of West Hartlepool, who had particularly strong and personal motivation following their town's bombardment in 1914, raised more per head of population.[49]

Position	Town/City	Total Subscribed (£)	Total per Head of Population (£ s d)
1	West Hartlepool	2,367,333	37 0 0*
2	Huddersfield	2,680,899	24 17 3
3	Leith	1,722,565	21 0 2
4	York	1,522,963	18 11 2
9	Bradford	4,050,000	13 15 8
10	Glasgow	14,503,704	13 5 1
25	Leeds	1,521,702	3 9 5

* adjusted from £35 10s per head after the poster advertisement was printed

185

War Weapons Week

Tank Week was such a success that there were two similar initiatives in 1918 and annual one during World War II. Next was War Weapons Week, from Wednesday 3 to Wednesday 10 July 1918 a lower-key affair than Tank Week, with the incentive that if Huddersfield purchased £250,000 in War Bonds a tank would be named after the town.

The opening ceremony in St George's Square was timed for the arrival of the latest trainload of wounded soldiers destined for the Royds Hall War Hospital. It was conducted from the top of the 'bank', a tramcar 'specially decorated and well covered with pictorial appeals for support' and 'fitted up for investors in War Bonds and War Savings Certificates.' Predominantly stationed in St George's Square, the tramcar bank also made daily visits to outlying districts where members of the War Savings Committee addressed meetings at the various termini.[50]

> The brilliant red of the car decoration and the streamers flying from the trolley, with vari coloured posters in the windows, presented a striking appearance and the rolling of drums by Boy Scouts on the top of the car brought out many spectators along the route.[51]

War Weapons Week raised £604,902 in war bonds and war savings certificates and the *HDE* proclaimed that Huddersfield had 'again realised the hopes entertained of the borough – to go one better than was proposed.'[52] Huddersfield had earned its tank, the second piece of military hardware named after the town, as the Chamber of Commerce had presented the Canadian High Commissioner, Sir George Perley, with a Sopwith Camel for his country's airforce in February 1918.[53]

Thanksgiving Week

The country's financial problems did not end at the Armistice, and the Government tapped into the carefree celebratory indulgence with 'Thanksgiving Week', Huddersfield and district responding with a further £1,739,850. War bonds were still advertised well into 1919, and by March of that year Huddersfield had contributed £12,300,130 in War Loans and £1,338,694 in War Savings Certificates the total of £13,638,824 approximating to £100 per head.

Sir RM Kindersley, Chairman of the National War Savings Committee, praised not only 'the skill and resourcefulness with which your appeal was made, but also … the patriotism of those to whom it was directed.'[54]

This patriotic financial support was far from naïve and unquestioning. It was also laced with self interest, and with healthy awareness and scepticism, as expressed in the following rhyme from the *HDE* of 16 August 1919.

Precept and Practice
by
Anon

The government preaches economy, yet
It practises not what it preaches;
But spends with both hands till the National Debt
An amount that is staggering reaches.

A million or two is of no consequence
To those who this country are running;
But you must be careful of shillings and pence,
All forms of extravagance shunning.

By denying yourself, save what money you can,
And then to the Government lend it.
Who will quickly bring forward some new-fangled plan,
The object of which is to spend it.

The poem has a certain timeless quality, as indeed do the War Bonds and the War Savings Certificates, which were renamed National Savings Certificates in 1920. In 1932 Neville Chamberlain's Government called in the 5% war loan, offering cash or an option of continuing the loan at the lower rate of 3.5%. In 2014 there was, nationally, still close to £2 billion outstanding in unclaimed war loans. Although interest is still paid on them at 3.5%, their face value does not keep pace with inflation. A War Bond purchased for £100 during the Great War was worth about £80 in 2014.[55]

The Mayor's Cigarette Fund

Whilst the savings schemes encouraged frugality, one of the most popular funds of the war, the 'Cigarette and Tobacco Fund', indulged the troops. Established by the Mayor, Alderman Joseph Blamires in March 1915, within six months the fund had raised £720 from donations, flag days, collections and concerts, and sent out 2,024,000 cigarettes, 10,000 ounces of tobacco and 1400 tins of sweets.[56]

Report on the latest meeting of the Mayor's Cigarette Fund Committee from the *HDE* 4 November 1915

One of the first recipients, on 2 May, was Private Freddie Smith of the 5th Dukes:

> Tuesday night ... our sergeants and corporals came along the traverses and trenches with a very much appreciated gift of 6 packets of Woodbines for each man, and pleased were we when told that the Mayor of our own town had sent them out to us.[57]

By the end of the war the cigarette count alone had topped 10 million. The fund was regularly replenished by donations and the occasional specific event, such as a flag day in May 1917 which raised well over £300.[58]

In February 1916 the fund provoked a row about wartime priorities and Lord's Day observance. The Watch Committee refused permission for a fundraising show on a Sunday at the Empire Picture House on religious grounds. A row erupted at the next Town Council meeting, and Alderman Schofield represented the popular view:

> There ought to be more broad-mindedness (Hear, hear) ... the concert could have contributed something like £30 to £40 to the Mayor's Cigarette Fund.[59]

The local press encouraged generous contributions to the fund by publishing letters of appreciation from the front. In January 1916 Second-Lieutenant A Pontefract of the 1st Battalion KOYLI described the arrival of their cigarette parcel in Salonika:

> ... they simply went wild when their favourite Woodbines arrived ... They made one cigarette into about five by having say two puffs at it, then docking it, putting it behind the ear, then doing a bit of good hard digging. Then out would come the matches, and one man would say to his pals, 'One more pull, Paddy?' Then out would come a cloud of smoke.[60]

Lecturing from the front, Ada Ward observed:

> Out here, wherever one sees a lad in khaki, one sees also, as part and parcel of him, hi‍
> precious cigarette. In the thick of the fight, in the weary waiting time in the long marche‍
> Tommy is happy with his fag. I have seen him myself, brought down straight from the battl‍
> … blood-stained and maimed, but with the little tube of comfort between his lips.[61]

Lance-Corporal F Horsfall described cigarettes as 'The greatest comfort Tommy gets out here.'‍
'Nothing seems to be better for the nerves than tobacco', wrote GA Marriot, Kings Royal Rifles.‍
Cigarettes were expensive at the front, so it was particularly 'opportune' if a cigarette parcel arrive‍
when stocks were low, a couple of days before the troops' 'weekly issue.'[64]

Parcels were also sent to Huddersfield prisoners of war. Able-Seaman Clifford Appleyard o‍
Hillhouse, was one of several local men who sent 'heartiest thanks for your most welcome presen‍
from the prisoner of war camp at Döberitz.[65] A similar letter was received from Sergeant JW Clarke‍
KOYLI, a prisoner of war at Schneidemühl.[66]

A Cigarette for "Tommy"
by
J Prise, Huddersfield

For "A Cigarette for 'Tommy'" I have found a little time
To write a "begging letter," which I'm putting into rhyme,
In the hope that you will read it, for I think that if you do,
You'll realise that "Tommy" has a claim on even YOU.

"A cigarette for 'Tommy'"! Just consider what it means
To someone in the trenches, who of home and England dreams;
When a cheerless watch he's keeping, in the dark and cold and wet,
He won't feel half so lonely with a pipe and cigarette.

It maybe you enjoy a pipe or like a good cigar
(I can't afford the latter, at least, not since the war),
If so, I needn't ask you (though, of course, you may "forget")
To see that every "Tommy" has his pipe or cigarette.

Or you may not be a smoker (not that I complain of that);
Your "arguments" 'gainst smoking, I admit, might "floor me flat";
But if you don't like tobacco, you surely won't refuse
A cigarette for "Tommy," though it is against your "views".

It may be, like myself, you have a lad who's had to go
To take his place, with others, in the field against the foe.
That it broke your heart to lose him I can quite well understand;
But now he's gone to him I am sure you'll "lend a hand".

To help the Mayor's "bacca" fund, as very soon you'll see,
A Matinee at the Hippodrome next week there's going to be;
If you'd "do your bit" for "Tommy," and give yourself a treat,
Hurry up and buy a ticket, or (still better) BOOK A SEAT.[67]

A legacy of the war was an increased number of men who smoked, many acquiring the habit o‍
active service. Yet, even with 21st century knowledge about the toxicity of tobacco, it is difficult t‍
argue against contemporary wartime opinion that the psychological benefits of smoking outweighe‍
the physiological harm to the Tommies.

The most telling local testimony came from Dr Louis Petro Demetriadi, who had joined th‍
Territorials in 1897 as Medical Officer to the 5th Dukes and went to France with them in April 1915‍
Until January 1917 he served as Lieutenant-Colonel in charge of a Casualty Clearing Station, whic‍
was 'constantly under German shellfire.'[68] From there he wrote several letters of thanks to the Mayo‍
for generous provisions of cigarettes …

I have noticed what a wonderful soothing effect tobacco has when men are in pain. It certainly acts as a sedative … in shell-shock cases the cigarette soothes the nerves, and patients often go to sleep at once with the cigarette only half smoked.[69]

In June 1916 he wrote:

I am convinced no fund has helped to cheer the patients up more than your cigarette fund has done.

One young fellow the other day had all his lower jaw blown away with a bomb … I thought he wouldn't be able to smoke, or even to find his mouth for bandages, but he said. "Can I please have a packet of cigarettes?" … we just managed to find a way to his mouth, where we put the spout of the feeding cup, and he smoked two packets straight off, and said they had done him more good than anything he had had since he came up – although he has no lower jaw left he will get better, and I am certain his recovery has been due in no small way to the Huddersfield cigarettes. Again, ladies and gentlemen, thank you very VERY much …[70]

Has anybody taken your temperature to-day, my man?
I don't know—but I missed a packet o' fags first thing this morning!

By September 1916 Dr Demetriadi and his medics were treating the wounded from an 18-mile stretch of the front line from La Bassée to Touchez.

As the men arrive the first thing they want is a drink of water – Then they ask for a cigarette, which, thanks to you, we can always give them. Then they often fall asleep, and perhaps the half-burnt cigarette falls out of their mouth and it burns a little hole in the blanket! But we don't care about this … I have seen men smoking what you have sent them from Huddersfield, and die within an hour of coming in … I am certain many of the last hours of a number of wounded men have been made happier by your committee … The last thing that a lot of the men have done in this world is to smoke one of the Huddersfield cigarettes.[71]

Dr Demetriadi came home in January 1917, ostensibly on leave, but he was unwell. Returning to his role as Conservative Councillor for Marsh, he was 'cheered for his efforts on the battlefield' at his first Town Council meeting. He had performed most of his duties within range of German shells and had been mentioned in dispatches by both Lord French and General Sir Douglas Haig. He told the council that he 'had seen horrors … that he never thought he would … in this world.'[72]

In March 1917 he spoke to a meeting of local fund-raisers at Huddersfield Town Hall, urging them to continue sending cigarettes to the front. He also recounted a harrowing tale about an elderly soldier who begged to help carry a stretcher from the battlefield. When asked why, he replied: 'There were three of us together in the field – myself and my two sons. My eldest son was killed and my youngest son is on the stretcher.' When the doctor looked on to the stretcher, his youngest son was dead too.

Another soldier had asked the doctor to post two letters to his mother and sweetheart.' The letter had to be censored and he had written:

Lieutenant-Colonel Dr Louis Petro Demetriadi

I have not been frightened out here before but I am frightened now. We are going over the parapet this afternoon at 2 o'clock, and I shall be hit and I shall die at 8 o'clock tonight.

The soldier was killed at 7.55 that evening.[73]

Dr Demetriadi was unable to return to France. His health deteriorated and in January 1918 he relinquished his commission on the grounds of ill-health.[74] He was transferred to Southport to convalesce, but died in Huddersfield on 26 October 1918, two weeks before the Armistice, aged 55. He was buried with full military honours at Lindley Parish Church, where he had been a church warden. The Demetriadi name lives on at Outlane Golf Club where he was the first club captain from 1906 to 1908. Members still compete for the Demetriadi match-play trophies, the men's cup presented by the doctor in 1908 and the women's cup by his wife in 1912.[75]

Whilst cigarettes were a great source of comfort and relaxation, YMCA Huts provided the troops best opportunity for communal relaxation. About 350 of these were erected in France, of which Huddersfield supplied two at £500 each. Some were converted into hospitals but the majority of them were havens of food, entertainment, religious services, shelter and rest. Open night and day, they were a sanctuary from the horrors just a few miles away.[76] Reverend George Evans, Pastor of Golcar Baptist Church, spent five months with the YMCA in France, and had no doubt that the concerts and other activities in the YMCA huts were vital to the troops' well-being. The experience of the front line 'got on men's minds.' When a soldier returned from duty he was often 'moody', very disturbed by what he had witnessed, and in need of 'something to keep him from thinking of yesterday and tomorrow.'[77]

In April 1916 the Mayoress organised a Flag Day for the YMCA which raised £1560.[78] Three months later she started an appeal for £150 to send out a Huddersfield Concert Party to perform for the troops.[79]

Such concert parties were the brainchild of London actress and theatre manager, Ms Lena Ashwell, who led 25 different troupes from around the country between February 1915 and the autumn of 1918. On 24 October 1916 she spoke at Huddersfield Town Hall, when preparations for the Huddersfield Concert Party were underway. Each party was usually comprised of seven artists – a soprano, contralto, tenor, bass, violinist or cellist, an entertainer and an accompanist. Each performed three concerts per day – 3pm in a hospital and two in a camp, beginning at 5.30pm and ending at 9.30pm. The soldier appreciated serious as well as light entertainment and she had seen *Macbeth*, Handel and Bach well received. The War Office was initially suspicious that such entertainments 'might undermine or disrupt military discipline.' They had been proved wrong. She had seen …

> … fine men going up the line and battered wrecks coming down … could they realise what a concert, a few hours of normal life, meant to these men, after months and months of … nothing but desolation and horror? A few moments of beauty … could always wipe out evil and misery could always be kept away by healthy laughter.
>
> … a doctor and … a padre, had thanked her – by crying … they had felt so deeply the necessity of music, art and beauty.[80]

The Huddersfield Concert Party, led by Lena Ashwell, arrived in France in March 1917. Fitting into the routine of three concerts per day, they performed at a variety of YMCA huts, French halls, camps, canteens, garages, convalescent hospitals, an ammunition depot and 'endless other places.' Invariably there was standing room only. One hut was …

> … so packed that men hung onto the railings which supported the roofs, and even found places on the cross beams. We are all deeply affected by the enthusiasm displayed … it was the first hour of brightness they had had for a long time, and likely to be the last for another long period.[81]

Accompanied by 'clever pianist', Haydn Sandwell, they opened with a song by the whole company, after which they introduced themselves as 'The Huddersfield Concert Party.' This was generally greeted by shouts of 'Good old Huddersfield' and, at one performance, 'Play up, Wagstaff!'[82] The programme proceeded with a mix of comedy, serious songs and community singing. They were always well received, and Private Wesley Wilman was proud to overhear comrades discussing them as 'the best they had ever heard.' After 70 performances over 'four busy and trying, but memorable weeks', they returned home in April. One final homecoming performance in Huddersfield Town Hall was rapturously received by the local audience, which had a 'reputation of not being too easily "drawn" from their cold, critical and undemonstrative attitude.'[83]

Ada Ward saw first-hand the value of such concerts. In a letter home she summed up Huddersfield's support for the war effort:

> I am more and more amazed at the ever-widening and deepening channel of human kindness which flows from the generous heart of Huddersfield ... First came the National Relief Fund, the local relief fund ... help for the starving and outraged Belgians.
>
> As local trade gradually recovered from the first overwhelming chaos, or fear of chaos, so a generous stream of wealth was poured on all in need. A War Hospital is mentioned. At once a magic wand waves over Royds Hall and transforms its grounds into a city of healing ... A whisper suggests that a gymnasium will materially help recovery and a perfectly equipped building rises obediently to the call.
>
> The Y.M.C.A. pleads for a special Huddersfield hut for the firing line, and immediately enough money is raised for two!
>
> ... Nothing seems forgotten or overlooked – the babies, the young girls, the Serbians, the Poles, the Russians, the horses, the coffee vans, the Y.W.C.A. ... the glorious Red Cross, Belgian Field Ambulance, Scottish Tommies, Soldiers' and Sailors Comforts, Cinderella Fund.[84]

Ada Ward made her own generous contribution towards the end of her sell-out lecture tour of Canada and the United States in 1917, sending £100 to Lena Ashwell to support further concert parties at the front.[85]

In March 1919 the *HDE* listed 49 wartime charities that Huddersfield had supported to the tune of £209,905.[86] Two of the three women who spearheaded these efforts, former Mayoress Mary Blamires, and Miss Emily Frances Siddons, were awarded the MBE in 1918. Mrs Blamires was cited for her leadership and organisation skills and both had shown sustained commitment to a wide range of war-related work. In addition to her duties chairing the Huddersfield's Women's Suffrage Society, Emily Siddons' contributions included:

- recruitment for the forces
- helping to settle Belgian refugees
- organisation of comforts and supplies to the troops
- founding the scheme to help wives and families of men who enlisted at the start of the war
- chairing the Huddersfield Board of Guardians which placed a large hospital at the disposal of the authorities, and equipped it with additional resources
- helping to build and open the YMCA hut at Royds Hall
- vice-president of the War Pensions Committee
- president of Honley Auxiliary Hospital.[87]

Their awards reflected the voluntary contributions across the district. In Huddersfield's long, proud history, the unstinting voluntary commitment by so many, from all walks of life, to the charities and patriotic causes of 1914-18 will remain one of its crowning glories. Humanity's most brutal and horrific conflict had inspired soaring communal compassion, underpinned by an indomitable spirit which, perhaps, shone brightest following the Allies' desperate retreat in the spring of 1918. On 24 April 1918 the *HDE* reported:

> The recent evacuation of territory by our troops has entailed the abandonment of over fifty of the Church Army (YMCA) recreation huts, tents, and clubs at the front. A meeting at the Temperance Hall yesterday afternoon and evening started a campaign to raise £2000 for four more huts.

Chapter 18

1917: Passchendaele

German Withdrawal

After the battles of The Somme and Verdun were closed down there was a lull in the fighting. Both sides licked their many wounds, counted the cost and considered how best to break the enemy without sustaining such heavy losses of life and limb.[1] A number of local troops spent Christmas at home and noticed significant differences in Huddersfield. Shortages of food were becoming acute as Germany attempted to starve Britain into submission.[2] This objective would underpin German military strategy on the western front in 1917 – playing for time.

Throughout the war, the attacking army had lost more troops than the defensive line. Now Field Marshal Paul von Hindenberg decided to concede ground, retreating to a defensive line designed to be impregnable, comprising three rows of barbed wire, yards deep, strategically positioned pillbox machine gun posts, fortified craters and, in places, deep, wide trenches. This formidable barrier was known to the Germans as the Siegfried Line, and to the Allies as the Hindenberg Line. As they retreated the Germans adopted a scorched earth policy, leaving little that could be of use to their pursuers.[3]

On 1 February 1917, in conjunction with this defensive strategy, the Germans resumed unrestricted warfare on merchant shipping. They gambled that the United States would not enter the war and that if they did, German submarines would prevent significant numbers of their troops crossing the Atlantic. The U.S. President, Woodrow Wilson – known as 'Wouldn't Row Wilson' to British troops – was clearly reluctant to get involved.

The British aim for the year was to drive the Germans back from a line three miles west of Baupame and Arras, towards Douai and Cambrai. The method would be a series of strategic attacks designed to capture specific areas of high ground.[4]

Another Winter at the Front

The 5th Dukes were back in the front line at Berles-au-Bois in early January, the freezing weather causing great discomfort.

> Everything – boots, brushes, soap – was frozen stiff – sleeping blankets had a ridge of icicles on them near the mouth of the sleeper ...[5]

Soldiers who had suffered trenchfoot after long periods in damp, muddy boots in 1916, were particularly susceptible to frostbite. Apart from 'the odd patrol encounter', the cold was the greatest hardship in this quiet tour of duty.[6] The little news that reached the *HDE* was increasingly censored and bland. Old Volunteer, in his typically patriotic weekly column, blamed 'Germany's ... particularly detestable form ... of espionage' but concluded that 'I am sure the people at home would rather remain in complete ignorance ... than ... giving of the slightest advantage to our unscrupulous enemies.'[7] He was, however, sensitive to the strain relatives at home felt at this lack of news.

> ... those whose duty it is to wait at home suffer the greatest anxiety. The men at the front are kept too busy, either by duty or by games during their periods of relaxation, to mope. They know the worst that is happening, and, therefore do not conjure up imaginary terrors, as so many of us at home can scarcely help doing.[8]

The anguish was acute for relatives of servicemen reported 'missing'; this meant probably, but not certainly, killed.

Missing

by

'V' of Holmfirth

Oh, word of dread and anguish,
Seared upon my brain!
When will the waiting finish?
When will end the strain
Of watchful day and waking night?
Will he come home again?
And bid my cares diminish,
Turning sorrow to delight.[9]

This poem surely struck a chord with the parents and fiancé of Second Lieutenant Norman Eyre Bentley of Fenay Bridge. On the day that it was published, 13 February 1917, they received a letter from his Brigadier General. It informed them that, on duty in No Man's Land, Norman's patrol …

> … had to retire and in getting back through our wire the sergeant of the patrol got caught. Your son stayed behind to assist him, and has not been heard of since. It was a gallant act. We all hope that he may have been taken prisoner, and his life saved.[10]

The 2/5th Dukes head for the Front

Meanwhile, numerous local troops were heading for France, Old Volunteer reporting on 16 February:

> I saw a small body of men go from Huddersfield this week. Most of them had been out before, and knew what they were going to. There was no flag wagging. This business has become much too serious for that. But the men were calm and self-possessed, and one could not help but admire the quiet determination with which they faced the future, with its unknown perils and dangers.

Many second line battalions were also being shipped to the front, to replace, relieve and support the depleted veterans of The Somme. The new arrivals included the 2/5th (Huddersfield), 2/6th (Skipton), 2/7th (Colne Valley) and 2/8th (Halifax) Dukes. Together they comprised the 186th (2/2nd West Riding) Brigade which was part of the 62nd (2nd West Riding) Division.[11]

In training since November 1914, the 2/5th Dukes had periodically provided drafts to their first line battalion, the 5th Dukes, and had been a familiar sight route marching around Huddersfield in 1914-15. Since then they had trained at several camps, including Derby, Doncaster and Salisbury Plain. For most of 1916 they had been on coastal defence duties at Henham Park near Lowestoft, where there were regular Zeppelin sightings.

Docking at Le Havre on 12 January 1917, they spent their early weeks in hard labour, repairing infrastructure destroyed in the Battle of the Somme. This included building narrow-gauge railways, repairing roads, maintaining ammunition dumps and burying cables.'[12] Interspersed were short visits to the front line east of Hébuterne to learn the lie of the land and to take instruction in trench warfare from experienced officers.[13]

On 12 February they entered the front line at Berm Work near Beaumont Hamel, where the remains of a Somme battlefield were frozen several inches deep. Conditions deteriorated when a thaw set in three days later. The land 'returned to a condition of slough and quagmire even worse than that of the previous autumn.'[14]

> Trenches as such did not exist, for they had been obliterated … The front line was held by a series of posts and dug-outs which somewhat resembled islands in a sea of mud. Shell holes pock-marked the ground, often overlapping one another and where pathways existed between them they were but a few inches wide. The holes were full of water and more than one man lost his life through slipping off the narrow pathway into the slimy mess which engulfed him.

The 62nd Division worked hard to deepen and widen their trenches, but 'roads, disintegrated by the frost, broke up', and 'the sides of trenches fell in.'[15]

In Pursuit of the Germans

The German withdrawal to the Hindenberg Line began on 22 February. The Allies' task was to disrupt the retreat, inflicting casualties, and denying time for the Germans to dig in and destroy resources. The enemy vacated Serre in front of the 62nd Division's positions at Beaumont Hamel on 25 February. At 8pm two days later, Lieutenant PR Ridley led an advance. Three patrols crossed 800 yards of difficult and unfamiliar terrain to rush and capture a German trench at Orchard Alley. By the early hours the last German resistance had withdrawn and the 2/5th Dukes had consolidated with defensive outposts on the Puisieux to Achiet-le-Petit sunken road. At dawn they entered and occupied the village of Puisieux, eventually dislodging the most stubborn Germans from the village church.[16]

Among very few fatalities was Private Joe Taylor from Milnsbridge.

> He was a well-known athlete, having won numerous prizes for running and walking. He also played as a wing-threequarter with the Huddersfield [Northern Union Rugby] 'A' team.[17]

Huddersfield had lost another of its young sportsmen.

This remarkably clean and successful beginning earned the 2/5th Dukes' first honours. Lieutenant Ridley was awarded the Military Cross and Lance-Corporal Hubert Priestley, who pressed forward with his bombing party despite a head wound, the Military Medal.[18]

After a fortnight of trench-digging at Forceville, the 62nd Division took over the line at Miraumont, north-west of Puisieux, on 15 March. Led by Captain Joseph Walker, 'B' Company of the 2/5th Dukes held Resurrection Trench, south of Achiet-le-Petit, where they were heavily bombarded for two days and 'suffered severe casualties.' On 17 March the 2/5th Dukes advanced, tasked with securing the villages of Achiet-le-Petit, Achiet-le-Grand and Gommecourt.

> An hour before dawn … two battle patrols were despatched to the flanks of the town [Achiet-le-Petit], followed by the rest of B Company. Some opposition from machine-guns was encountered, but the village was quickly occupied and passed through, the company immediately consolidating and digging in at a sunken road on the north side of the village with the other three companies pushing in behind in support trenches.[19]

At midday the 'Corps Pigeoner' arrived with a basket of birds, and reports were attached to them to be flown back to headquarters.[20]

Pressing on beyond a German barrage that destroyed much of Achiet-le-Petit, the 2/5th Dukes approached Achiet-le-Grand. 'A' Company faced the perils of clearing well-concealed German detachments from Logeast Wood. 'B' and 'C' Companies had to create a path for the cavalry by cutting the barbed wire of the Bihucourt Line. It was '100 yards in depth in three broad belts, and so thick that it had to be dug up in parts.' Missions accomplished, these three companies advanced to capture enemy positions north west of Achiet-le-Grand.

Meanwhile, 'D' Company pushed on towards the village of Gommecourt. The Germans' strategic withdrawal, Operation *Alberich*, was well underway, and the village was conceded with only token resistance. At 4.30am on 18 March the 2/5th Dukes occupied Gommecourt. Everything in the village bar a booby-trapped chateau and a billet of 50 wire beds had been destroyed …

> … every road junction had been blown up, fruit trees were either cut down or incisions made to cut the arteries and prevent the sap from rising. All the wells were blown in and one had been poisoned with arsenic.[21]

This was the Huddersfield lads' first taste of the Germans' scorched-earth policy. Ahead of them, the Germans were devastating every resource and facility as they withdrew 'to an immensely powerful and shorter line, positioned to take every tactical advantage of ground.'

Parts of the front…

> … had now moved several miles, leaving the devastated 1916 Somme battlefield and the razed ground of Alberich behind the British front. New place names began to appear in British news … they would soon assume as sinister an air as the villages and woods of the Somme.[22]

The pursuit became necessarily cautious. Every advance required the re-building of basic infrastructure, particularly the supply lines of roads, railways and bridges, making unprecedented demands of the Royal Engineers. Much of the manual work continued to fall to the battalions 'at rest', including the 62nds. A constant eye was kept for covert German detachments covering their retreat, occupying high ground and firing opportunistically. German counter-attacks also seemed more likely after 6 April, when the United States declared war on Germany.

The U.S.A. Enters the War

The United States had severed diplomatic relations with Germany in February, after the renewal of attacks on merchant shipping. In April, British intelligence intercepted a telegram from German foreign minister Herman Zimmermann to the Mexican government and released it to the American press. The telegram promised that Germany would annex Texas and Arizona as Mexican territory if Mexico would attack the United States.

The USA began a massive programme to increase their army from 100,000 to over three million. Although it would be over a year before their troops could make a significant impact, the United States' powerful industries and economy were now part of the Allied war effort. Germany's strategy of playing for time was in danger of back-firing.[23]

With Russia in political and military disarray, and a mutiny in the French army, perhaps the spring of 1917 should have been the time to attack the armies of Britain and her Commonwealth Allies.

The Arras Offensive: the Battle of Vimy

One part of the line the Germans were reluctant to relinquish was a 17-miles stretch from Vimy Ridge in the north to the Messines to Wytschaete Ridge in the south, from which they had overlooked the Ypres Salient since May 1915. The Battle of Arras, Haig's offensive to flatten this line by capturing the high ground east of Ypres, began on 9 April 1917 with the Battle of Vimy Ridge. Aided by a British creeping barrage and tunnels to evade shellfire, the Canadians captured Vimy Ridge in three days. It was the most spectacular Allied success of the war so far, the Germans retreating not just from the ridge but from the many acres of land to the east that it overlooked.[24]

Casualties numbered 20,000 Germans and 14,000 Canadian[25], including Privates AB Shearman and T Lawson, respectively of the 46th and 49th Canadian Regiments. They were transported to Huddersfield for treatment at the Royds Hall War Hospital, but in the last week of April both died from their wounds.

On 1 May a huge funeral procession left Royds Hall. It included all the walking wounded from Royds Hall and the district's auxiliary hospitals, most of the staff, all of the town's civic leaders and the Reverend Herbert Gwyer, who had returned to Huddersfield as the Chaplain of Royds Hall since his escape from the *Lusitania*. The cortege passed through crowded streets via Marsh to Edgerton Cemetery, where Reverend Gwyer took the service.[26] Later that day he wrote to the *HDE*:

> An impressive ceremony, though a sad one, took place today, when two Canadian soldiers were laid to rest with full military honours in the Huddersfield cemetery. These men, with every prospect of a brilliant career in front of them, had come thousands of miles to defend, among other things, the citizens of Huddersfield. In doing so they met their deaths, as many others have done … All the patients at the War Hospital and auxiliary hospitals came of their own free will to pay a last respect to their comrades from overseas, but many of the spectators seemed to view the procession in the light of a spectacle, rather than a solemn ceremony. There were numbers, large numbers I regret to say, who did not even take the trouble to remove their pipes from their mouths, much less their hats from their heads, as the cortege went by. Disrespect to the dead is always disgraceful, but how much more so when those to whom it is shown have come from a far off country and given their lives in the great cause. Most of us have lost friends or relatives in this war … It is for this reason that the scandalous indifference shown by so large a section stands out so prominently.[27]

War Graves of four Canadian soldiers from the Great War in Edgerton Cemetery (left).
The grave of Private AB Shearman is second from the left, and in close up (right).

Whilst exploits at Vimy Ridge captured the headlines, the 1/5th Dukes were on regular patrol duty in the Rue du Bois region, north east of Festubert.[28] Here, Lieutenant Albert E Taylor, the formidable soldier from Paddock who had earned the DCM for gallantry at the First Battle of Ypres in 1914, and been gassed then wounded home in 1915, was killed.[29]

More fortunate were Corporal Albert Scholes, a wireless operator with the Flying Corps, and Private Ernest Sykes of the 27th (Service) Battalion (4th Tyneside Irish) Northumberland Fusiliers.

19-year-old Corporal Scholes was a telegraphist at Huddersfield Post Office before signing up in 1915. In September 1916 he had received the Military Medal for 'efficiency in keeping up communications with an aeroplane while under heavy shell fire.' On 4 April 1917 his medal saved him

> A shrapnel bullet struck the bar of his military medal, and glanced off, entering his chest about an inch above the heart. Had it not for this obstruction, the shot would in all probability have proved fatal.[30]

Private Sykes was in the front line near Arras on 9 April. His regiment progressed 300 yards ahead of the British line when heavy gunfire on three sides forced them back. Many wounded comrades fell as they vacated the recently captured land.

> Regardless of the peril that menaced him, Mr Sykes went forward on the humane mission of rescuing the wounded. He made four dangerous journeys into the gun fire, each time bringing in a wounded man.

'Prepared for a further ordeal', Ernest went out for a fifth time.

Left: His Majesty King George V presents Ernest Sykes with the Victoria Cross, 8 June 1917
Right: Ernest, back row, fourth right, returns to a civic reception at Mossley Station, 13 July 1917

196

Under conditions which appeared to be certain death, he remained out until he had bandaged all those who were too badly injured to be moved. Only by a miracle, it seemed, did he survive the incessant gun fire from enemy rifles and machine guns.[31]

On 8 June 1917 His Majesty King George V presented Ernest Sykes with the Victoria Cross.

Employed on the London, Midland and Scottish Railway, Ernest also had a locomotive named in his honour, 'The Ernest Sykes V.C.' Although he hailed from Mossley, Huddersfield was proud to claim him as one of her own after he moved to live in Milnsbridge in 1921. The *HDE* provided extensive coverage of his invitation to a dinner by the Prince of Wales in 1929, and of the Royal British Legion laying a wreath on his grave in Lockwood Cemetery in 1956, seven years after his death.[32]

The Arras Offensive: the Battle of Bullecourt

Simultaneously with Ernest Sykes' heroics, the men of the 1/5th Dukes were training Portuguese troops in trench warfare, and the 2/5th Dukes were in the front line preparing to attack a German stronghold at Bullecourt. Their attack, on 11 April, stalled owing to lack of planned support from tanks and an Australian regiment, and they suffered heavy losses. On 15 April they lost more men defending a German counter-attack at Lagnicourt.[33] The *HDE* dutifully listed the casualties, but with no counter-balancing detail of morale-boosting progress, other than vague reassurances of 'great advances.'

> Of the local units little is heard and less can be said. The casualty lists show us that the great events of the past few days are being dearly bought.

Two local privates who had lied about their age were sent home from Bullecourt for being 'too young.' One of them had a German helmet, and when asked if he had bought it replied, 'Now, I haven't 'bout it ... him 'at owned this is dead naah.'[34]

Whilst the Allies progressed to the north and south, Bullecourt remained fiercely defended. During the second half of April the 62nd Division trained for a renewed attack on this village which began on 3 May. Three Brigades advanced abreast, 186th Brigade (4 battalions of the second line Dukes) in the centre, flanked by the 185th Brigade (4 battalions of the West Yorkshire Regiment) on their right and the 187th Brigade (2 battalions of KOYLI and two battalions of the York and Lancaster Regiment) on their left. The 185th Brigade was to help the Australians take Bullecourt, the 186th Brigade was to take the Hindenberg Line north of Bullecourt and press on to Hendecourt, and the 187th Brigade was to form a defensive flank, interlocking with the third army to the north.[35]

At zero hour, 3.45am, the barrage began and the tanks advanced, followed by the three brigades. The 186th Brigade crossed a sunken road, an obvious 'gathering point'which was heavily bombarded by the Germans. With each soldier weighed down by equipment that included a rifle, grenades, sandbag, rations and a mat to lay over and flatten barbed wire, they progressed about 100 yards every three minutes, at least until a strong breeze blew dust disturbed by their own barrage back into their faces. The ground across the road afforded very little cover and they lost their bearings. Fighting their way up the other side towards a ridge north of Bullecourt, they came under 'decimating machine-gun fire from hidden concrete emplacements and a terrific barrage of high explosives and shrapnel.'[36]

Bodies fell like ninepins. Among them was brilliant Cambridge scholar, 22-year-old Lieutenant Eric Sykes of Honley. Wounded at 4am in his right hip and arm, he was patched up and was organising a counter-attack when he was mown down by machine gun fire.[37] Another to fall was Private George Fletcher, a well-known local footballer and club professional cricketer who taught at Slaithwaite Wesleyan Sunday School.

Through the mayhem, a few of the 2/5th Dukes on the southern edge of the 62nd Division, and the 2/7th Dukes just inside them, reached the first line German trenches, occupying them for seven hours. The successes were too isolated to be sustained but, faithful to their original orders, these troops continued to advance. A re-appraisal would have been safer.

> ... those who were left of the 2/5ths were rallied and continued to press forward into the "Hindenberg Line" through a tornado of bullets. At this point Lieutenant G Walker, of Lindley, was killed as he was charging, rifle in hand, at the head of his platoon, through the German wire.

With a handful of men left, Captain Joseph Walker led B Company in a successful assault on a German strong point, which was defended by more hidden emplacements. But behind them, the rest of the 186th Brigades were bombed out of the German trenches and forced to retreat, first to shell holes for refuge, then back to the sunken road. B Company was cut off, surrounded by Germans.[38]

Taking refuge in a German gun emplacement, they were pinned down by continuous bombing and shelling. They survived into the next day, 4 May, when an enemy attempt to take them prisoner was repelled, but without water and with only their iron rations for sustenance their situation was becoming increasingly desperate. On 5 May their position was 'badly blown in', leaving it 'untenable.' It was broad daylight, but Captain Walker had no choice. He ordered an immediate return through the German outpost line to the British lines. Shot at from all sides, Walker and his walking wounded improvised a fire and movement retreat over the ridges, taking refuge in the blood-soaked craters. Hour after hour they dodged the shells and bullets, their difficulties compounded by Germans disguised in captured British helmets and tunics. By 'some miracle', after nine tortuous hours, they arrived back at the British lines.[39]

It was a rare triumph in three days when the 62nd Division suffered 881 fatalities, including 80 from the 2/7th Dukes and 176 from the 2/5th Dukes. Such was the chaos, that of these 176, only five have known graves. The remaining 171 are commemorated on the Arras Memorial to the Missing.[40]

The 62nd Division was relieved on 5 May, but the battle and its heavy casualties continued until 17 May before the Germans were driven out of Bullecourt by the 58th London Division.[41]

Desertion in the French Army

Haig felt that he had been pushed into the Battle of Arras by the French. It was intended as a diversion to a French attack in the Aisne further south, where Nivelle's offensive failed catastrophically. In three weeks the French suffered 187,000 casualties to the Germans' 168,000. Many French soldiers had been denied leave for three years. Now 30,000 of them deserted and half of the rest refused to obey orders. Nivelle was replaced by General Philippe Pétain, who restored order by offering better food, home leave and longer rest periods. The French Army's domestic difficulties left Haig to pursue his preferred option of attacking on the Ypres Salient in Flanders.

The Battle of Messines

Haig's first target was the 9-miles long ridge on the eastern outskirts of Ypres. It stretched from the village of Wytschaete, which overlooked Ypres and all the British positions on the salient, south eastwards to the village of Messines, a vantage point above the valley of the River Lys. Held and fortified by the Germans since 1914, it was arguably their strongest position on the whole front. For 18 months, the British had dug tunnels leading to chambers packed with explosives under the German strong points or

352 Siege Battery Ammunition Column; Douglas Clark is on the front row, second from the right.

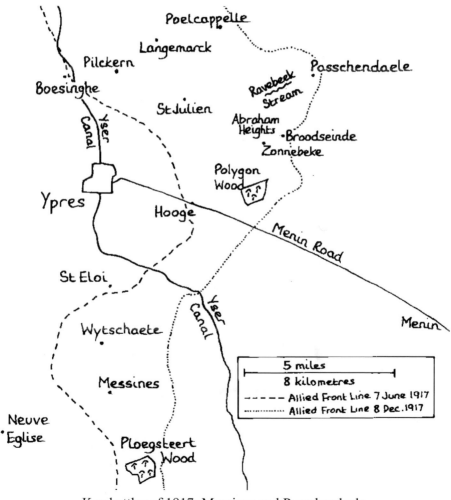

Douglas Clark's military driving certificate, issued by the War Office

this ridge.[42] From 21 May, 17 days prior to the eruptions, the British bombarded the German lines. Douglas Clark, Huddersfield's Great Britain international northern union rugby forward, had just arrived on the front line. Based at 7th Siege Park, a munitions depot on the Ypres Salient, he was an NCO with the 352 Siege Battery Ammunition Column of the Army Service Corps (ASC) Motor Transport, delivering supplies to the front line. The first entry in his diary from the front reads:

I shall never forget Messines … the bombardment simply awful.[43]

Key battles of 1917: Messines and Passchendaele

At 2.50am on 7 June, the bombardment stopped. The Germans fell into the trap. Expecting a charge, they rushed to their front line positions. At 3.10am the British began the detonation of 19 mines, in sequence. 450 tons of high explosives killed 10,000 Germans. Then, protected by a creeping barrage artillery and gas attacks, the infantry advanced. After a week of attack and counter-attack the Messine ridge was in Allied hands. Holding it was a further challenge, and land continued to change hands.[44]

None of the local battalions was involved at Messines, but the artillerymen further enhanced their reputation. They had already rendered excellent service during 1917, at Louvencourt in January, at Arras and at Messines, where they had supported the 11th Division's attacks on Wytschaete Ridge in May.[45] Their latest successes came at a price. On 13 June Douglas Clark watched these 'Batteries from Huddersfield, each distressed, coming from the Messines battle.' He recognised and acknowledged about 200 of them, and there was 'plenty of "Play up Huddersfield"' to lift their spirits.[46]

It was a busy and dangerous time for Douglas in the 352 Siege Battery Ammunition Column. Away from the immediate front line, the motor transport units were thought to be on a 'soft number' by some of the infantry, but as the use of spotter planes and observation balloons increased and the accuracy of longer range artillery fire improved, motor transport convoys were increasingly targeted.

Douglas experienced the perils of the job for the first time on 12 June when he set out with a convoy of five lorries to deliver ammunition to 156 Battery at Ploegsteert Wood, eight miles south of Ypres. On arrival they found that the Battery had moved. Delayed by German bombing of a nearby farm, which was hit and ablaze, they had to abandon one lorry which sank up to its axle in mud.

Eventually they moved on, but were halted by an officer who 'cursed' them for bringing the lorries up in broad daylight. Douglas quickly understood why. 'We can easily see Fritz's observation balloons and watch events with a very wary eye.' The Battery Officer reluctantly allowed them to unload at the ammunition dump before dusk, but they had just completed this when …

> … a German shell landed right on Dump, wounding Sgt of Battery in back. I would be 100 yards away on open road. Fritz shrapnel bursting all around … find myself on ground knocked off footboards by drivers of lorry running to cover ... Fritz is trying to get it. We lay flat in a ditch, shrapnel bursting all over our heads past lorries. Battery want us to remove vehicle, but my drivers refuse. A bit of shrapnel hits door covering my legs [with debris]. run to lorry and try to take it to cover past our Battery, only to receive a curse from officer for drawing fire on them. I reverse it right back to Tree Avenue and Battery men give me a good cheer. Then officer thanks me. As soon as I get lorry under cover they stop shelling.[47]

On 16 June, Douglas was on the road for 21 hours. Again heading south, his ammunition column salvaged shells from an abandoned Battery position, then transported Royal Garrison Artillery men to Le Bizet. En route, near 'Shrapnel Corner', he spotted someone signalling as each lorry passed.

> I consider every person in civvies a spy round here and I am not alone on this point.

Shortly afterwards they were 'heavily shelled' and the small car that accompanied them was 'badly ditched.' Pulled out, its clutch was damaged, and it had to be towed back to the Siege Park.[48]

On 7 July Douglas and the 352 Siege Battery Ammunition Column was moved to a Siege Park on the southern outskirts of Ypres. The 'nasty rumours concerning our new position' were borne out by regular delays on congested roads and frequent bombardments of gas bombs, sounding 'like some monster giant wheel crushing everything in its wake.' A narrow escape on 16 July precipitated daily gas drills,[49] but these did not help Douglas on 24 July.

> We are about to unload. Fritz sends over shrapnel. Gets in Dump which spreads all over lorries and, of course, we get it. He kills one man and two lose their arms. I am very weepy We help bandage poor fellow up. He sends over his beastly Chlorine gas. We put them in lorry. Driver missing. I take helmet off to call for driver, but have to put it on again. Driver turns up and takes wheel, nearly ditches us. I take off my helmet to drive, manage to get to hospital. Find two of wounded dead. I collapse and taken to gas hospital. Eyes, chest, throat very bad. Sick, sick.[50]

Even the robust constitution of a professional rugby player took time to recover from the insidious gas and Douglas was under treatment for the next ten days.[51]

A Nomadic Summer with the 1/5th Dukes

Whilst Douglas Clark and Huddersfield's artillerymen were engaged around Ypres, the 1/5th Dukes of the 49th Division were re-introduced to the fray in support of the 57th Division towards the southern end of the British line near Fleurbaix. It was a lengthy section of the line, defended by lightly manned, isolated posts which were usually quiet but potentially vulnerable. On 5 June, a post defended by Corporal B Siswick and three privates was attacked by an enemy raiding party of 60 to 70. The Huddersfield men faced surrender or death, but with a combination of ingenuity and calmness they repulsed the attack, gaining the battalion 'a great deal of kudos.'

Later in June the 49th Division was moved a little further north to support the 6th Division at Hulluch in the St Elie mining district. Although mostly employed guarding the shaft heads, they also took refuge in 'deep shafts and subterranean passages' during frequent gas shell attacks.[52] On 28 June, dummy raids in this sector helped to distract the enemy and aided the success of attacks along the Souchez River.[53]

Operation *Hush*

On 13 July the 49th Division was dispatched north for their next assignment in this most varied summer, destination Nieuport on the Belgian coast. They were one of four British divisions involved in Operation *Hush*, a coordinated amphibious and land offensive at Lombartzyde intended to capture this part of the coastline. This would reduce the U-boat threat to merchant shipping and to channel crossings, and deny the Germans key channel port bases from which to launch an invasion of Britain.[54]

Unfortunately, the plan was in tatters before the 49ths even arrived. The opposition was formidable - three Marine Korps divisions, including highly trained stormtroopers, 24 coastal batteries, including eight large calibre naval gun batteries with a range of 18 miles, and a coastline of trenches and wire supported by 33 concrete machine gun nests spaced every 1,000 yards.

The French Corps handed over to the British on 20 June, but the Germans smelled a rat. On 10 July they launched a pre-emptive strike. Unprepared, the most easterly of the British forces were overwhelmed. On 18 July the 49th Division inherited the precarious defence of a two miles by 1000 yards strip of dunes between the coast and the wide Passchendaele Canal.[55] Attacked by heavy and accurate shelling 'from all sides', a direct hit exploded much of their ammunition on 21 July.

On the same day, the 1/5th Dukes were among those 'deluged' by a new, sinister and deadly type of shell – mustard gas. Colourless, almost odourless apart from a faint garlic or mustard scent, it was virtually undetectable until breathed in. From a slight irritation of nose and throat, the victim deteriorated to sneezing and vomiting, inflamed, painful eyes, temporary blindness, internal and external bleeding, followed by either a week of debilitating coughing or death.

After repelling two German attacks, the 1/5th Dukes were moved to the Lombarzyde sector on 8 August where they endured a fortnight of further intense shelling, 'chiefly of … mustard gas.'

> It was here that a disaster occurred to the bulk of the battalion headquarter staff, who were entombed in a large dug-out by an ammunition dump being blown up close by.[56]

About twenty were killed, casting 'a gloom' over the whole battalion. Among the dead was Sergeant-Major Charlie Tiffany, who was suffering from gas poisoning 'but could not be induced to go sick.' Cool under fire, he had led them brilliantly through the desperate recent days. All were laid to rest 250 yards away from their dug out. On 17 August the 49th Division was relieved and began a month's rest along the coast at La Panne.[57]

Sport behind the Lines

During rest periods, formal training was punctuated by sporting activities. The *HDE* printed regular requests for equipment, as in September 1917 when 'Bombardier Atkinson' pleaded for a football.

> We don't care whether it is round or oval, oblong or square, so long as it can be kicked ... not that we need much exercise – we have plenty of that – but we like a game of football.[58]

In the same month, Signaller George W Freer, from Linthwaite made a similar request as they had 'quite a large number of the old Fartown and Town followers among us, and footballs will keep the old spirit up.'[59] Laurie Magnus in *The West Riding Territorials in the Great War*, observed:

> … how quickly sport succeeded war … in all units … the typical Battalion Sports' Office would get a move on very quickly … converting … the shell-pocked field … into a football ground, with its holes neatly patched and darned, and its goalposts and other appurtenances requisitioned as urgently as ammunition.

In 1915 Private J Lamb of the 5th Dukes wrote to thank Mr S Grimshaw of Uppermill for posting out to him three cricket balls and a bat. The Dukes played several inter-platoon matches on 'a decent pitch' in an orchard.

> You can bet we were soon wielding the willow. Last night we came into the trenches again … but we are looking forward to our next time out and a game of cricket.[60]

In February 1918 a number of Huddersfield lads transferred to the 9th Dukes had 'a battle royal' northern union match against troops from Wigan.

> The respective teams were played on to the field by the band to "She's a lassie fra' Lancashire" and "The Moonlight Bay," which habitués of Fartown will remember in the old days.[61]

Douglas Clark's diary records regular sporting fun at the siege parks of the ASC, where he wrestled and enjoyed games of chess, cricket and football – at least until 27 October when a bombardment destroyed their goalposts. On 16 October he delivered a talk about the 1914 British Northern Union tour of Australia.

In the summer of 1917, Divisional Sports at Achiet-le-Petit helped the 2/5th Dukes to recuperate from the ordeals of Bullecourt. The venue for many of their events and entertainments was an ingenious 2000-seat ampitheatre, 'The Coliseum', which they constructed inside a huge crater that had formed when a German ammunition dump exploded.[62]

On 14 June performances by the Divisional Band and concert party were interspersed with boxing contests in the arena's 18-feet ring. Top of the bill was a bout between star boxer of the 2/5th Battalion, CSM Schofield, DCM, and Private Hayhurst of the 2/6th (Skipton) Dukes. Two days later a gymkhana was held outside the arena, the 2/5th Dukes winning four events out of five.[63] These included three events on horseback - dribbling a football with a pick handle, driving a second horse round a course, and picking

Douglas Clark in his
Great Britain shirt and cap

up a series of stones to drop into a bucket. There were also 100 yards sprint and mile races, although it 'was not exactly a Fartown sports day. The ground was very heavy, and as mud stuck to the pumps it made the going very trying.'[64]

A number of events were designed to practise combat skills, including 'firing grenades' and 'speed shooting.' The 62nd Division's best marksmen could disperse a party of Germans at 1200 yards. Later in the summer, the 2/5th Dukes won the Divisional Football Cup, beating a Royal Engineers and RAMC team 6-1 in the final. As Laurie Magnus commented, with 'play imitating work', morale was restored and 'the spirit of Bullecourt' renewed.

> The old saying about the playing-fields of Eton and the battle of Waterloo recurs to memory … The preparation for war in sport was illustrated again and again.[65]

The fitness of the 2/5th Dukes earned a special mention in divisional orders when they dug 600 yards of trenches, 3 feet wide and 3 feet deep, on 2 July. In early August they occupied the hazardous

The Coliseum ampitheatre, constructed by the troops inside a huge crater that had formed when a German ammunition dump exploded

Apex' near Reincourt, where the Germans' advanced outpost was just 30 yards away. All means of attack – grenade, rifle, machine gun and trench mortar – were employed by both sides. Further exploiting this proximity, the 2/5th Dukes were ordered to hurl propaganda leaflets into the enemy lines. This somewhat optimistic initiative invited any German wishing to surrender to approach the British lines at dawn calling "cuckoo." 'No cuckoos were collected by the battalion.'

The 2/5th Dukes enjoyed rare culinary variety when, wearing gas helmets, they raided 40lb of honey from a beehive in their Vraucourt billets. At the end of August they were moved back to Bullecourt to salvage munitions and equipment from the battles of the spring. Motivated by competition, they collected so much that 'they went to the head of the divisional salvage list.'[66]

The Battle of Passchendaele

Whilst the 49th Division was engaged in the north at Nieuport and the 62nd Division held the line to the south, Douglas Clark witnessed preparations for the most infamous battle of 1917, the Third Battle of Ypres, better known as the Battle of Passchendaele, scheduled to commence on 31 July.

On 30 July, six days after inhaling chlorine gas, he returned to hospital at Poperinge.

> … eyes not quite as well today. Guns quiet. RAMC men prepare for 50,000 wounded, marquees all along road. We receive our instruction re moving of guns after advance … bombardment to commence after midnight. After dusk, roads full of limbless and Red Cross. 12pm [midnight] Mr Preedy and myself take up our position to watch bombardment from top of lorries …
> … at 3.50am witness the sight of our lives. 3 mines go off and guns open in full. Such a bombardment the like of which this war has ever seen. Then the line just looks white hot and Fritz is soon in trouble sending SOS Green and Red star shells up along the front.
> I have never seen fireworks half so beautiful. We all feel for poor old Fritz. He replies with shrapnel, but soon stops. The bombardment has not ceased for one moment, it is now 11am. We all wonder if it's possible for a human being to live in it ... but the left flank of enemy holds fast. We bombard this flank all day ... our men advance … but owing to such bad state of no-man's land, we cannot take guns up to support, and our men have to retire and start digging in 2 miles down. We bombard all night, but rain sets in. Conditions awful, out of question going over.[67]

On 1 August, Douglas wrote: 'It never stops raining … ground awful', and on 2 August, 'Rains all day. Cook house blown down.' A 15-inch naval gun opened fire behind them, becoming an immediate target for German shells which whistled directly over their Siege Park. On 3 August, Douglas resumed duties, driving 200 rounds of pipe to 352 Battery and returning past the Cloth Hall in Ypres.

It is enough to turn anyone grey, the destruction of this town.[68]

There would be only brief respites from the rain over the next four months. The Allies pounded the 13-mile battle front with 4.25 million shells until mid-August, but alongside their successes they destroyed many of the dykes and ditches that drained the low-lying, clay-based terrain. It created the worst underfoot conditions for an attacking force in the history of the British army.

Tanks were negated, fire and movement – any sort of movement – was problematic, and the deepest German lines were six miles away. The water table was so high that there were few manned German trenches. Instead, the land was defended by dozens of pillbox machine gun posts with overlapping fields of fire. Relatively stationary, protected by these outposts and by their deeply wired first, second and third Hindenberg Line defences, the Germans quickly disrupted attempts by the Allies to coordinate artillery, tanks and infantry in the same attack.[69]

On 16 August Douglas Clark received a widely circulated extract from a 'Zurich telegram.'

We must hold our positions between the seas and our lines or we shall lose the war entirely. The fate of Germany is now being decided in Flanders.

That day he delivered 800 rounds of ammunition to three different batteries, but noted that the guns were 'not going forward.'[70]

Allied plans for the Battle of Langemarck (16 to 18 August) were wildly ambitious, and minor gains were dwarfed by the number of casualties. The Germans retaliated on 22 August, Douglas recording:

Early morning. Great bombardment raging which shakes our hut just like the endboards of a box cart.

Shortly afterwards he was part of a munitions convoy that drove through Ypres to 352 Battery's position. He was unloading when ...

… a shrapnel shell … burst over my head. I gave myself up as a goner, about 15 pieces hit my steel helmet and my back. I thought of home, but luck was with me and my helmet.

Shrapnel fairly splintered off it and nearly choked me with smoke. Cox was 10 yards from me and gave me up as lost. Pleased to report only damage, a cut on little finger, so I carry on …'

Douglas Clark on the 352 SBAC's motor bike; the photograph was taken behind the lines at Poperinge in September 1917

The disaster at Langemarck saw General Gough replaced by the more conservative Sir Herbert Plumer. He began the cagier tactic of taking the German's lightly defended outer positions, and digging in.[72] This method secured ground at the battles of Menin Road Bridge and Polygon Wood between 20 September and 3 October, after which the Allies possessed the ridge east of Ypres.[73]

On a foggy 30 September, Douglas Clark set off from Ypres along the Menin Road to deliver ammunition to 352 Battery on the front line. Either side were dead bodies and improvised graves from the recent battle, and not just those of infantrymen.

> Fritz is knocking hell out of it … man's greatest friend the horse, poor beasts, are lying dead or dying on this road this morning … would turn anyone.[74]

"Ilium"
by
'Salient'

> Fair was your city, old and fair,
> And fair the Hall where the Kings abode.
> And you speak to us in your despair,
> To us who see but ruins here,
> A crumbled wall, a shattered stair,
> And graves on the Menin Road.
>
> It was sweet, you say, from the City Wall
> To watch the fields where the horsemen road;
> It was sweet to hear at evenfall
> Across the moat the voices call;
> It was good to see the stately Hall
> From the paths by the Menin Road.
>
> Yea, Citizens of the City Dead,
> Whose souls are torn by memory's goad;
> But now there are stones in the Cloth Hall's stead,
> And the moat that you loved is sometimes red,
> And the voices are still and laughter sped,
> And torn is the Menin Road.
>
> And by the farms and the House of White,
> And the shrine where the little candle glowed,
> There is silence now by day and night,
> Or the sudden crash and the blinding light,
> For the guns smite over as thunders smite,
> And there's Death on the Menin Road.[75]

Continuing his journey, Douglas Clark arrived at his Battery just as the British guns began a bombardment.

> It's hellish awful, poor Bosch. I watch effects of barrage … Fritz balloons up, look as near as ours, a beautiful sight indeed … Every make of gun in play, from 15 inch to rifle. Guns everywhere you look blending fire. This is a real war, a wonderful, splendid, inspiring, awful sight I shall not forget.[76]

Although a local battalion was still to participate in these attacks, Douglas was one of many Huddersfield lads involved in the push for Passchendaele. Among the *HDE*'s daily casualty lists was Captain Arnold Sykes of the York and Lancaster Regiment, whose death 'cast a gloom over the whole town.' He wrote and performed for the Huddersfield Amateur Operatic Society, and wrote gentle satirical, humorous poems. He left a wife and three children.[77] Rifleman CH Cocker, a stretcher bearer with the King's Royal Rifles, 'had his left tunic sleeve blown off by concussion from shells' as he tended a wounded man. 'But he still carried on his work until he received a direct hit as he was trying to carry his comrade away.'[78] Sergeant Norris Crossley was another who would be sadly missed. Ordinary Seaman Fred Taylor dedicated the following poem to him.

Her Son

by

Ordinary Seaman Fred Taylor

There's a grave out there in Flanders,
In the sound of booming guns,
Where lies to-day, beneath the sod,
One of Britain's noblest sons.
He fought and died for country's sake,
And a cause he thought was right.
Now his body lies out in Flanders,
But his soul has taken flight.

There's a home he left behind him,
Where now stands a vacant chair.
And a mother sad who grieves all day,
For her son who is not there.
She gave her lad for country's sake,
And a cause she knew was right.
And though she grieves, she still is proud,
That the Huns he went to fight.

There's a home far from the cottage,
And away from Flanders too;
We know not where, but there abide
All the loyal and the true.
And in that land of light and love,
Away from the booming guns,
One day a meeting there will be –
Mother and noble son.[79]

On 23 September the 49th Division began to march from the Belgian coast back to the Ypres region. Arriving on 4 October, they relieved the Wellington and Otago Battalions on recently captured land in the Ypres Salient, and on 8 October repulsed a German attack.

Meanwhile, Generals Plumer and Gough recommended that the front between Ypres and the Passchendaele Ridges, almost six miles away, should be closed down, at least until it dried out. Rejecting this advice, Field-Marshal Haig's next attack would involve eleven Divisions taking the village of Poelcapelle. These included the 49th West Riding and the 66th East Lancashire divisions which were ordered to advance along two parallel spurs. Between them should have been the Ravebeek stream, but it had become an impassable 50-yards wide swamp.

At 7pm on 8 October, the 49ths and 66ths left Ypres, allowing them five hours to march the two miles to the front line at Abraham's Heights, and five hours' rest before zero hour. Laden with 60lb of equipment, reaching their positions by midnight was impossible. The duckboards over the morass of mud were covered in slime and were broken every few yards. In the darkness, the troops slipped, concertinaed, collided, fell and slithered into water and mud-filled craters. The porridge-like sludge acted like quicksand and several were sucked under and needed rescuing. It took both divisions ten hours to cover the two miles, barely 400 yards per hour. They arrived exhausted and 'covered from head to foot in mud and slime.'

The creeping artillery barrage that should have led their attack was equally disrupted. Gun platforms continually slid and sank, and the wheels of the guns were up to their axles in mud, impeding aim and adjustment. Pack mules which carried their ammunition had difficulties reaching the batteries. Each shell had to be cleaned to make it fit for firing. In the circumstances, the barrage was understandably feeble.'

Dawn broke to reveal an alien landscape: shattered tree stumps where woods once stood; piles of bricks from ruined buildings; scores of impact craters, many overlapping, and all glistening with mud. As the rain continued the routes deteriorated, further churned up by each trip to the front line. The prospect of regular supplies or relief troops reaching them or, should it be necessary, a controlled retreat, diminished by the minute.

In the circumstances, the 1/5th Dukes in the 147th Brigade was fortunate to be ordered into Divisional Reserve whilst the 146th and 148th Brigades led the attack. Of these, only the 146th Brigade was able to cross the Ravebeek swamp. The 148th Brigade sought an alternative route which left them exposed to enemy fire.

At 1.30pm on 9 October, eight hours into the attack, the 1/5th Dukes were sent into battle to support the 148th Brigade. Captain Keith Sykes set an 'inspiring example of courage' that afternoon, earning a mention in despatches. During the evening they were heavily shelled, which is probably when Private Fred Hey, a twice-wounded hero of the Somme who worked in Huddersfield but hailed from Ravensthorpe, suffered multiple shrapnel lacerations. Fred was evacuated, a tortuous journey involving a 'marathon' relay of 16 stretcher bearers, with every chance of one of them slipping and tipping him into a swampy grave. After several hours he arrived at a Casualty Clearing Station, where his left leg was amputated. From there he was moved to a base hospital at Wimereux, north of Boulogne. One of the hospital matrons wrote to Fred's sister to report his amputation, and wounds to his shoulders and to his right leg. Fred 'sent his love' but was unable to write. He would never see his sister. After four agonising days Fred died on 13 October from 'gas gangrene and amputation of the left leg.' He is buried at Wimereux Communal Cemetery.[80]

Across the Ravebeek Stream was Second-Lieutenant Harry Coverdale of the 11th Battalion, Manchester Regiment. Leading his platoon in an attempt to capture an enemy strong point, he killed a German officer and captured two soldiers who were sniping at him. He then rushed and eliminated two machine-gun positions, killing or wounding the occupants. Circling back, Harry reorganised his platoon to capture another position, only retreating when they were endangered by the British artillery barrage. Several hours later, his company attacked and took out a German patrol, but suddenly came under severe rifle fire from a German counter-attack. Using all the limited time available, Harry ordered his men to withdraw one by one, until he was the last to retreat. These remarkable actions at the Battle of Poelcapelle earned Harry the Victoria Cross, to add to the Military Medal awarded to him earlier in the year.

Harry Coverdale moved to Huddersfield in the early 1920s, becoming Chief Engineer at Joseph Lumb and Sons of Folly Hall Mill and serving as an officer in the local Home Guard in World War II. He died in 1955 and is buried at Edgerton Cemetery.[81]

Against the odds, the attack of the 49th and 66th Divisions achieved one of its two objectives, driving the Germans a little further back to establish a new front line on the Belle Vue Spur overlooking Passchendaele. But the Divisions were in no condition to progress further and the cost was high. Casualties in the 1/5th Dukes alone numbered eight officers and 200 other ranks. In total the three Brigades lost 2585 men including 654 fatalities, most of these in the 146th and 148th Brigades that led the attack.

Relieved on 10 October after enduring the worst conditions of the war, they retired 'thoroughly exhausted' to an 'uncomfortable' camp at St Jean 'where everyone had to sleep in shell holes.'

On 12 October the New Zealand Division attacked ahead of St Jean, but with little success and so many casualties that, despite their exhaustion, three officers and 150 men of the 1/5th Dukes immediately volunteered to act as stretcher bearers, 'to go and reclaim their wounded from the battlefield.'

This was the last action of Major-General Perceval CB with the battalion. Having led them since 1915 at Ancre and on the Somme, he took his leave of them on 18 October and was succeeded by Major-General Neville JG Cameron CB, CMC of the Cameron Highlanders, until the end of the war.[82]

Gallantry of the Motor Transport Drivers
The M.T. A.S.C.*
by

B Haigh, Huddersfield, M.T. A.S.C., 18 May 1917
(who has been to over 200 breakdowns in two years in France)

Some say we're not in danger –
The M.T., A.S.C.
But as a motor driver
I don't at all agree

Who takes the big guns up the line,
And ammunition, too;
And food for men and horses,
And brings back wounded, too?

Who has to travel awful roads
Which they have never seen
Without a light to lead them on,
And shell-holes in between?

Who helps our Tommy on his way
When weary and footsore,
And takes him to his "little home,"
Right to his dug-out door?

Who is it that goes up the line
To a place as hot as hell
For officers' cars and ambulances
That have been hit by shell?

Tis I, a first aid driver,
Have all this work to do,
And with wee Jock, my pal, to help
We've got them dozens through.

Let those who love to run us down
Just read these lines right through
And then I think without a doubt
They'll give praise justly due.[83]

* The Motor Transport, Army Service Corps

On 26 October, the Canadians, some of the best troops in the Allied armies, progressed to within 500 yards of Passchendaele.[84] That afternoon Douglas Clark and the 352 Siege Battery Ammunition Column made several deliveries, the last of them to the 352 Siege Battery almost a mile beyond Prazinburk Ridge, near St Jean. As Douglas recorded, their orders were taking them ever-closer to the front line.

> Death on every side. 12 tanks destroyed … count 20 horses and 8 men dead. Wounded coming in. Splinters from Fritz shell hit my legs. Flying everywhere. Our Battery is in line with field guns. 4.30, we see our lot going up, then all guns open up on poor Bosch guns, wheel to wheel. Pours with rain and up to knees in slush, no words could explain condition, still we all see what Salient looks like. We return to Park … have supper and turn in wet through.[85]

That evening Douglas met his Fartown teammate Ben Gronow, who was Acting Sergeant with the 275th Section Heavy Artillery Motor Transport, and handed a German bayonet to him to be forwarded home.

Three days later, Douglas was again unloading at 352 Battery's dump when …

> … Fritz starts shelling, simply hellish. We have to unload ourselves as men have taken cover horses and men flying for their lives. Grenadier Guards … are detailed to unload us. After one lorry they scoot and we never see them again. I have never seen anything so awful as this before, death at every side.

Then a shell struck part of the dump where the Guards' captain and some of his men were sheltering. Douglas tried to organise a rescue, but …

> … Three officers and lots of men refuse to help me, they run like March Hares.

Entering alone, he found them 'badly wounded from some burning cartridges,' and helped them on to the relative safety of his lorry, before continuing his journey of deliveries.

> I breathe a silent prayer for four hours and think every minute my last. Words fail to express this scene, blood everywhere you look, dead men and wounded. Those fine stretcher bearers.

The pack mule drivers of the RFA unloaded on Prazinburk Ridge, as it was 'not fit to take horses further' yet Douglas and his colleagues delivered to 352 Battery a mile further along the same road. There, the Battery men refused to leave cover to help as the lorries were unloaded.

> There's not a soul in sight excepting men trying to find a better hole … You can see shell explode long before you hear the noise of shell travelling through air and explosion.

Shell fragments set fire to some of their shipment of cartridges. He and his co-driver fled, fearing a major explosion, but returned when their wounded passengers could not make their escape. Extinguishing the blaze, they returned to their Siege Park.

> The awfullest day in my life so far. My lucky star.[86]

Field-Marshal Douglas Haig was aware of such valour. In his Passchendaele despatch he referred to:

> Particularly good work … by the Motor Transport drivers who have shown the greatest gallantry and devotion to duty … under heavy shell fire and during long hours of exposure.

For how long could Douglas's luck hold out? Their next delivery to the same area was two days later. Six lorries left at about 5.30pm. Approaching Prazinburk Ridge the Military Police informed them that the shelling was worse there than over the ridge, so they proceeded over the ridge, keeping 200 yards between each lorry. As an extra precaution, they planned to wait until each lorry had not just unloaded but returned before the next one started out on the last 200 yards.

> It is now quite dark and wind favourable for Fritz gas. All guns his side of Bavaria House in action … Mr Preedy and I rode on first vehicle. We had not gone very far until we found the gas very bad … so we pulled up to warn drivers, Mr Preedy going back to following lorries. I took ours forward to unload … the place was deserted, so first and second driver and myself started unloading. I pulled off my helmet 3 times, doing so I was almost overcome. At this point one of Fritz's green lights flared up, and then the place was turned into hell. I doubt if ever Fritz has sent over so many shells on such a small stretch as he did round us, even putting the shelling of the previous days in the shade. I received a nasty wound in the left arm and I thought it certain all would be killed. I ordered boys to go back and take cover near the other lorries. Here I found Mr Preedy and reported I was wounded. He wanted to take me to hospital, but I refused to leave lorries. Shells were falling in front, behind and on all sides … we decided to get lorries out of this …

With some difficulty, Douglas turned his lorry round. Then …

> … a shell burst, hitting me in the abdomen and chest and throwing me some distance.

The blast threw him over a hedge into a pool of water.

> I was bleeding very heavy from stomach and having lost my gas helmet, thought the end must be near. Its then a man starts to think of the dear ones at home and I prayed I might just be able to see them to say "goodbye", when another shell threw me back onto the road …

As the men emerged from cover they found Douglas 'lying on the road with almost all of his clothing torn off by the force of the explosions.'

> … I was picked up and taken to Ypres Dressing Station (the Prison) and my wounds dressed. The journey left me very weak from loss of blood, it was simply murder.

From there he was moved to Number 10 Casualty Clearing Station outside Poperinge. Doctors found that eighteen pieces of shrapnel had penetrated his left arm, abdomen and chest, one piece penetrating perilously near his heart.' Douglas's only chance was an immediate operation.[87]

Local Artillerymen and the Capture of Passchendaele

A bloody October ended with the Allies just 300 yards from Passchendaele village. The final push to capture it commenced with the deployment of some of the Allies' best infantry – the Canadian 1st Division – supported by some their best artillery – the 168th Brigade, raised in Huddersfield at the start of the war.[88] Interviewed at Royds Hall at the end of 1917, Company Sergeant Major McKee of the Royal Irish Rifles described the 168th Brigade as …

> … the best men in France. We have been covered by several bodies of artillery, and very often we were tightly pressed. Some other brigades have closed down their guns. But the 168th never did. They always fought right up to the last until they silenced 'Jerry's' guns … Often … they have "saved our mutton". When we had to storm the trenches and take our gruel they were at their very best …

> … on one occasion … it was left to some other artillery to cover us. Their fire was no effective enough and … we lost a lot of lads. But … "our own lads," as we came to look upon the 168th … came up behind and … gave 'Jerry' what Paddy gave the drum. They are fine not only in the way they man their guns, but in the accuracy with which they use them .. Every shell they send tells, and they continue sending them until they silence the opposing artillery, and then send a few more …

> … They are amongst the best men in France or in any other theatre of war and have proved it conclusively.[89]

Although 168th Brigade was depleted when B Battery lost five guns on 1 November, A, C and D batteries took their revenge five days later, unleashing devastating fire in support of the Canadian 1st Division. Passchendaele Ridge was stormed and the village – obliterated but for its church – was captured. Fighting continued until 10 November when the last ridge was taken, the local artillerymen expending 2240 rounds from their 16-pounders and 75 rounds from their howitzers on the final day of the Battle of Passchendaele.[90]

Field-Marshal Haig commended the artillery, which had, in the most atrocious conditions 'never failed to dominate the German batteries… practically without protection of any kind … under a continuous bombardment of gas and high explosive shell.'[91]

Germany had lost its strategic positions on a 12-mile front from Messines to Passchendaele. For the Allies, the Ypres Salient was no longer an overlooked deathtrap, but the whole operation had been more difficult, time-consuming and costly than anticipated. They had inflicted 260,000 German casualties, but suffered 310,000 in return.[92]

Douglas Clark's Injuries

Among these was Douglas Clark, who came round from his operation to remove shrapnel from his chest and abdomen at 4am on 1 November, about eight hours after receiving his injuries. He endured a 'very bad' 48 hours, but skilful surgery combined with the strength, endurance and determination developed as a coalman, rugby footballer and wrestler saw him through.[93] On 9 November he was well enough to be transported to base hospital at Boulogne, where the ward was 'a large marquee with 32 beds and very comfy considering wild elements.' Three days later he was marked 'for blighty.' He sailed from Boulogne to Dover on 14 November and by 17 November was in the Northern General Hospital, Lincoln.[94]

On 27 November his parents arrived from Douglas's home village of Ellenborough on the Cumberland coast, just as he learned that his courage had earned him the Military Medal. He was transferred to Huddersfield's Royds Hall War Hospital on 17 January 1918, and on to Honley District War Hospital ten days later where he completed his convalescence.[95]

Invalided out of the war, Douglas was told that he would jeopardise his life if he returned to his rugby and wrestling careers. He defied medical advice. Later in 1918 he rejoined his Motor Transport Unit on the western front. In 1919 he resumed his position in the Huddersfield pack, helping the club to win the Yorkshire League, Yorkshire Cup and Challenge Cup, before setting sail for Australia with the 1920

Great Britain Northern Union touring team. He played for Huddersfield until 1929, his retirement from rugby league at the age of 38 coinciding with the first formal organisation of professional wrestling in Britain. Amidst an upsurge in interest, Douglas twice became the All-in Wrestling Heavyweight World Champion in the 1930s. Reputedly 'the strongest man on the planet', he toured Australia in 1934 and 1936, eventually retiring in 1941 at the age of 50. Douglas died suddenly from influenza in 1951, aged 59. In 2005 he became one of 17 inductees to the Rugby League Hall of Fame.[96]

Christmas 1917

The end of the Battle of Passchendaele did not mark the end of Huddersfield casualties for the year. Moved around the front line, the heroic 168th Brigade suffered 30 fatalities from accurate German shelling in December.[97] The 1/5th Dukes sustained regular injuries defending the line at Broodseinde Ridge, just east of Zonnebeke, from mid-November until the New Year, when they enjoyed a delayed Christmas lunch,[98] compensation for Christmas Day when one officer wrote:

> I have just had my Christmas dinner – cold beef, a bit of dry bread, and some cold water … We are in the front line and it is snowing hard … please excuse my writing, as my hands are so cold I don't know whether I am holding a pencil or not.[99]

At the end of 1917, both sides were involved in a race against time. Britain was in danger of being starved into submission by U-boat attacks on merchant ships. Civilians in Germany were experiencing similar austerity from the blockade. Germany needed to exploit a temporary numerical advantage resulting from Russia's military, political and economic implosion,[100] and from the redeployment of five British and six French Divisions to bolster the Italian army, which had retreated 70 miles from mountain-top positions in the Alps to the River Piave. Germany's desperation to achieve a decisive breakthrough before the arrival of three million troops from the United States would dictate the next phase of the war.[101]

(*Above*) Christmas Dinner 1917 in the Sergeants' Mess of the Tank Corps contrasted with that on the front line

(*Right*) Cartoon from *The Salient* newspaper, Christmas 1915 edition.

Chapter 19

1917: Cambrai

Tank Attack

In late summer 1917 General Haig was persuaded, mainly by Sir Julian Byng, commander of the British Third Army, to sanction an attack towards Cambrai later in the autumn. Although not top of the Allies' priorities, Cambrai was a junction of rail, road and canal/river transport that supplied the German lines and would be a significant capture. It would involve punching through the hitherto unbreached Hindenberg Line, and capturing the strategically valuable heights of Bourlon Wood and Bourlon Village, which overlooked the Baupame to Cambrai road and a sizeable area south and west of Graincourt.

Byng proposed a fast, surprise attack, led by the largest tank force the world had ever seen. Tanks had proved not only ineffective but highly vulnerable in the muddy terrain east of Ypres. By comparison, the approaches to Cambrai were across relatively undamaged, rolling chalk land. Haig agreed, but set a two-day deadline for the capture of all objectives.

The Hindenberg Line in front of Cambrai

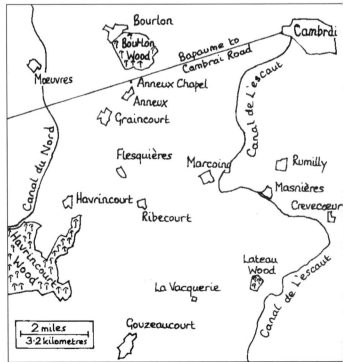

The Battle of Cambrai: the 186th Brigade featuring the Huddersfield and Colne Valley battalions made a record advance for one day, from Havrincourt Wood to Anneux Chapel

From mid-October the 62nd West Riding Division, which included the second line territorial battalions from Huddersfield (2/5th Dukes) and the Colne Valley (2/7th Dukes), joined several other divisions in intense attack training, developing their physical endurance and their shooting skills in platoon competitions.[1]

Five infantry divisions were to attack across a five and a half mile front stretching from La Vacquerie, Lateau Wood and Les Rues des Vignes in the south to Moeuvres and Bourlon in the north. The 12th (Eastern) and 20th (Light) divisions were allocated the easier terrain to the southern end of this front, paving the way for the cavalry to round Cambrai and cut it off from the rear. The 51st (Highland), 62nd (West Riding) and 36th (Ulster) divisions were to attack across the more difficult terrain on the centre-north of the front, advancing through Bourlon and on to Cambrai. The 62nds were to take Havrincourt, the strongest point in the German line. There were three infantry divisions in reserve.

The tanks would lead for much of the way, camouflaged by a creeping artillery barrage, heavy in smoke, fired over them. Rapid advances in trigonometry and munitions manufacture had facilitated precise calculation of sights, elevation and position. There would be no preliminary artillery barrage and no range-finding shots. The first shot was to be accurate and intended to count.

On 18 and 19 November, Byng's force of 476 Mark IV tanks and supporting artillery moved into the area, masked by aircraft engines and diversionary troop movements that suggested attacks elsewhere.[2]

In the foggy early morning of 20 November, the three brigades of the 62nds left billets at Bertincourt. Only their officers knew of the plans, as they assembled on the edge of Havrincourt Wood, six miles from Cambrai, in the following formation:

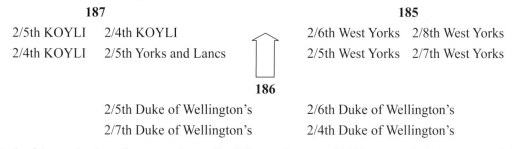

187			185	
2/5th KOYLI	2/4th KOYLI		2/6th West Yorks	2/8th West Yorks
2/4th KOYLI	2/5th Yorks and Lancs		2/5th West Yorks	2/7th West Yorks

186

2/5th Duke of Wellington's	2/6th Duke of Wellington's
2/7th Duke of Wellington's	2/4th Duke of Wellington's

Each of the twelve battalions was short of its full complement of 1000 troops, their force comprising about 10,000 men in total.[3]

Advance of the 62nd Division

Zero hour was 6.20 am, but the 62nd's tanks were late. Advancing without them, the 185th and 187th brigades entered Havrincourt Wood and within minutes came under heavy machine gun and rifle fire from a German strong point, protected by barbed wire. Overcoming this resistance, they reached the first Hindenberg Line barrier. It comprised thick barbed wire, tens of yards deep, with trenches, including 14-feet wide anti-tank trenches and machine gun posts. Beyond this was a second, similar barrier and, 200 yards behind that, a third line of support and anti-tank trenches.

The tanks caught up. Looming through the fog and smoke towards the panicking Germans, they crushed paths through the barbed wire that the infantry and artillery crossed with ease. Anti-tank trenches were bridged by laying large, tightly bound bundles of brushwood. The 185th and 187th Brigades captured Havrincourt Wood, neighbouring Chateau Wood and Havrincourt village, suffering 51 fatalities, but inflicting a similar number on the enemy and taking 200 prisoners.

The 186th Brigade, commanded by 25-year-old Brigadier-General RB Bradford, VC, followed closely behind, led on the left by the 2/5th Dukes, with the 2/7th Dukes behind them, and on the right by the 2/6th (Skipton) Dukes followed by the 2/4th (Halifax) Dukes. Despite the success of the first two brigades, lurking pockets of German resistance remained in the woods, one of which opened fire on the 2/5th Dukes as they approached Chateau Wood on the road from Havrincourt Wood to Havrincourt village. Several of them suffered bullet wounds, a handful of men were captured and their

British Mark IV Female Tanks being loaded aboard flat-bed railway trucks at Plateau Station for transportation to the British lines prior to the opening of the Battle of Cambrai.

commanding officer, Lieutenant-Colonel TA Best, DSO, was shot as he tried to negotiate a gap in the wire. Lieutenant Bodker fell next to him. Both were killed, and are buried side-by-side in Ruyaulcourt Military Cemetery. The 62nd's Divisional Commander, General Sir Walter Braithwaite, described Best as 'one of the finest soldiers and the most perfect gentlemen' he had ever commanded.[4]

> Captain and Adjutant HS Jackson took command of the battalion and endeavoured to reorganise. Captain T Goodall, officer commanding "D" Company … entered the wood to locate the point from which the casualties were being sustained, and having done this signalled to Lieutenant Douglas Black to advance with his platoon. The strong point was rushed, one officer and 58 other ranks and two machine-guns were captured … many Germans were killed and two British officers [from the 2/4th KOYLI] rescued.[5]

Captain Goodall was awarded the DSO for leading this assault which eliminated a stubborn obstacle to their advance.

Among the ruins of Havrincourt village, they came under further heavy fire. Captain CS Moxon identified the key German position and directed a tank to advance and fire on it. Along with Lieutenant Black, he led Number 14 Platoon in capturing the position, killing five Germans and taking three prisoners. The rest of the German garrison fled towards Graincourt but were 'annihilated by Lewis gun fire.'[6] The capture of Havrincourt was later described by General Haig as 'a most gallant and remarkably successful advance',[7] and helped to earn Captain Moxon the DSO and Lieutenant JH Irons, formerly an assistant in the Huddersfield Town Clerk's office, the Military Cross for 'astute leadership and fighting qualities.'[8]

As the advance continued a young Huddersfield officer recalled:

> The men … went forward with absolute fearlessness ... The Bosches made several counter-attacks, shoulder to shoulder, eight lines deep, cavalry behind. Our artillery had a splendid target. They blazed into them at practically point blank range, and simply mowed them down.

62nd West Riding Division in captured German trenches at Havrincourt

Encountering a besieged British tank crew, they beat off the German attackers. Then, hastening across country towards Graincourt, D Company captured and held a German trench known as Kangaroo Alley, the other three companies passing through them. Tanks accompanied them, blasting two anti-tank guns at Graincourt and paving the way for the 62nds to secure the village. At 5.30pm they moved on to Anneux Chapel on the Baupame to Cambrai Road.[10] They could have pressed on, but their extraordinary progress had created a sharp salient that dangerously exposed their right flank where the 51st Highland Division had been delayed for several hours by stubborn resistance at Flesquieres.[11]

Across the five divisions, the advance of 20 November cost 4000 Allied lives, but they took 5000 prisoners and inflicted thousands of casualties. The 62nds alone captured a large array of weaponry and over 2000 prisoners from six different German divisions.[12] Of these, the 2/5th Dukes captured 353 prisoners, and also killed and wounded scores of Germans. Their own casualties were 13 killed, 57 wounded and four missing.

Victory Bells

The average advance for the day was three to four miles. The 62nds had exceeded this, advancing four and a half miles, extraordinary progress with each man carrying an average of 60 pounds of equipment.

> The advance of 4½ miles in one day under battle conditions was a record that was not to be beaten by the rest of the British army during the remainder of the war.[13]

With skilful, courageous support from tanks and artillery, they had punched through two lines of the Hindenberg defence and taken possession of three villages. Field-Marshal Douglas Haig assessed it as 'a brilliant achievement.' The *HDE* saluted the 'discipline, valour and steadiness of all ranks' which was 'beyond praise.'[14] For the first time in the war, on 23 November 1917, victory bells pealed across Britain in celebration.

The *HDE* suggested that the order of the 62nd Division's commanding officer should be read in all schools and ...

> ... a holiday should be given at as early a date as possible ... impressing on the younger generation the achievement of their parents and relatives.[15]

The log book of South Crosland National School for 21 December records:

> Closed school for Xmas Holiday at 9.30am; an extra day has been granted to celebrate the gallant conduct of West Riding troops in the recent advance on Cambrai.

Celebrated across all ages, the events of 20 November became part of Huddersfield's folklore.

The Tank
by
Dorothy Irwin, aged 10, Standard III, Birkby Council School

The Tank is a monster huge and black,
When the Germans see it they hurry back,
It does its work you'll all agree,
It is doing its bit for you and me.

It laughs at the bullets and bayonets, too;
And the wires and walls it pushes through;
And when the Tank has cleared the way
Our soldiers follow and shout hooray.

Its guns peep out from its sides of steel;
Of the damage they've done we've heard a great deal;
They save the lives of our father's and brothers,
Who wish they were at home with their sisters and mothers.

By saving the pennies we used to spend
We're helping to bring the war to an end,
And we hope before long we'll have a lot more
To help to finish this dreadful war.[16]

The Battle for Bourlon Wood

Following the death of Lieutenant-Colonel Best, Lieutenant-Colonel Frank Brook took command of the 2/5th Dukes, and was confirmed in the role after his brilliant leadership on 20 November. Captain Goodall was second in command.

Now 'in the lee of the hill crowned by Bourlon Wood', their objective for 21 November was the high ground to the west of Bourlon Wood and Bourlon village. Ahead of them lay a third Hindenberg obstacle of partly-completed support line trenches, then a 1000 yard rush down a long slope from Anneux, a sunken lane, and a rise up to the wood.[17]

Zero hour was 10am, but, for the second consecutive day, the tanks designated to help them were late. Instead of moving forward over crushed wire, the battalion improvised a bombing assault along the German support-line trench. They were opposed by the first enemy reinforcements rushed to the area.[18]

> ... continuous machine-gun fire rained down in places where the trenches were only part completed and shallow ... In a determined bid to drive the enemy along the trench, Lieutenant JE Ridgway of A Company led a rush for a strong point, which was captured along with 40 prisoners, but Ridgway was killed and Captain Moxon injured.[19]

A mid-afternoon impasse was broken when Lieutenant-Colonel Brook commandeered a stray tank and directed its fire on the Germans who, at length, 'fled in disorder.' Continuing to advance, the tank met ...

> ... a furious counter-attack by large German forces, just managing to escape whilst inflicting further heavy casualties on the enemy ... By darkness the battalion were in possession of the whole of the Hindenberg support line in this sector.

The 2/5th battalion now occupied a stretch of sunken road north-west from Anneux Chapel, taking their advance to six miles in two days, and their tally to 1138 prisoners, 34 field guns and 38 machine guns. Ahead of them was a slope upwards towards Bourlon Wood, their most stubborn obstacle so far. Elsewhere the British line had to be reinforced by dismounted cavalry and the 2/6th Dukes, which was being held back for an assault on the village.

During the evening, an enemy patrol was captured, and one of the prisoners informed them of 'an impending and massive counter-attack.' It commenced half an hour later and appeared to be broken up by Lewis gun and rifle fire, but this was only the beginning.[20]

The odds were stacking against the British. Haig's two-day deadline was up. German high command was rattled and had diverted considerable reserve forces to the Cambrai sector, including at least one division from Russia and seven divisions from their impending journey to fight the Italians at Piave. 179 British tanks were now out of action, destroyed, disabled or broken down. The volume of tanks, artillery, wagons and cavalry traffic was quickly disintegrating the rain-sodden roads on which the British were transporting supplies and, if necessary, would need for their retreat. The success of the 62nds had been remarkable, but they were exhausted. Unless the heights of Bourlon Wood could be captured quickly, their overlooked position would become untenable.

Compounding their problems, they were exposed on a deepening salient. Attacks at the southern end of the line had failed. Crucially, a bridge over the Canal de L'escaut near Masnières had collapsed under the weight of the first tank, preventing the cavalry even approaching Cambrai to attack it from the rear.[21]

Lieutenant Walter Mangham, an ex-surveyor for Holmfirth District Council, was part of the southern assault, in command of the tank *The Fighting Fifth*. Walter's worst fears were realised at Rumilly where his tank broke down. A sitting duck, it was heavily shelled, and Walter was seriously injured. Somehow, he got the engine started and manoeuvred it ponderously back to camp. Hospitalised for nine months in Dolgelly, Walter wrote a paper on 'Lessons of the war as applied to roads and bridges.' He had surveyed over 20 miles of trenches and reported on impressive German engineering, particularly the 'immense strength of the many ferro-concrete vaults, dug-outs, and gun emplacements left behind in the German retreat in the Arras sector. Ferro-concrete bridges had proved to be practically indestructible.' The paper was presented to the Institute of Municipal Engineers in June 1918, one of many examples of the Great War accelerating the understanding of technology. Despite his traumatic experience, Walter's resolute opinion was that trust in the effectiveness of tanks 'was not misplaced.'[22]

On the evening of 21 November, Field-Marshal Haig faced a difficult decision. Although capturing Cambrai was beyond them, possession of the ridge at Bourlon Wood would be success in itself. Reluctant to relinquish their spectacular gains, he decided to continue the attack. In hindsight, it was a mistake. In stark contrast to the first day of the battle, every yard was now bitterly contested.

In the early hours of 22 November the 62nds were relieved in the front line trenches by the 185th brigade and returned to Havrincourt Wood and then to billets in Bertincourt. In their absence, the 40th

Division took over on 23 November and, supported by 100 tanks, briefly captured most of Bourlon Wood and village. But, driven back by increasingly formidable German reinforcements, they were in danger of capitulation and the 62nds were ordered back into the line on 25 November.

Surviving heavy shellfire on the journey up, the 2/5th Dukes arrived coated in mud and very cold. They took over the line towards the southern edge of Bourlon Wood, now a tangle of blast-damaged undergrowth, fallen branches and mangled bushes, perfect nests for snipers and machine gunners. Their objective was the railway line east of Bourlon village. After a day and night of heavy snow, sleet and shelling, they attacked in the early morning darkness of 27 November. An immediate tornado of fire ripped through the wood from locations they could not identify. Scores fell as they retreated to their line. Hampered by a shortage of ammunition, they fired trench mortars until their supply was expended. Communication wires were 'blown to ribbons' and Signaller Lieutenant William Hinchcliffe, resorted to sending Morse code messages by lamps.

A three-hour German barrage inflicted further heavy casualties. Meanwhile, an attack by the 187th brigade had failed on their right, and a battalion of guards had been driven back on their left, leaving them dangerously exposed on both flanks. Acquiring much-needed ammunition, they withstood several counter-attacks until relieved by dismounted cavalry.

The 2/5th Dukes retired into support lines in Bourlon Wood. It had been a bad day. They had taken 2 prisoners, but had lost 20 men killed, and 145 were missing. After two days in close support, they retired further to the Hindenberg support line where the combination of extreme cold and lack of dug-out accommodation proved a greater hardship than the Germans' heavy but inaccurate artillery fire. On December they returned to billets.

Little Land Lost or Gained

By then the tide had turned. Between 28 and 30 November, concentrated barrages of gas shells, followed by swift counter-attacks using storm troopers, drove the British from Bourlon Wood. Between and 7 December the British were forced into a controlled retreat. Ultimately, with a little ground lost in the south and a little gained in the north, the line resembled that before the attack started. The entire operation had cost 44,207 casualties, about 20,000 of them killed, 6000 taken prisoner and the rest wounded. German losses are estimated at 45,000.[23]

Lieutenant Hinchcliffe wrote:

... I have passed through one of the most thrilling and exciting times in my life, and have realised to their fullest extent the horrors of war. We have been in the line for nine days, and never had a minute's sleep … It was a great experience, and one that I would not have missed for anything. But I certainly think I am lucky to be alive.

Although the Battle of Cambrai had achieved little, the 62nd Division's reputation had been enhanced, a captured German officer commenting:

This division is always put in the line when the English intend making an attack.

Back at billets, a Somerset Quartermaster added:

Give me Yorkshire lads and I'll go anywhere and everywhere they go.[24]

Among the severely wounded was Lieutenant Douglas Black, returning to hospital for a third time, having previously been gassed and wounded. The casualty lists were followed by the honours – DSOs and 6 MCs for the officers and 24 Military Medals and one bar to a Military Medal for other ranks, presented by General Braithwaite at a battalion parade at Bailleul aux Cornailles on 4 January 1918. Added to these, in the King's New Year's Honours List, was a posthumous bar to his DSO for Lieutenant Colonel Best.[25]

The Cambrai operation had provided further clues to breaking the deadlock. The success of the initial attack had demonstrated the value of surprise and speed, of tanks co-ordinated with infantry, and increasingly accurate creeping barrages and predicted fire from the artillery. The Germans had seen the effectiveness of storm troopers infiltrating between the strong points of enemy lines rather than a full frontal assault. Both sides understood a little more about how to open up the conflict into the more mobile war that they desired.

Chapter 20

1917-18: Rationing

Food Economies and Inflation

The predictable panic-buying of essential commodities, particularly food, at the outbreak of war was quickly arrested by a combination of reassurances from the authorities and common sense from shopkeepers. Local shopkeepers were familiar with their regular customers and their spending habits and began to refuse excessive purchases, allowing customers only 'their usual amounts.'[1]

The Government was determined that, as far as possible, it would be 'business as usual' and that food shortages at home would not become demoralising. Yet profiteering, hoarding and the black market were all features of the inflationary wartime economy as demand outstripped supply and prices outstripped pay.

Locally, there was sporadic unrest about prices, as in January 1915 when the Huddersfield Trades Council organised a demonstration to voice their concerns about the 'high and rapidly advancing prices of bread, flour, coal, meat and other necessities of daily life.' The Council claimed that the working classes were struggling for 'subsistence' and urged the Government to intervene and put an end to the 'unjust and extortionate prices.'[2]

Yet the situation remained remarkably normal until the summer of 1916. There was a stoical acceptance by the public that economising was a patriotic duty. Spending less would eke out the increasingly scarce resources, and leave more money for the purchase of War Savings Certificates. It was informal self-regulated rationing, although it increasingly favoured those who could afford their regular quantities as prices rose.[3]

> Careful use of all commodities, the sparing use, indeed the cutting away, of all extravagances, the entire denial of luxuries, the "do without" whenever we can, the placing with the Government of as much money as our economies can bring us … is … our simple duty .. Save and we shall win the war.[4]

Economise
by
Charles Lunn

Economise, economise,
Fulfil your obligation;
Spend not by stealth your surplus wealth,
But lend it to the nation.

Economise, economise,
And stifle foolish cravings;
Take not delight in appetite,
But in your "War Loan Savings."

Economise, economise,
Avoid all ostentation;
Just set aside all paltry pride,
And wear last year's "creation."

Economise, economise,
Deny yourself some pleasure;
Your country needs unselfish deeds,
In full and generous measure.[5]

U-boat Attacks on Merchant Shipping

In June 1916 a shortage of sugar, which was entirely imported, was the first significant effect of attacks on merchant ships by German U-boats.

Britain's food crisis escalated that autumn. In September the *HDE* reported that eggs were disappearing from mealtimes in many households.' By October there had been a 33% increase in food prices since the start of the war. A month later this had risen to 78%.[6] By the end of the year the real-term prices of barley and oats were the highest since the Napoleonic Wars a century earlier. Between January 1914 and January 1917 overall expenditure for a 'typical working class family' rose by 60%, with food prices the main contributor.[7]

In February 1917 Germany resumed and intensified unrestricted submarine warfare, aiming to 'break Britain's back' through starvation. The following month 25% of all Britain-bound shipping was sunk.[8]

Restraint – The Briton's Duty
by
Charles Lunn

For generations we have sung
With valiant heart and strenuous lung
"Britannia rules the waves":
And still it is our proudest boast
The Navy keeps our well-loved coast
Free from invading knaves.

But now a new, insidious foe
Infests the sea, and sails below
To sink just what he may.
We have not got his measure yet,
But he is racking up a debt
Which soon he shall repay.

But if we would upset his plan
To starve us out, then every man
Must curb his appetite;
And eat what will but just suffice,
Or we may pay an equal price
To Germany's sad plight.[9]

U-boat sinkings peaked in April 1917. Convoys – groups of merchant ships flanked by a protective naval escort, initially used in 1916 in the North Sea to cover trade with neutral Norway and Holland,

Stark advertisement from the *HDE* 8 March 1917,
highlighting the value of space on merchant ships.

were used for Atlantic crossings from May 1917. The strategy negated U-boat damage to commercial shipping to such an extent that Germany switched her attacks to outbound vessels, prompting convoys in both directions from August 1917. The convoys were an essential intervention in the nick of time. Britain had just six weeks' supply of grain left, and food supplies were further threatened by the reassignment of increasing American tonnage to the transportation of American troops.[10]

In the *HDE*, news stories about food shortages increased ten-fold in the spring of 1917. In May the Mayor issued a circular on 'Food and General Economy', identifying four causes for the 'immense catastrophe':

1. The withdrawal of men from their work on the land.
2. The diversion of commercial shipping to uses of war.
3. A shortage resulting from failure of last year's crops at home and abroad.
4. Submarines sinking food ships from abroad.[11]

Bread Rationing

Despite the reduced effectiveness of the U-boats, prices continued to rise and there were creative attempts to make the most of dwindling supplies. 'War-bread', for example, which included more of the millers' 'offal', tasted 'better than feared.'[12]

The regulation of bread by central Government was particularly contentious. To maintain stocks they reduced the rations for soldiers home on leave and, in February 1917, a new Bread Order regulated the size and composition of bread.

The Order placed restrictions on cakes so that ingredients could be prioritised to make bread, but the legislation betrayed an ignorance of local variations. When news arrived that Yorkshire teacakes and hot cross buns had been banned, there was uproar in Huddersfield. Local bakers protested that teacakes and hot cross buns were bread, and the Chief Constable was reduced to threats of prosecution if they persisted in baking them. The Huddersfield and District Bakers' and Confectioners' Association reluctantly discontinued teacakes and hot cross buns, pending a court ruling on whether or not they were bread. If so, were they 'rolls' and if they were 'rolls', were they bigger than the maximum size allowed?[13]

Forcefully presenting their case, local bakers posted teacakes to the Ministry of Food in London along with written representations. A key argument was that teacakes were made from yeast-based dough.[14] They highlighted how the Huddersfield mill worker would 'start from home with two or three teacakes in a handkerchief for his meals ... the teacake for dinner ... a meat sandwich', concluding that the teacake is far different to the prohibited 'fancy cakes.'[15]

On 19 April the Food Controller added to the confusion by banning 'crumpets and muffins.' There was relief for all a week later when, after due consideration, and with the Arras Offensive in full swing cross the Channel, the House of Commons decreed that Yorkshire teacakes were bread, and were permitted. This set the bar for similar products.[16]

Bread was again to the fore at a Workers' Conference held in Huddersfield's Friendly and Trade Club on 19 May 1917. Attended by local MPs and 79 Trade Unions and 31 Co-operative Societies representing 160,000 people, the meeting called on the Government to commandeer and make available all foodstuffs, means of production and transport at fair prices, claiming they had allowed too much profiteering. In effect, they were asking for measures that would have been incendiary in peacetime - rationing and price-fixing. They also warned that recent suggestions of bread rationing to two ounces per meal failed to understand the physicality of work in Yorkshire, where bread is the 'stuff of life.'[17]

They got their wish in the autumn. Bread rationing began on 11 October, families limited to two 2lb loaves and one 4lb loaf per person per week. On 2 November the Local Food Controller, considering 'communication from the Ministry of Food', decided that all local bread should be of uniform quality and sold at 2½d per lb loaf, 4½d per 2lb loaf and 9d per 4lb loaf. All temporary licences to sell other breads were to be withdrawn. On 12 November detailed adult rations were published for a range of foodstuffs and, as requested by the Workers' Conference, the quantity of bread allowed was greater for manual workers.[18]

Adult Rations per Head per Week
BREAD

Class	Men		Women	
	lb	oz	lb	oz
Very heavy industrial work or agricultural work	8	0	5	0
Ordinary industrial or other manual work	7	0	4	0
Unoccupied or sedentary work	4	8	3	8
Men and women other rations				
Other cereals	0	12		
Meat	2	0		
Butter, margarine, lard, oils and fats	0	10		
Sugar	0	8		

N.B. Bread includes all 'flour' whether used for bread or cooking.[19]

Still the food crisis deepened, and on 10 December 1917 an emergency Bread (Use of Potatoes Order) was passed, allowing bakers to use potatoes as a bulking agent in their loaves. The nutritional value of bread took a further hit on 15 January 1918 when the Ministry of Food removed the limit on the percentage of potato that could be included in a loaf.[20]

Sugar Shortages and Alcohol

Shortages in Huddersfield were exacerbated by the increasing number of war workers and the temporary settlement of several thousand wounded soldiers in August 1917, when the Food Controller agreed to allocate additional sugar to the district.[21] One 'wag' in a railway carriage of newspaper readers asked if they had seen the list of patriots who had given up the use of sugar. After much turning of pages to find the information, the wag pronounced, 'Look in the death column!'[22]

As essentials were prioritised over luxuries, the sugar shortage was cited by the temperance movement in a growing campaign against the production and importation of alcoholic drinks. In April 1917, a prohibition meeting at the Town Hall, chaired by Joseph Turner, JP, the Chairman of British Dyes and Huddersfield Northern Union Rugby FC, was attended by representatives of the Church of England, the Free Churches, and Temperance and Social Workers. It urged the Government to ban alcoholic drinks to preserve foodstuffs for essentials. Alcohol, they claimed, was hindering the war effort by:

- delaying our food supplies; since the war began it has consumed over 3,500,000 tons of food, with sugar enough to last the nation 100 days. It uses up more sugar that the Army.
- cutting through the efficiency of the nation; it weakens our fighting forces and must lengthen the war
- hindering the Army; it is the cause of … delay within munitions; it keeps thousands of men from work every day
- hampering the Navy; it delays transports, places them at the mercy of submarines, slows down repairs, and congests the docks
- threatening our mercantile marine; it has absorbed during the war over two hundred million cubic feet of [shipping] space, and it retards the building of ships to replace our losses.
- shattering our moral strength; its temptation to women involves grave danger to children and anxiety to thousands of soldiers.[23]

W Jacques of Huddersfield challenged the Mayor to confront the issue:

> … we are asked to economise in lighting, clothing, furnishings, amusements, holidays: but there is no mention of beer.[24]

H Townsend of Birkby Baptist Church decried the use of fertile land for growing hops to make beer, although others believed there was plenty of alternative land to use.[25] Despite support amongst politicians, the clergy and the Royal Family, restrictive tax increases and reduced licensing hours, the Government continued to baulk at direct rationing or a ban on alcohol.

Horse Racing

Horse racing was also accused of wasting resources. In April 1917 the War Cabinet cancelled all racing after the spring meeting at Newmarket, owing to 'the shortage of oats … no large quantity can be imported before the new harvest.'[26] Persuaded by the powerful racing lobby of 'the national importance of horse breeding', the War Cabinet backtracked, allowing a limited amount of horse racing and increasing the allowance of oats per horse but, to conserve fuel, no special trains or motor vehicles were to be run to race meetings.[27] To facilitate this, meetings were largely restricted to Newmarket.[2] This did not satisfy Thomas B Black, whose letter to the *HDE* complained that, while many were foregoing food, warmth and recreation, others are not making comparable sacrifices.

> For the moment … food value is the primary necessity … How foolish it is to feed good oats to racehorses … under the pretence that these creatures may somewhere and somehow be of military value on the shell-wrecked surface of France and Flanders whilst… we are killing off half-fed cattle and sheep because we cannot spare the grain to complete their fattening.[29]

Hoarding and Profiteering

There was universal condemnation of hoarding and profiteering. The Government gradually introduced greater controls of supplies which helped to reduce hoarding – 'nothing less than a crime' – and overconsumption. A scheme of voluntary rationing was introduced, with the general public encouraged to monitor their usage, a sacrifice adopted by the Royal Family to encourage support for it.[30] Furthermore, there were regular patriotic appeals, reminding the public that it was:

> … the duty of all … to adhere to the prescribed quantity of food, and thus to show the world the spectacle of a united people ready to deny themselves in order that a victory for civilisation and liberty may be rendered swift, certain and decisive.[31]

Consumers, meanwhile, accused the authorities of tardiness in protecting them against profiteers exploitation of wartime shortages along the supply chains of various foodstuffs.[32] From early 191 the authorities began to fix prices to keep essential foods affordable. Potato farmers immediately complained that the Potatoes (Minimum Crop Prices) Order of February 1917 – £11 10s per ton – left hardly any profit.[33]

Hort Commons

by

Charles Lunn

We're running short of this and that,
Food prices are still soaring;
Some profiteers are waxing fat
By food control ignoring.
The price is fixed for honest tea
(The brew that is so cheering),
But when we ask for them we see
The cheap blends disappearing.
Of high-priced tea there is no lack
At certain shops we visit;
It's all one value, green or black.
Come, tell me this! How is it?
The butter price is fixed, except
For what they call real Danish;
So now no other brands are kept,
For reasons which are plainish.
And so we suffer, day by day
In spite of regulations;
But if I just could have my way,
There'd soon be alterations.[34]

222

In March 1917 local farmers from Kirkburton and Highburton were fined 10 shillings for selling milk at a price contrary to the Price of Milk Order 1917.[35] In 1918, two local bakers were fined £5 each for breach of the Bread Order 1918, selling loaves that were underweight.[36]

James Cockhill, a grocer from Sheepridge was summoned for inaccurate recording of the butter he sold. Although found to be careless rather than deliberately fraudulent, he was fined £40 for 'absolute disregard of the requirements of the Rationing Order.'[37]

The regulations also stifled honest dealings. A Paddock greengrocer often supplied nurses and visitors with provisions for the wounded at Royds Hall. In September 1917 he was fined 5s for serving a local customer after the 6pm restriction. When asked if he could continue to serve hospital-related customers – visitors who arrived in the district or staff who were off-duty – after his permitted opening hours the Chairman of the Police Court replied, 'regulations are regulations.'[38]

From April 1917, public eating houses where meals cost more than 1s 3d were banned from serving meat on Wednesdays and Fridays, and potatoes could only be served on those two days. Provisions were also made for less bread to be served.[39] In the same month the Food Controller banned any food on 'Whitsuntide Treats.' Just before Christmas 1917 the Mayor and other members of the Food Control Committee appealed for a suspension of afternoon teas, Sunday school and parish teas, and 'old folks' treats.'[40]

In January 1918, the obituary of 72-year-old Thomas Jenkinson of Marsh, a popular, cheerful horse-cab driver for 52 years, further emphasised the food crisis.

> His sympathies were not only for the horses of the cab-rank, but for all animals, and especially for the pigeons in St George's Square. He used to collect the crumbs from the station porter's dining rooms to give to the birds. Lately he used to say that the men were so careful that there were not many crumbs left to give.[42]

As well as food, tobacco was also now in short supply, and cigarettes for the troops took priority.

Unnamed Poem
reprinted in the *HDE* from the *Daily News*

My Tuesdays are meatless,
My Wednesdays are wheatless,
I am getting more eatless each day.
My home it is heatless,
My bed it is sheetless –
They're all sent to the Y.M.C.A.

The bar-rooms are treatless,
My coffee is sweetless,
Each day I get poorer and wiser.
My stockings are feetless
My trousers are seatless –
My, how I do hate the Kaiser![41]

The Last Straw
by
Anon

I've suffered much in silence
I'm an uncomplaining man;
Nor ever I in prose or rhyme
Suggested a new plan.
For dealing with the shopping queue,
Or profiteering "stunts";
I never even aired my views
Regarding butter-hunts.
But when we're warned tobacco stocks
Are running very low,
My whole scheme of existence rocks –
I stagger 'neath the blow.
Potatoes, tea or margarine –
I was content to wait
Till some controller should subvene
And put the matter straight.
But if they stop my daily smoke,
Then gone is my restraint;
I'll join with all the grousing folk,
And loudly make complaint.[43]

Digging for Victory

In addition to restraint, rationing and combinations of price and stock controls, the major response to food shortages was a huge land conversion scheme – 'Digging for Victory.' In March 1917 the Government released a circular stating that local food production was top priority and allotment plans were to go ahead.[44]

District authorities could assume control over huge areas of available land for cultivation. In 1917 alone, 2.5 million acres of land were converted to the use of farming. As a large number of farm workers had enlisted for military service, women, conscientious objectors, and those unable to serve in the military, were directed into agricultural work, which was added to the 'starred' industries 'of national importance.' The West Riding authorities in food and agriculture strongly supported military exemptions for farmers.[45]

In December 1916, following Government encouragement to 'grow food where we can', the military took the lead in Huddersfield by digging up a large vacant area adjacent to the Drill Hall. Cultivated by soldiers passing through or waiting to be sent to their battalions, this allotment was a very productive 'potato patch.'[46] The potato was the staple crop of many of the new allotments, for the same reasons that it 'underpinned' the Industrial Revolution. It was a cheap source of calories, more reliable than alternatives which were susceptible to inclement weather, and able to grow in relatively crude locations.

District councils were quick to begin their endeavours. In January 1917, Linthwaite acquired land for allotments and Holmfirth invited allotment applications. Golcar, seeking ten acres for conversion, ploughed up a recreation ground earmarked as a site for a new school at Swallow Lane.[47]

A review of Huddersfield Corporation land in January 1917 found that 10-12 acres were suitable. This was split into allotments of 200 square yards and rented out at 2s 6d per annum for the duration of the war. The Council nurtured the project by purchasing five tons of potato seed to sell on to tenants, supplying fertiliser from the sewage works and organising a Town Hall lecture, 'Gardening in Wartime', by Mr AS Galt, lecturer in Horticulture at Leeds University. The lecture, on 24 January 1917, was 'well attended by all classes of society.'[48]

Education initiatives were a feature of allotment support for the remainder of the war. Regular columns in the *HDE* instructed readers on how to plant their own beetroot, kidney beans, onions and other vegetables. Various figures, from professional teachers to the Town Council Chairman, delivered lectures and demonstrations on how to preserve foodstuffs by, for example bottling and canning fruit and vegetables.[49]

Mr Galt emphasised that choice of location was very important for allotments, confirming that the 'atmospheric conditions in the vicinity of British Dyes' were not just 'distinctly bad' for growing vegetables, but deadly to almost any form of plant life, as one glance at the devastation on Kilner Bank confirmed. In addition, much of the higher land in the region was 'old and poor grassland' likely to yield poor crops.

Before the end of January 1917 allotments at Woodfield (Lockwood), Royds Hall, Hollin Carr (Marsh), Luck Lane and Salendine Nook were ready for planting. By September there were about 800 new local allotments. These included several at Huddersfield Golf Club, where parts of a fairway had been dug up.[50] The 'brown up-ploughed field' had become a 'salient feature of the landscape .. no longer the exception but rather the rule.'[51] Such rapid progress was a surprise to all. In September 1917 the *HDE* commented:

> Probably no-one last November, when the Food Production committee first began its work .. with little guidance save for its own good sense, expected quite so much from the allotments as actually has been achieved … [The initiative has been] … seized upon with enthusiasm … with a fine spirit of mutual cooperation difficulties were quickly overcome, and the gardeners surprised themselves by their unexpected achievements.[52]

Production was also stepped up on farmland and, in February 1917, to address the need for

The women's land army at work during World War I

additional labour, the National Land Council appealed for 50,000 women to assist 'in saving the country from famine.' Scepticism about women's capacity for the manual work required on allotments and farms was soon allayed and in July, reduced rail fares were introduced as an incentive for women land workers.[53] In December 1917 the *HDE* reported ...

> ... innumerable testimonies received during the past few months as to the utility of women labour in tractor and horse ploughing and threshing work, as well as in lighter forms of farm labour.

There was also prejudice. The HDE found it ...

> ... astonishing ... that there should still be some farmers who refuse to employ women for one or other of these objects.

Such farmers were told that if they refused to employ the women workers allocated to them they risked the withdrawal of their certificates of exemption.[54]

During the springs and summers of 1917 and 1918, the Minister of Munitions and Department of Food Production encouraged the release of skilled ploughmen from munitions work to agriculture, particularly during the sowing and harvesting seasons.[55]

Back to the Land
by
Charles Lunn

Oh! It's back to the land for we English just now,
And the man who can handle a tractor or plough,
Who can clean up a furrow, or manage a cow,
He must ever go back to the land.

Oh! It's back to the land for the smart city clerk,
He is digging and hoeing each evening till dark.
As a keen cultivator he's making his mark,
He is bending his back to the land.

Oh! It's back to the land for my dear Lady Fay,
She has taken it up as a new form of play;
But e'er long she'll be ready to welcome the day
When she's turning her back to the land.

But it's back to the land in keen earnest for those
Whose ambition it is to disgruntle our foes,
And when they've succeeded the shires will disclose
Welcome peace coming back to our land.[56]

Bending their backs to the land

A combination of the reconstruction of agriculture, price fixing and the wettest August for almost 40 years produced some unintended anomalies. Whilst cereal crops struggled, root crops thrived. The autumn of 1917 saw a potato surplus of two million tons. Logically, this should have reduced their price, but with traders disinclined to pay the Government's fixed minimum price of £6 per ton or to break the law, many potatoes were taken back to farms unsold. On 1 November the *HDE* scoffed:

> Three hours and more were spent by the House of Commons wandering up and down the potato patch … discussing … the best way of dealing with the bountiful crop which has upset the scheme of the Food Controller and made the minimum price ridiculous.[57]

The potato surplus was testimony to a widespread commitment to growing food, although not all were enamoured of this zeal, one correspondent to the *Examiner* complaining of:

> … allotment holders [who] are becoming a little trying … the bare faced way these plotters will gloat over the prospect of a wet weekend … a drenching day finds them purring about a "nice drop o' rain" and a weekend like the last, with lowering skies and intermittent showers, reduces them to a state almost prayerful in their anxiety for a steady incessant downpour. Reproach them … and they hurl at you with withering disdain one word – potatoes.[58]

In addition to the farms and allotments, many gardeners sacrificed luxury for utility by transforming their flower beds into vegetable patches.

In February 1918, the Huddersfield Allotment Holders' quarterly meeting reported a further increase from 383 pre-war allotments to 1500, but the Board of Agriculture wanted a further 1000.[59] When the council proposed a conversion of half of the Municipal School's playing field into allotments, FW. Merlin asserted that playing fields were also 'of national importance – the play of boys in an industrial town … fresh air and exercise are only secondary to food in building up a healthy adolescence.'[60]

Vegetable displays at the Floral and Horticultural shows of 1918 'exceeded all expectations'[61] in quantity and quality. The annual Town Hall event in August had 154 exhibits, an increase of 44 from the previous year, and 29 classes of vegetable, an increase of 22, produce yielded by a landscape that in places was barely recognisable from that of 1916:

Fields previously bearing nothing but rough grass have been converted into pleasurable and profitable sources of food supply … Corporation and other tips, which until recently were the haunts of rodents, have become green and pleasant places. All this has been accomplished in two short years, in which other pre-occupations have been numerous and pressing.[62]

My War-Time Garden
by
Charles Lunn

In by-gone days when war-dogs slept,
My garden was so trimly kept;
In bed and border treasures grew,
Of every shape and every hue.

But now, instead of gorgeous blooms,
And their delicious, sweet perfumes,
Is seen the strangest state of things,
One of the changes wartime brings.

I've columbines and kidney beans,
Carnations bold, and curly greens;
I've peas next to the pansy bloom,
While Brussels sprouts surround the broom.

My roses I could hardly spare,
But radishes sown with great care
Fill the spaces in between,
While here and there a swede is seen.

I've artichokes where once I grew
Anchusas of the heavenliest blue;
While picotee and poppy strives
For pride of place with cos and chives.

My garden, once a place of dreams,
A sheer delight in colour schemes,
Instead of soothing wearied eyes,
The inner man now satisfies.[63]

Food Queues

Despite these successes, shortages of some essential foods continued. Until late 1917 food was sold on a first come first served basis and food queues, usually for butter, lard, sugar, tea and meat, were a wearying feature of daily life. The queues, and frustrations at uncontrolled and often unfair distribution of scarce commodities, led to a growing clamour for further food controls.

On 29 November 1917 the Mayor, Alderman Jessop, received a deputation representing the Huddersfield Trades and Labour Council and the Workers' Union, protesting against food queues. They suggested that butter, lard, sugar and tea should be systematically distributed from 15 centres. The Mayor promised to take the suggestions to the Food Committee.[64]

The following morning, the food queues issue was brought into sharper focus. At 7.15am a Lockwood mother left her three children, aged four, seven and eleven, in bed as she went 'searching for butter.' After ten minutes in the queue she was urged to return home as 'something was wrong.' Gladys Pearson, the eldest child, was afraid of the dark and as there was no gas upstairs, tried to light a candle. She set her bedclothes and herself on fire. Neighbours, using wet towels as protection against the heat and smoke, rushed upstairs. Opening a window to let the smoke out, they found and rescued the two younger children. Gladys was unconscious on her side and severely burned. She died before they could take her downstairs.

The coroner returned a verdict of 'accidental death.' A juryman commented:

> 'It is a wonder there are not more of these cases as the women have to be out now.'[65]

The *HDE* added that the case …

> …directs attention to the serious consequences entailed by the present method of food distribution … this sad occurrence … does not exhaust the evil side of food queues … In weather such as we expect to experience at this period of the year it is a saddening spectacle to see long queues of women and children waiting outside provision shops for the necessary food for their families. What this exposure may mean in future illnesses can easily be imagined.[66]

On 17 December 1917 the district awoke to five inches of snow. Daytime temperatures plummeted to minus 9°C and rarely rose above freezing over the next few weeks. It was the start of the coldest winter for years. The ice and frosts lasted well into April and the queues, predominantly women, were chilled to the bone. As discontent escalated, Lord Rhondda, the Food Controller, announced: 'Food queues must and will be stopped', suggesting that, as the Huddersfield Trades and Labour Council and the Workers' Union had recommended nine months earlier, more general rationing was the solution.[67]

'Old Volunteer' reflected the depressing drudgery:

> … the men from the front, who come home on leave, almost without exception, are struck by the apparent depression of spirit they found prevailing around them, and it is quite a common remark amongst them that they prefer the more cheerful surroundings at the front.[68]

Experiencing no change since their requests to the Mayor, on 15 December the Trades and Labour Council organised a protest meeting in St George's Square. Over 2000 people gathered 'tired of this nonsense about the queue system' and passed a resolution demanding that the Town Council or Food Control Committee be given powers to take control of all foodstuffs coming into the town, and to organise its equal distribution. Failing this, 'the workers were recommended to consider adopting industrial action.' They wanted queues abolished and the Hoarding Act enforced. The Mayor responded that the Committee would meet every day to find a way of remedying the 'serious evil' of queuing.[69]

Still the Government's response was piecemeal, the latest 'crisis' food being margarine. Even one of Huddersfield's 'aristocrats' was …

> reduced to the ignominy of waiting in the margarine queues. The shawl-headed women standing near her referenced her presence there; and she explained, "Of course, I only require the margarine to grease the tins," whereupon another replied; "Aye, an' aw nobbut want mahr to grease mi clogs."[70]

Food queues lined
the streets.

O Margarine

by
'OTEA'

O margarine, O margarine
I went in vain for thee,
The various shops in town have got
No bacon, lard, or tea.
I stood in queues in drenching rain,
I felt rheumatics gripping,
And when I landed home again
My weeping wife said – "dripping?"[71]

Just before Christmas, Lord Rhondda gave Food Control Committees the power to regulate local supplies of margarine and to arrange its 'equitable distribution.'[72] The Huddersfield Food Control Committee immediately commandeered three tons of margarine from a firm in King Street. Half of it was redirected to the War Hospitals, 15 Co-ops and various other stores 'all over town.' Customers were required to register with a single retailer, and merchants were obliged to divide their margarine equally among their customers. Butter, lard, sugar and tea were next on the list.[73]

Food Rationing

The Government introduced ration cards on 23 February 1918, bringing countless local initiatives under national control. To prevent the hoarding of food before rationing took effect, an amnesty was offered before the authorities checked suspected premises. Any more than two to three weeks' supply would be considered hoarding.[74]

Ration cards were distributed to retailers by the 25 Food Control Committees that covered Huddersfield and its outlying districts. Each customer was limited to a quarter of a pound of butter, margarine or a combination of them, per week. Almost four tons of butter and margarine – a paltry 1½ ounces per head – was distributed across the district in the first week.[75]

There were also growing concerns in Huddersfield about supplies of fresh meat. There was little local cattle production, the district's butchers buying most of their supplies from markets in Leeds, Wakefield and Liverpool. The Government's Cattle (Sales) Order of December 1917 tried to address soaring prices by controlling the quality and wholesale price of cattle sold for slaughter. This had the effect of reducing farmers' profits and, consequently, cattle were held back. Leeds Market reacted to the shortage by selling only to Leeds-based butchers, and supplies of meat at Wakefield Market decreased by 50 percent. The upshot was an immediate shortage in other towns that relied on these markets. The largest of these towns was Huddersfield.

On 3 January 1918 local butchers met at the Plough Hotel, and wrote a strong letter to the authorities:

> Unless the … Order is altered immediately there will be no meat for sale in Huddersfield during the coming week. As Huddersfield is a large munition centre we hope you realise the seriousness of our position.[76]

Some butchers closed, having sold out, and supplies of tinned meat were in great demand. The Ministry blamed the crisis on over-buying around Christmas and promised stocks would be restored soon.[77]

Huddersfield's meat supplies in January were expected to be half of those of the previous October. Chilled meat and some mutton was brought in for sale, but yet more tedious food queues lined the streets.[78] With no sign of improvement and the government intransigent, Huddersfield's Food Control Committees assumed control. Butchers were limited to how much they could buy or sell per week. Meat did not initially appear on the new ration cards as it was too time-consuming to cut it up into the precise small amounts, but a national meat-rationing scheme was introduced in April.[79]

Weekly fluctuations in the imports, production and distribution of rationed foods made shopping an anxious and uncertain experience. In the first week of March there was a surplus of margarine in Huddersfield, and the Golcar Food Control Committee defied the Food Controller by increasing the ration from four ounces to six. They were severely reprimanded as they could have thrown the 'whole scheme into confusion.' All surpluses of goods were to be unsold, a painful reality under the inflexible bureaucracy of rationing.[80]

On 20 March the Government fixed Huddersfield's margarine allocation at 5 tons per week. This was less than 2 ounces per head and representations were made that it was inadequate.[81]

Meat coupons, released on 8 April, were worth varying, barely adequate weights of different meats, such as four ounces of bacon or ham, or 12.5 ounces of poultry, although heavy manual labourers were allowed more. Coupons could also be used for a meat meal at restaurants. The *HDE* praised the locals as there had been …

> …very little grumbling … diners are wisely and patriotically accepting the meatless dinners with good grace.

Most abandoned eating out, preferring to eke out the remains of their meat through improvised and inventive cooking. The Huddersfield Grocers' Association condemned the meat coupon system as 'causing great hardship for the working classes',[82] and the Huddersfield Master Bakers' and Confectioners' Association protested at the inclusion of 'meat pies, sandwiches and such like goods' in the Meat Rationing Order. Rationing the working man's packed lunch could create …

> …a very grave spirit of dissatisfaction and unrest, which may become a serious calamity to the nation in this critical hour.[83]

Sacrifice as the keystone of victory was the theme of 1918 on the home front. In April Lord Rhondda expressed gratitude for the public's compliance, 'goodwill and good temper.'

> The old emotion and unity which we had [in] 1914 are back again in the hearts of all … A black week brings out the best in us … character is what a man is in the dark … British character … blazes out in the blackest moments.
> Rationing means fair play; each having … no more than his common share at the common table.[84]

On 14 July, the ration cards were replaced by a General Book Rationing Scheme. Included in the colour-coded books were: sugar (yellow); fats – butter, margarine, lard – (blue); and meats – butchers' meat and bacon – (red). Spare pages were left for new categories, such as tea.[85] Errors on the application forms of about 2000 locals left staff unable to send their books to them. They had to queue to pick their book up in person, or face 'considerable difficulty in obtaining proper supplies of rationed food.'[86]

The books had a limited lifespan – 14 July to 27 October – to allow for changing circumstances. The price of jam doubled in July, owing to a poor yield of plums and apples, as well as difficulty obtaining sugar. However, rhubarb growers in the West Riding profited, as the plant was used to supplement jam production. July also saw increased rations of bacon and ham. Rations of butchers' meat were lowered slightly to compensate, but there was a slight net increase in the quantity of meat allowed.[87]

July 1918 also saw the introduction of 'National Kitchens' where families could buy a cheap meal. The Huddersfield 'Kitchen' was opened at the Aspley on 30 July.

> By the time the opening ceremony was concluded, there was a long queue, and throughout the dinner hour the attendants at the kitchens were kept very busy by the demands made upon them … if the kitchen continues to receive the same measure of support the committee will have to consider the extension of the scheme to all the town's districts.

Food at the kitchen included, for 3d, a Cornish pasty or vegetable pie, whilst 2d would buy boiled rice or rhubarb and custard.[88] The Kitchen's popularity was unabated as food prices continued to rise, now significantly affected by the flood of United States troops crossing the Atlantic, many on merchant ships that previously transported grain, meat, sugar and syrup, a popular sugar substitute.[89]

In October 1918, the ration of butter was halved to one ounce per head per week and the Ministry of Food issued its food outlook for the winter. A continuation of 'food economy' was essential. 'Digging for Victory' had eased some of the anxiety about vegetables, but the outlook for meat, butter, cheese, cereal crops and fresh fruit was bleak. It was now an offence to feed animals with any grain fit for human consumption.[90]

Coal and oil were in similar short supply. Almost all of Britain's oil was imported. It fuelled ships, planes, transport and industry, and military requirements took priority. As the U-boat attacks began to bite, coal replaced oil where possible. Petrol rationing was introduced in July 1916, the measures including tax increases, tokens to monitor individuals' usage and a ban on motor cycling. Tram and train services were reduced. In January 1918, the new Motor Spirit and Gas Restriction Order restricted the use of motor spirit or gas for any journey unless 'expressly authorised.'[91]

Owing to its large coal mining industry, Britain was able to avoid coal rationing until 1918. Even though coal production had decreased by the end of 1915, it continued to supply almost all the coal of France and Italy in addition to its own domestic, commercial and military demands.[92] The Government nationalised the industry in December 1916 to alleviate potential shortages, but fuel prices rose sharply, and by February 1917 some coal-powered mill owners were regretting that …

> … cumbersome waterwheels have been taken out. At three Holme Valley mills water turbines have been installed with good effect and a fourth is to be put down at a Holmfirth Mill.[93]

If all the Coal & steam were saved on Wash day — How many Trains would it drive?

IT may need only a few shovelsful of coal to keep the copper fire going but remember there are fifty-two wash-days in the year, and a few hundred shovelsful can be reckoned in hundredweights, and there are millions of homes with wash-days in the United Kingdom. But the saving can start next wash-day in your own home, if you will give the matter a thought, or rather give Rinso, the Cold Water Washer, a trial.

Rinso washes while you sleep. It saves the cost of coal—the bother of a copper fire—the unpleasantness and waste of steam.

You soak the clothes in cold water and Rinso overnight—Rinse and hang to dry in the morning—that's all! Rinso is the easy washer—easy for the housewife—easy for the clothes.

In 2d. & 1d. Packets everywhere.

RINSO
THE DIRT DISPELLER

R. S. HUDSON LIMITED.
LIVERPOOL, WEST BROMWICH AND LONDON.

Advertisement exploiting the coal shortage from the *HDE*, 20 March 1917

Notwithstanding the extensive mining operations on the western front, the folly of sending 75,000 skilled miners to war, reducing annual output of coal by over 22 million tons, was becoming apparent.

The Coal Rationing Order came into effect in July 1918, restricting the use of gas, electricity and coal for domestic purposes and non-military industry. The measures included further reducing the number of passenger trams, prohibiting lights in shop windows, banning cooked food in public eateries after 9.30pm, and limiting the opening times of theatres, music halls, cinemas and other 'places of amusement' to between 1pm and 10.30pm. Three local fish and chip shop owners were prosecuted for serving after hours, breaching the Lighting, Heating and Power Order.

Domestic coal rationing was to be proportionate to the number of rooms in the house and its location, as some areas were colder than others. Yorkshire's allowance, higher than the southern counties, was roughly one ton per room per year, with a minimum of three rooms and maximum of twenty.[94]

In the spirit of voluntary rationing, the *HDE* regularly urged readers to use less than the prescribed amounts. Announcing a shortfall of 36 million tons per year, the Controller of Coal suggested his own conservation measures, including:

- mix coke with it
- consider how many fires you can do without
- cook fewer hot meals
- reduce the number of hot baths
- put firebricks in grates where possible
- never use a gas stove for boiling water if there is a fire in the house
- see that all kettle and saucepans are free from soot.[95]

In the autumn of 1918 restrictions were extended to articles which could washed in a public laundry. The embargo included luxuries such as blouses, silk underwear, elaborate lingeries and lace curtains. The target group was the newly affluent migrant women workers who 'are sending such articles on a scale undreamed of in pre-war days.'[96]

As austerity seeped ever-deeper into everyday life, a resigned public had little choice but to stick with it. There was considerable trepidation about the oncoming winter, particularly with the deadly Spanish Influenza virus sweeping the country.

A Chilly Prospect
by
Charles Lunn

In a deck chair I'm reclining,
With the summer sun a-shining
Far above me in an arc of cloudless sky;
But my thoughts are far from pleasant –
I have left behind the present,
And am thinking of the winter drawing nigh.

Of the days with north winds blowing,
When it's raining or it's snowing,
And the sun is hiding from our wistful gaze;
When the water pipes are freezing,
When we're shivering and sneezing,
And we dare not poke the fire to make a blaze.

So I try to plan (devising
Ways of coal economising)
How to make our ration last the winter through
"Can we do it?" is the question.
Will you give me a suggestion
How to make a ton give out the heat of two?

Then I put it down in writing –
So much heating, so much lighting –
And read again Form F.H.F.I.A.,
Till my poor brain sings a tune, it's
Tons and cubic feet and units –
And I wish the Coal Controller I could slay.[97]

Other shortages also encroached into daily life. In March 1917, posters advertising newspapers and periodicals were banned because of a paper shortage. Simultaneously, the *HDE*, which had been reduced to just four pages from the early days of the war, discontinued its 'Special Edition' and began regular advertisements offering payment for old newspapers and magazines to be recycled.[98]

In March 1918, the cost of the *Weekly Examiner* was increased as their allowance of paper was little more than one third of the amount they were consuming. In June the Region's Paper Controller in Bradford appealed for 'anything that can be made into paper.'[99] Incongruously, he asked for 'anyone who discovers instances of waste paper' to 'communicate with him by letter.' Several people replied on full-sized notepaper to suggest that a waste of paper could be avoided by reporting to him by telephone.[100]

The directive to textile firms to manufacture civilian clothes from thinner, lighter-weight cloth to decrease consumption, was most untimely alongside fuel rationing.[101]

Whenever the end of the war came – and in early autumn 1918 no one knew when that would be – supplies of food, fuel and other goods and materials could not be restored overnight. However long the war lasted, the shortages, rationing and self-denial would be longer. Demands on the tenacity, fortitude and endurance of the nation were far from over.

But despite this grim outlook, the frustrations of the food queues, clumsy Government interventions in the market and periodic unrest, Britain was not starving. The country had pulled together. Rationing, 'Digging for Victory', self-denial, the courage of the merchant sailors and the success of the convoys had left Britain in a healthier state than most continental combatant nations, including Germany. Whatever the quantity and quality of the food, victory would make it taste all the sweeter.

War-Time Breakfast
by
Charles Lunn

Each morning as I breakfast, I glance o'er the latest news,
Taking first official telegrams, and then the experts' views,
And when I read "The French advance, more villages retaken."
I masticate a morsel of the most delicious bacon.

When I in my poor rationed paper read in black and white.
Of how the British gained the day in some unequal fight.
With grim determination that did neither halt nor waver;
I ask "Whence came this coffee, dear? 'Tis exquisite in flavour."

Some days there are when news is not as good as one would wish.
Then I can find no pleasure in one single breakfast dish;
When we retreat through tactics weak, or strategy that's faulty,
I swear the coffee's burnt or smoked, the bacon far too salty.

But when I see across the page, in letters bold and plain.
That fighting days are over and glad peace has come again,
And know that industry once more will take the place of slaughter,
I'll breakfast in contentment on a crust and cup of water.[102]

Chapter 21

1918: From the Jaws of Defeat

Ludendorff targets the British Forces

At the beginning of 1918 the Allies' position was precarious. Even as the bells rang out to celebrate the initial attack at Cambrai in November 1917, far more significant events were taking place in Russia that jeopardized the Allies' position. The Bolsheviks, led by Lenin, took control after the second Russian Revolution of the year and announced peace with Germany. The price for Russia was significant territory and supplies, ratified by the Treaty of Brest-Litovsk on 3 March 1918. The price for the remaining Allies was a Germany able to concentrate resources on one major European front. Through the winter of 1917-18 Germany raced half a million troops westwards by train. By the spring the Allies on the western front were outnumbered by 250,000.

Ludendorff – now effectively Germany's military and political leader – regarded Britain as the major obstacle and devised a spring offensive – the *Kaiserschlacht* – to eliminate Britain from the war before the impending troops from the Unites States could take effect.

He had three plans of attack. Operation *George* involved attacking Plumer's 2nd Army in the north close to the Belgian border near Armentières. The British were strongest here, holding strategically valuable land and protecting the Channel ports that supplied the British army. Operation *Mars* would concentrate an assault on the 1st and 3rd British armies at Arras in the centre of the British line. Operation *Michael* would target General Gough's 5th Army at the southern end of the British line east of Amiens, punching through between British and French forces and exploiting opportunities that arose, with the possibility of turning north to force the British back to the Channel ports.

Already weakest in this southern sector, the British had taken over an additional 25 miles of poor quality front line trenches from the French, extending the British front to 126 miles. The Allies agreed that, if necessary, the British could afford to concede ground in this sector, providing the Germans were made to fight for it. This compromise was partly because Prime Minister Lloyd George had deprived General Haig of some of the conscripted troops who were in training. Lloyd George had lost faith in his military commander and, whilst lacking the authority to remove him from office, was determined to reduce his 'wasting of lives.'[1] It was a dangerous development. As Germany assembled 'a weight of men and guns unequalled in the history of warfare', Britain's man-power was much reduced.[2]

1/5th Dukes Disbanded

The British Army adapted by reorganising at the end of January 1918. One hundred and fifteen battalions were disbanded, their men reassigned to restore the remaining battalions to a full complement of 1000. In addition, 38 battalions were amalgamated to form 19. With the exception of the Australians, New Zealanders and Canadians, brigades were reduced from four battalions to three. This impacted directly on the 1/5th and 2/5th Huddersfield battalions of the Duke of Wellington's West Riding Regiment.[3]

The 2/5th Dukes of the 62nd Division spent January south east of Arras, enduring heavy snow and a sudden thaw that flooded their front line trenches and hampered their labouring duties building roads and railways. Fifty miles further north, the 1/5th Dukes of the 49th Division manned the line east of Ypres. Their duties included the erection of a 4000 yards barbed wire apron across the whole divisional front.[4]

On 27 January the 1/5th Dukes moved back to Hondheghem, near Hazebrouck, 'and spent two days in the melancholy task of dismembering the battalion.' Many stayed in the 49th Division compulsorily transferred to other West Riding Regiments. Of these, eight officers and 195 men joined the 1/6th (Skipton) Dukes.

Twelve officers and 200 men travelled south, joining the 2/5th Dukes in the British Third Army at St Aubin near Arras. They were renamed the 5th Duke of Wellington's West Riding Regiment. In command was Lieutenant-Colonel Best Joseph Walker, formerly of the 1/5th Dukes. Lieutenant-Colonel Frank Brook, who had assumed control of the 2/5th Dukes on the death of Lieutenant-Colonel Best in the attack on Cambrai, was second in command. The 2/5th troops formed the new A and B companies, with the 1/5th forming companies C and D.[5]

During February they manned the front line at Gavrelle, north-east of Arras, interspersed with route marches and firing-range practice. By 9 March they were a little further north, close to Vimy Ridge, where they observed increased enemy aircraft and artillery movements. The anticipated German offensive was imminent, just to the south of them.[6]

The western front battles of 1918 would see local troops cover more ground than at any time in the war.

The Battle of St Quentin

From his three attacking options, Ludendorff had chosen Operation *Michael*. At 4.40am on 21 March the Germans began a five-hour bombardment across a 27-miles front from Arras to Gouzeaucourt west of Cambrai, firing one million shells – over 3000 shells per minute. At 9.40am, assisted by fog and smoke that hampered the British artillery and snipers, they charged across No Man's Land, the old Somme battlefields of 1916. It was a charge unlike any the Allies had seen.

The Germans had hand-picked their strongest, most athletic men and trained them as 'storm troopers.' Carrying only their weaponry, which included flamethrowers, they travelled lightly and quickly, able to punch through sections of the British line to the reserve lines, before turning to attack from the rear. The ensuing chaos was exploited by regular troops in close support.

The intensity of the attack shocked the British, but even at such speed, attacking well-manned defensive positions was perilous and on 21 March both sides suffered about 40,000 casualties. Gunner F Webster, a bell-ringer at Meltham Parish Church, had seen many battles in France, but described this assault as …

> … unparalleled … Wave after wave came over only to get mown down time after time. Our boys killed so many that they were simply tired of seeing them keep coming on ... the Boche cannot boast of a great victory at Arras. He did not take sufficient ground to bury his thousands of dead. If the German people knew the cost of the ground they have taken they would ask for peace tomorrow … at any price.

Gunner Webster's battery maintained an unceasing barrage for two days and nights until they were specifically targeted. Over the next two days their 'guns were silenced in succession.' On 24 March Webster was struck in the shoulder. Their one remaining officer shook him by the hand, saying 'Well done, Webster.'

> I went, leaving him with about seven men and two guns still carrying on as if nothing had happened. That is one battery amongst hundreds which have shown … great … pluck and tenacity … We'll beat them to the last man if necessary.[7]

24-year-old Private Harry Roebuck of Holmfirth, a northern union rugby footballer at Underbank Rangers, was less fortunate. Showing 'bravery and utter disregard for danger' he prevented several men of his company 'being completely surrounded by the enemy' before he was fatally wounded.[8]

Vastly outnumbered, the British 5th Army retreated unsteadily. Dangerous salient developed but were flattened as the wings fell back. Units became mixed, but adapted, some battalions improvising 'barriers of their own dead.' Somehow, touch was just about maintained between brigades and the retreat retained a semblance of control, all the time sapping the enemy.[9]

By 23 March, two days into Operation *Michael*, the Germans had advanced 12 miles in the south and a rapturous Kaiser declared 24 March a national holiday in celebration. Ludendorff now targeted Amiens, a key railway junction linking Paris to the Channel coast, as a strategic gain to reflect the territory taken.[10]

The First Battle of Bapaume

Meanwhile, the waves of withdrawal had reached the 62nd Division in the British 3rd Army near Arras. Moved south, they entered the line at Achiet-le-Petit at 4pm on 24 March. The 186th Brigade, including the 5th Dukes, was on the right, with the 185th Brigade on the left. Their orders were to prolong the battle in Logeast Wood north of the village, but they marched into a rapidly deteriorating situation.

> Large numbers of retiring troops, utterly worn out, from five different divisions, passed through the brigade as they advanced.

Alarming information that 'the enemy was advancing steadily in large numbers' was confirmed at dusk when the local battalion saw thousands of Germans 'on the high ground above Irles' to the south. The 62nd Division had just one gun for artillery support and the confusion behind the lines offered little prospect of more.

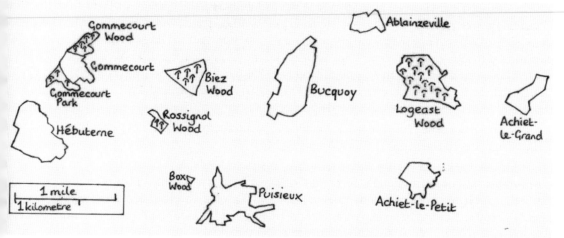

Key locations in the Battle of Bapaume

Their hopes depended greatly on the tactical nous of Divisional Commander, Major-General Walter Braithwaite, who had taken over command of the front in this sector. To protect their exposed right flank, the General ordered the 62nds to retreat to high ground between Bucquoy and Puisieux. On 26 March the Germans adjusted from a westerly to a north westerly advance to re-expose and attack the right flank of the 186th Brigade. Two 186th battalions, the 5th Dukes and the Pioneers, withdrew a short distance to face south east, their right flank now on Rossignol Wood, just west of Hebuterne, to screen the retreats from Puisieux. Using his initiative, Second-Lieutenant SR Morton of the 5th Dukes moved his platoon to an advanced position at Puisieux and frustrated the German advance for 45 minutes, enabling several companies to withdraw to a stronger position that extended the screen beyond Rossignol Wood. The Second-Lieutenant, who had assumed command of his company after the loss of three senior officers, was awarded the Military Cross for this action. Meanwhile, Australian and New Zealand battalions plugged a gap between the 62nd and 12th Divisions in the nick of time.

Suffering numerous losses in the screening operation, the right flank of the 5th Dukes was again attacked on 27 March. Operating from some old trenches, their rifles and Lewis guns held their own across open ground, but the storm troopers created havoc, swarming through the trenches, bombing and maiming. Between 1pm and 5.30pm, the 62nds repulsed four such assaults from the cream of the German troops, two at Rossignol Wood and two at Bucquoy, sustaining many casualties. Gradually, more artillery and tanks came to their assistance and the line held. This resistance was arguably the 5th Dukes' most important and courageous contribution of the war.

The First Battle of Arras 1918

The following morning, 28 March, a German bombardment preceded an advance along the whole front. They were delayed by a counter-barrage, and by accurate shooting from an advanced post held by a platoon of the 5th Dukes. As the battle developed this platoon became isolated. They were still holding out at 1pm, and support reached them in mid-afternoon, but it was too late. The local men had fought 'back-to-back' to the last man, but had been completely overwhelmed. All were dead.[11]

During the afternoon, storm troopers captured Rossignol Wood and the ridge east of Hebuterne, but towards evening the German attack 'waned and finally collapsed.'[12] A Huddersfield Territorial wrote:

> Our battalion has been very highly congratulated … We stopped the progress of the Boches, and thereby saved a very critical situation, but not without a good many casualties.

One of his officers added:

> … the old Hun seems to have been held on our bit of front better than anywhere.

A Huddersfield private reinforced the scale of their resistance:

> Jerry was bound to get on a bit with all the men he had against us. But I think we have got him by the short hairs now, and I think this will go a long way towards winning the war.[13]

237

The coastal Field Hospital at Étaples was flooded with casualties, many of them from the 62nd Division. Between 25 and 31 March the Division lost 98 officers and 2084 other ranks killed, wounded or missing, of whom nine officers and 206 other ranks were from the 5th Dukes.[14] Among Huddersfield's casualties were Second-Lieutenant J Sugden and Second-Lieutenant Geoffrey Woodcock, both killed at the front of their platoons, and Second-Lieutenant GF Lockwood, who was taken prisoner, having 'fought splendidly and held his position until surrounded.'[15] Bombardier John T Gee from Outlane, a successful local sprinter, was hospitalised after heroically giving 2.5 pints of blood to save a comrade.

> The major called for volunteers. I couldn't see the poor fellow die. I have been very weak, but am now convalescent … I saved a man's life.[16]

The Underbank rugby club suffered further casualties. Private Walter Bray, who was also a much-respected bowler in the Huddersfield Cricket League, was killed, and two relatives of rugby international Harold Wagstaff, both gunners in the RFA, were invalided home with gas poisoning. Harold's brother Norman, who played briefly for Huddersfield, was hospitalised at Folkestone and his cousin, also called Harold Wagstaff, was treated at Southport.[17]

The 62nd Division was relieved at the beginning of April, just as the German advance in the northern sector of Operation *Michael* ran out of steam. Ludendorff now embarked on Operation *Mars*, advancing on Arras, ten miles north of Bucquoy, but the Germans made little headway. He briefly re-opened Operation *Michael*, but the attack floundered at Villers-Brettoneux, ten miles east of Amiens. German supply lines were becoming stretched and discipline broke down into looting and drunkenness when their hungry troops came across the relative riches of Albert. The casualty toll of Operation *Michael* was 250,000 German, 77,000 French and 178,000 British and Commonwealth soldiers. Roughly one third of these were fatalities.[18]

Germany had moved the front line westwards, but had not broken through. Now she was running out of time. Austria was close to bankruptcy and starvation. Turkey was impoverished, the Ottoman Empire crumbling with the loss of Baghdad and Jerusalem to the British who were close to driving Turkish forces from Mesopotamia, Syria and Palestine. When 1500 stretcher cases arrived in Frankfurt from the First Battle of Bapaume, 5000 Germans demonstrated outside the city's hospital, demanding an end to the war.[19]

The Battles of the Lys: The Battle of Messines

Needing a breakthrough more urgently by the day, on 9 April Ludendorff launched Operation *Georgette* – revised from Operation *George* – in the valley of the River Lys, where there was potential for progress after a dry spring. A four and a half hour bombardment preceded an attack across a 12-mile front by 14 German divisions, and a massive assault shattered the resistance of a thinly spread Portuguese Division just north of Neuve Chapelle. On 10 April these gains were extended north of Armentières to Wytschaete and Hollebeke, forcing the British to abandon the Messines Ridge.

Additional troops were rushed to the area. These included the 49th Division, with its scores of reassigned Huddersfield troops who had been holding the line on the Ypres Salient. That night they desperately defended Nieppe, near Armentières.

Key locations in the Battles of the Lys

The following day Armentières fell and the Germans pressed on through Nieppe. A German tide was sweeping across Flanders, the Allies' most strongly defended area. The key railway junction at Hazebrouck was just five miles away – one day at the current rate of advance. At this darkest of hours, the 49th Division listened gravely as Field-Marshal Haig's desperate Special Order of the Day was read to them:

> Victory will belong to the side which holds out the longest ... Every position must be held to the last man: there must be no retirement. With our backs to the wall, and believing in the justice of our cause, each one of us must fight on to the end. The safety of our homes and the freedom of mankind depend alike upon the conduct of each one of us at this critical moment.[20]

The destiny of the war was at hand.

With Our Backs to the Wall
by
Charles Lunn

The command has been given to stay the retreat;
To take a firm stand, and the hammer blows meet;
Every soldier is bidden to hold or to fall,
To fight for dear life with his back to the wall.

They have heard the grim order, and hold on till death,
Sinking down when their bodies no longer hold breath;
Every man like a hero has answered the call,
And a Briton fights best with his back to the wall.

The issue is vital. The future is bright
Or dark with the blackness of uttermost night;
As goes the stern battle. So kneel one and all,
And pray for our men with their backs to the wall.

In this hour of grave trial let none feel dismay,
For ever 'tis darkest before break of day,
Keep a stiff upper lip, and whatever befall
Trust in God and your sons with their backs to the wall.[21]

The Battles of the Lys: The Battle of Bailleul

The Germans also thrust northwards from Armentières towards Mount Kemmel, the strategically vital summit dominating the land south of Ypres. Falling back from Nieppe, battalions of the 49th Division occupied trenches to the north of Neuve Èglise, a village two miles from Mount Kemmel, where they were subjected to artillery bombardment and infantry harassment throughout 11 April. Early next day, the Germans launched a concentrated infantry attack which penetrated the southern part of the village. Ejected from their positions, the West Yorkshiremen together with the Worcesters mounted a counter attack in the early hours of 13 April. Ferocious street fighting drove the enemy 150 yards beyond the village.

Elsewhere there were mixed fortunes. On 12 April the Germans had struck westwards, crossed the River Lys between Merville and Steenwerk, and reached the outskirts of Hazebrouck. They were halted there by stern resistance from the British 31st Division. But on 15 April the British abandoned Passchendaele Ridge, and the towns of Bailleul and Wulverghemfell.[22]

On the same morning, four days of heroic resistance by the 49th Division at Neuve Èglise was finally overcome. One young Huddersfield officer called 'the remnants of his platoon' together. When he saw how few were left he wept in front of them. Their efforts earned official commendation from General Haig:

> ... no troops have done harder work since the beginning of the battle on April 9th. They helped to retake Neuve Èglise no fewer than four times in the bitter struggle for that place ... a heavy price has been paid ... but ... this will be as fine a page as has been written in the history of the war.[23]

Huddersfield private EE Peace, who had been rushed to France from Italy, was horrified to see terrified civilians trapped in these battleground villages:

> … screams … made by the shells passing over … homes of peasants wrecked … Women and children homeless … running for shelter towards a cellar whenever the Boche drops the shells in the vicinity; a woman carrying one child in her arms and perhaps two or three tiny toddlers clinging to her skirts and hurrying as fast as their little legs can take them. This is the picture that makes a man thank God that his wife and children or parents are not situated in circumstances such as these.[24]

The Battles of the Lys: The First and Second Battles of Kemmel

The 49th Division retreated from Neuve Èglise, fought, retreated and fought again, regrouping for further resistance around Bailleul. On 16 April the Germans captured the villages of Meteren, west of Bailleul, and Wytschaete. Ypres itself, regarded as the gateway to the Channel ports, was now in sight.

French reinforcements arrived to take over a nine-mile stretch of the front, renewing hopes that the British resistance and sacrifices had not been in vain, but on 25 April the French lost Mount Kemmel to the Germans. With Allied forces concentrating south of Ypres, Ludendorff renewed his attempts to reach Amiens with an attack on Villers-Bretonneux, but was again frustrated by French and British resistance.

Both sides were now close to exhaustion. Many new British replacements were teenagers, and a desperate Government, relenting on the supply of troops, waived virtually all exemptions from conscription. On 29 April, Ludendorff launched an attack on Ypres from the south across a five mile front from Dranoutre to Voormezeele, centred on Mount Kemmel. It failed before nightfall, and Operation *Georgette* was abandoned.[25]

For 21 days the Allies had battled to straighten the bends and plug the fractures in their last line of defence. Somehow, it had held. The 49th Division was in the line throughout, a Huddersfield private describing it as:

> the worst … days of my life … I can't reckon up yet, why or how I got out with my life … We never gave up an inch of ground without orders.[26]

It was the second blow to German morale in just over a week. On 21 April the seemingly invincible Baron Manfred Albrecht Freiherr Von Richtofen, the famous 'Red Baron', destroyer of over 70 Allied aircraft, had been shot down over the Somme battlefield.[27]

The Battle of the Tardenois

It was a month before the Germans were ready to launch another offensive. Operation *Blucher* also known as the Third Battle of the Aisne, began with an artillery bombardment against the Chemin des Dames Ridge, north-west of Reims on Monday 27 May. Taken by surprise, the Allies frantically rushed troops to the area but were outnumbered. They lost several bridges across the Aisne and 12 miles of territory as the Germans marched through a 25 miles wide gap in the Allied lines. By 30 May the Germans had captured 50,000 prisoners.[28]

A week into the operation, the Germans' rate of progress continued to surprise the Allies, a Huddersfield private writing:

> Little did we think last Sunday afternoon that a battle was imminent. At seven o'clock … we were playing badminton on the lawn of a lovely old chateau, and at eight o'clock we were on our way to the line.
>
> … Civilians … forsook their homes and fled from the enemy … people with little children walking along whilst German shells and machine gun bullets were flying around them.[29]

The following day, Monday 3 June, the Germans bombarded Paris with a salvo from 'Big Bertha', a huge gun mounted on a train 75 miles north-east of the capital. First unleashed on 21 March, its 820 kilogram shells were the first man-made objects to reach the stratosphere. They caused considerable damage and 250 deaths in Paris, excellent for German propaganda and morale, but contributing little to capturing the city. That was down to the infantry who continued to advance in that direction, but at great cost.

In addition to casualties inflicted by the Allies, thousands of German troops were being struck down by the first wave of Spanish Influenza. Tired, dirty and malnourished, the armies were a fertile breeding ground for the virus. On 11 June a counter-attack, bolstered by new arrivals from the United States, drove the Germans back close to their starting point at Chemin des Dames.[30]

General Foch, appointed Supreme Commander of the Allied Armies, shrewdly anticipated Ludendorff's next move. Convinced that Germany now posed little threat in Flanders, he requested an additional four British Divisions to strengthen the junction of the French and British armies. Haig sent the 15th, 34th, 51st and 62nd Divisions, constituting the XXIInd Corps, under Lieutenant-General Sir Alexander Godley. As well as the West Riding troops, the 62nd Division now included the 2/4th Hampshires and 1/5th Devons.[31]

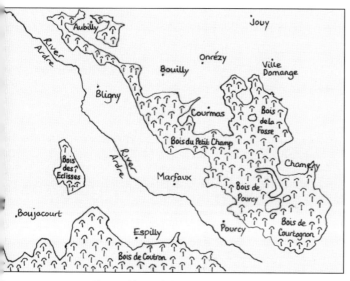

The Valley of the River Ardre

Repeatedly cheered through the towns and villages on their train journey south via Paris, these Divisions arrived at Reims on 17 July, just as 32 German Divisions attacked the French 4th Army to the east of the city and 17 German Divisions attacked the French 6th Army west of the city. Frustrated in the east but successful in the west, the Germans crossed the River Marne and advanced four miles across a nine-mile front before a combination of French, British, United States and Italian troops arrested their progress.

The next day, 18 July, Foch launched his counter-offensive along the River Ardre, which rises south of Reims and flows north-west between high ridges and spurs. It was a valley of deceptive beauty. The wooded terrain on the tops, the vineyards and hamlets on the slopes, and the golden crop fields, sunken roads, banks and villages in the valley bottom offered countless concealments for machine-gun nests.

On a successful first day, 24 Allied Divisions reduced the German salient by five miles. On 19 July, the 62nd Division continued the attack on the south side of the Ardre, with the 51st Highland Division on the north side. The fighting was 'bitter.' German prisoners trickled out, but there were also casualties to machine gun and shell fire. On 20 July, as the 5th Dukes dodged a series of shell attacks, its various units lost sight of one another and were in danger of becoming isolated. Realising the problem, Captain Keith Sykes of Huddersfield ventured alone into the undergrowth and guided them together again.[32]

Multiple officer casualties left Second-Lieutenant William McLintock of Thongsbridge suddenly in command of a large sector. Quickly deeming it too dangerous to advance any further, he …

> … rallied his men and those of other companies who were without a commander, and formed a line of posts in communication with the neighbouring units, in spite of the continued fire

Caricature of Captain Keith Sykes

241

from the infantry and machine-gunners. He was thus able to retain the territory taken after great struggle … he conducted himself magnificently.[33]

Both Sykes and McLintock were congratulated for their gallantry in General Berthelot's 5th French Army Orders.

Extract from General
Berthelot's
5th French Army Orders
commending
Captain Keith Sykes.

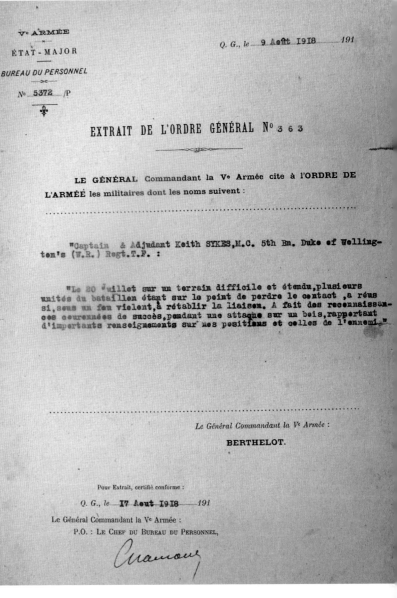

Threatened with isolation on the salient created by their earlier attacks, the Germans retreated up the valley, pursued by the Allies. On 22 July the 62nd Division encountered several German nests on a thickly forested spur of the Bois du Petit Champ near the village of Bligny. The German machine gunners, well-hidden in thickets, fired in the direction of sound and the 62nd's advance became deadly game of stealth and deception. Prowling, creeping, circling approaches climaxed in sudden close range attacks – and numerous casualties. Stalking what appeared to be the main strongpoint, the front company of the 5th Duke's left column was outmanœuvred, drawn into hand-to-hand combat and surrounded. Captain JB Cockhill and eight men fought their way through the rear of the encirclement retreated, reorganised and attacked again, capturing the strongpoint's garrison and freeing their captured comrades. The remnants of resistance were cleared from the wood under a creeping barrage the following day. The 5th Dukes captured over 200 prisoners and 40 machine guns, whilst the 'utterly defeated' 123rd German Division was withdrawn.[34]

During the next week the 186th Brigade, with the Highland Division to their north and a French Division to their south, repeatedly took villages 'by storm', harrying and driving the Germans back. Rapid progress over such testing terrain put great pressure on the signallers to maintain communication lines. One such was Second-Lieutenant Thomas Aspinall of Lockwood, serving with KOYLI. On 27 July he pushed ahead alone to establish a line from the village of Courmas to battalion headquarters. He then followed the attackers through a heavy barrage to supervise a similar operation at Espilly. His courage earned him the French Croix de Guerre with gold star.[35]

With the battle won, the 62nd Division was withdrawn from the line on 29 July. The Division had suffered substantial casualties – 118 of 338 officers and 3865 of 9401 other ranks. Of these, the 5th Dukes had lost 13 officers and 400 other ranks. They had also taken over 1300 prisoners and advanced more than four miles.[36] Among their casualties was Sergeant Reginald Field of Huddersfield. Awarded the Military Medal for helping to capture an objective on the Ardre, he was one of several to be captured in a counter-attack.[37] Another casualty was Lieutenant Reynold Donkersley of Almondbury. His valour in a patrol skirmish earlier in the year had earned him the Military Cross, but he was killed during the battles on the Ardre. His family placed one of the first war-related 'In Memoriam' poems in the *HDE*.

> He did not stop to reason
> When first the war began,
> But went and did his duty,
> Like a soldier and a man.
> In the bloom of youth God took him,
> In the pride of his boyhood days,
> None knew him but to love him,
> None mentioned his name but with praise.[38]

There were hundreds more 'In Memoriam' messages and poems in the local press in 1918 and 1919. The courage and tenacity of the local troops, and the significance of this victory, were reflected in a long list of honours published in the *HDE* on 9 September 1918. A Huddersfield private wrote:

> everyone had pulled his last ounce … we had done our share in one of the decisive victories of the war. [39]

The tide had turned. Germany's manpower and resources were stretched. She had suffered over one million casualties since the start of the spring offensive. In Germany, a shortage of metal was betrayed when centuries-old church bells and lead pipes from the streets were requisitioned and melted down for weaponry.[40]

The 62nd Division returned north to their old billets at Authie, west of Bucquoy for rest, training and the integration of a large number of new, predominantly very young, drafts.[41]

Throughout August, emboldened by U.S. troops who gave the Allies an increasing numerical advantage, General Foch ordered a succession of rolling attacks, switched to different sectors in turn to keep the Germans on the retreat and off-balance. Applying the lessons of the war, the Allies integrated tanks, aircraft, artillery and infantry, attacking at speed and targeting clear, achievable goals. It was a combination never mastered by the Germans.

On 8 August, the first day of the Battle of Amiens, the Canadians advanced eight miles in a joint attack with the Australians and British. The Huddersfield men in the 168th Brigade of the RFA fought fiercely alongside them, further enhancing their fine reputation. 18,500 German prisoners, many of them exhausted, hungry and dispirited, were captured but, in addition, both sides suffered 9000 casualties.[42]

On 23 August the local artillerymen supported the 97th Brigade in a successful attack on Herleville. Driving the Germans out of the village the following day, they created an opening to force them back to the Hindenberg Line in this sector.[43]

The Battle of the Scarp

Simultaneously, 20 miles further north, the 62nd Division's rest period was cut short by the British advance north of Albert. They took over the front line at Achiet-le-Grand and, at 9am on 25 August, attacked due east. They met no opposition at Behagnies or Sapignies, but the Germans had established a strong defensive position in old trenches across the Bapaume to Arras road. Leading the attack in the 5th Dukes' sector, B and C companies incurred heavy casualties from machine gun fire. Lieutenant LM Tod, the battalion intelligence officer, went ahead under 'the heaviest fire' and returned with information that enabled A and D companies to maintain the attack.[44] This was spearheaded by Sergeant-Major W Fisher of Moldgreen, who led a bombing squad up a communication trench, drove the Germans back and exploded a machine gun position with rifle grenades. With two platoon commanders killed, Fisher took charge of both and led the advance until, just east of the Favreil to Mory light railway, he called a halt. The 37th Division to their right and the 2/4th York and Lancaster Regiment on their left had not kept pace, their flanks were exposed and consolidation was necessary.

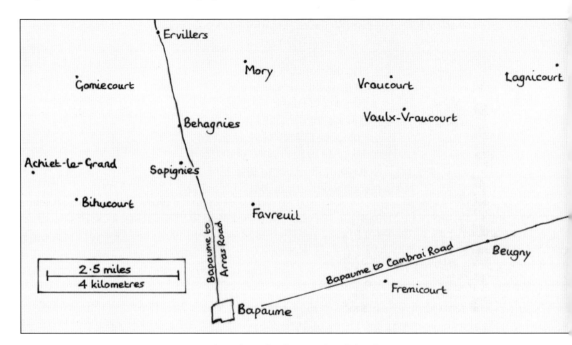

Key locations in the Battle of the Scarp

Fisher organised defensive lines, but at 5pm the Germans targeted their position with shrapnel and gas shells. Just over an hour later the Germans counter-attacked. Expending artillery, rifle and Lewis gun fire, the 5th Dukes repulsed the enemy and bought critical time, but at a cost of 254 casualties, including 35 fatalities. Lieutenant Tod was awarded the Military Cross and Sergeant-Major Fisher a bar to his DCM for their courage in this action.[45]

Two days later, on 27 August, the 5th Dukes led an attack by the 62nd Division that drove the Germans out of Mory. It was their last act under Major-General Walter Braithwaite who was knighted, promoted to Lieutenant General and appointed to command IXth Corps as reward for his successful leadership of the 62nd Division. He was replaced by Major-General Sir RD Whigham, KCB DSO.[46]

As the advance continued, Lieutenant Tod made another 'fearless reconnaissance' to ascertain the lie of the land on 28 August. This enabled Private R Jennings of Huddersfield and two comrades to run across open country behind Germans who were attacking the 5th Dukes' trenches. Surprising the enemy, they knocked out a strong machine gun position and returned with 20 prisoners. All three were awarded the Military Medal.[47]

The following day the 5th Dukes were ordered to capture another troublesome German strong point in a double trench system south-west of Vaulx Vraucourt. A and D Companies fought with bomb and bayonet, but the resistance was fierce until Sergeant-Major Fisher once again inspired the breakthrough. Leading a bombing party, he personally killed five Germans and 'was largely responsible for the success gained, which included the capture of trenches, 100 prisoners, 16 machine-guns and two trench mortars.' But for his actions, the battalion would almost certainly have suffered more than their 30 casualties from this confrontation. The Sergeant-Major was awarded the Military Cross to add to his other distinctions.[48]

The pattern of advance, punctuated by pockets of resistance, continued. On 30 August the 5th Dukes progressed a mile, captured 100 prisoners and suffered 22 casualties. On the night of 31 August, Second-Lieutenant James Huffam, a young officer from Berwick, rushed an enemy machine gun post with three other men. They captured the position but were then heavily attacked and forced to withdraw. Huffam fought his way out carrying a wounded comrade. Later that night the 5th Dukes were delayed by another enemy machine gun at a farm. Rushing it, Huffam and two others captured eight prisoners, enabling the advance to continue. Second-Lieutenant Huffam was awarded the ultimate honour, the Victoria Cross, for these actions, one of only two earned by the 5th Dukes during the war.[49]

Second-Lieutenant James Huffam, VC

On 2 September, Lieutenant Tod provided yet more life-saving information. With a counter-attack looming, he advanced alone onto high ground in front of the line, ascertained the general situation, and advised on new defensive positions which proved effective, saving many lives. Shortly afterwards, the 62nd Division was relieved. In nine days they had forced the Germans back 12 miles, from Achiet-le-Grand to roughly halfway between Bapaume and Cambrai.[50]

Similar encouraging progress was being made across the front. By the end of August the Huddersfield Artillerymen occupied the west bank of the Somme south of Peronne. Continuous pressure from the Brigade assisted the 97th Division in crossing the river by Brie Bridge on 6 September. Four days later they supported attacks around villages west and north of St Quentin. The Hindenberg Line was now in their sights, as it was for the 62nd Division when they returned to the front line on familiar territory on 12 September. Their objective was Havrincourt, the village they had captured the previous November on the glorious first day of the Battle of Cambrai.

The Battle of Havrincourt

Zero hour was 5.30am. B and D companies of the 5th Dukes attacked to the right of the Brigade front. Beating off heavy resistance and several counter-attacks, they captured numerous prisoners and suffered over 100 casualties, but by 11.30am they had secured the north-east quadrant of Havrincourt Wood. The Allies' first breach of the Hindenberg Line since the Battle of Cambrai, this was a significant psychological blow, but not yet a strategic breakthrough. Reinforced since 1917, the Hindenberg Line now comprised three formidable belts of barbed wire, superbly engineered dug-outs, shelters, gun emplacements and fortified villages, stretching from Lille to Metz. Overcoming it would significantly shorten the war and diminish Germany's post-war bargaining position.[51]

On 13 and 14 September, A and C companies of the 5th Dukes made a succession of bombing raids. Informed by a 'daring reconnaissance of advanced positions' by Captain Keith Sykes, their strategy yielded 57 prisoners at the expense of just one casualty and earned the Captain a bar to his Military Cross.[52]

Elsewhere in the battle, Corporal Elliot Hirst of Berry Brow, serving with the 9th Dukes, earned the Military Medal by moving his Lewis gun section to a position of great tactical advantage which expedited the capture of key objectives. When his officer and sergeant became casualties, he took command, reorganised the platoon and consolidated their position.[53]

Over the following week the 62nd, 37th and New Zealand Divisions battled their way south eastwards. At one point, Corporal Harvey Hinchcliffe of Golcar, serving with KOYLI, was the only surviving member of his Lewis gun team, but continued to his objective, expending all his ammunition. Later, he took another section into No Man's Land 'under terrible fire' and rescued two of his Lewis gun comrades who had lain wounded for 60 hours. He too was awarded the Military Medal.[54]

The Battle of the Canal du Nord

On 28 September, as news arrived that the U.S. and French armies were making great progress south of Verdun, the 62nd Division renewed attacks on the Hindenberg Line in the sector where the Cambrai offensive had floundered in 1917 – the Marcoing crossing. Despite heavy rain and mud that made movement difficult, the 5th Dukes combined with the 2/4th Hampshire Battalion to overcome stiff resistance in the village of Marcoing before midday.[55]

Progressing south east towards the Canal de L'escaut, they were delayed by machine gun fire until Private Henry Tandey crawled forward with a Lewis gun team and knocked out the German strong point. Breaking through the second line of the Hindenberg defence system, they reached the deathtrap of the canal, the most hazardous obstacle to their advance. It fell to the 5th Dukes to force the crossing. As expected, the bridges were down, but Private Tandey 'restored the plank bridges under a hail of bullets.'

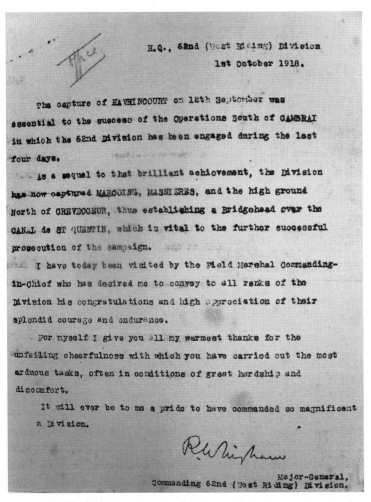

Letter of gratitude to the 62nd Division from their Commanding Officer, Major-General R Whigham

Bullets continued to sweep the canal as the 5th Dukes made their perilous way across. Still extremely vulnerable on the east bank, they were counter-attacked with heavy shell and machine gun fire. Rather than remain trapped on the bank, they opted to attack, immediately running into 'greatly superior numbers of the enemy.' In the ensuing battle, stretcher bearer Private HOK Asquith of Huddersfield 'worked continuously ... in getting in the wounded and attending to them under the heaviest ... fire.' He was awarded the Military Medal for 'unselfishness and bravery ... beyond all praise ... he undoubtedly saved many lives.'

Amidst flying bullets and grenades, and ruthless bayonet and hand-to-hand fighting, Private Tandey and eight others were surrounded by 'an overwhelming number of Germans.' Their position appeared hopeless, but Tandey 'led a bayonet charge through them, fighting so fiercely that

37 of the enemy were driven into the hands of his Company.' Twice wounded, Tandey 'refused to leave till the fight was won.' The 5th Dukes not only repelled the Germans, but captured 400 prisoners, 23 machine guns and gained vital ground, establishing a more defendable position. Private Henry Tandey, who hailed from Leamington and had already been decorated with the DCM and Military Medal, became the second 5th Dukes' soldier to be awarded the Victoria Cross.

By crossing the waterways east of Marcoing and, further north the Canal du Nord, the Allies forced the Germans to abandon Cambrai and pull back to the River Selle. The 5th Dukes captured Masnières and high ground north of Crèvecoeur, establishing a vital bridgehead over that part of the St Quentin Canal before they were relieved on 1 October. Their achievements earned glowing plaudits in Sir Douglas Haig's official communique, an extremely rare distinction for an individual battalion.[56]

The Battle of the St Quentin Canal

Twenty miles to the south, the Huddersfield Artillerymen were helping to breach the St Quentin Canal at Bellinglise, which was also part of the Hindenberg Line. Attached to the 46th Division, they bombarded the approaches to the Riqueval Bridge, paving the way for 1/6th Battalion of the North Staffordshire Regiment to overrun the outer German defences and storm across the bridge in the nick of time. On the far side German engineers were about to blow up the bridge, but Captain AH Charlton captured a machine-gun post and cut the wires to the explosives. Without the bridge, there would have been carnage trying to force a crossing down the canal's deep, exposed ravine.[57]

30 September 1918: 137th (Staffordshire) Brigade (46th North Midland Division) on the east bank of the St. Quentin Canal, addressed by Brigadier Campbell from the Riqueval Bridge. Their brilliant assault on this part of the Hindenburg Line the previous day was aided by the Huddersfield men of the 168th RFA.

One member of the North Staffordshire Regiment who missed this success was 25-year-old Lance-Corporal Allen Brown from Hepworth. On 23 October he was charged at Holmfirth Police Court with desertion. The Lance-Corporal confessed, but in mitigation he had served for four years. 'I have done my whack!' He was remanded to await a military escort and convicted by court-martial on 28 November. Along with 'cowardice', desertion could carry the death penalty; of 20,000 convicted servicemen, 3,000 were sentenced to death and 306 were executed. Lance-Corporal Brown was not executed and it is likely that he served a prison sentence.[58]

Along the front line, the Allies' unrelenting pursuit denied the Germans time to regroup. The Beaurevoir Line, the recently reinforced third belt of the Hindenberg Line, had been breached in places, taking Allied troops further east than at any point in the war. To add to Germany's woes, the Allies had smashed through the Bulgarian lines in Macedonia, and the Bulgarians were suing for peace. Ludendorff knew the game was up and on 1 October suggested peace proposals to his shocked senior staff.[59]

On 8 October, the 62nd Division, in bivouacs at Havrincourt, had another rest period cut short. They had to start marching to keep in touch with the advance.[60] They arrived in new billets at Carnières, five miles east of Cambrai just as, a couple of miles north-east, the 49th Division was driving the Germans out of Saulzoir.

> The cellars were full of civilians, taking refuge, who welcomed their liberators with cognac and coffee.[61]

Even further north, Major RW Brooke of Huddersfield commanded patrols that cleared the last Germans from the town of Tourcoing.

> … crowds swarmed the officer's vehicle with cheers, 'Merci, merci, chers Anglais', 'vive les Allies!' Flags were tied to the car … I have never seen such expressions of affection and gratitude; even the babies seemed to be smiling.[62]

The Battle of the Selle

On 17 October the 62nd Division relieved the 2nd Coldstream Guards in the front line at St Python, just west of Solesmes, which was occupied by Germans who had retreated from the 49th Division's attack at Saulzoir. Attempting to minimise civilian casualties, the 5th Dukes and Guards Divisions led a furtive attack on Solesmes in the early morning darkness of 20 October. They waded across the 'unfordable' River Selle, up to their waists in places, scrambled over dense hedges and barbed wire fences and silently entered the outskirts of the village.[63]

Lance-Corporal Harry Darlington of Dalton turned a corner ahead of his section. Suddenly a German light machine gun opened up at close range. Without hesitation, Harry rushed the post and bayonetted the gunner. Four other Germans attacked him, but Harry grappled and brawled until his section arrived and captured them. It sparked a full scale battle. The 5th Dukes fought through the streets as civilians took cover from machine gun volleys, rifle fire and vicious hand-to-hand fighting. Sergeant Franklin Draper from Lepton led his section to eliminate two German machine gun posts and capture over 30 prisoners, as the Allies took the village and a strongly fortified command position on high ground two miles beyond. They sustained 34 casualties, killed over 100 Germans and captured 300 prisoners. Lance-Corporal Darlington and Sergeant Draper were both awarded the Military Medal.[64]

During October, the Allies had progressed 20 miles east of the Hindenberg Line, but had suffered 20,000 casualties and their supply lines were stretched. A quick end to the war on the western front was highly desirable, and seemed more likely on 2 November when it ended in the east. On 30 October the Allies signed an Armistice with Turkey at Mudros. Three days later 57 Allied Divisions – 51 Italian, three British, two French and one U.S. – captured Tagliamento, signalling the end of Austro-Hungarian resistance. [65]

The Battle of Valenciennes

The Huddersfield gunners in the 168th RFA continued to support the attacks north east of St Quentin, a direct hit on a troublesome enemy battery assisting the 11th Infantry Brigade to take the village of Levergies.[66]

To the north, the Canadians launched an assault on Mont Houy, key to capturing Valenciennes. On their southern flank was the threadbare 49th Division, in which the combined three battalions of the 146th Brigade had been reduced from 3000 men to less than 1000. Ordered to attack, they shinned along tree trunks lain across the Rhonelle River, then proceeded eastwards, entering the village of Préseau.[67] Immediately, Rifleman Albert Sheard of Newsome was hit, but opted to stay at his post at the battalion report centre. All day he braved shell and machine-gun fire, carrying important orders from company headquarters and returning with valuable information. Within 48 hours 146th Brigade had captured the villages of Préseau and Maresches, along with 700 prisoners.[68]

Keeping pace with the eastward tide, on 4 November the local Artillerymen were at Ors, supporting the Royal Sussex and Manchester Regiments and the Lancashire Fusiliers in the hazardous crossing of the Oise-Sambre Canal.

Unleashing concentrated, accurate barrages across the canal, the artillery kept the Germans pinned down as the infantry constructed temporary bridges. Sadly, their firepower could not prevent the death of a 25-year-old Second-Lieutenant leading his unit in the 2nd Battalion Manchester Regiment. He was Wilfred Owen, arguably the greatest of the war poets.

The Oise-Sambre Canal was the last major obstacle in the sector. Once across, the artillerymen could see the devastation they had caused.

> For over a thousand yards there was scarcely an area twenty yards square without its shell-hole ... the teams lying on the road side showed that some of the shells had found victims.

Beyond this battleground, the land was unblemished, paradise after weeks of ploughing through the old battlefields.

> Nobody at home can ... appreciate the relief ... after travelling over 70 miles, and living under the most primitive conditions for four months, to see once more an undamaged countryside. An ordinary – very ordinary – cottage by the road side was indeed a thing of beauty.

Large, abandoned German guns betrayed the speed of their retreat as, unhindered by mud, craters and debris, the advance accelerated into a pursuit.[69]

The Battle of the Sambre

Whilst the artillerymen crossed the Oise-Sambre Canal, to the north, the 5th Dukes in the 62nd Division, alongside the 37th Division, fought fiercely to capture the walled town of Le Quesnoy and its German garrison of 1000 men. They then marched eastwards across 'intricate country' and, with the New Zealand troops, captured several villages. Just south of them, the last major German resistance was crumbling in the Forest of Mormal.

Over the next five days the 62nd Division advanced 18 miles, much of it in drenching rain, but with dwindling opposition. They arrived at the outskirts of Maubeuge on 9 November, predictably finding the bridges over the Sambre blown up. They crossed over a temporary plank bridge at 2am and, when the town awoke, were greeted with 'great enthusiasm.' The civilians had vivid memories of the German bombardment, siege and plundering in the first month of the war, and had been under German occupation for over four years.[70] Appropriately and symbolically just north of Maubeuge, Mons had also been reclaimed.

Armistice

As the 62nd Division occupied Maubeuge, a much diminished Kaiser Wilhelm was forced to abdicate. The following day he fled into exile in neutral Holland. A German delegation had already crossed Allied lines to discuss Armistice terms with Marshal Foch. The terms amounted to unconditional surrender.

The Armistice was signed on behalf of the new Republic of Germany in a railway carriage in the secluded Forest of Compiègne at 5.30am on 11 November 1918. Germany agreed to evacuate France and Belgium in two weeks, and to disarm by forfeiting her U-boat and naval fleets, 2000 aeroplanes, 5000 artillery pieces, 30,000 machine guns, 5000 locomotives, 150,000 rail wagons and 5000 trucks. She would also pay compensation. The Allies would maintain the blockade for the immediate future, and occupy the west bank of the Rhine.

The ceasefire would begin at 11am.[71]

The 62nd Division received the news in Maubeuge. The 49th Division was at

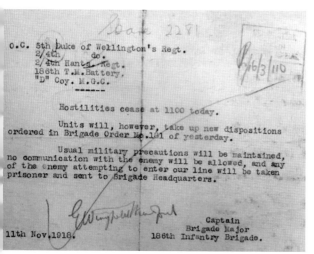

The official notification of the Armistice sent to the 186th Brigade of the 62nd Division.

rest back in Douai. The 168th Brigade of the RFA were in barns and stables at Grand Fayt, further east than any other artillery brigade. One of the artillerymen recalled:

> How quietly that information was received. Not a cheer, scarce a shout – just a deep sigh of relief as the load of anxiety fell off shoulders that had borne it … That night, for the first time for ages, lights were lit and shamelessly exposed, for there was no fear of the droning of an enemy aeroplane and the cry "Lights Out".[72]

A young Huddersfield private wrote:

> I don't seem able to realise it yet. All the guns have stopped, and everything seems unreal … Even the General has just said 'Good morning' to me, so it MUST be over.[73]

The news reached the *HDE* offices in Huddersfield at 10.50am. A message was immediately posted outside and the Red Ensign, the first victory flag in the town, was flown from the window. On the footpath outside the offices, a Belgian woman stopped a reporter and asked tremulously …

> "Ees it true?" "Yes, quite true," was the response. "Oh! le bon Dieu! Den I can go home, is dat not true?"

As word spread from mouth-to-mouth, handshakes and congratulations were exchanged among a crowd gathering outside the Town Hall to witness the hoisting of the flags of the Allies.

> … all establishments where flags, rosettes and streamers could be obtained, were quickly doing a roaring trade, and almost everybody in the streets wore some decoration of national colours.[74]

The flags and bunting displayed from churches, public buildings, private houses and across the thoroughfares reflected just part of the spectrum of emotions. Schoolgirl Vivien Hirst heard the news as she emerged from a photographic studio.

> I danced along beside Mummy, holding her arm, exclaiming with joy, but received a douche as there was no responding happiness in her face. She only murmured "we should have marched into Berlin, this is not complete victory."[75]

Not all were so bitter, and the *HDE* captured the mood of the town.

> The sense of relief in … the civilian population was evident in their demeanour. There were no extravagant exhibitions of delight, little or no dancing about the streets in the ecstasy of the moment. Parties of boys and girls soon appeared in the streets waving flags, singing and shouting, but the more responsible members of the community bore themselves with great restraint. They evidently realised that the occasion was one more for quiet joy than for unseemly exuberance. They felt a sense of relief from some mighty incubus that had depressed the mind and the spirit a long period. They remembered, too, that there are many who cannot rejoice, many whose dear ones had fallen in the task of bringing the present consummation. Tears were shed unashamedly because of the bright young lives which cannot take any part in today's celebrations, and will long remain a green and fragrant memory by reason of the sacrifice they have made. Truly it was an occasion on which to weep with those that weep, or to rejoice with those that rejoiced.[76]

The Mayor posted an invitation in the *HDE* for everyone to attend a Thanksgiving Service in their local church that evening. At 7.30pm, less than nine hours after the news reached the town, there was standing room only in churches across the district. At Huddersfield Parish Church, Canon Tupper Carey said:

> We owe it to our dead, to the men who laid down their lives, to make the world brighter, cleaner, better than it has been in the past.[77]

Perhaps the greatest joy was reserved for the parents of Private George Wharton of Paddock. George was reported killed on the Somme in September 1916 but, like so many, his body and possessions were not recovered. His mother never gave up hope and, in a last desperate attempt to find him, wrote to the King of Spain, Alfonso XIII, to ask if he 'was in his territory.' Shortly after the Armistice she

Like all who survived the war, both servicemen and civilians, George faced a challenging period of readjustment, but at least he was alive. As British Officer Richard G Dixon wrote:

No more slaughter. No more maiming. No more mud and blood. No more shovelling bits of men's bodies and dumping them into sandbags. No more writing those dreadfully difficult letters to the next of kin. A strange and unreal thought was entering my mind. I had a future.[79]

FIGHTING ENDED ON ALL FRONTS

GERMANY SIGNS THE ARMISTICE.

DELAY FOR EVACUATION PROLONGED.

PREMIER'S STATEMENT.

ENTHUSIASTIC SCENES IN LONDON AND THE PROVINCES.

The Prime Minister makes the following announcement:—

The armistice was signed at five o'clock this morning, and hostilities are to cease on all fronts at 11 a.m. to-day.

(French Government Wireless.)

Hostilities will cease on the whole front as from November 11th at 11 o'clock (French time). The Allied troops will not, until a further order, go beyond the line reached on that date and that hour.

(Signed)   Marshal Foch.

EVACUATION DELAYED.

German plenipotentiaries to the German High Command, to be communicated to all the authorities interested.

The armistice was signed at five o'clock in the morning (French time). It comes into force at eleven o'clock in the morning (French time). Delay for evacuation prolonged by twenty-four hours for the left bank of the Rhine, besides the five days: therefore thirty-one days in all. Modifications of the text compared with that brought by Helldorf will be transmitted by radio.

(Signed)   ERZBERGER.

THE ARMISTICE TERMS.

EVACUATION, REPATRIATION, SCRAPPING OF OLD PEACE TREATIES.

The Prime Minister announced the terms of the armistice in the House of Commons this afternoon. On entering the House Mr. Lloyd George was received with great cheering, all members rising. The terms of the armistice which he read are:—

THE KING'S "THANK GOD."

HOSTILITIES AT AN END AND PEACE WITH IN SIGHT.

Addressing the vast crowd from the balcony of the Palace to-day, the King said: "With you I rejoice and thank God for the victories which the Allied Armies have won and brought hostilities to an end and peace within sight."

The speech provoked great cheering.

RECEPTION OF NEWS.

JUBILANT SCENES IN AND ABOUT HUDDERSFIELD.

"Is it true at last?" was the enquiry made from many quarters as one passed along the streets this morning. "It is true," was the most welcome answer. There was a smile and a glow upon many faces that have not been so lighted up during many weary months past. Of all news this great announcement was the most acceptable, and its effect was electrical.

The news reached the "Examiner" Office at 10-50, and a message was immediately posted on a notice outside the office. The Red Ensign was also flown from an upper window, and it was the first flag to be hoisted in Huddersfield on receipt of the great news. The news spread quickly from mouth to mouth, and very soon animated groups gathered in front of the "Examiner" office. But the occasion was not without touches of pathos, as, when one Belgian woman stopped an "Examiner" representative with the question, uttered in broken English, and in a manner that betrayed great emotion—"Ees it true?" "Yes, quite true," was the response. "Oh! le bon Dieu! Den I can go home, is dat not true?" was the fervent rejoinder.

WHEN THE BOYS COME HOME!

There was much hand-shaking and congratulation. "We shall have the lads home soon," said one old dame hastening up Ramsden Street carrying a bundle of flags with which to decorate her home. Very quickly the people gathered in groups outside the Town Hall in order to witness the hoisting of the Union Jack. As it was run up a sailor going down Ramsden Street saluted the flag, and thereby unconsciously perhaps expressed the relief of our fighting men for the removal of the terrible burden that has lain upon them during the past four and a quarter years. And who more than our sailors, soldiers, and airmen could really rejoice? They have withstood the hardships and horrors of a long and arduous campaign, and it was no detraction from their bravery to notice the sense of relief that came into the faces of the men when they heard the news. The Stars and Stripes, the French Tricolour, and the Belgian flag were also flown from the balcony window of the Town Hall.

SCENES IN THE STREETS.

The sense of relief in the minds of the civilian population was evident in their demeanour. There were no extravagant exhibitions of delight, little or no dancing about the streets in the ecstasy of the moment. Parties of boys and girls soon appeared in the streets waving flags, singing and shouting, but the more responsible members of the community bore themselves with greater restraint. They evidently realised that the occasion was one more for quiet joy than for unseemly exuberance. They felt a sense of relief from some mighty incubus that had depressed the mind and the spirit a long period. They remembered, too, that there are many who cannot rejoice, many whose dear ones have fallen in the task of bringing about the present consummation. Tears were shed unashamedly because of the bright young lives which cannot take any part in to-day's celebrations, and which will long remain a green and fragrant memory by reason of the sacrifice they have made. Truly, it was an occasion on which to weep with those that weep, as well as to rejoice with those that rejoiced.

Toy shops, fancy goods shops, and all establishments where flags, rosettes, and streamers could be obtained, were quickly doing a roaring trade, and almost everybody in the streets wore some decoration of national colours, or bore one or more flags. The display of flags in the streets within an hour of the news becoming known was much greater than at any other time during the war period, and certainly more extensive than on the well-remembered morning when the Huddersfield Territorials left for their training camps.

Flags were hoisted on the different churches and

The *HDE* reports the Armistice in its edition of 11 November 1918

Chapter 22

1918-19: Transition and Legacy

Exit Wilhelm II
by
F.B.

You are gone – and earth sighs in her gladness,
Foul destroyer, who challenged the world.
You have taught us new meanings of sadness,
As upon us your wrath has been hurled.

You have gambled for kingdoms and empires;
You have drunk of the blood of the slain;
You have nourished an army of vampires,
And compelled them our chalice to drain.

You have wagered the life-blood of millions,
And have aimed at the seat of a god;
You have butchered your soldier-civilians,
The dumb slaves who have fought at your nod.

You have thrown – and the stake has been paid for
By the world – at a measureless cost.
It shall never again be thus played for;
You have hazarded all – and have lost.

Demobilisation

As this poem from the *HDE* of 20 November 1918 suggests, there was universal loathing for the German high command, but more sympathy for the German civilian foot-soldiers. Reports from the army of occupation revealed a Germany where many were 'broken in body and in spirit by slow starvation', requiring 'many months of well-balanced nourishment and care' to 'reverse the deterioration.'[1] Letters to the *HDE* were compassionate towards the impoverished German civilians.

> Germany waited until near-capitulation before surrendering … We must at the earliest moment come to her assistance, as we are not waging a war against humanity, but for humanity.[2]

Large numbers of local servicemen witnessed this German suffering. On 18 November the 62nd Division and the 168th Brigade RFA marched from their respective billets at Maubeuge and Grand Fayt for the Rhine Province, part of the army of occupation that would oversee the Armistice terms.[3] Both were repeatedly cheered through decorated Belgian streets. The artillerymen arrived first and their 15-mile cavalcade was installed by 14 December. The Dukes' Battalions marched across the German frontier to their Regimental March at Potean on 17 December. The Regimental colours, sent from Huddersfield, reached them at Blumenthal on 23 December, and they reached their final destination, Mechernich, on Christmas Day. They were the only Territorial formation selected to occupy the Rhine bridgeheads.

The 62nd Division on the march

Meanwhile, the Huddersfield troops who had remained in the 49th Division in the reorganisations of January 1918 were demobilised and headed for home.

As the Army of occupation settled into peacetime routines of parades and training in the morning and sports in the afternoons, the *HDE* published several requests from local troops for sports equipment, games and books.[4]

The least enviable post-Armistice military tasks fell to labourers' battalions, clearing the French and Belgian battlefields of debris, unexploded shells and corpses. Many shell holes, especially on the Somme and at Passchendaele, had to be 'pumped clear of water before bodies could be recovered.' Soldiers hastily buried in the heat of battle were disinterred, identified, and any possession discovered on their bodies carefully put to one side to be sent home to their relatives. The bodies were then preserved in mortuaries for burial in a nearby war cemetery, prepared by the Imperial War Graves Commission.[5]

In December 1918 woollen spinner Private Albert Abby of Golcar began such a tour on the battlefields. Terrible dangers lurked, some on the surface and some concealed by mud, rubble and rotting vegetation. On his third day Private Abby was killed by an explosion.[6]

The 5th Dukes remained with the 62nd Division in Mechernich, and learned they were to be disbanded in March. Inter-Company football competitions were concluded and, on 9 March, the battalion band played for the last time at Mechernich's Peliceum Theatre. On 29 March the 5th Dukes were reduced to a Cadre establishment of 5 officers and 46 other ranks. The rest were either demobilised or, if 'retainable in the army', transferred to the 2/4th (Halifax) Dukes, among them Captain JB Cockhill DSO, MC, and Captain GV Bennays MC both of whom volunteered to serve another 12 months in Germany.

The demobilised troops returned to Huddersfield …

> … not with bands playing and colours flying as some people have imagined … but in driblets… Many people have pictured … a triumphant march … and they find it difficult to reconcile those pictures … with the quiet breaking up of various units, so that the first intimation they have of the return of men in their neighbourhood is, in many cases … that they are going quietly about their business, just as they did in pre-war days, except for their bronzed faces and the more serious demeanour which their experiences … have left behind …

The bearing of many of these men had altered little nine months later. In December 1919, the *HDE* commented:

> Men are coming back to civil life often with jarred nerves and tempers sharpened by the strain of war. The outlook on life of many of them has been rudely shaken, and sufficient time has not elapsed to allow of a readjustment of vision.[7]

For many of them, the war would never truly be over. Haunted by nightmares, they rarely talked about their experiences. In stiff upper lip 20th century Britain, the only place men displayed raw emotion in public was on the football terraces.

Particularly affected was Dr Daniel Stuart. He had served at Gallipoli and was one of the last two medics to leave in the evacuation of Suvla Bay. He was 'not a surgeon, and the blood troubled him. He had grieved very much about what he had seen.' On 11 November, as the Armistice was announced, he was found lifeless in his Huddersfield home. He had committed suicide.[8]

During April the Cadre of the 5th Dukes was attached to the 5th Division at Pleurus, near Charleroi. It included one officer – Captain Keith Sykes – and five other ranks who went out with the 5th Dukes in April 1915, and one officer – Lieutenant-Colonel James Walker – and 11 other ranks from the 2/5th Dukes who went out in January 1917. They were the last of about 5500 troops who had served with the 5th Dukes. The rest had been killed, wounded, captured, transferred or demobilised.[9]

The Cadre returned to Huddersfield with the colours at 5.45pm on 9 May. At last there were heroes returning en masse to acclaim. The Parish Church bells rang from 5.30pm and they were greeted by the Mayor Alderman Carmi Smith, by past and present members of the battalion, and by the band of the 2nd Dukes. Dense crowds cheered loudly, and Lieutenant-Colonel Walker spoke briefly.

Demobilisation provided new opportunities for advertisers. These were printed in the *HDE* on 29 May 1919 (top left), 14 February 1919 (top right) and 20 March 1919 (bottom).

The people of Huddersfield have every reason to be very proud of the manhood they sent to the front. Nothing could daunt it in the darkest days, and nothing could stop it when it was unleashed last year.

The Mayor responded:

You have kept the enemy away from us, and we feel, as citizens of Huddersfield that we are very proud of you and proud of the work you have done.

They then marched to the Town Hall for a civic tea with the Mayor and Mayoress.[10]

9 May 1919: the Cadre of the 5th Dukes marches out of Huddersfield Station led by Captain Keith Sykes (left) and Lieutenant-Colonel James Walker

Demobilisation of the 168th RFA of the 32nd Division, which was kept at full strength as part of the army of occupation on the Rhine, took longer. The release of local artillerymen began in the spring of 1919. The last detachment returned in December and was marked by a meal for 400 artillerymen at the Town Hall and another 200 in the Masonic Hall, generously provided by Sir William and Lady Raynor.[11]

Demobilisation also marked the end of the line for the Motor Volunteers. They closed their rest room at Huddersfield Railway Station, and their last late-night arrival was driven home on 22 March. Since the innovation of their service in January 1917, they had served an estimated 70,000 servicemen and war hospital visitors in the rest room, 1000 staying the night there. In addition, 30,000 servicemen had been driven home in night time journeys totalling 100,000 miles.

War honours continued to be presented to local servicemen for several months after demobilisation. Captain Cecil Lockwood was presented with his Military Cross and Captain Keith Sykes the bar to his Military Cross by the King at Buckingham Palace in May 1919.[12] In his four years with the 5th Dukes Captain Sykes had been promoted to Adjutant on 27 October 1915, Temporary Captain in January 1916 and Substantive Captain in June 1916. In addition to his MC and Bar, he received the French

255

Croix de Guerre avec Palme, a citation in French Army Orders, and two mentions in despatches, for being 'a good platoon leader' and for his 'inspiring example of courage to his men at all times.'[13]

Lance-Corporal Tandey attended Buckingham Palace for the presentation of his VC in December 1919. At that time there were a further 40,000 still waiting to receive their war honours. Lance-Corporal Tandey and fellow VC-winner Lieutenant Huffam were made honorary members of the 5th and 7th Dukes' Old Comrades Association.

Now that the time has come for you to leave the Army and go back to civil life, I wish, both personally and officially, to thank you for the service which you have given.

You take away with you the priceless knowledge that you have played a man's part in this great War for freedom and fair play. You will take away with you also your remembrances of your comrades, your pride in your Regiment, and your love for your country.

You have played the game, go on playing it, and all will be well with the great Empire which you have helped to save.

I wish you every prosperity and happiness.

Brigadier General,
Commanding 186th Infantry Brigade.

Captain Keith Sykes' demobilisation certificate from the Brigadier General

Spanish Influenza

Whilst the armed forces gradually demobilised, civilian life reverted to a peacetime footing. Immediately after the Armistice, all call-up notices and appeals to the Military Service Tribunals were terminated. Work ceased in most mills and workshops, many remaining closed for the next two days. The Chief Constable received permission from the military for celebratory fireworks and bonfires, and for church bells to be rung at all times for a week.

The packed church services on the evening of 11 November were followed by a Thanksgiving Service at the Town Hall the following afternoon. This was so well attended that many were turned away and a parallel service was conducted in Ramsden Street from the Town Hall balcony. The Mayor paid tributes to 'not only the soldier and sailor at the front ... but every man and woman at home congratulating in particular 'the women of Huddersfield.'[16]

There was a cruel irony to the commemorations and celebrations. In the relief and joy of victory the district – and indeed the whole country – let down its collective guard against an even deadlier threat, Spanish Influenza.[17]

This lethal virus had emerged as the war and its many related difficulties peaked in the spring and summer of 1918. It was named Spanish Influenza because it appeared to have originated in Spain. In fact, it had just been reported more freely from Spain, a neutral country, than elsewhere. Its origin may have been an outbreak of a flu-type virus in the British field hospital at Etaples in 1916. Another theory is that it came from China, where a similar outbreak occurred in November 1917 shortly before 94,000 Chinese men were shipped via Canada to work as labourers behind the Allied lines in France. In March 1918 there was a lethal outbreak where they had been billeted in Canada, and shortly after their arrival in France, troops began to fall ill.[18] The timing also coincides with the arrival of American troops from Fort Riley in Kansas, where there had also been a deadly outbreak.[19]

The virus found fertile breeding grounds on the squalor of the battlefields. It spread quickly, assisted by the increased mobility of the armies in 1918. The transportation of thousands of casualties back to their homelands, quickly escalated Spanish Flu into an international epidemic.

Ode to Spanish Flu

by

Charles Lunn

All hail! Thou germ of Spanish blood,
Thou joy of all creation,
That com'st across the Channel flood
To plague our stolid nation.

We, who were always proud and free,
Who felt no man's oppression;
We bow down one and all to thee,
As slaves in thy possession.

Thou com'st unseen, unheard, unknown,
To torture and to pillage.
Thy hordes, to countless numbers grown,
Sack every town and village.

Thou makest us to sneeze and cough,
And ticklest throats so tender,
We fling all bravado off
And make complete surrender.

Reckless despot, Spanish Flu,
That tramplest on tradition;
Grim Knight o' the Order of Atchoo,
Hear our one meek petition:

Oh mighty tyrant, from thy tower,
Go seek the German vulture,
And, having got him in thy power,
Then give the flu to Kultur.[20]

Victims deteriorated rapidly and in extreme cases could be healthy at breakfast and dead by teatime. Survivors began to recover after 48 hours. Outbreaks spread across Britain in June 1918 and in the last week of the month there were seven deaths in Huddersfield, with hundreds more ill. On 4 June Spring Grove Council School had 200 absentees, and only 11 of Brierley Wood's 50 primary school children attended. At David Brown's engineering works 25% of the employees were ill. Yet even within Huddersfield the spread was uneven. Other large employers were virtually unaffected and Birkby and Lindley were comparatively free of the virus.[21]

The disease's grip on the district tightened, claiming 18 victims in the first week of July. Day schools and most Sunday schools were closed, and absenteeism caused a fall in production in many factories. A 'disappointing' £123 raised on Lifeboat Day was blamed on a low turn-out of voluntary workers and fewer people on the streets than usual.[22] Despite the precautions, the virus killed a further 17 over the next seven days as Huddersfield's weekly death rate soared to 40 per thousand, compared to a national average of 21. A medical report to the Town Council described it as 'the severest and most malignant epidemic that has visited the town' for at least 50 years.

The outbreak abated in early August. The total number of local deaths was estimated at 75 to 100, but was not entirely clear as several people had died from complications of existing medical conditions, although pneumonia was often a common factor. Most who became ill had recovered and were lucky not just to survive, but because their antibodies provided immunity as the virus mutated to become even more virulent and lethal.[23]

The first notification of the next wave was the closure of Hillhouse Higher Elementary School in the last week of September 1918. Initially only students at the school were affected. Then, on 8 October, Oakes Council School was closed. Two days later the Huddersfield Education Committee closed every school and play centre in the district.[24] This prompt action helped to contain the spread but 310 deaths in Glasgow that week and the arrival of three wounded soldiers with the virus persuaded the Huddersfield authorities to remain cautious.[25]

The last week of October brought a surge of seven local deaths and an increasing number of cases often in the same household.[26] The military authorities banned all servicemen from attending theatres, concert halls and cinemas to prevent them catching or spreading the virus.[27] The local Medical Officer Dr SG Moore recommended that the general public should avoid such places, provoking a defiant joint letter from the managers of the Hippodrome, Theatre Royal and Palace Theatre. They had a combined staff of over 140 and only one of these was ill. Factories and workshops had 'immensely higher rates.'[28] This did not prevent the prejudices of the town's moral guardians surfacing. Huddersfield's much maligned cinemas were singled out and instructed not to admit under-14s.[29] Meanwhile, the temperance movement objected to advice that whisky was an effective narcotic and relieved some of the suffering.

The Armistice celebrations almost certainly contributed to a further spike in the number of fatalities from 14 in the preceding week to 23.[30] The outbreak peaked at 27 local deaths in the second week of December.[31] Suddenly it subsided, and after 11 weeks local elementary schools re-opened their doors on 30 December, with secondary schools following in the New Year. Over 100 formerly healthy local people had died and many others, already weakened by ailments, died from complications.[32] Nationally, in the last quarter of 1918 there were 241,218 deaths, compared to 114,000 in previous quarter. Deaths exceeded births for the first time since records began in 1851.[33]

A third, yet more virulent wave struck at the end of January 1919. The *HDE* advised that masks should be worn and crowded places avoided.[34] Then, in early February 'a number of army medical doctors working in France' claimed to have isolated the virus.[35]

To an Influenza Germ
by
Charles Lunn
At last we've tracked you to your lair,
You spiteful little pest;
We know just how and when and where,
You make your little nest;
We know your weight and shape and size,
The colour of your hair and eyes,
And ugly face unblessed.
We'll put you in test tubes till
You're ready for inspection;
And when your brood the glasses fill,
We'll make a choice selection;
For some great scientific mind,
Experimentally inclined,
Who some new antidote will find,
To minimise infection.
So when you once again appear,
We'll know just how to meet you;
No more shall we be filled with fear,
With serum we'll defeat you;
Then you will quite as harmless be,
As our old friends the gnat and flea,
And as a germ from danger free,
We can afford to treat you.[36]

INFLUENZA!

Advertisement for 'Formamint, the germ killing throat tablet' from the HDE 6 December 1918

It raised false hopes. There was no effective antidote at this time. To compound the problem, many workers could not afford to take further time off, most schools tried to stay open and the virus was rampant. On 11 February the *HDE* reported 46 deaths directly or indirectly attributable to flu during the previous week. Doctors were 'run off their feet.' By mid-February school attendances were low and a number of teachers were absent ill.[37] The safest place in the district was the Deanhouse Institution workhouse in Netherthong, owing to 'its excellent isolation from the outside world.'[38]

In the last fortnight of February 1919 the virus accounted for 114 local victims, 'more deaths ... than the last epidemic of smallpox in the borough during its whole course.' Huddersfield's death rate per thousand was the second highest in the country, and funerals were delayed as the gravediggers were unable to meet the demand. Some of the 500 special constables, enrolled to make up a shortfall of local officers in April 1918, were drafted in to help them.[39] All schools and evening classes were belatedly closed, and Dr Moore wrote a despairing letter to the *HDE*.

> ... people meet together ... without regulation – trains, trams, churches, theatres and so on ... It is not uncommon to see a person sitting or standing in a crowded tramcar or train, sneezing, blowing the nose, coughing, perhaps hoarse, and presenting all the well-known symptoms of influenza. Other passengers apathetically remain on the tram, or in the train. They do not get off or go out, neither do they insist on the plague-infected individual doing so.
>
> ... what would happen if instead of the obvious signs of influenza, the individual presented obvious signs of smallpox. But influenza kills more people than smallpox ever did.[40]

Subsequent letters brought the lack of communal hygiene into sharp focus. Why bother to disinfect the trams before leaving the depot every morning when ...

> ... overlooked is the obnoxious spitting in tramcars, especially the early workmen's cars ... it is disgusting to see this habit allowed to continue?

The correspondent advised enforcing the 40 shillings' fine 'stated on the side of the cars.' Meanwhile, 'Ratepayer' was revolted by human excrement in the street:

> Last week two men were removing one of the tubs of the Huddersfield Corporation Sanitary Department, and finding it rather too heavy I saw them deliberately pour some of the contents into the roadway – It lightened the burden, no doubt, but is it healthy? It is not the first time ...[41]

Infected soldiers returning from the front remained a concern. At the beginning of March Private Fred Turton arrived from a labourers' battalion in France with Spanish

Flu and pneumonia. He was admitted to Holmfirth Auxiliary War Hospital which, along with the other auxiliary hospitals, was due for closure. Fred was Holmfirth's last patient. The hospital closed when he died on 11 March.[42]

By then, stringent local precautions were in place. From 1 March it was an offence 'for any person suffering from dangerous infectious disease' to go to 'any public place.' All were advised to avoid places 'where there are a number of persons – churches, parties, theatres … and so forth.'[43] The number of local flu-related deaths per week declined dramatically during the month – 56, 41, 21, 12, 7. The epidemic died out in April.[44]

About 250 local people died in this third outbreak, bringing the total victims since June 1918 to almost 450. Deaths from complications of existing ailments made the exact number impossible to quantify. Worldwide, Spanish Flu killed about two million people, roughly double the number of combatants who died during the whole of the war.

Rationing

Individual and collective resistance to the epidemic was weakened by the rationing of food and fuel 'Dogged resolution' and 'commendable moderation' eked out scarce resources beyond the Armistice after which restrictions were very gradually relaxed as the national and European food crises eased.[45]

Increased produce from merchant ships, no longer impeded by U-boats, was available by the end of November, when white bread re-appeared in the shops and the fixed maximum price for oranges and lemons was removed.[46] Meat rations were doubled for Christmas 1918, when 'coupon 7' (18-25 December) was worth 8 ounces of meat rather than the usual 4 ounces.[47] From 29 December all meat coupons were worth 5 ounces, and pork, poultry and rabbit were coupon-free. Meat rationing finally ended on 30 June 1919. All restrictions on the sale and distribution of livestock for slaughter were removed three months later.[48]

In January 1919 ration books were discontinued and the amount of sugar and butter sold per individual was increased.[49] The sale of 'sweetmeats' was no longer restricted to small traders who depended on them for their livelihoods. Chocolate returned to the shelves, and was once again sold in theatres from 18 February.[50] It remained illegal to use jam for pastry, but jelly and marmalade could be used.[51]

The Public Meals Order was revoked on 7 October 1919, so that catering establishments were no longer restricted on what they could serve. At the same time, the Food Hoarding (Amendment) Order was revoked. Households were no longer capped at a seven day requirement and could stock their cupboards, relaxing the burden of weekly frugality before the next allowance. Even so, planning a household budget was far from straightforward in the volatile and inflationary post-war economy, as prices and wages rose rapidly but inconsistently.[52] Parliamentary Secretary to the Ministry of Food, Mr McCurdy, blamed public pressure for these difficulties.

> We were told to get rid of DORA and all her works … This – prices determined entirely by supply and demand – is the result.[53]

The abandonment of food controls was popular, but the British Medical Journal also felt that the Government had relaxed too many controls too soon.[54] By August 1919 the avoidance of a winter famine was dependent on a successful harvest, and most shopkeepers reverted to allowing only reasonable amounts to their customers.[55] There was no famine, but this transitional period of unpredictable and erratic supplies and prices continued into the 1920s.

Controls on the use of paper were discontinued on 1 May 1919 and fuel regulations were also gradually relaxed as stocks of coal and oil were re-established. By 9 December 1918, limited street lighting and the use of lights in shop fronts, made Huddersfield more welcoming in the evenings, in time for carol singing.[56]

> The streets have for so long been quiet and deserted after nightfall that it came as somewhat of a shock to hear a band breaking blatantly into the silence of the night on Christmas Eve.[57]

Demobilisation and Adjustment in War Industries

Demobilisation plans were announced for munitions and textile workers three days after the Armistice. First were those who would withdraw voluntarily, followed by those who could be readily absorbed into their previous or another occupation, then bad timekeepers, and finally those who had worked in the industries for the shortest time. The Board of Control of Wool Textile Production was to facilitate the early demobilisation from the forces and reintegration of textile workers whose skills qualified them as 'pivotal men.'[58] This would save money for the Government which allowed up to four weeks' furlough (leave on full pay) on demobilisation for those who did not immediately find or return to work. After that they would receive the 'out of work donation.'[59] By April 1919 almost 1.1 million people, including almost 400,000 ex-servicemen, were receiving this forerunner to unemployment benefits, which were formalised by the Unemployment Insurance Act (1920), the first such universal benefits in the world.[60] Although many demobilised soldiers were re-absorbed into the workforce, over 300,000 of them were still unemployed on the first anniversary of the Armistice.[61]

On 1 September 1919 the out of work donation period was extended and the amounts increased, and the Government encouraged firms to commit to a scheme to employ disabled ex-servicemen.[62] Whilst many did, some munitions companies were accused of exploiting the Munitions of War Act which gave them one year from the Armistice to restore normal trading practices.

> some … invite trouble by … for the sake of additional profit, taking the fullest advantage of the time limit. The act is tying on both employers and employees, but industrial action is likely as employees feel exploited by deliberate and unnecessary delays.[63]

The textile industry was less tardy. Khaki orders for the British Army stopped when the Armistice was signed, and partially completed contracts were renegotiated.[64] An army surplus of over five and a half million square yards of cloth was sold in large quantities to the highest bidders for the manufacture of civilian clothing. The Surplus Government Property Disposal Board economised by controversially not allowing householders to purchase smaller quantities for their own use.

> To sell in small amounts would entail the setting up of establishment and staffs all over the country – at a time when Government staffs are being reduced to 250,000.[65]

This was a busy period for Sir Charles Sykes. Chairman of the Board of Control of Wool Textile Production, he stood as a Coalition Liberal candidate in the December 1918 General Election and was elected as MP for Huddersfield. The 69% turnout was among the highest in the country, reflecting the locality's engagement with the political process.[66]

In this transitional year, Huddersfield's textile industry was buffeted by difficulties in obtaining materials, by inflation, and by coal and railway strikes. Industrial action was avoided in textiles by the Industrial Councils. Established in 1919 as workplace partnership forums for employees and employers, the Councils successfully dealt with requests for shorter hours and additional wages.

Sir Charles Sykes

By June 1919 confidence in textile prices was restored and French import restrictions had been lifted. By December the Colne Valley manufacturers were 'booked up for six to nine months ahead.'[67]

> Throughout the year there was never any difficulty in selling goods. The difficulty was rather to hold off the buyers. There is still, and likely to remain, a huge unsatisfied demand for woollen and worsted cloths, and it is an accumulating demand, for … more people than ever, even amongst the semi-civilised races, are wearing or desiring to wear these cloths.

The adaptability and resilience of the textiles industry displayed during and immediately after the war would be repeatedly tested by the economic vagaries of the inter-war years. The decline and demise of the industry after World War II was caused in part by some of its customer 'races' using and adapting British technology to produce woollen textiles more efficiently and cheaply.

The Roles of Women

Among the greatest industrial, social and political post-war issues were the rights, freedoms and opportunities for women. Despite proving their capabilities in many traditional men's roles, most notably in factories and on farms, thousands of women were no longer required in the workplace and faced a period of readjustment. Most immediately, many munitions factory workers were demobilised into unemployment and insecurity. Others were compelled, as agreed when taken on, to surrender their jobs to men returning to their original employment. The Post Office filled the gaps of men who did not return by offering some women the opportunity of continued employment, but in lower-grade positions.[68] The *HDE* reported that nationally, of 1.5 million additional women in the workforce as a result of the war, 12% were out of work by Christmas 1918.

Most of Huddersfield's large migrant wartime workforce returned home on demobilisation and some women were happy to return to a life of domesticity. But many sought alternative employment and applications at local employment exchanges for traditional female roles exceeded the number of jobs available. In April 1919 there were 750 local women and girls, mainly former munitions workers, receiving 25s per week from the 'out of work pay scheme.'[69]

Compounding fears of a complete resumption of traditional gender roles, the local Aldermen threatened compulsory 'return to domestic service.' Women who had acquired a taste for non-domestic work would not be so easily persuaded, but as women's rights activist Mary McArthur stated, 'The new world looks uncommonly like the old one.' By 1 January 1919 one third of adult women were employed, the same percentage as in 1914.[70] At a meeting of the Huddersfield branch of the National Union of Women's Suffrage Societies on 12 March 1919, Mrs Oliver Strachey, their national Parliamentary Secretary, highlighted two main causes – equal pay for equal work, and employment in a greater variety of industries and professions.

Some ex-servicemen felt similarly aggrieved. Not all promises that they could resume their original employment were kept, and they returned to a much-changed town. Some found their work, or the work of former male colleagues, taken by women. There was a deep suspicion that women were being employed because they were cheaper, and that men's wages were being depressed as a result. The hostility by some men to women in the workplace was as understandable as it was unfair.

The government attempted to reduce the pay differences between the sexes by setting and subsidising minimum wage levels for women war workers. Even so, in July 1919 average women's wages were only around 35s per week, about two-thirds of the average wage for men.[71] The new minimum wages for female farm workers in Huddersfield and district were 7d per hour, 9d per hour at weekends and 10d per hour overtime on Sundays.[72] Although the land army was officially disbanded during the autumn of 1919, many local women continued to flourish in their work on the farms, the *HDE* commenting …

> … their service to that industry has been proved ... Women ... have learned to love work in the open air, they have enjoyed the sense of guardianship of livestock they have tended, and because they have carried out their work so efficiently employers are anxious to retain them whenever it is possible to do so.[73]

Nationally, by December 1919, 75% of the women who had worked on farms during the war were still in that employment.[74]

Women were also moving into more senior white collar jobs and professions. In June 1919 a report by the Women's Advisory Sub-Committee of the Ministry of Reconstruction, suggested:

> Women should be eligible for all grades of appointment in the Civil Service on the same terms and conditions as men.[75]

The tide was turning. In 1918 the Representation of the People Act had granted the first limited voting rights to women, and a bill was passed to allow women to work as solicitors.[76] Armitage Sykes LLP of Huddersfield became one of the first solicitors to employ female staff.[77] A Bill allowing women to become Justices of the Peace was passed on 25 June 1919, albeit with an amendment to restrict this to women aged thirty years or older.[78] In December 1919, the Sex Disqualification (Removal) Act was passed. It stated:

> A person shall not be disqualified by sex or marriage from the exercise of any public function, or from being appointed to or holding any civil or judicial office or post, or from entering or assuming or carrying on any civil profession or vocation …[79]

Marriage could no longer be a bar to employment, although senior positions in the civil service remained closed to married women until 1946. Universities could no longer bar women from their degree courses, and doors were opened to occupations that were previously closed. In 1922 Mary Sykes of Huddersfield became one of the first four women to begin training as a solicitor. Qualifying in 1925, she became the second woman to enter the profession. She went on to become a Justice of the Peace, secretary of the Huddersfield Law Society and, in 1945, the first woman appointed as Mayor of Huddersfield.[80]

Like men in the armed services, wartime necessities brought women together. In the workplace and in voluntary organisations they had formed life-long friendships and memories. The final meeting of the Huddersfield and District Women's Committee for Soldiers and Sailors was held on 13 February 1919. Mrs Mary Blamires, former-Mayoress and founder, was in the chair, and reflected:

> They had passed through a period of anxiety, strain, and sorrow, and there were in that room those who had lost their nearest and dearest … it was almost with feelings of regret that they now came to the parting of the way.

It is doubtful whether their extraordinary combined voluntary efforts have ever been surpassed locally, and the bonds that had grown between them were almost tangible.[81]

The Women's Committee, along with the town's other war charities, was grateful to Ernest Woodhead, proprietor of the *HDE*, who had 'done everything in his power' to promote their work and 'to help win the war.'

Many women also adapted their homes to take in refugees. A letter to the family of Mr Stanley Battye from M Annessens of Antwerp in December 1918 was one of many received from grateful Belgian lodgers.

> We are all full of gratitude and admiration for all that England has done for the benefit of humanity, and especially for little Belgium. We never have despaired, because your mighty and generous country was there.

> I can assure you that every day and every evening when going to bed, we have spoken of you, your house, your way of being, and your kind attention. You have done so much for us in such a nice way that we never can forget you. I hope to come to England and see you as soon as possible.

> My kind regards, please, to Mr. Woodhead, the newspaper director, who worked so much for the relief in Belgium. Tell him that without the Committee for Relief in Belgium nobody would have survived.[82]

Political and Social Legacies

Collectively, women surpassed all expectations in the war. It was widely acknowledged that without their capacity to combine many additional workplace, home and voluntary responsibilities, the war could not have been won. Locally and nationally they had earned a new respect. They had also developed collective confidence and expectations of equality and opportunity that could not be reversed.

Change to the old order was afoot. The war encouraged many to doubt and challenge the assumptions that underpinned the British way of life. The aristocratic and capitalist elites had been exposed as fallible and, at times, incompetent. They could no longer expect unquestioning deference and obedience. The spread of education and literacy produced more people who disputed and mocked patriotism and authority in print, most specifically why men had been ordered to fight and endure such slaughter. Political comment, satire, allegorical fiction, and poetry thrived during and after the war. Writing, along with art and music, became much freer, symbolising and accelerating the erosion of Britain's restrictive, autocratic, Victorian, class-based structures.[83]

Huddersfield's tradition of questioning authority resurfaced with further left-wing, libertarian support for conscientious objectors in 1919. In March, the Huddersfield and District Council for Civil Liberties organised a conference at which religious, co-operative, trade union, Labour, and Socialist organisations from across the district were united in expressing ...

> ... condemnation of the continued imprisonment by the government of a large number of conscientious objectors to military service.

They demanded 'their immediate and unconditional release.'[84] The town's radical traditions, and the close links between community organisations which fostered an acceptance of non-conformist and anti-establishment views, were alive, kicking and ready to ride the oncoming wave of social change.

Aid for the Vulnerable

Part of that change involved humane, practical support for the most vulnerable in society. The war had created a large and potentially disaffected underclass of widows, disabled men and orphans, and the state had a duty of care. A State Pension Scheme for war widows and dependents of disabled servicemen was debated in the House of Commons in August 1916. It was set at two-thirds of pre-war income capped at £104 per year (£2 per week) for dependents of the partially disabled and £130 (£2 10s per week) for dependents of the totally disabled and deceased, 'enormously in advance of anything any other country had ever done.'[85]

Local assistance for impaired ex-servicemen and bereaved families also began before the end of the war. The Huddersfield Association of Discharged and Demobilised Sailors and Soldiers, the 5th and 7th Dukes' (Old Comrades) Association, was founded on 17 July 1917. War widows could apply to be honorary members for assistance with pensions. By March 1919 the association had 1000 members.[86] The Ministry of Pensions funded classes at Huddersfield Technical College so that discharged soldiers could learn trades within their physical capacity, including boot-making and repairing, electrical engineering, tailoring and commercial work. Forty discharged soldiers began these classes in June 1918 and, in addition, could attend the classes of 'ordinary students.'[87]

On Christmas Day 1918, house-to-house collections by an army of volunteers, including many schoolchildren, raised £434 for the St Dunstan's Society, which worked tirelessly for blind veterans. Sir Arthur Pearson of St Dunstan's wrote to thank and congratulate the Mayor on the 'wonderful achievement' in raising so much after more than four years of war.[88]

All this praiseworthy assistance did not allay the concerns of the Huddersfield Board of Guardians about some discharged servicemen 'drifting into vagrancy.' By August 1919 one local man, impaired by injuries sustained at Loos in 1915, and discharged as 'honest, sober, hardworking', had been reduced to vagrancy as he was unable to live on his 'utterly inadequate' pension of 13s 9d per week.[89]

The Old Comrades Association was dismayed by local indifference towards ex-servicemen and their families, particularly the apathy of committeemen purportedly working on their behalf.

> Promises were plentiful during the recruiting period, but if a return of the attendances at these committees could be given ... since the Armistice it would ... tell a remarkable story of the lack of interest in the work ... to deal directly with ex-servicemen and their grievances.[90]

Their observations induced renewed efforts on their behalf, and the following poem.

A Plea for the Disabled
by

Charles Lunn

Ay! Celebrate with all your might,
Shout with your loudest voice, and sing;
For Britain made a gallant fight,
And victory is a glorious thing
But don't forget the debt you owe
The men who vanquished Britain's foe.

Forget not those who heard the call
And answered it; who freely gave
Their health, their strength, their fight, their all,
Your country and your homes to save.
Forget not, and let action show
You mean to pay the debt you owe.

Can you replace the shattered limb?
Then make the pathway broad and smooth.
Can you restore the sight grown dim?
Then try the tortured nerve to soothe.
Lies gratitude within your heart?
Then pay the debt, if but in part.

'Tis not for charity they ask,
That you and I should freely give;
'Tis Britain's debt and Britain's task
To give each man the chance to live
A life full worthy of the name,
Regretting not he played the game.

Guard the traditions of your race,
Justice and honour, and fair play,
And suffer not the deep disgrace
That any man who lives should say
I fought for Britain in her need,
'Twer better for that I had died,
My cry for help they do not heed,
I'm broken and am cast aside.[91]

War orphans were also assisted by legislation. The Ministry of Pensions created a Special Grants Committee tasked with accelerating the restoration of order and normality to orphans' lives by maintaining some form of family or, if this was not possible, finding foster parents. Local sub-committees comprising half male and half female members selected suitable homes 'resembling as near as possible the ideals of British home life.' Where possible, siblings would be kept together in families of the same religious denomination as their parents.[92] Instructions about this scheme and its implementation were received by the Huddersfield authorities in October 1919.[93]

Fundraising

These initiatives to support the vulnerable would be expensive, particularly the war pensions and the embryonic benefits payments. In addition, the military's tasks were far from over, and a post-war force would be maintained. The swift demobilisation of all that could be spared from the military and from industry saved money but two days after the Armistice, Chancellor Bonar Law emphasised that the country still required a weekly minimum of £25,000,000 in War Bond savings.

... peace and plenty will come in time; at first it will be peace and scarcity.[94]

'Thanksgiving Week', the next push to sell War Bonds and War Savings Certificates, began on 25 November. St George's Square was 'decorated' with artillery guns behind sandbag emplacements, 'camouflage' and a projected image of a ruined Belgian church. The Royal Dragoons' Band played a civic procession into the Square before proceedings were opened 'by the sounding of the "Cease Fire."' The Chancellor's national target was £1,000,000,000 of which Huddersfield's share was £3,500,000. Ambitiously, £2,000,000 of this was to be raised during Thanksgiving Week, with the rest over subsequent months. The first day yielded £606,000, mostly from the banks and other large companies.[95] By Saturday, that had risen to £1,739,850, short of the target but, as the *HDE* happily declared, 'more than Halifax', even though Huddersfield had held a War Weapons Week in July while Halifax had not.[96]

Increases in taxation were also inevitable. In March 1919, the Government proposed a 'Bachelor Tax' which was, in part, an attempt to socially engineer a population increase in the wake of the war and Spanish Influenza.

The Bachelor Tax
by
Charles Lunn

The Chancellor now takes the view
That when in search of revenue
To pay the price of war,
No one can pay so well as he
Who toils but for himself, so we
Must tax the bachelor.

So very soon 'twill come to this,
That when he sees a dainty miss
The bachelor will say,
"Shall I enchain myself for life
By taking to myself a wife,
Or for my freedom pay?"[97]

Music, Theatre and Cinema

Alongside the often unsettling transitions in the aftermath of war, the public was anxious to share the communal pleasures of peacetime. Many were wary of crowds during the Spanish Flu epidemic, but from the spring of 1919 they flocked to post-war entertainments at Huddersfield's theatres, music halls, concert halls, cinemas and sports' grounds.

The opening of the Grand Picture Theatre on Manchester Road in March 1921 was symbolic of a thriving local entertainment industry.[98] The choirs and orchestras of the local music societies were soon back to their full complement, and many of them went from strength to strength.

The brass bands of Marsden, Meltham and Meltham Mills, Slaithwaite, and Brighouse and Rastrick, all founded in the 19th century, are still going strong in the 21st. The latter won the country's two premier competitions at Belle Vue in 1929, was the most successful in the land in the 1930s, and has remained among the most prestigious ever since.[99]

The Huddersfield Choral Society became an early pioneer of recorded music with Columbia Records in 1927, and continued its associations with leading figures in classical music. In 1936 they performed the first of their periodic commissioned works, *Dona Nobis Pacem*, a cantata by Vaughan Williams, performed in Huddersfield Town Hall and accompanied by the Hallé Orchestra with the composer present. This was one of 14 world premiers that are sprinkled through the society's illustrious history.[100]

The Huddersfield Glee and Madrigal Society built on its enhanced wartime reputation. Like the Choral Society and the annual Mrs Sunderland competitions, it has been a mainstay of vocal music in the town since the 19th century. Embracing more modern times, it was renamed the Huddersfield Singers in 1985 as the local music scene expanded to encompass music from all styles and eras, notably in the town's annual music festival.[101]

On 15 January 1919 the *HDE* proclaimed 'a return of interest in sports', adding that it was to be hoped that players would demonstrate the same 'wholehearted spirit as they have fought in the war.' The FA and the Northern Rugby Football Union both lifted restrictions on the payment of players, but Huddersfield NURFC was not ready to participate in the first post-war competition, the Yorkshire League, which commenced soon after the Armistice. Given the virulence of Spanish Influenza in the district this was, by accident or design, a wise decision.[102]

By the spring of 1919, the core of the Team of all Talents from 1914-15 had returned. There was 'a very general desire to see "Waggie" in harness again ... and ... the old bewildering movements ... dash and verve that left the opposition in a state of mystified speculation.'[103]

Leading the forwards in the first post-war match at Fartown, a 23-6 win over Hunslet, was Douglas Clark. Fully recovered from his horrific Passchendaele injuries 18 months earlier, he was greeted rapturously by the 7000 crowd.[104]

The supporters had to wait to welcome home Australian winger Albert Rosenfeld. Whilst in Persia he contracted Malaria and, on arriving home, was admitted to the Huddersfield War Hospital with influenza. Even when discharged on 1 May 1919, he was classed as physically unfit owing to the effects of heat stroke, a disability rated at 30%. Albert Rosenfeld resumed his rugby career but, even allowing for the passage of time, was a shadow of the player that scored the all-time record 80 tries in the 1913-14 season. The war had taken its toll with a vengeance on a great sportsman.[105]

Herbert Banks was another loss. The powerful forward had smashed an ankle working in the reserved occupation of coal mining in 1917, and had been unable to work since. The club staged a successful benefit match for him and his family in May 1919.[106]

Even without Rosenfeld, Banks, the deceased Fred Longstaff, and Jim Davies who had returned to Wales, Huddersfield were strong enough to win the first post-war competition they entered, the Yorkshire Cup, in the spring of 1919. Their players were four years older, but buoyed by massive and enthusiastic crowds – over 32,000 attended their Easter home matches against Hull and Wigan – much of the spark was still there.[107]

The Yorkshire Cup returned to its autumn slot in the 1919-20 season and Huddersfield won it again, becoming the only club to win it twice in the same calendar year. They went on to win the 1919-20 Yorkshire League and Challenge Cup before five of their star players set sail for Australasia with the Great Britain squad, captained by Wagstaff. Bereft of their stars, Huddersfield were narrowly beaten by a late Hull try in the Championship Final, depriving them of all four cups in the same season for a second time.

Huddersfield's Great Britain Northern Union tourists of 1920: Ben Gronow, Harold Wagstaff, Johnny Rogers, Gwyn Thomas and Douglas Clark

The 1919-20 season was the last hurrah for the Team of all Talents. Their average age was now 30 and their best sporting years had been spent on the battlefields. Their generation began to make way for the next as the Huddersfield team entered a period of transition. For the next four decades there were periodic successes, but nothing to match the Team of all Talents. Then, from the mid-1960s to the mid-1990s the club's fortunes plummeted alongside those of its fan base in the town's sinking manufacturing industries. Revived by municipal and private capital, notably from Ken Davy who became Chairman, the club embraced professional sports' new corporate, commercial age, reflected in a change of name to Huddersfield Giants, summer rugby, and the town's all-seater stadium, named after its respective sponsors McAlpine, Galpharm and John Smith's.

Whilst the professional rugby club made a swift and healthy recovery after World War I, the same could not be said for the amateur game. Several Northern Union teams that folded in the first months of the war did not re-form. Fartown was made available for junior league matches to support the valiant effort to encourage junior rugby, but it was a work in progress that as yet filled only some of the gaps vacated by the pre-war players.[108]

Number of Amateur Clubs Identified Pre and Post-War in Huddersfield and District

	1913-14	1919-20
Association Football	30	68
Northern Union Rugby Football	14	6*
Cricket	46	49
Crown Green Bowling	42	49

*In addition, 6 other clubs only in Under 21 league and three other clubs only in Under 17 league.

The town's sole rugby union club, Huddersfield Old Boys RUFC also re-started in the spring of 1919. There was some trepidation about their prospects after the wartime deaths of six players, including their Yorkshire star Rowland Owen, but the club christened their new ground at Salendine Nook with a couple of victories that promised 'a successful future for the club.' It too has enjoyed a continuous existence into the 21st century.[109]

Association football flourished after the war. It had been the most popular sport behind the lines, easier to organise and safer to play than either code of rugby. As a truly national sport it provided commonality for troops from different parts of the country thrown together in the same regiment. Only 39% of Huddersfield's soldiers served with the local battalions, and even Harold Wagstaff found himself playing left back for the anti-aircraft section of his regiment in Egypt, where the climate was 'far too disagreeable' for rugby.[110] Post-war, football helped to release the ex-servicemen's well-honed combative instincts, to replicate the camaraderie from the forces that many missed in civilian life, and to maintain contact with comrades. Cricket clubs, many of them fielding two or three teams, fulfilled similar needs in the summer.

Huddersfield Town FC, having sustained a reasonably strong team in the Football League's wartime Midland Section, entered the revived West Riding Senior Cup Competition in May 1919. They began the 1919-20 season where they had ended 1914-15, in Football League Division 2, but emboldened by lofty ambitions 'to secure a place in the First Division.' They had only been in the Football League since 1910-11, but fully intended to emerge from the shadow of Fartown's northern union stars in the town's affections.

In the first post-war season, 1919-20, Huddersfield Town won promotion from Division 2 and were runners-up in the FA Cup. Continuing to progress, they finished 17th, 14th, and 3rd in their first three seasons in Division 1, and beat Preston North End 1-0 in the 1922 FA Cup Final. The appointment of Herbert Chapman as manager in 1921 was a masterstroke. Inspired by his tactical innovations, Huddersfield became the first club to win the First Division title in three consecutive seasons (1923-24 to 1925-26). Runners-up in the next two seasons and FA Cup winners again in 1928, the 1920s remains the best decade in the club's history. The club's post-war aspirations were no idle boast.[111] They remained in the top division until 1952 and most of their seasons since then have been in the second and third tiers of English football.

Golf also enjoyed a revival to pre-war numbers in 1919.[112] The course at Meltham was in fine condition, and the Huddersfield club was confident that their course at Fixby, where ten acres had been ploughed up for allotments, would be quickly restored – not least because the club's wartime debts had been paid off by the 'generosity of the members.'[113] Some of the players had difficulty finding their old enthusiasm. Too often, on the walks between tee and green, minds slipped out of the moment onto distressing memories and affairs that made the game seem insignificant.

... the men who have come back undamaged find themselves coming quickly back to form, but few of us talk about the game nearly as much as we did five years ago ... I think for most men who played golf before the war the game will never be quite the same ... The keenness of zest cannot be revived to its old fullness. But evidently the new beginner can be carried away as completely as ever was the golfer in the former days.[114]

Local cricket was integral to the district's community life in the summer. Its leagues, minus some of their clubs, had been sustained for the duration of the war, and resumed with a full complement of clubs for the 1919 season, although some were at full stretch to field all their teams. Almondbury, for example, had 56 members who served in the forces, six of whom were killed, four were prisoners-of-war who returned debilitated and some of the rest were in regiments that were demobilised after the beginning of the 1919 season.[115] The vast majority of these clubs continue to play in the Huddersfield League and the Huddersfield Central League in the 21st century.

Crown Green Bowls had enjoyed a resurgence of interest in players and spectators before the end of the war. In July 1918 the Huddersfield Amateur Individual Merit Competition had a record 595 entries and record crowd of 2000 watched the final at the Hillhouse and Birkby club.[116] Post-war, entries to club and individual competitions continued to exceed expectations, boosted by the re-entry of Yorkshire to the Crosfield (County) Cup Competition after a three-year absence. Local athletics, cross-country and cycling clubs were also boosted beyond their wartime numbers.

Emboldened by their expanding roles in society, more women were participating in sport. Pre-war women had been largely restricted to tennis, golf, swimming and cycling, but during the war factory girls in numerous towns and cities had formed their own charity football teams. The best of these was the Dick, Kerr Ladies of Preston, who had visited West Yorkshire to play two decent Bradford teams, Manningham Ladies, founded at Lister's Mill, and Heys Ladies, a brewery team.

The Huddersfield Atalanta Ladies Sports Club followed their example. Established in November 1920, they organised netball and football practices for their members, acquiring the Sandhouse field at Crosland Moor for football. After a few weekly practice matches played in all weathers, Huddersfield Atalanta began to play competitively.

Their first match, a 1-0 win over Bath Ladies at Leeds Road on Good Friday, 1921 attracted a crowd of 15,000, swelling the post-war distress funds of the Mayor, Alderman James Woolven, who was more than happy to become President of the club. The local girls' style of play was surprisingly robust, and the Bath forwards required the 'services of the woman trainer upon two occasions owing to the havoc caused ... by the vigorous Miss Hilda Clark', Atalanta's right back from Thongsbridge.

The club proceeded to raise further funds with matches against St Helens Ladies at Thrum Hall and the Dick, Kerr Ladies at Hillsborough. Anxious to further exploit this money-spinner, the Mayor arranged the visit of a French touring team Fémina of Paris, to Fartown on 18 May 1921. The local girls lost 1-0, but the gate of £424 8s 6d delighted the Mayor.

In 1922 Atalanta affiliated to the English Ladies FA (ELFA) and entered the ELFA Cup. They defeated a new local team, Huddersfield Ladies at Moor End, Lockwood, in Round 1, and Chell from Stoke in Round 2 before losing to Doncaster and Bentley in the semi-final. There was also a third Huddersfield women's team, Huddersfield Alexandra, possibly Atalanta's reserve team. In the face of hostility from the men's game, most women's football teams disbanded in the 1920s. Atalanta's pavilion was bought by Broad Oak Cricket Club in 1926.

The Dick, Kerr Ladies was one of the few clubs that sustained women's football into the 1960s when a combination of the women's liberation movement and England's men winning the 1966 World Cup began a momentum that saw many thousands of women playing football in the 21st century. Both codes of women's rugby followed football's lead, establishing their governing bodies in the 1980s. Huddersfield Atalanta and the other post-World War I clubs all helped to sow the seeds for this future participation.[117]

Women's cricket enjoyed a similar flowering in the late 1920s. In 1931 Huddersfield, Holme Valley and Brighouse – which had fielded a women's team as early as 1898 – were among twelve clubs that founded the Yorkshire Women's Cricket Federation. In 1935 the Federation amalgamated with its Lancashire counterpart to form the England Women's Cricket Federation, which in turn was eventually absorbed into the England Women's Cricket Association.[118]

The Treaty of Versailles

For the first six months of 1919, local affairs were played out against the backdrop of the international peace-terms negotiations which began in January 1919. Twenty seven countries met in Paris, although the big decisions were made by the Council of Four – Georges Clemenceau of France, Lloyd George, Woodrow Wilson of the United States and Vittorio Orlando of Italy. Germany and her allies were not invited, but the victors were less united in peace than they had been in war. France wanted Germany restrained for the sake of French security, Italy wanted land, Lloyd George wanted to safeguard the British Empire, and Wilson wanted a fair new world order of justice and democracy for all.

All wanted recompensing for the cost of the war. France owed Britain and the U.S. billions for financing her war. Britain could not afford to waive the debt and the U.S. would not, Wilson believing that Germany should learn the lessons of waging an unjust war.

Germany had to pay, and therefore had to accept the blame for causing the war. On 7 May 1919 the German delegation arrived to sign and was horrified by the terms, particularly the war guilt clause which underpinned the entire treaty. The bill was immense, but nothing less than the general public amongst the Allies expected.[119]

Payment
by
Charles Lunn

You prate of your war of defence,
You lie to your countrymen still.
But you cannot deceive the informed,
And the world is at work on your bill.
Each item in that must be met,
From full payment you can't get away.
You must learn that when Kaisers make war,
There is always the 'Devil to pay.'[120]

The world, meanwhile, did not stand still. The French repossessed Alsace-Lorraine, and new frontiers were established in Eastern Europe. Poland carved out a vast new territory from Germany and Russia. Czechoslovakia took land from Austria and Hungary. Serbia founded her own Slav state, Yugoslavia. Faced with these fait accompli, the peace talks ratified them, but did not create them.

Germany reluctantly signed the Treaty of Versailles on 28 June 1919, five years to the day after the assassination of Archduke Ferdinand.

The war had many lasting legacies. Wilson achieved his first world forum, the League of Nations, the forerunner to the United Nations, and the United States had been confirmed as a world power. The world map moved from empires to nation states, particularly in eastern Europe where the Hapsburg, Ottoman, German and Russian empires were broken up. Canada, Australia and New Zealand all gained confidence in their national identities. Russian desperation crystallised in revolution that launched the

270

world's first communist state. The principles over which the war was fought – democracy, liberalism and nationalism – have endured.

The war also left dangerous loose ends. Grievances in the Middle East, the Balkans and Ireland were unresolved. German and Austrian militarism had been contained, but the peace terms had humiliated them. In addition to the loss of her territories, Germany was ordered to pay 2.5 billion German marks per year from 1921 to 1961, mainly to repair the wastelands of north eastern France and Belgium. Such servitude, and the enforcement of it, was unsustainable. The payments ended in 1926.

German propagandists and historians began to rewrite history. Germany was not to blame for the war. Her gallant troops had defied the world and had not lost, but been betrayed by the surrender of self-serving, cowardly politicians. In Germany these myths persisted until exposed by research in 1961.

Germany's economy floundered through the 1920s and collapsed in the Great Depression of the early 1930s. Resentful Germans, craving self-respect, prosperity and, in some cases, revenge, were fertile territory for the extreme nationalism of Hitler's Nazi Party. As the shrewd French General Froch said on the signing of the Treaty of Versailles:

This is not peace. This is an Armistice for 20 years.[121]

The signing of the Treaty was received in Huddersfield with little enthusiasm. A few national flags were hung from town centre buildings, there was a modest display of coloured ribbons, and a number of youngsters set off fireworks. For one man, the highlight was an acquaintance who was notorious for his short arms and deep pockets 'standing drinks all round.'[122]

War Memorials

Internationally, the war cost ten million military lives, plus unknown numbers of civilians in occupied France and Belgium, on the eastern front, in the flight of the Serbs in 1915, in the Armenian massacres and in Africa. Of the 20 million wounded, no one knows how many never fully recovered or how many died prematurely.[123]

Of Huddersfield's population – probably about 115,000 by 1916 – about 12.5% served in the forces. For a town with such extensive war industries, this was remarkably close to the national average of 12.6%. Researching her book *All Our Yesterdays*, Margaret Stansfield quantified that:

- between 14,000 and 15,000 Huddersfield men and women served in the forces
- about 5500 (39%) of these served with the 5th Dukes
- of all those who served, about 23% were killed – 3438 men and one woman, Nurse Ada Stanley (this represents the loss of about 2.9% of Huddersfield's population, compared to a national average of about 1.7%)
- of the deceased, 3333 served in the army, 64 in the Royal Navy and Merchant Navy, 40 in the air service, and two were civilians who died in explosions, one in a munitions factory and the other as a Mersey Harbour pilot
- a further 130 local servicemen died from 1919 to 1921 as result of wartime injuries.[124]

Huddersfield and its surrounding districts had erected several memorials before the war had ended, mainly financed by public subscription. In July 1918 a stained glass window was installed adjacent to the south aisle of St. Bartholomew's Church, Marsden.[125] The names of 98 servicemen, 18 of whom had lost their lives, were engraved onto a shrine in Dock Street, where all but one house had contributed at least one man to the forces.[126] Shortly before Christmas 1918, a memorial to over 230 servicemen, including 53 fatalities, from Duke Street, Cross Grove Street, Swallow Street and Upperhead Row was unveiled at the bottom of Swallow Street. At the top of its centre panel was a brass figure of Christ, saved from the ruins of a church in France.[127]

Some communities continued this pattern in 1919. Almondbury, for example, quickly settled on a purpose-built memorial which was unveiled in the churchyard of the local Parish Church in May 1919.[128]

In other districts there were conflicting ideas about the use of public money. Former soldier Joshua Chadwick of Golcar, thought that memorials were 'scandalous'; it was more important to take care of 'widows, mothers and other dependents.'[129] Some wanted functional memorials. Suggestions for a Milnsbridge Memorial included a free library and a memorial hall.[130] Proposals for the main Huddersfield Memorial included a library, art gallery and country holiday homes for 100 to 200 children ...

> ... celebrating and remembering the past in such a way that the future of Huddersfield's community and citizens will benefit.[131]

Golcar Councillor, Edgar Sykes, thought such ideas were disrespectful pragmatism. He wanted a 'distinct and permanent' monument as it 'might be the only tomb that some people would ever be able to look upon for those they had lost.' The most persuasive voices in these debates agreed with him. They came from the 5th and 7th Dukes' Old Comrades Association, representing fallen and wounded heroes.

> This association unanimously protests in the strongest possible manner against the premature action of the Corporation of Huddersfield in deciding to erect a public library, and art gallery as a memorial to our fallen heroes. This association emphatically protests against the name of 'fallen heroes' being used to collect money for an object which should be provided by the municipality.[132]

Almondbury War Memorial: a central cross and, on the semi-circular wall behind, tablets inscribed with the names of Almondbury men who served

They wanted a purpose-built monument. Major Coben, who lost both of his legs in the war, was a persuasive advocate. Officers and soldiers at the front 'did not think much of death; they thought more of comradeship.' A memorial was a commemoration of their heroic lives as brothers in arms, a reminder of the courage and sacrifice of fallen heroes, and of the values of humanity and justice for which they had fought.[133]

By mid-November 1919 an elevated piece of ground had been selected in Greenhead Park, and a memorial construction designed that met the approval of the Old Comrades Association.[134] Authorised by the Mayor, James Woolven, the Memorial was eventually completed and opened in 1924.[135]

Meanwhile, on the desolate battlefields of France and Belgium, whilst towns were rebuilt and fields were reclaimed as farmland, beautiful, peaceful cemeteries, and monuments to the unidentified and missing, were constructed under the auspices of the Imperial War Graves Commission. Visits were arranged for relatives of the fallen, the first before the end of 1919.

The Huddersfield War Memorial in Greenhead Park

The other major initiative that recognised the sacrifices of so many was 'Victory Day.' Delayed until the Treaty of Versailles had been signed, it was arranged for Saturday 19 July 1919. It was also another opportunity for the Treasury to raise money. War Savings Associations were still going strong across the country, including 271 in Huddersfield and district.[136] Huddersfield's Victory Loans Week ran from 7 to 12 July and received a midweek boost from a parade of naval heroes who had served at Jutland. By Saturday evening Huddersfield had saved £4,072,124, representing £37 per head of population, one of the highest in the country and in contention for the prestigious 'King's Flag', awarded to the most lucrative town or city.[137]

PEACE

Celebrate Peace in a practical manner by investing to the utmost limit of your resources in Victory Loan. Subscribe to the Victory Loan and place our credit in such an overwhelming position that we may gather the full fruits of glorious Victory.

Subscribe to the Victory Loan to create Trade, to increase employment, and to replace scarcity by plenty.

Do not let this great day in Britain's History pass without going to your Banker, your Stockbroker, or your Post Office, and buying as much as you can to signalise our triumph in War and to secure our Prosperity in Peace.

Victory Loan

You can buy Victory Loan at any Bank or Trustee Savings Bank, from your Stockbroker, or at any Money Order Post Office. Local War Savings Committees will give any information.

Advertisement from the *HDE*, 24 June 1919

On Victory Day the following Saturday, a special tea was provided for the children of the town and there was a 'peace bonus for the old folk.' Villages around the district held commemorations, and about 25,000 people lined the streets to witness the main event in Huddersfield. A dignified procession from the Town Hall to Greenhead Park featured the 5th and 7th Dukes, the 168th RFA, and all medical, charity, voluntary and council-run organisations which had contributed to the war effort.

> In consequence of the number of disabled men in their ranks the ... Discharged and Demobilised Soldiers [Old Comrades] fell in at the main entrance to the park, and marched at the head of the procession.

> In the Park 150 musicians and speakers led a moving memorial service.[138]

Victory Day was almost an embarrassment for the organisers, as the Old Comrades Association came close to boycotting it.

Planning the event, the town's civic leaders betrayed a disconnection between those who worked on the home front and those who had served in the forces. The councillors envisaged Victory Day as the denouement of all the town's efforts, the glorious celebration of victory that so much of their recruitment and fundraising propaganda had promised. They allocated £5000 to fund a two-day festival of concerts and fireworks.

The Old Comrades protested in the strongest terms. Coming a fortnight after their objections to the war memorial proposals, they were ever-more convinced that the town's civic leaders had little empathy with their experiences and the reality of modern warfare. For them, the war was about personal stories, tragedies, stark, harrowing memories and the comradeship that had seen them through. There was much to be thankful for and to commemorate, but little to celebrate.

'Victory Day' in Huddersfield

… give the kiddies a treat by all means, see to it that the dependents of those who have fallen are not forgotten … display as much as you like the spirit of thanksgiving, but don't let us have any triumphal marches.[139]

They also viewed any celebration as disrespectful to the 500,000 British men still serving around the world, overseeing the last throes of the war. Much of Europe and Asia was still 'in a state of upheaval.' The work of many war hospitals, including Royds Hall, continued.[140] Unless the proposals for Victory Day were toned down, it would take place without them.

Similar views were expressed around the country, and the Government reduced Victory Day from two days to one. Locally, its budget was halved to £2500. There would be no fireworks. Local schools, already granted permission to close on Friday 18 July, held a Fancy Dress Competition, not for 'Victory', but for 'Peace.'[141] Saturday's main events, the procession and memorial service were, as the Old Comrades had requested, a moving commemoration.

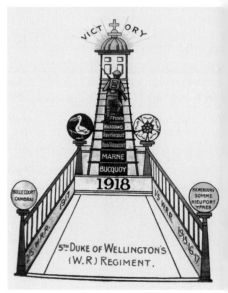

The 5th Dukes' Battalion Christmas Card, 1918.

They were right. The national search for significance found little succour in victory and freedom from likely oppression. For all the might of the nations and their firepower, it was the personal stories, particularly the personal, family tragedies and suffering, which resonated loudest. The nation found enduring, tangible symbolism in the Cenotaph and in the body of the Unknown Soldier. Exhumed in France, he represented our boy – comrade, brother, husband, son. It was a very personal war.[142]

In Memoriam, in loving memory of Private Fred Hardy,
of Brownhill Lane, Holmbridge, from his Father, Mother, and Sisters.
With aching hearts we clasped his hands,
Tears glistened in our eyes;
We wished him luck, but never thought
It was our last "Goodbye."
Could we have stood beside his grave,
And seen him laid to rest,
The pain would not have been so bad
For those who loved him best.
In a far and distant graveyard,
Where the trees and branches spread.
Lies a true and loving son and brother,
Numbered there amongst the dead.
We think of him in silence,
And his name we oft re-call,
But there's nothing left to answer
But his photo on the wall.[143]

References

Abbreviations used in References

Articles

A Canadian Soldier's Grave in Upperthong	Rumsby, John; *A Canadian Soldier's Grave in Upperthong and The Story of Holmfirth Auxiliary Hospital;* Huddersfield Local History Society Journal Issue No 24, May 2013
British Unemployment 1919-1939	Garside, WR; *British Unemployment 1919-1939: A Study in Public Policy,* 2002
ICI at 50	Reader, William J; *ICI at 50: Some reflections on ICI's early history*
The Huddersfield Music Society: A Short History	Norcliffe, Hilary; *The Huddersfield Music Society: A Short History,* Huddersfield Local History Society Issue No 24, May 2013
VAD Life	Light, Sue; *VAD Life*
Women Post Office Workers in Britain	Crowley, Mark, *Women Post Office Workers in Britain: The Long Struggle for Gender Equality and the Positive Impact of World War II,* 2012.

Books: Local

A History of Honley Cricket Club	Davies, Peter; *Pagodas and Potato Salad: A History of Honley Cricket Club,* 2010
A History of Meltham Golf Club	Holdsworth, Jack; *A History of Meltham Golf Club and Thick Hollins Hall,* 2001
A Village Goes to War	Tattersall, David; *A Village Goes to War: A History of the Men of Ravensthorpe who fell in the Great War,* 2000
All Our Yesterdays	Stansfield, Margaret, *All Our Yesterdays,* 2014
Family of Four	Hirst, Vivien; *Family of Four,* 1993
Colne Valley Folk	Lockwood, Ernest; *Colne Valley Folk: The Romance and Enterprise of a Textile Stronghold,* 1936
Comrades in Conscience	Pearce, Cyril; *Comrades in Conscience: The story of an English community's opposition to the Great War,* 2014
David Brown's	Desmond Donnelly; *David Brown's: The Story of a Family Business, 1860-1960,* 1960
Huddersfield: A Most Handsome Town	Haigh, EA Hilary (Ed); *Huddersfield: A Most Handsome Town: Aspects of history and culture of a West Yorkshire town,* 1992
Huddersfield RUFC: 1909-2009	*Huddersfield RUFC: 1909-2009 one hundred years of rugby union;* 2009
My Milnsbridge	Wood, GM; *My Milnsbridge,* 1984
Nostalgic Memories of Huddersfield	Mitchell, Andrew, Ainsworth, Steve, O'Neill, Brendan; *Nostalgic Memories of Huddersfield,* 2011
Outlane Golf Club Centenary	*Outlane Golf Club Centenary,* 2006
Royds Hall	Free, Lynn F; *Royds Hall,* 1996
The First Thirty Years	*The First Thirty Years,* Thomas Broadbent and Sons Ltd
The Great War 1914-18: Meltham & District	Various; *The Great War 1914-18: Meltham & District: The Souvenir Book and Memorial,* 1920
The West Riding Territorials in the Great War	Magnus, Laurie; *The West Riding Territorials in the Great War;* 1920

Books: Non-Local

Britain's Civilian Volunteers	Thekla Bowser; *Britain's Civilian Volunteers: Authorized Story of British Voluntary Aid Detachment Work in the Great War,* 2010
Catastrophe: Europe Goes to War, 1914	Hastings, Max; *Catastrophe: Europe Goes to War, 1914,* William Collins, 2013
Dye-makers of Great Britain 1856-1976	Fox, Maurice R; *Dye-makers of Great Britain 1856-1976: A history of chemists, companies, products and changes;* Imperial Chemical Industries PLC, 1987
In a League of Their Own	Heywood, Brian, Heywood, Freda, Heywood, Malcolm; *In a League of Their Own: Cricket and Leisure in 20th Century Todmorden,* 2010
Military Operations France and Belgium	Miles, Wilfred, Captain; *Military Operations France and Belgium, 1916,* 1938
Missing in Action	Mather, Tom; *Missing in Action,* 2005
Naval Operations	Corbett, Sir Julian S; *Naval Operations,* 1923
The Great War: A Pictorial History	Hill, Duncan/Daily Mail; The Great War; *A Pictorial History,* Atlantic Publishing, 2013
World War I in Photographs	Whittle, Paul (Ed); *World War I in Photographs,* Eagle Editions, 2003

DVDs

The Great War 1914-1918	*The Great War 1914-1918,* The National Archives/Go Entertainment Group Ltd, 2013
WWI: The Bloody War WWI	*The Bloody War, Military History,* E & E Home Video, 2004

Education Schemes

Bradford City Football Club A Scheme of Work	*Bradford City Football Club: A Scheme of Work for Primary Schools,* Sports Inspire Educational Publishing, 2010

Newspapers

HBTCVG	Hebden Bridge Times and Calder Valley Gazette	HWE	Huddersfield Weekly Examiner
HDE	Huddersfield Daily Examiner	Leeds Mercury	Leeds Mercury
HWC	Huddersfield Weekly Chronicle	The Worker	The Worker

Original Sources

Ds Clark's War Diary	*Douglas Clark's War Diary, 1917-18,* courtesy The Imperial War Museum
Brierley Wood School Log Book	*Brierley Wood Council Infants School Log Book 1906-1922,* courtesy of Kirklees Archive Service
Captain Keith Sykes' Scrapbook	Sykes, Captain Keith, MC, *Scrapbook,* courtesy of Duke of Wellington's West Riding Regiment and Kirklees Archive Service
Crow Lane School Log Book	*Crow Lane School Log Book 1897-1937,* courtesy of Kirklees Archive Service
Greenfield, Wilfred, WWI Letters	Greenfield, Wilfred, *World War I Letters,* courtesy of Caroline Courtney
Smith, F, WWI Letters	Smith, Freddie, *Collection, World War I Letters,* courtesy of Kirklees Archive Service
Owen, Roland H, WWI Letters	Owen, Roland H, Collection, *World War I Letters,* courtesy of Kirklees Archive Service
S Crosland School Log Book	*South Crosland National School Log Book 1914-1919* courtesy of South Crosland J and I School

Presentations

The Holme Valley Lads   Cooksey, Pam; *The Holme Valley Lads* presentation to Huddersfield U3A, 03/03/2014

Radio Programmes

The Great War of Words   Portillo, Michael; *The Great War of Words*, BBC Radio 4, 2014

The Long, Long Trail   *The Long, Long Trail*, BBC Radio, 1961/2014

First World War in 100 Objects   Hughes-Wilson, John, in association with the Imperial War Museum, *A History of the First World War in 100 Objects*, 2014

Television Programmes

A Necessary War   Hastings, Sir Max, *A Necessary War*, BBC Television, 2014

Britain's Great War   *Britain's Great War*, BBC Television, 2014

Kate Adie's Women of World War I   *Kate Adie's Women of World War I*; BBC Television, 2014

Railways of the Great War   Portillo, Michael, *Railways of the Great War*, BBC Television, 2014

The First World War   Strachan, Hew *The First World War*, Channel 4/Hamilton Film, 2003

This Week   *This Week*, BBC Television, 2014

War Walks   Holmes, Richard (writer and presenter); *War Walks* BBC Television, 1996

World War I   *World War I*, BBC Television, 2014

The First World War from Above   Keane, Fergal (presenter) *The First World War from Above*, BBC Television, 2010

Chapter 1: War is Declared

1 *World War I in Photographs; The Great War: A Pictorial History*

2 *HDE*, 20/01/1914

3 *HDE*, 06/02/1914

4 *HDE*, 12/03/1914

5 *World War I in Photographs; The Great War: A Pictorial History*

6 *World War I in Photographs; Catastrophe: Europe Goes to War, 1914*

7 *World War I in Photographs; The Great War: A Pictorial History*

8 *World War I in Photographs; The Great War: A Pictorial History*

9 *HDE*, 19/08/1914

10 *HDE*, 06/08/1914

11 *HDE*, 07/08/1914

12 *HDE*, 09/11/1914; *HDE* 23/01/1918

13 *Supplement to the HWE*, 23/03/1919

14 *HDE*, 31/07/1914

15 *HDE*, 03/08/1914

16 Owen, Roland H, *WWI Letters*

17 *HDE*, 04/08/1914

18 undergroundhistories.wordpress.com

19 *World War I in Photographs; The Great War: A Pictorial History*; *HDE*, 05/08/1914; *The Long, Long Trail; Catastrophe: Europe Goes to War 1914*

20 *The Great War: A Pictorial History*

Chapter 2: 1914: Raising an Army

1 *Family of Four*

2 *HDE*, 05/08/1014; Supplement to the HWE, 29/03/1919

3 *HDE*, 31/07/1914; *HDE*, 10/08/1914

4 *HDE*, 22/04/1918

5 *Supplement to the HWE*, 29/03/1919

6 *World War I in Photographs*

7 The West Riding Territorials in the Great War

8 HDE, 06/08/1914

9 *World War I in Photographs*; *HDE*, 17/08/1914

10 *World War I in Photographs; Huddersfield: A Most Handsome Town*: Chapter 7

11 *This Week*, 09/01/2014

12 *HDE*, 04/09/1914

13 *HDE*, 01/02/1915

14 *HDE*, 06/10/1914

15 *HDE*, 26/08/1914

16 *HDE*, 28/08/1914; *HDE*, 02/09/1914

17 *HDE*, 04/09/1914

18 *HDE*, 04/09/1914

19 *HWE*, 31/10/1914; Supplement to the HWE, 29/03/1919

20 *HDE*, 14/09/1914; Supplement to the HWE, 29/03/1919

21 *The Worker*, 15/08/1914; undergroundhistories.wordpress.com

22 *HWC*, 29/09/1914

23 www.huddersfieldhistory.org.uk/wp-content/uploads/2012/04/luddite-trail-leaflet-final.pdf

24 *HDE*, 24/08/1914

25 en.wikipedia.org/wiki/Representation_of_the_People_Act_1918

26 *HDE*, 31/08/1914

27 commons.wikimedia.org/wiki/File: Lieutenant_ Rowland_Owen_2_ Battalion_West_Riding_Regiment

28 *HDE*, 31/08/1914; www. kingscollections.org/warmemorials/ guys-hospital/memorials/knaggs-francis-henry; www.geni.com/people/Francis-Knaggs

29 *HDE*, 05/01/1915

30 *HDE*, 31/09/1914

31 *HDE*, 02/09/1914

32 *HDE*, 10/09/1914

33 *HDE*, 03/12/1914

34 hansard.millbanksystems.com/written_ answers/1915/feb/11/football- matches-during-war

35 *HDE*, 10/03/1915

36 www.1914-1918.net/derbyscheme; www.firstwordlwar.com.atoz/ derbyscheme.htm

37 *HDE*, 09/03/1915

38 *HDE*, 16/10/1914; *HDE*, 10/05/1918

39 *HDE*, 09/09/1914

40 *HDE*, 16/11/1914

41 www.bbc.co.uk/bradford/sense_of_ place/remembrance_huddersfield. co.shtml

42 *HDE*, 05/10/1914

43 *HDE*, 30/12/1915

44 *HDE*, 14/08/1916; gameofthepeople. com/2014/01/03/1915-when-football-seemed-unimportant

45 *HDE*, 24/09/1914; HDE, 28/08/1914

46 *HDE*, 25/09/1914

47 *HDE*, 20/11/1914

48 *HDE*, 24/09/1914

49 *Supplement to the HWE*, 29/03/1919

50 *HDE*, 05/01/1915; *HDE*, 06/01/1915

Chapter 3: 1914: To War

1 *The Great War; A Pictorial History; World War I in Photographs p13-14; The Long, Long Trail*

2 *HDE*, 04/09/1914

3 *HDE*, 01/02/1914

4 *HDE*, 04/09/1914

5 *HDE*, 15/01/1919

6 *HDE*, 25/01/1915

7 *HDE*, 10/05/1918

8 en.wikipedia.org/wiki/Siege_of_ Antwerp_(1914); www.firstworldwar. com/battles/antwerp.htm

9 *HDE*, 01/02/1915

10 Owen, Rowland H, *WWI Letters*; en.wikipedia.org/wiki/Battle_of_Le_Cateau

11 *HDE*, 27/08/1917

12 *HDE*, 03/12/1915

13 *World War I in Photographs* p17; www. bbc.co.uk/history/worldwars/wwone/ battle_marne.shtml

14 *HDE*, 27/07/1915

15 *HDE*, 03/12/1915

16 *HDE*, 06/10/1914; HDE, 01/02/1915; www. firstworldwar.com/battles/aisne1.htm

17 *HDE*, 10/11/1914

18 *HDE*, 06/10/1914

19 *HDE*, 10/11/1914

20 *HDE*, 01/02/1915

21 *HDE*, 06/10/1914

22 *World War I in Photographs; The Great War; A Pictorial History*; www.1914-1918.net/bat1.htm

23 *HDE*, 26/01/1916

24 www.firstworldwar.com/battles/aisne1.htm

25 *A Necessary War*

26 *World War I in Photographs*; www.firstworldwar.com/battles/ypres1.htm

27 *HDE*, 27/07/1915

28 www.firstworldwar.com/battles/ypres1.htm

29 *HDE*, 10/11/1914

30 *HDE*, 20/11/1914

31 *HDE*, 23/11/1914

32 *HDE*, 01/02/1915

33 www.1914-1918.net/bat1.htm; www.firstworldwar.com/battles/ypres1.htm

34 *HDE*, 04/06/1915

35 *World War I in Photographs*

36 *The First World War from Above*

37 *Huddersfield: A Most Handsome Town*: Chapter 7

38 *World War I in Photographs*; *The Great War; A Pictorial History 5*; *World War I*, Ep 7, Blockade

39 *HDE*, 05/01/1915

Chapter 4: 1914: Kindling the Home Fires

1 *HDE*, 16/02/1917

2 *HDE*, 06/08/1914

3 *HDE*, 14/08/1914; *HDE*, 18/08/1914

4 *HDE*, 07/08/1914

5 *HDE*, 13/08/1914; *HDE*, 28/08/1914; *Supplement to the HWE*, 23/03/1919; *Supplement to the HWE*, 05/04/1919

6 *Supplement to the HWE*, 29/03/1919

7 *Supplement to the HWE*, 05/04/1919

8 *HDE*, 13/08/1914; *HDE*, 17/08/1914

9 *HDE*, 01/01/1915

10 *HDE*, 26/08/1914

11 *HDE*, 04/09/1914

12 *HDE*, 10/08/1914

13 *HDE*, 11/08/1914

14 *S Crosland School Log Book* 18/09/1914; 19/09/1914

15 *HDE*, 13/08/1914

16 *HDE*, 18/08/1914

17 *HDE*, 22/09/1914

18 *HDE*, 01/09/1914; *HDE*, 22/10/1914; *HDE*, 30/11/1914

19 *HDE*, 08/10/1914

20 *Crow Lane Schl Log Book* 1897-1937

21 *HDE*, 22/10/1914; *HDE*, 30/11/1914

22 *HDE*, 30/10/1914

23 *Supplement to the HWE*, 26/04/1919

24 *HDE*, 30/10/1914

Chapter 5: 1914-15: The U-Boat Menace

1 en.wikipedia.org/wiki/HMSPathfinder_(1904)1914-1918.invisionzone.com/forums/index; www.naval-history.net/WW1NavyBritishBVLSaRN1408.htm

2 *HDE*, 30/09/1914; en.wikipedia.org/wiki/HMS_Aboukir_(1900); en.wikipedia.org/wiki/Action_of_22_September_1914; www.worldwar1.co.uk/cressy.htm

3 *HDE*, 06/01/1915; en.wikipedia.org/wiki/HMS_Formidable_(1898); www.burtonbradstock.org.uk/History/Wrecks%20off%20Burton%20Bradstock/HMS%20Formidable

4 *HDE*, 13/01/1915

5 en.wikipedia.org/wiki/HMS_Formidable_(1898); www.burtonbradstock.org.uk/History/Wrecks%20off%20Burton%20Bradstock/HMS%20Formidable

6 *HDE*, 11/03/1915; www.theempressofireland.com/#salversgoal/c9so; www.pb.org/lostliners/empress.html

7 trove.nla.gov.au/ndp/del/article/45355129

8 *HDE*, 10/05/1915

9 www.gwpda.org/naval/lusika05.htm; www.rmslusitania.info/people/second-cabin/herbert-gwyer/; First World War in 100 Objects

10 *HDE*, 01/05/1917

11 *HDE*, 17/06/1915; *HDE*, 19/07/1915; *Britain's Great War*, Ep 2, The War Machine

12 *HDE*, 10/05/1915

13 *HDE*, 19/05/1915

14 *The Holme Valley Lads*

15 *Britain's Great War*, Ep 2, The War Machine

16 *HDE*, 26/11/1915; *HDE*, 27/08/1917; www.epsomandewellhistoryexplorer.org/HMHSAnglia.html;1914-1918.invasionzone.com/forum/indexgreatwarnurses.blogspot.co.uk/2009/11/sinking-of-hospital-ship-anglia.html

Chapter 6: 1915: A Bloody Stalemate

1 *HDE*, 03/06/1915

2 *HDE*, 01/02/1915

3 *HDE*, 24/08/1915

4 *HDE*, 08/02/1915

5 *HDE*, 14/04/1915

6 *HDE*, 24/11/1915

7 *HDE*, 12/11/1915

8 *HDE*, 17/11/1915

9 *HDE*, 24/08/1915

10 *HDE*, 07/05/1915

11 *HDE*, 01/12/1915

12 *HDE*, 19/05/1915

13 *HDE*, 24/08/1915

14 *HDE*, 10/01/1916

15 *HDE*, 22/04/1918

16 www.1914-1918.net/bat11.htm

17 *HDE*, 03/06/1915

18 *HDE*, 31/03/1915

19 www.1914-1918.net/bat11.htm

20 *HDE*, 22/01/1918

21 *HDE*, 20/05/1915

22 *HDE*, 04/03/1915

23 Smith, F, *WWI Letters*, 15/04/1915

24 *Supplement to the HWE*, 29/03/1919

25 *HDE*, 17/05/1915

26 *HDE*, 04/06/1915

27 *Huddersfield RUFC: 1909-2009*

28 *HDE*, 17/05/1915

29 *HDE*, 20/05/1915

30 *HDE*, 17/05/1915

31 *HDE*, 04/06/1915; *The West Riding Territorials in the Great War*

32 *HDE*, 20/05/1915

33 *HDE*, 16/04/1917; www.cwgc.org

34 www.firstworldwar.com/battles/ypres2.htm

35 *HDE*, 18/01/1915

36 *HDE*, 04/05/1915

37 *Supplement to the HWE*, 29/03/1919

38 *HDE*, 19/05/1915; *HDE*, 20/05/1915; *HDE*, 26/05/1915

39 Smith, F, *WWI Letters*, 24/04/1915

40 Smith, F, *WWI Letters*, 07/05/1915

41 Smith, F, *WWI Letters*, 13/05/1915; 'early June'

42 Smith, F, *WWI Letters*, 26/05/1915

43 www.firstworldwar.com/battles/ypres2.htm

44 Smith, F, *WWI Letters*, 02/06/1915; 04/06/1915

45 Smith, F, *WWI Letters*; 'early June'

46 Smith, F, *WWI Letters*, 14/09/1915

47 Smith, F, *WWI Letters*, 23/08/1915

48 Smith, F, *WWI Letters*, 01/07/1915

49 Smith, F, *WWI Letters*, 19/06/1915

50 *HDE*, 13/07/1915

51 *HDE*, 13/07/1915

52 Smith, F, *WWI Letters*, 12/07/1915

53 *HDE*, 16/07/1915

54 *HDE*, 23/07/1915

55 *HDE*, 29/07/1915

56 *HDE*, 09/08/1915

57 *HDE*, 03/08/1915

58 *HDE*, 21/07/1915

59 *HDE*, 21/07/1915

60 *HDE*, 20/10/1915

61 Smith, F, *WWI Letters*, 06/07/1915; 16/07/1915

62 Smith, F, *WWI Letters*, 03/08/1915

63 Smith, F, *WWI Letters*, 01/08/1915

64 Smith, F, *WWI Letters*, 18/09/1915

65 Smith, F, *WWI Letters*, 07/08/1915

66 Smith, F, *WWI Letters*, 21/07/1915; 07/08/1915

67 Smith, F, *WWI Letters*, 18/08/1915

68 Smith, F, *WWI Letters*, 05/07/1915

69 Interview with William Heywood, 1985

70 Smith, F, *WWI Letters*, 'early September'

71 Smith, F, *WWI Letters*, 21/07/1915

72 Smith, F, *WWI Letters*, 'early September'

73 Smith, F, *WWI Letters*, 12/09/1915

74 Smith, F, *WWI Letters*, 16/09/1915

75 Smith, F, *WWI Letters*, 18/09/1915

76 www.1914-1918.net/bat13.htm

77 www.firstworldwar.com/battles/loos.htm; www.westernfrontassociation.com/great-war-on-land/61-battlefields/312-poi-gas-loos.html; www.webmatters.net/txtpat/?id=716

78 www.1914-1918.net/bat20.htm

79 *HDE*, 07/10/1915

80 *HDE*, 05/11/1915

81 Smith, F, *WWI Letters*, 18/09/1915

82 Smith, F, *WWI Letters*, 17/08/1915

83 Smith, F, *WWI Letters*, 23/08/1915

84 Smith, F, *WWI Letters*, 18/09/1915

85 Smith, F, *WWI Letters*, 10/10/1915

86 Smith, F, *WWI Letters*, 14/10/1915

87 Letter from Freddie Smith's pals, 17/10/1915

88 Letter from 2nd Lieutenant Gledhill, 18/10/1915

89 Letter from Freddie Smith's pals, 17/10/1915

90 Letter from Private A Senior, 18/10/1915

91 Smith, F, *WWI Letters*, 01/10/1915

92 www.1914-1918.net/bat13.htm

93 *HDE*, 25/11/1915

94 www.history.com/this-day-in-history/italy-declares-war-on-austria-hungary

95 *HDE*, 10/05/1916

96 *HDE*, 03/12/1915

97 *HDE*, 28/07/1915

Chapter 7: 1915-16: Gallipoli

1 www.1914-1918.net/Gallipoli.htm;
   www.anzacsite.gov.au/1landing/why;
   www.firstworldwar.com/battles/
   landingsapr15.htm; *A Village Goes to War*
2 *HDE*, 27/05/1915; *HDE*, 02/06/1915
3 *HDE*, 27/05/1915
4 *HDE*, 27/05/1915; *HDE*, 02/06/1915;
   A Village Goes to War
5 *HDE*, 14/06/1915
6 www.1914-1918.net/hamiltons_gallipoli_
   despatch_1.htm; www.1914-1918.net/
   Gallipoli.htm; www.firstworldwar.com/
   battles/landings_apr15.htm
7 www.anzacsite.gov.au/5environment/
   timelines/100-events-gallipoli-campaign/
   june-july-1915.html
8 www.1914-1918.net/Gallipoli.htm

9 *HDE*, 15/07/1915
10 *HDE*, 02/12/1915
11 *HDE*, 31/01/1916
12 *HDE*, 01/09/1915
13 *HDE*, 07/01/1916; en.wikipedia.org/
   wiki/Landing_at_Suvla_Bay; *A Village
   Goes to War*
14 *HDE*, 02/12/1915
15 *HDE*, 29/11/1915
16 www.anzacsite.gov.au/4panels/
   opt5.html
17 1914-1918.invisionzone.com/forums;
   British Journal of Nursing, 08/01/1916
18 *HDE*, 20/01/1916
19 www.firstworldwar.com/battles/_
   evacuation_dec15.htm

20 *HDE*, 08/02/1916
21 *HDE*, 09/03/1916
22 *HDE*, 08/02/1916; *HDE*, 09/03/1916
23 *HDE*, 09/03/1916
24 *HDE*, 14/11/1916
25 *HDE*, 04/07/1918
26 *HDE*, 09/03/1916
27 *HDE*, 08/02/1916
28 *HDE*, 11/10/1916
29 *HDE*, 14/11/1916
30 *HDE*, 11/05/1917
31 www.1914-1918.net/Gallipoli.htm
32 *HDE*, 21/03/1917
33 *HDE*, 28/01/1916

1 *In a League of Their Own*
2 *Comrades in Conscience*
3 *Supplement to the HWE*, 12/04/1919
4 *HDE*, 01/05/1917
5 *HDE*, 02/11/1914
6 *Colne Valley Folk*
7 *Supplement to the HWE*, 12/04/1919
8 *HDE*, 01/02/1917
9 *HDE*, 02/11/1914
10 *HDE*, 11/01/1917
11 *HDE*, 31/01/1917; en.wikipedia.org/
   wiki/John_Dickson-Poynder,_1st_
   Baron_Islington
12 *HDE*, 16/01/1917
13 Supplement to the *HWE*, 12/04/1919
14 *HDE*, 02/11/1914
15 *Britain's Great War, Ep 2*, The War Machine

Chapter 8: A Khaki Economy

16 *HDE*, 20/04/1915
17 *HDE*, 17/06/1915
18 *HDE*, 01/07/1915
19 *HDE*, 25/06/1915
20 *Comrades in Conscience*
21 *HDE*,10/09/1917
22 *HDE*, 07/04/1916; *HDE*, 10/09/1917
23 *Comrades in Conscience*
24 *HDE*, 13/12/1917
25 *HDE*, 03/01/1919
26 *HDE*, 20/06/1917
27 *HDE*, 19/07/1917
28 *HDE*, 27/07/1917
29 *HDE*, 26/04/1916
30 *HDE*, 06/01/1915; *HDE*, 16/01/1917
31 *HDE*, 02/06/1916
32 *HDE*, 24/04/1917

33 *HDE*, 05/05/1916
34 *HDE*, 19/04/1915; *HDE*, 05/01/1916
35 *Supplement to the HWE*, 12/04/1919
36 *News*, BBC TV, 19/08/2014; *HDE*,
   01/08/1917
37 *HDE*, 22/09/1915
38 *HDE*, 02/01/1917
39 *HDE*, 16/02/1917
40 *HDE*, 24/10/1917
41 *HDE*, 02/05/1917
42 *HDE*, 22/05/1917
43 *HDE*, 24/10/1917; *Supplement to the
   HWE*, 12/04/1919
44 *HDE*, 12/12/1917
45 *Supplement to the HWE*, 12/04/1919
46 *Family of Four*

1 *Britain's Great War, Ep 2*, The War Machine
2 *HDE*, 16/08/1916; *Kate Adie's Women of
   World War I*
3 *HDE*, 05/07/1916
4 *Nostalgic Memories of Huddersfield*
5 *David Brown's*
6 *The First Thirty Years*
7 *Dye-makers of Great Britain 1856-1976*
8 *HDE*, 20/08/1915
9 *Supplement to the HWE*, 12/04/1919
10 *Dye-makers of Great Britain 1856-1976*
11 *HDE*, 03/06/1915
12 *Dye-makers of Great Britain 1856-1976*
13 *HDE*, 23/02/1917
14 *Dye-makers of Great Britain 1856-1976*;
   HDE, 26/01/1972; *HDE*, 04/03/1972;
   HDE, 11/03/1972
15 *HDE*, 21/05/1966
16 *ICI at 50*
17 *HDE*, 28/06/1916; *HDE*, 01/06/1916
18 *HDE*, 14/06/1916
19 *HDE*, 06/06/1916
20 *HDE*, 20/07/1916
21 *HDE*, 14/11/1916
22 *Dye-makers of Great Britain 1856-1976*
23 *HDE*, 08/11/1916
24 *HDE*, 17/01/1917
25 *Britain's Great War, Ep 2*, The War Machine
26 *Family of Four*
27 *HDE*, 14/03/1917
28 *HDE*, 02/07/1918; *Kate Adie's Women of*

Chapter 9: Munitions Factories

World War I
29 *HDE*, 28/11/1917; *HDE*, 13/12/1917
30 *HDE*, 20/09/1917
31 *HDE*, 14/02/1917
32 *HDE*, 07/04/1916
33 *HDE*, 20/02/1917; *HDE*, 23/02/1917;
   HDE, 18/03/1917
34 *HDE*, 20/02/1917
35 monologues.co.uk/musichall/songs-W/
   Where-Are-The-Lads-Of-The-Village.
   htm; *HDE*, 21/12/1917
36 *HDE*, 16/07/1917
37 *HDE*, 25/07/1917
38 *HDE*, 14/08/1917
39 *HDE*, 21/07/1916
40 www.eyes-and-ears.co.uk/pennione/etailsasp?
   Title=Treating+Strictly+Prohibited
41 *HDE*, 31/03/1915
42 *HDE*, 16/04/1917
43 *Dye-makers of Great Britain 1856-1976*
44 *HDE*, 21/01/1915
45 *HDE*, 07/04/1916
46 *HDE*, 31/03/1915
47 www.eyes-and-ears.co.uk/pennione/detailsasp?
   Title=Treating+Strictly+Prohibited;
   Britain's Great War, Ep 2, The War Machine
48 *HDE*, 11/11/1915
49 *HDE*, 15/11/1915
50 *HDE*, 26/01/1915
51 *HDE*, 20/12/1915
52 *HDE*, 24/10/1916; *HDE*, 19/01/1916

53 *HDE*, 07/02/1917; *HDE*, 06/11/1917
54 *HDE*, 08/02/1917
55 *HDE*, 30/01/1917
56 *HDE*, 16/01/1917
57 *HDE*, 14/06/1918
58 *Britain's Great War*, Ep 3, The Darkest Hour
59 *Brierley Wood School Log Book*
60 *HDE*, 05/07/1916
61 *HDE*, 26/01/1917
62 *HDE*, 05/06/1916
63 *HDE*, 08/06/1916
64 *HDE*, 05/06/1916; *HDE*, 07/06/1916
65 *HDE*, 04/09/1916
66 *HDE*, 07/06/1916
67 *HDE*, 28/07/1916
68 *HDE*, 10/08/1916
69 *HDE*, 23/08/1916; *HDE*, 25/08/1916
70 *HDE*, 01/01/1919
71 *HDE*, 10/09/1917
72 *HDE*, 24/08/1916; *HDE*, 10/09/1917
73 *HDE*, 07/08/1917
74 *HDE*, 14/08/1917
75 *HDE*, 14/01/1917
76 *HDE*, 27/03/1918
77 *HDE*, 01/07/1918
78 *Colne Valley Folk; My Milnsbridge
   HWC*, 24/07/1915; *HWC*, 18/12/1915
79 *HDE*,22/01/1917; www.faversham.org/history
   explosives/greatexplosion1916.aspx; en.wikipedia
   org/wiki/faversham_explosives_industry

80 http://www.bradfordhistorical.org.uk/antiquary/third/vol03/lowmoor.html; *Leeds Mercury*, 04/03/1924

81 *HDE*,09/10/1916; *HDE*, 24/04/1918

82 *HDE*, 18/01/1918; *HDE*, 24/04/1918

83 www.elhas.org.uk/reports/barbowt.htm; www.barwickinelmethistoricalsociety.com/4746.html

84 *HDE*, 22/01/1917; history.co.uk/study-topics/history-of-london/ww1-1917-silvertown-explosion

85 *HDE*, 15/06/1917; *HDE*, 13/07/1917

86 en.wikipedia.org/wiki/National_Shell_Filling_Factory_Chilwell; www.bbc.co.uk/insideout/eastmidlands/series2/blast_chilwell_somme.shtlm

87 *HDE*, 25/07/1917

88 www.blackcatfireworks.co.uk/history; www.yorkshirepost.co.uk/news/maintopics/local-stories/a-blast-from-the-past

Chapter 10: Zeppelins and the Blackout

1 *HDE*, 01/11/1916

2 *Britain's Great War*, Ep 1, War Comes to Britain

3 *The Great War of Words*, Ep 1

4 *HDE*, 01/04/1919

5 www.1914.org/news/victims-of-the-first-airship-raid-on-britain-remembered/

6 www.firstworldwar.com/airwar/bombers_zeppelins.htm

7 *Supplement to the HWE*, 24/05/1917

8 *Supplement to the HWE*, 24/05/1917

9 *HDE*, 19/06/1917

10 *HDE*, 03/02/1916

11 *HDE*, 26/04/1916

12 www.greenwichmeantime.co.uk/daylight-saving-time/history-william-willetts.htm;en.wikipedia.org/wiki/Daylight_saving_time

13 *HDE*, 25/05/1916; *HDE*, 27/06/1916

14 *HDE*, 26/09/1916

15 aircrashsites.co.uk/history/zeppelin-airship-l21-over-lancashire-2/; In a League of Their Own

16 *HDE*, 03/10/1916

17 *HDE*, 16/01/1917

18 *HDE*, 16/10/1916; *HDE*, 02/11/1916

19 *HDE*, 12/09/1917

20 *HDE*, 11/08/1916

21 *HDE*, 26/09/1916

22 *HDE*, 28/11/1916

23 *HDE*, 13/12/1916

24 *HDE*, 08/01/1917

25 *HDE*, 04/12/1916

26 *HDE*, 22/12/1916

27 *HDE*, 23/01/1917

28 *HDE*, 04/12/1916

29 *HDE*, 23/01/1917

30 *HDE*, 24/01/1917

31 *HDE*, 19/03/1917

32 *HDE*, 28/03/1917

33 *HDE*, 12/09/1917

34 *HDE*, 18/09/1917

35 *HDE*, 13/03/1918; *HDE*, 20/02/1918

36 www.nationalarchives.gov.uk/education/lesson32.htm; www3.shropshire-cc.gov.uk/roots/packages/war.htm

37 *HDE*, 13/03/1918

38 www.wiganworld.co.uk/album/photo

39 *Supplement to the HWE*, 24/05/1917

Chapter 11: War Hospitals

1 *Royds Hall* p7

2 *Britain's Civilian Volunteers*; www.redcross.org.uk

3 *HDE*, 04/02/1915

4 *HDE*, 04/05/1915

5 *HDE*, 11/05/1915

6 *HDE*, 19/05/1915

7 *HDE*, 21/05/1915

8 *Supplement to the HWE*, 26/04/1919

9 *HDE*, 16/11/1916

10 *HDE*, 29/07/1916; 1914-1918.invisionzone.com/forums/index.php?showtopic=51072

11 *HDE*, 06/09/1917

12 *HDE*, 04/08/1916

13 *HDE*, 02/02/1917; *HDE*, 26/07/1917

14 *HDE*, 02/02/1017

15 *HDE*, 06/09/1917

16 *Supplement to the HWE*, 26/04/1919

17 *HDE*, 13/09/1917

18 *HDE*, 27/08/1917; hansard.millbanksystems.com/commons/1918/feb/18/motor-spirit-order

19 *HDE*, 02/02/1917

20 *Supplement to the HWE*, 26/04/1919

21 *HDE*, 31/01/1918; *Supplement to the HWE*, 26/04/1919

22 *HDE*, 09/02/1917; *HDE*, 16/02/1917

23 *HDE*, 09/08/1917

24 *HDE*, 21/05/1915; *HDE*, 28/03/1918

25 *Family of Four*

26 *Supplement to the HWE*, 10/05/1919

27 *HDE*, 05/10/1915

28 *VAD Life*; www.scarletfinders.co.uk; *Supplement to the HWE*, 10/05/1919

29 *HDE*, 07/01/1918; www.pathsoc.org/index.php/grants-lectures-awards/lectures-awards/115-sims-woodhead-medal

30 *HDE*, 04/10/1915

31 *Supplement to the HWE*, 10/05/1919

32 *Supplement to the HWE*, 26/04/1919

33 *Britain's Civilian Volunteers* p.17

34 *Royds Hall*

35 *HDE*, 11/10/1915

36 *HDE*, 18/10/1915

37 *HDE*, 09/08/1917

38 *HDE*, 04/02/1916

39 *HDE*, 20/03/1918; *Supplement to the HWE*, 10/05/1919

40 *HDE*, 17/02/1915

41 *HDE*, 07/07/1916

42 *A Canadian Soldier's Grave in Upperthong*; *HDE*, 18/09/1916

43 *A Canadian Soldier's Grave in Upperthong*

44 *HDE*, 02/11/1916

45 *Supplement to the HWE*, 26/04/1919

46 *The Great War 1914-18: Meltham & District*

47 *Supplement to the HWE*, 10/05/1919; *HDE*, 02/03/1917; *HDE*, 23/07/1917

48 *Supplement to the HWE*, 10/05/1919

49 *Royds Hall*

50 *HDE*, 30/04/1918

51 *HDE*, 09/06/1915; *HDE*, 07/06/1916; *HDE*, 20/07/1916; *HDE*, 01/02/1917; *HDE*, 30/07/1917; *HDE*, 29/07/1918; *HDE*, 09/08/1918; *Supplement to the HWE*, 10/05/1919

52 *HDE*, 23/11/1915

Chapter 12: Recruitment and Conscription

1 *HDE*, 05/02/1917

2 en.wikipedia.org/wiki/Annie_Kenney; spartacus-educational.com/Wdrummond.htm

3 *HDE*, 05/02/1917

4 *Comrades in Conscience*

5 *Supplement to the HWE*, 29/03/1919

6 *HDE*, 10/01/1915

7 *HDE*, 04/06/1915; *HDE*, 07/06/1915; Comrades in Conscience

8 *HWE*, 07/08/1915

9 *HDE*, 27/09/1915; *HDE*, 04/10/1915

10 *HDE*, 03/08/1915

11 *HDE*, 08/07/1915

12 *HDE*, 13/07/1915

13 *HDE*, 13/12/1915; *HDE*, 14/12/1915

14 www.1914-1918.net/msa1916.html

15 *HDE*, 07/02/1916

16 *HDE*, 21/02/1916

17 *HDE*, 24/02/1916

18 *Comrades in Conscience*

19 *Family of Four*

20 *HDE*, 24/10/1916

21 *HDE*, 04/05/1016

22 *Comrades in Conscience*

23 *HDE*, 20/03/1916

24 *HDE*, 24/02/1916

25 *HDE*, 02/03/1916

26 *HDE*, 15/03/1916; *HDE*, 27/03/1916; *HDE*, 03/04/1916

27 *HDE*, 08/03/1916

28 *Comrades in Conscience*

29 *HDE*, 02/02/1916

30 *HDE*, 04/02/1916

31 *HDE*, 07/02/1916

32 *HDE*, 01/03/1916

33 *HDE*, 06/03/1916

34 *Comrades in Conscience*

35 *HDE*, 21/03/1916

36 *Comrades in Conscience*

37 *HDE*, 23/03/1916

38 *Comrades in Conscience*

39 *HDE*, 23/03/1916; *Comrades in Conscience*

40 *Comrades in Conscience*; www2.
kirklees.gov.uk/you-kmc/MAYOR/
former/pre1974.asp?area=huddersfield;
www.bbc.co.uk/programmes/p01s6fbd

41 ir.lawnet.fordham.edu/cgi/
viewcontent.cgi?article=1210&context=
facultyscholarship

42 *Comrades in Conscience*

43 *HDE*, 17/02/1916; *HDE*, 19/04/1916;
explore.bfi.org.uk/4ce2b71895f58

44 *HDE*, 01/05/1916

45 *HDE*, 01/05/1916

46 *The Worker*, 08/02/1917

47 *The Worker*, 26/02/1915

48 www.ppu.org.uk/coproject/guide

49 *HDE*, 07/08/1916

50 *HDE*, 16/05/1916

51 *Supplement to the HWE*, 29/03/1919

52 *HDE*, 15/05/1916

53 *HDE*, 05/06/1918

54 *HDE*, 27/06/1916

55 *HDE*, 13/06/1916

56 *HDE*, 09/03/1917

57 *HDE*, 26/02/1917

58 *HDE*, 23/07/1917

59 *HDE*, 16/03/1916

60 *HDE*, 14/05/1918

61 *HDE*, 11/09/1916

62 *HDE*, 13/02/1917

63 *HDE*, 28/03/1917; *HDE*, 30/03/1917;
HDE, 16/04/1917

64 *HDE*, 07/05/1917

65 *HDE*, 24/05/1917

66 *HDE*, 02/08/1917

67 *HDE*, 07/05/1917

68 *HDE*, 23/02/1917

69 *HDE*, 14/03/1917

70 *HDE*, 22/04/1918

71 *Supplement to the HWE*, 29/03/1919

72 *The Great War 1914-1918*, 1918:
Germany's Last Gamble

73 *Comrades in Conscience*

Chapter 13: 1916: The Somme

1 *The Great War 1914-1918*, 1916:
Stalemate; *WWI: The Bloody War*, Battle
of the Somme; Battle of Verdun

2 *HDE*, 16/03/1916

3 *HDE*, 02/05/1916

4 *HDE*, 03/02/1916

5 *HDE*, 16/03/1916

6 *A History of Honley Cricket Club*

7 *HDE*, 26/04/1916

8 *Supplement to the HWE*, 31/05/1919

9 *HDE*, 15/02/1916

10 *HDE*, 15/02/1916

11 *HDE*, 10/05/1916

12 *HDE*, 02/05/1916

13 *HDE*, 02/06/1916

14 *HDE*, 02/10/1916

15 *HDE*, 31/01/1916

16 *HDE*, 05/10/1916

17 *HDE*, 08/01/1917

18 *HDE*, 30/05/1916

19 *HDE*, 02/05/1916

20 *WWI: The Bloody War*, Battle of the
Somme

21 *Supplement to the HWE*, 31/05/1919

22 *HDE*, 05/10/1916

23 *The Great War 1914-1918*, 1916:
Stalemate; *WWI: The Bloody War*, Battle
of the Somme; *War Walks*: The Somme;
The First World War, Ep 6, Breaking the
Deadlock

24 *HDE*, 21/07/1916

25 *HDE*, 06/07/1916

26 *WWI: The Bloody War*, Battle of the
Somme; *War Walks*: The Somme

27 *HDE*, 21/07/1916

28 *HDE*, 04/09/1916

29 *WWI: The Bloody War*, Battle of the
Somme; *The First World War from
Above*; *War Walks*: The Somme

30 *HDE*, 03/07/1916

31 *HDE*, 06/07/1916

32 *HDE*, 31/07/1916

33 *Supplement to the HWE*, 31/05/1919;
War Walks: The Somme

34 *HDE*, 05/10/1916

35 *HDE*, 29/06/1916; *HDE*, 30/06/1919

36 *HDE*, 18/08/1916

37 *HDE*, 19/07/1916

38 *HDE*, 21/07/1916; *HDE*, 14/08/1916

39 *HDE*, 05/01/1917

40 *HDE*, 20/07/1916

41 *HDE*, 21/07/1916

42 *HDE*, 08/08/1917

43 *HDE*, 08/08/1916

44 *HDE*, 18/08/1916

45 *HDE*, 10/08/1916

46 *HDE*, 16/08/1916

47 *HDE*, 18/08/1916

48 *HDE*, 18/08/1916

49 *HDE*, 24/08/1916

50 *HDE*, 30/08/1916

51 *HDE*, 22/08/1916

52 *HDE*, 14/09/1916

53 *HDE*, 15/09/1916

54 *HDE*, 14/09/1916; *HDE*, 29/06/1919;
HDE, 30/06/1919

55 *HDE*, 22/09/1916

56 *HDE*, 29/06/1916; *HDE*, 30/06/1919

57 *HDE*, 11/09/1916

58 *HDE*, 15/09/1916

59 *HDE*, 02/10/1916

60 en.wikipedia.org/wiki/File:Roses_of_
picardy_sheet_music_01.jpg

61 *HDE*, 29/09/1916

62 *HDE*, 29/06/1919; *HDE*, 30/06/1919

63 *HDE*, 09/10/1916

64 *HDE*, 06/10/1916

65 *HDE*, 02/10/1916

66 *HDE*, 12/09/1916

67 *HDE*, 02/10/1916

68 Greenfield, Wilfred, *WWI Letters*;
11/09/1916; 14/09/1916; 21/09/1016;
30/09/1916; 'Tues'/10/1916

69 www.1914-1918.net/haigs_somme_
despatch.htm

70 www.worcestershireregiment.com/
wr.php?main=inc/h_transloy_ridges

71 www.cwgc.org/somme/content.
asp?menuid=30&id=30&menuname=
Le+Transloy&menu=main;
en.wikipedia.org/wiki/Battle_of_
Le_Transloy; *Military Operations
France and Belgium*; www.
scarboroughmaritimeheritage.org.uk/
greatwar

72 *HDE*, 23/07/1917

73 *HDE*, 23/11/1916; *HDE*, 29/06/1919;
HDE, 30/06/1919

74 *Supplement to the HWE*, 31/05/1919;
HDE, 30/05/1916

75 *HDE*, 27/08/1917

76 addingham.info/somme/; *HDE*, 03/11/1916

77 *HDE*, 14/12/1916

78 *HDE*, 30/11/1916; *HDE*, 19/04/1917

79 *The Great War 1914-1918*, 1916:
Stalemate; *WWI: The Bloody War*, Battle
of the Somme; *War Walks*: The Somme;
The First World War, Ep 6, Breaking the
Deadlock; *A Village Goes to War*

80 *HDE*, 18/09/1916

81 *The Great War 1914-1918*, 1916:
Stalemate, *WWI: The Bloody War*, Battle
of the Somme; War Walks: The Somme;
The First World War, Ep 6, Breaking the
Deadlock

Chapter 14: 1916: Jutland

1 *HDE*, 04/02/1916

2 *HDE*, 17/04/1916

3 *HDE*, 20/04/1916

4 *HDE*, 06/06/1916; 07/06/1916

5 www.northeastmedals.co.uk/britishguide/
jutland/hms_queen_mary_casualty_
list_1916.htm

6 *HDE*, 05/06/1916; *HDE*, 07/06/1916

7 *HDE*, 07/06/1916;www.
dreadnoughtproject.org/tfsH.M.S._
Warspite_at_the_Battle_of_Jutland

8 www.dreadnoughtproject.org/tfs

9 *HDE*, 06/06/1916

10 www.northeastmedals.co.uk/
britishguide/jutland/hms_black_prince_
casualty_list_1916.htm

11 *Naval Operations*; www.kiplingsociety.
co.uk/rg_seawarfare_jutlandfighting.
htm; www.northeastmedals.co.uk/
britishguide/jutland/hms_tipperary_
casualty_list_1916.htm; archive.org/
stream/fightingatjutlan00fawcuoft_djvu.
txt; en.wikipedia.org/wiki/HMS_Tipperary_
(1915); www.dreadnoughtproject.org/tfs/
index.php/H.M.S._Tipperary_(1915); www.
dreadnoughtproject.org/tfs/index.php/
Charles_John_Wintour

12 *HDE*, 07/06/1916; archive.org/stream/
fightingatjutlan00fawcuoft_djvu.txt

13 *HDE*, 06/06/1916

14 *HDE*, 07/06/1916; www.northeastmedals.
co.uk/britishguide/jutland/hms_
sparrowhawk_casualty_list_1916.
htm; en.wikipedia.org/wiki/HMS_
Sparrowhawk_(1912)

15 *HDE*, 23/10/1916

16 archive.org/stream/
fightingatjutlan00fawcuoft_djvu.txt

17 *HDE*, 05/06/1916

18 *HDE*, 06/06/1916

1 www.examiner.co.uk/news/
  west-yorkshire-news/snapshot-of-
  huddersfields-cinema-history; www.
  arthurlloyd.co.uk/HuddersfieldTheatres.
  htm; huddersfieldhistory.files.wordpress.
  com/2010/09/discovering-old-
  huddersfield-v2.pdf
2 *HDE*, 13/08/1914
3 *HDE*, 18/04/1916
4 *HDE*, 18/08/1914
5 *HDE*, 13/07/1915
6 *HDE*, 06/03/1916
7 *HDE*, 27/07/1915
8 *HDE*, 04/01/1916
9 *HDE*, 25/01/1916
10 *HDE*, 24/12/1917
11 *HDE*, 07/01/1918
12 *HDE*, 21/01/1918
13 *HDE*, 04/08/1916
14 *HDE*, 22/05/1916; *HDE*, 08/02/1917;
   www.arthurlloyd.co.uk/Huddersfield
   Theatres.htm
15 *HDE*, 22/04/1918
16 *HDE*, 02/05/1916; downthetubes.net/dtt-
   old/features/film/british_comics_films.html
17 *HDE*, 16/08/1916; *HDE*, 12/09/1916
18 *HDE*, 20/02/1917
19 *HDE*, 22/10/1917
20 *HDE*, 04/02/1918; *HDE*, 12/02/1917
21 *HDE*, 14/04/1916
22 *HDE*, 19/09/1917; www.
   huddersfieldchoral.com/media/page_
   content; www.examiner.co.uk/whats-on/
   review-huddersfield-choral-society-
   huddersfield-4974040
23 *HDE*, 01/11/1916
24 *HDE*, 18/06/1918
25 *HDE*, 07/01/1918; *HDE*, 15/01/1918
26 *HDE*, 17/12/1917
27 *HDE*, 18/12/1917
28 *HDE*, 25/05/1916; en.wikipedia.org/
   wiki/Vladimir_Rosing; en.wikipedia.
   org/wiki/Arthur_Eaglefield_Hull; *The
   Huddersfield Music Society: A Short
   History*
29 *HDE*, 15/10/1917
30 *HDE*, 26/06/1918; *HDE*, 28/08/1918
31 *HDE*, 02/07/1915
32 *HDE*, 12/08/1915; *HDE*, 05/11/1915;
   HDE, 14/04/1916
33 *HDE*, 15/03/1915; en.wikipedia.org/
   wiki/Clara_Butt
34 *HDE*, 05/06/1916; *HDE*, 23/08/1916
35 *HDE*, 27/09/1915
36 *HDE*, 23/08/1916
37 *HDE*, 03/04/1918
38 *HDE*, 03/06/1915; *HDE*, 05/03/1917;
   A History of Meltham Golf Club

39 *HDE*, 28/02/1917; *HDE*, 08/03/1917;
   HDE, 31/05/1917
40 *HDE*, 24/10/1917; *HDE*, 25/03/1918
41 *HDE*, 12/08/1915;
42 *HDE*, 24/08/1917
43 *HDE*, 19/09/1917
44 *HDE*, 29/07/1915; *HDE*, 15/08/1917;
   In a League of Their Own
45 *HDE*, 25/08/1915
46 *HDE*, 04/09/1916; *HDE*, 30/07/1917
47 *HDE*, 17/05/1916; www.terramedia.co.uk/
   reference/law/entertainmentstax.htm
48 www.huddersfieldrlheritage.co.uk/
   Archive/Written
49 *HDE*, 02/10/1914
50 *HDE*, 28/09/1914
51 *HDE*, 30/11/1914
52 *HDE*, 01/02/1915
53 www.huddersfieldrlheritage.co.uk/
   Archive/Written
54 *HDE*, 03/05/1915
55 *HDE*, 24/09/1915
56 *HDE*, 17/01/1915
57 *HDE*, 30/07/1918
58 *HDE*, 14/02/1915; *HDE*, 27/11/1915
59 *HDE*, 24/09/1915
60 *HDE*, 14/02/1916
61 *HDE*, 24/02/1915
62 *HDE*, 08/11/1915
63 *HDE*, 10/04/1916; *HDE*, 15/09/1916
64 *HDE*, 30/08/1916
65 *HDE*, 07/06/1916; www.wafll.com/
   leeds-statistics/ leeds-1915-16.html
66 *HDE*, 20/12/1915
67 *HDE*, 25/09/1917
68 *HDE*, 09/10/1916
69 *HDE*, 23/10/1916
70 *HDE*, 06/11/1916
71 *HDE*, 27/11/1916
72 *HDE*, 04/12/1916
73 *HDE*, 14/11/1916
74 *HDE*, 27/12/1917
75 *HDE*, 22/12/1916
76 *HDE*, 16/04/1917
77 *HDE*, 27/08/1917
78 *HDE*, 17/12/1917
79 *HDE*, 10/04/1916
80 *HDE*, 04/04/1916
81 www.huddersfieldrlheritage.co.uk/
   Archive/Written/Players/AlbertRosenfeld
82 www.bbc.co.uk/bradford/sense_of_place/
   remembrance_pals; *Missing in Action*;
   www.huddersfieldrlheritage.co.uk/
   Archive/Written/Players/FredLongstaff;
   www.huddersfieldrlheritage.co.uk/
   Archive/Written/Huddersfield/Hudds_
   NU_WW1; Interview with Sue Allen, Gt.
   Niece of Fred Longstaff

83 www.huddersfieldrlheritage.co.uk/
   Archive/Written/Huddersfield/Hudds_
   NU_WW1
84 www.examiner.co.uk/news/west-
   yorkshire-news/tragedy-huddersfield-
   town-star-larrett; johndoxey.100freemb.
   com/Silverwood/larrett-roebuck
85 *HDE*, 08/08/1916; *HDE*, 14/08/1916;
   HDE, 05/10/1916; *HDE*, 03/11/1916;
   HDE, 30/08/1918
86 *HDE*,18/08/1916;johndoxey.100freemb.
   com/Silverwood/larrett-roebuck
87 www.examiner.co.uk/news/west-
   yorkshire-news/tragedy-huddersfield-
   town-star-larrett
88 www.wafll.com/leeds-statistics/
   leeds-1915-16.html; www.wafll.com/
   leeds-tatistics/leeds-1916-17.html; www.
   wafll.com/leeds-tatistics/leeds-1917-18.
   html; www.wafll.com/leeds-tatistics/
   leeds-1918-19.html
89 *HDE*, 28/04/1916
90 *HDE*, 15/03/1916
91 *HDE*, 19/08/1918; 1914-1918.
   invisionzone.com/forums
92 *HDE*, 30/09/1915
93 *HDE*, 05/07/1915; *HBTCVG*
   21/06/1901 to 29/09/1911
94 *HDE*, 05/05/1916
95 *HDE*, 21/06/1916
96 *HDE*, 19/04/1917
97 *HDE*, 15/07/1915
98 *HDE*, 27/09/1915
99 *HDE*, 20/04/1916; *HDE*, 20/04/1916;
   HDE, 05/05/1916
100 *HDE*, 10/07/1916
101 *HDE*, 08/08/1916
102 *HDE*, 21/09/1916
103 *HDE*, 04/05/1917
104 *HDE*, 10/05/1918
105 *HDE*, 08/09/1915
106 *HDE*, 05/08/1915; *HDE*, 11/10/1915;
    HDE, 29/06/1916
107 *HDE*, 27/09/1915
108 *HDE*, 26/03/1915
109 *HDE*, 08/11/1915
110 *HDE*, 03/07/1917
111 *HDE*, 12/09/1917
112 *HDE*, 19/02/1918
113 *HDE*, 11/02/1918
114 *HDE*, 22/12/1918
115 *HDE*, 06/05/1918
116 *HDE*, 02/10/1916; *HDE*, 01/10/1917
117 *HDE*, 12/09/1917

Chapter 16: Women: Vindication for Emancipation

1 *HDE*, 18/02/1918
2 *HDE*, 22/03/1915
3 *HDE*, 20/04/1915
4 *HDE*, 13/05/1915; *HDE*, 08/09/1915;
  Railways of the Great War, Ep 4; *On
  Track to Victory*
5 *HDE*, 28/07/1915
6 *HDE*, 27/08/1915
7 *HDE*, 03/11/1915

8 *HDE*, 18/07/1916; HDE, 26/09/1917
9 *HDE*, 24/04/1917
10 *HDE*, 18/08/1915
11 *HDE*, 08/12/1916
12 www.edwardianpromenade.com/war/wwi-
   wednesday-women-ambulance-drivers/;
   www.cliochronicles.com/2012/07/29/
   the-home-front-wwi-part-ii/; *Kate Adie's
   Women of World War I*

13 *HDE*, 30/03/1917; www.
   hud.ac.uk/news/2014/march/
   wwihuddersfieldtechnical
   collegeandthegreatwar.php
14 www.dailymail.co.uk/home/books/
   article-2629582
15 *HDE*, 30/03/1917
16 *HDE*, 02/08/1916
17 *HDE*, 30/03/1917

18 *HDE*, 05/06/1917

19 hansard.millbanksystems.com/ commons/1917/jun/19/clause-4- franchises-women; en.wikipedia.org/ wiki/Representation_of_the_People_ Act_1918

20 *HDE*, 04/03/1918

21 kirkleeslibdems.org.uk/en/ article/2007/077676/100-years-of- women-in-council

22 *HDE*, 10/05/1916

23 *HDE*, 26/05/1916; *HDE*, 15/07/1916

24 *HDE*, 29/05/1918

25 *HDE*, 14/04/1916

26 *HDE*, 19/01/1917

27 *HDE*, 09/08/1916

28 *HDE*, 14/04/1916; *HDE*, 14/02/1917; *HDE*, 06/06/1917

29 http://archive.spectator.co.uk/article/1st- december-1917/19/war-and-population

30 *HDE*, 27/06/1917

31 *HDE*, 09/07/1917

32 *HDE*, 11/06/1918

33 *HDE*, 17/06/1918

34 *HDE*, 08/12/1916; *HDE*, 16/01/1917

35 *HDE*, 05/06/1917

36 *HDE*, 22/01/1917

37 *HDE*, 04/07/1916

38 *HDE*, 21/05/1917

39 *HDE*, 05/06/1917

Chapter 17: Appeals and Alleviating Distress

1 *HDE*, 19/07/1915; *HDE*, 05/07/1915; *HDE*, 19/01/1917

2 *HDE*, 12/07/1915

3 *HDE*, 21/07/1915

4 *HDE*, 07/03/1919

5 *HDE*, 23/02/1916; *HDE*, 06/02/1917

6 *HDE*, 21/05/1917

7 *HDE*, 12/07/1915

8 *HDE*, 25/03/1915

9 *HDE*, 25/03/1915; *HDE*, 14/04/1916

10 *HDE*, 26/07/1915

11 *Supplement to the HWE*, 05/04/1919

12 *HDE*, 25/08/1915

13 *HDE*, 12/10/1915

14 *S Crosland School Log Book*, 20/11/1916; 30/01/1917; 15/03/1917

15 *Family of Four*

16 *HDE*, 04/11/1915; *Supplement to the HWE*, 05/04/1919

17 *HDE*, 07/05/1917; *Supplement to the HWE*, 05/04/1919

18 *HDE*, 02/01/1919

19 *HDE*, 10/05/1918

20 *HDE*, 01/08/1917; *HDE*, 10/05/1918; *HDE*, 09/06/1919

21 *HDE*, 08/11/1916

22 *HDE*, 01/08/1917

23 *HDE*, 12/09/1917

24 *HDE*, 27/09/1917

25 *HDE*, 07/05/1917; *HDE*, 10/05/1917; *Supplement to the HWE*, 05/04/1919

26 *HDE*, 05/07/1915; *HDE*, 31/07/1916; *HDE*, 04/12/1916; *Supplement to the HWE*, 05/04/1919

27 *HDE*, 09/10/1917; *HDE*, 05/12/1917; *HDE*, 03/04/1919

28 *Colne Valley Folk*

29 *HDE*, 16/04/1917; *HDE*, 23/07/1917

30 *HDE*, 23/07/1917

31 *HDE*, 12/10/1915

32 *HDE*, 04/09/1916; *HDE*, 11/06/1917

33 en.wikipedia.org/wiki/War_bond

34 *HDE*, 07/06/1916; en.wikipedia.org/ wiki/War_bond

35 *HDE*, 07/06/1916

36 *HDE*, 14/07/1916

37 *HDE*, 17/07/1916

38 *Supplement to the HWE*, 08/03/1919

39 en.wikipedia.org/wiki/War_bond; postalheritage.org.uk/page/savingsbank- warsavings

40 *S Crosland School Log Book*, 17/11/1916; 30/11/1916; 13/12/1918

41 *HDE*, 11/12/1917

42 *HDE*, 16/02/1917

43 *HDE*, 18/02/1918

44 *HDE*, 19/02/1918

45 *Crow Lane School Log Book*; *Brierley Wood School Log Book*

46 *HDE*, 19/02/1918

47 *HDE*, 20/02/1918

48 *HDE*, 22/02/1918

49 *HDE*, 25/02/1918

50 *HDE*, 04/07/1918

51 *HDE*, 05/07/1918

52 *HDE*, 10/07/1918; *Supplement to the HWE*, 08/03/1919

53 *HDE*, 08/02/1918; *HDE*, 12/02/1918

54 *Supplement to the HWE*, 08/03/1919

55 en.wikipedia.org/wiki/War_bond; postalheritage.org.uk/page/savingsbank- warsavings

56 *HDE*, 09/04/1915; *HDE*, 04/11/1915; *HDE*, 23/09/1915

57 Smith, F, *WWI Letters*, 07/05/1915

58 *HDE*, 07/05/1917

59 *HDE*, 17/02/1916

60 *HDE*, 28/01/1916

61 *HDE*, 24/07/1916

62 *HDE*, 04/11/1915

63 *HDE*, 12/08/1915

64 *HDE*, 24/09/1915

65 *HDE*, 24/09/1915

66 *HDE*, 16/06/1916

67 *HDE*, 12/05/1916

68 *Outlane Golf Club Centenary*; *HDE*, 18/01/1917; *HDE*, 16/01/1918

69 *HDE*, 04/05/1917

70 *HDE*, 16/06/1916

71 *HDE*, 28/09/1916; *HDE*, 04/05/1017

72 *HDE*, 18/01/1917

73 *HDE*, 28/03/1917

74 *HDE*, 16/01/1918

75 *Outlane Golf Club Centenary*

76 *HDE*, 10/05/1916; *HDE*, 03/04/1917

77 *HDE*, 08/01/1917

78 *HDE*, 10/05/1916

79 *HDE*, 14/07/1916

80 *HDE*, 25/10/1916

81 *HDE*, 07/03/1917; *HDE*, 20/03/1917; *HDE*, 28/03/1917

82 *HDE*, 13/03/1917

83 *HDE*, 09/03/1917; *HDE*, 20/04/1917; *HDE*, 25/04/1917

84 *HDE*, 24/07/1916

85 *HDE*, 12/09/1917

86 *HDE*, 07/03/1919

87 *HDE*, 13/06/1918; www.scarletfinders. co.uk/194.html

Chapter 18: 1917: Passchendaele

1 *The West Riding Territorials in the Great War*

2 *HDE*, 04/01/1917

3 *The West Riding Territorials in the Great War*

4 www.1914-1918.net/bat20.htm

5 *HDE*, 20/02/1917

6 *HDE*, 29/06/1919; *HDE*, 30/06/1919

7 *HDE*, 13/09/1917

8 *HDE*, 04/01/1917

9 *HDE*, 13/02/1917

10 *HDE*, 13/02/1917; *HDE*, 15/02/1917

11 *Supplement to the HWE*, 13/09/1919

12 *A Village Goes to War*

13 *Supplement to the HWE*, 13/09/1919; *The West Riding Territorials in the Great War*

14 *A Village Goes to War*

15 *A Village Goes to War*

16 *The West Riding Territorials in the Great War*; *Supplement to the HWE*,13/09/1919

17 *HDE*, 18/03/1917

18 *The West Riding Territorials in the Great War*

19 *Supplement to the HWE*, 13/09/1919

20 *The West Riding Territorials in the Great War*

21 *The West Riding Territorials in the Great War*; *Supplement to the HWE*,13/09/1919

22 www.1914-1918.net/bat20.htm

23 *The Great War 1914-1918*, 1917: Breaking of Armies

24 *The West Riding Territorials in the Great War*

25 www.1914-1918.net/bat20.htm

26 *HDE*, 01/05/1917

27 *HDE*, 02/05/1917

28 *HDE*, 29/06/1919; *HDE*, 30/06/1919

29 *HDE*, 16/04/1917

30 *HDE*, 16/04/1917

31 *Supplement to the London Gazette*, 08/06/1917; *Crow Lane School Log Book*, 12/11/1926

32 *HDE*, 26/10/1929; *HDE*, 26/06/1956

33 *The West Riding Territorials in the Great War*; *A Village Goes to War*

34 *HDE*, 19/04/1917

35 *The West Riding Territorials in the Great War*; *A Village Goes to War*

36 *A Village Goes to War*; *Supplement to the HWE*, 13/09/1919

37 *HDE*, 23/08/1917

38 *A Village Goes to War*; *Supplement to the HWE*, 13/09/1919

39 *Supplement to the HWE*, 13/09/1919; *The Bloody Battle of Bullecourt*; www. openwriting.com/archives/2009/01/the_ bloody_batt_1.php

40 *A Village Goes to War*

41 *The West Riding Territorials in the Great War*

42 *The Great War 1914-1918*, 1917: Breaking of Armies; *The First World War from Above*; www.1914-1918.net/ bat20.htm

43 *D Clark's War Diary*, 07/06/1917

44 *The Great War 1914-1918*, 1917: The Breaking of Armies; *The First World War from Above*; www.1914-1918.net/ bat20.htm

45 *Supplement to the HWE*, 31/05/1919

46 *D Clark's War Diary*, 13/06/1917

47 *D Clark's War Diary*, 12/06/1917

48 *D Clark's War Diary*, 06/07/1917

49 *D Clark's War Diary*, 07/07/1917; 12/07/1917

50 *D Clark's War Diary*, 24/07/1917

51 *D Clark's War Diary*, 27/07/1917

52 *HDE*, 29/06/1919; *HDE*, 30/06/1919

53 www.1914-1918.net/bat20.htm

54 *HDE*, 29/06/1919; *HDE*, 30/06/1919

55 www.1914-1918.net/haigs_pass_ despatch.html

56 *HDE*, 29/06/1919; *HDE*, 30/06/1919; www.1914-1918.net/haigs_pass_ despatch.html

57 *HDE*, 23/08/1917; *HDE*, 29/06/1919; *HDE*, 30/06/1919

58 *HDE*, 27/09/1917

59 *HDE*, 14/09/1917

60 *HDE*, 01/07/1915

61 *HDE*, 07/02/1918

62 *Supplement to the HWE*, 31/05/1919; *D Clark's War Diary*, various dates

63 *The West Riding Territorials in the Great War*

64 *HDE*, 19/07/1917

65 *The West Riding Territorials in the Great War*

66 *Supplement to the HWE*, 13/09/1919

67 *D Clark's War Diary*, 30/07/1917; 31/07/1917

68 *D Clark's War Diary*, 01/08/1917; 02/08/1917; 03/08/1917

69 *A Village Goes to War*

70 *D Clark's War Diary*, 16/08/1917

71 *D Clark's War Diary*, 22/08/1917

72 *A Village Goes to War*

73 *The Great War 1914-1918*, 1917: Breaking of Armies

74 *D Clark's War Diary*, 30/09/1917

75 The Salient (trenches newspaper) Christmas 1915

76 *D Clark's War Diary*, 30/09/1917

77 *HDE*, 05/09/1917

78 *HDE*, 01/11/1917

79 *HDE*, 27/08/1917

80 *A Village Goes to War*; *HDE*, 29/06/1919; *HDE*, 30/06/1919

81 www.traffordwardead.co.uk

82 *A Village Goes to War*; *HDE*, 29/06/1919; *HDE*, 30/06/1919

83 *HDE*, 29/05/1917

84 *A Village Goes to War*

85 *D Clark's War Diary*, 26/10/1917

86 *D Clark's War Diary*, 29/10/1917; www. huddersfieldrlheritage.co.uk

87 *D Clark's War Diary*, 31/10/1917; *HDE*, 13/11/1917; *HDE*, 21/12/1917

88 *The West Riding Territorials in the Great War*

89 *HDE*, 27/12/1917

90 *The West Riding Territorials in the Great War*; *The First World War from Above*; *Supplement to the HWE*, 31/05/1919

91 www.1914-1918.net/haigs_pass_ despatch.html

92 *A Village Goes to War*

93 *D Clark's War Diary*, 31/10/1917; 01/11/1917; 02/11/1917

94 *D Clark's War Diary*, 09/11/1917; 12/11/1917; 14/11/1917; 16/11/1917; 17/11/1917; *HDE*, 21/12/1917

95 D Clark's War Diary, 27/11/1917; 17/01/1918; 31/01/1918

96 www.huddersfieldrlheritage.co.uk

97 *HDE*, 22/11/1917; *Supplement to the HWE*, 31/05/1919

98 *HDE*, 23/01/1918; *HDE*, 29/06/1919; *HDE*, 30/06/1919

99 *HDE*, 02/01/1918

100 *A Village Goes to War*

101 *The Great War 1914-1918*, 1917: Breaking of Armies

Chapter 19: 1917: Cambrai

1 *Supplement to the HWE*, 13/09/1919

2 www.1914-1918.net/haigs_cambrai_ despatch.html; *Supplement to the HWE*, 13/09/1919; The West Riding Territorials in the Great War

3 *A Village Goes to War*

4 *A Village Goes to War*

5 *Supplement to the HWE*, 13/09/1919

6 *Supplement to the HWE*, 13/09/1919

7 www.1914-1918.net/haigs_cambrai_ despatch.html

8 *HDE*, 17/01/1918

9 *HDE*, 02/01/1918

10 *HDE*, 29/11/1917

11 *A Village Goes to War*

12 *HDE*, 05/12/1917

13 *A Village Goes to War*

14 *Supplement to the HWE*, 13/09/1919; *HDE*, 05/12/1917

15 *HDE*, 06/12/1917; *HDE*, 05/12/1917

16 *HDE*, 11/03/1918

17 *Supplement to the HWE*, 13/09/1919; www.1914-1918.net/haigs_cambrai_ despatch.html

18 *A Village Goes to War*

19 *Supplement to the HWE*, 13/09/1919

20 *The West Riding Territorials in the Great War; Supplement to the HWE*, 13/09/1919; *A Village Goes to War*

21 *The West Riding Territorials in the Great War; A Village Goes to War*

22 *HDE*, 14/06/1918

23 *The West Riding Territorials in the Great War; Supplement to the HWE*, 13/09/1919; *A Village Goes to War*; www.1914-1918.net/haigs_cambrai_ despatch.html; *HDE*, 13/12/1917

24 *HDE*, 13/12/1917

25 *Supplement to the HWE*, 13/09/1919

Chapter 20: 1917-18: Rationing

1 *HDE*, 06/08/1914

2 *HDE*, 25/01/1915

3 *HDE*, 22/09/1915

4 *HDE*, 07/06/1916

5 *HDE*, 11/12/1917

6 *HDE*, 12/09/1916; *HDE*, 11/10/1916; *HDE*, 16/11/1916

7 *HDE*, 16/01/1917

8 en.wikipedia.org/wikiU-boat_ Campaign_World_War_I

9 *HDE*, 01/05/1917

10 en.wikipedia.org/wiki/Convoys_ in_World_War_I

11 *HDE*, 16/05/1917

12 *HDE*, 09/01/1917

13 *HDE*, 08/03/1917; *HDE*, 15/03/1917

14 *HDE*, 19/03/1917

15 *HDE*, 24/04/1917

16 *HDE*, 19/04/1917; *HDE*, 26/04/1917

17 *HDE*, 21/05/1917

18 *HDE*, 11/10/1918; *HDE*, 02/11/1917

19 *HDE*, 12/11/1917

20 *HDE*, 10/12/1917; HDE, 15/01/1917

21 *HDE*, 21/08/1917

22 *HDE*, 20/03/1917

23 *HDE*, 16/04/1917

24 *HDE*, 16/05/1917

25 *HDE*, 05/03/1917

26 *HDE*, 30/04/1917

27 *HDE*, 05/07/1917

28 *HDE*, 30/04/1917; *HDE*, 05/07/1917

29 *HDE*, 13/02/1918

30 *HDE*, 16/02/1917

31 *HDE*, 12/02/1917

32 *HDE*, 24/10/1917

33 *HDE*, 03/01/1917; *HDE*, 16/02/1917

34 *HDE*, 30/10/1917

35 *HDE*, 28/03/1917

36 *HDE*, 09/10/1918

37 *HDE*, 06/11/1917

38 *HDE*, 17/09/1917

39 *HDE*, 05/04/1917

40 *HDE*, 17/04/1917; *HDE*, 04/12/1917

41 *HDE*, 23/01/1918

42 *HDE*, 23/01/1918

43 *HDE*, 04/12/1917

44 *HDE*, 19/03/1917

45 *HDE*, 03/09/1917

46 *HDE*, 07/12/1917

47 *HDE*, 09/01/1917; *HDE*, 12/01/1917; *HDE*, 23/01/1917

48 *HDE*, 18/01/1917; *HDE*, 25/01/1917
49 *HDE*, 17/04/1917; *HDE*, 27/07/1917; *HDE*, 21/08/1918
50 *HDE*, 09/08/1917
51 *HDE*, 25/01/1917; *HDE*, 03/09/1917
52 *HDE*, 10/09/1917
53 *HDE*, 02/02/1917; *HDE*, 18/07/1917
54 *HDE*, 05/12/1917
55 *HDE*, 16/03/1917; *HDE*, 18/01/1918
56 *HDE*, 15/05/1917
57 *HDE*, 30/10/1917; *HDE*, 01/11/1917
58 *HDE*, 05/06/1917
59 *HDE*, 04/09/1917
60 *HDE*, 08/02/1918
61 *HDE*, 22/02/1918
62 *HDE*, 10/09/1918
63 *HDE*, 26/08/1918
64 *HDE*, 30/11/1917
65 *HDE*, 03/12/1917
66 *HDE*, 04/12/1917

67 *HDE*, 18/12/1917; *HDE*, 19/12/1917
68 *HDE*, 17/01/1918
69 *HDE*, 19/12/1917
70 *HDE*, 12/03/1918
71 *HDE*, 05/02/1918
72 *HDE*, 21/12/1917
73 *HDE*, 24/12/1918
74 *HDE*, 12/02/1918
75 *HDE*, 16/01/1918; *HDE*, 07/02/1917
76 *HDE*, 02/01/1918; *HDE*, 04/01/1918
77 *HDE*, 07/01/1918
78 *HDE*, 11/01/1918
79 *HDE*, 23/01/1918; *HDE*, 05/04/1918
80 *HDE*, 06/03/1918
81 *HDE*, 20/03/1918
82 *HDE*, 11/03/1918; *HDE*, 10/04/1918
83 *HDE*, 12/04/1918
84 *HDE*, 16/04/1918
85 *HDE*, 22/04/1918; *HDE*, 12/06/1918
86 *HDE*, 10/07/1918

87 *HDE*, 29/07/1918; *HDE*, 07/08/1918
88 *HDE*, 30/07/1918
89 *HDE*, 22/08/1918; *HDE*, 11/09/1918; *HDE*, 15/10/1918
90 *HDE*, 02/09/1918; *HDE*, 15/10/1918; *HDE*, 07/11/1918
91 *HDE*, 14/06/1916; *HDE*, 02/02/1917; *HDE*, 15/01/1918
92 *HDE*, 04/07/1918
93 *HDE*, 07/12/1916; *HDE*, 06/02/1917
94 *HDE*, 20/03/1918; *HDE*, 04/06/1918; *HDE*, 04/07/1918
95 *HDE*, 14/08/1918; *HDE*, 21/08/1918
96 *HDE*, 05/09/1918
97 *HDE*, 21/08/1918
98 *HDE*, 02/03/1917; *HDE*, 19/03/1917; *HDE*, 20/07/1917
99 *HDE*, 06/03/1918; *HDE*, 24/06/1918
100 *HDE*, 17/04/1918
101 *HDE*, 12/12/1917
102 *HDE*, 24/07/1918

Chapter 21: 1918: From the Jaws of Defeat

1 *The West Riding Territorials in the Great War; A Village Goes to War; The Great War 1914-1918*, 1918: Germany's Last Gamble; *The First World War*, Ep 9, Germany's Last Gamble
2 *The West Riding Territorials in the Great War*
3 *A Village Goes to War*
4 *HDE*, 29/06/1919; *HDE*, 30/06/1919; *The West Riding Territorials in the Great War*
5 *HDE*, 14/02/1918; *HDE*, 07/03/1918; *HDE*, 29/06/1919; *HDE*, 30/06/1919; *The West Riding Territorials in the Great War*
6 *HDE*, 29/06/1919; *HDE*, 30/06/1919
7 *HDE*, 11/04/1918
8 *HDE*, 10/05/1918
9 *The West Riding Territorials in the Great War*
10 *A Village Goes to War*; *The First World War*, Ep 9, Germany's Last Gamble
11 *A Village Goes to War; The West Riding Territorials in the Great War*; *HDE*, 16/05/1918; *HDE*, 29/06/1919; *HDE*, 30/06/1919
12 *The West Riding Territorials in the Great War*; *HDE*, 11/04/1918; *HDE*, 29/06/1919; *HDE*, 30/06/1919
13 *HDE*, 11/04/1918
14 *HDE*, 29/06/1919; *HDE*, 30/06/1919; *A Village Goes to War; The First World War*, Ep 9, Germany's Last Gamble
15 *HDE*, 18/04/1918
16 *HDE*, 29/04/1918
17 *HDE*, 03/04/1918; *HDE*, 11/04/1918
18 *The West Riding Territorials in the Great War; A Village Goes to War; The First World War*, Ep 9, Germany's Last Gamble
19 *HDE*, 03/04/1918; *The First World War*, Ep 9, Germany's Last Gamble; *The First World War*, Ep 10, War Without End
20 *A Village Goes to War; The First World War*, Ep 9, Germany's Last Gamble
21 *HDE*, 16/04/1918
22 *A Village Goes to War; The West Riding Territorials in the Great War*; www.scarboroughsmaritimeheritage.org.uk/greatwar/s27-neuve-eglise
23 *HDE*, 02/05/1918; *HDE*, 09/05/1918
24 *HDE*, 27/05/1918
25 *A Village Goes to War; The West Riding Territorials in the Great War*; www.scarboroughsmaritimeheritage.org.uk/greatwar/s27-neuve-eglise; *The Great War 1914-1918*, 1918: Germany's Last Gamble
26 *HDE*, 02/05/1918

27 *The First World War*, Ep 9, Germany's Last Gamble; www.scarboroughsmaritimeheritage.org.uk/greatwar/s27-neuve-eglise
28 *A Village Goes to War; The Great War 1914-1918*, 1918: Germany's Last Gamble,
29 *HDE*, 13/06/1918
30 *A Village Goes to War; The Great War 1914-1918*, 1918: Germany's Last Gamble
31 *The West Riding Territorials in the Great War*; wikipedia.org/wiki/Ferdinand_Foch
32 *HDE*, 15/08/1918; *A Village Goes to War; The Great War 1914-1918*, 1918: Germany's Last Gamble; *The West Riding Territorials in the Great War*
33 *HDE*, 01/10/1918
34 *HDE*, 12/08/1918; *HDE*, 29/06/1919; *HDE*, 30/06/1919; *The West Riding Territorials in the Great War*; Special Order of the Day, 31/07/1918, Braithwaite, Major-General WP, Commanding 62nd Division
35 *HDE*, 15/08/1918; *HDE*, 12/02/1919; *The West Riding Territorials in the Great War*
36 *HDE*, 29/06/1919; *HDE*, 30/06/1919; *The West Riding Territorials in the Great War*
37 *HDE*, 05/09/1918
38 *HDE*, 12/08/1918
39 *HDE*, 15/08/1918; *HDE*, 09/09/1918; www.1914-1918.net/bat25.htm
40 *The First World War*, Ep 9, Germany's Last Gamble
41 *HDE*, 29/06/1919; *HDE*, 30/06/1919
42 *A Village Goes to War; The West Riding Territorials in the Great War; The Great War 1914-1918*, 1918: Germany's Last Gamble; *The First World War*, Ep 10, War Without End
43 *HDE*, 04/01/1919; *HDE*, 31/05/1919
44 *HDE*, 29/06/1919; *HDE*, 30/06/1919; *A Village Goes to War*
45 *HDE*, 09/09/1918; *HDE*, 14/10/1918
46 *The West Riding Territorials in the Great War*
47 *HDE*, 25/09/1918; *HDE*, 05/10/1918
48 *HDE*, 12/09/1918; *HDE*, 14/10/1918
49 *HDE*, 27/12/1918; www.dwr.org.uk/dwr.php?id=55; *Supplement to the HWE*, 25/01/1919; *The West Riding Territorials in the Great War*
50 *HDE*, 10/10/1918; *HDE*, 29/06/1919; *HDE*, 30/06/1919

51 *Supplement to the HWE*, 31/05/1919; *HDE*, 19/09/1918; *HDE*, 29/06/1919; *HDE*, 30/06/1919; *The West Riding Territorials in the Great War; A Village Goes to War*; www.cwgc.org/victory1918/content; *Captain Keith Sykes' Scrapbook* Special Order of the Day, 14/11/1918
52 *HDE*, 29/06/1919; *HDE*, 30/06/1919; *Captain Keith Sykes' Scrapbook*
53 *HDE*, 06/06/1919
54 *HDE*, 25/10/1918
55 *HDE*, 30/09/1918; *The Great War 1914-1918*, 1918: Germany's Last Gamble; *A Village Goes to War*
56 *HDE*, 30/09/1918; *HDE*, 10/10/1918; *HDE*, 29/10/1918; *Supplement to the HWE*, 25/01/1919; *The West Riding Territorials in the Great War; Captain Keith Sykes' Scrapbook* Special Order of the Day, 14/11/1918; Letter, 01/10/1918
57 *Supplement to the HWE*, 04/01/1919; *Supplement to the HWE*, 31/05/1919; www.cwgc.org/victory1918/content
58 *HDE*, 24/10/1918; en.wikipedia.org/wiki/Desertion
59 *The First World War*, Ep 10, War Without End; www.cwgc.org/victory1918/content.
60 *HDE*, 29/06/1919; *HDE*, 30/06/1919; *A Village Goes to War*
61 *HDE*, 29/06/1919; *HDE*, 30/06/1919; *The West Riding Territorials in the Great War*
62 *HDE*, 01/11/1918
63 *HDE*, 31/10/1918; *The West Riding Territorials in the Great War; Captain Keith Sykes' Scrapbook* Special Order of the Day, 14/11/1918
64 *HDE*, 31/10/1918; *HDE*, 18/11/1918; *HDE*, 27/12/1918; *HDE*, 29/06/1919; *HDE*, 30/06/1919; *Captain Keith Sykes' Scrapbook* Special Order of the Day, 14/11/1918
65 *The Great War 1914-1918*, 1918: Germany's Last Gamble; *A Village Goes to War*
66 *Supplement to the HWE*, 31/05/1919
67 *HDE*, 29/06/1919; *HDE*, 30/06/1919; *A Village Goes to War; The West Riding Territorials in the Great War*
68 *HDE*, 12/12/1918; *The West Riding Territorials in the Great War*
69 *Supplement to the HWE*, 04/01/1919; *Supplement to the HWE*, 31/05/1919

70 *HDE*, 29/06/1919; *HDE*, 30/06/1919; *A Village Goes to War; The West Riding Territorials in the Great War*; en.wikipedia.org/wiki/Siege_of_Maubeuge; *Captain Keith Sykes' Scrapbook* Special Order of the Day, 14/11/1918

71 *A Village Goes to War; The Great War 1914-1918*, 1918: Germany's Last Gamble; *The First World War*, Ep 10, War Without End

72 *Supplement to the HWE*, 04/01/1919; *The West Riding Territorials in the Great War*

73 *HDE*, 21/11/1918

74 *HDE*, 11/11/1918

75 *Family of Four*

76 *HDE*, 11/11/1918

77 *HDE*, 12/11/1918

78 *HDE*, 20/11/1918

79 *The First World War*, Ep 10, War Without End

Chapter 22: 1918-19: Transition and Legacy

1 *HDE*, 11/08/1919

2 *HDE*, 12/11/1918

3 *HDE*, 20/03/1919

4 *Supplement to the HWE*, 04/01/1919; *HDE*, 29/06/1919; *HDE*, 30/06/1919; www.1914-1918.net/62div.htm

5 *HDE*, 22/10/1919, 13/11/1919

6 *Huddersfield Examiner*, 09/11/2013

7 *HDE*, 09/12/1919

8 *HDE*, 13/11/1919

9 *Supplement to the HWE*, 29/03/1919

10 *HDE*, 06/05/1919; *HDE*, 07/05/1919; *HDE*, 12/05/1919

11 *HDE*, 13/03/1919; *HDE*, 09/12/1919; *HDE*, 10/12/1919

12 *HDE*, 31/05/1919

13 *Captain Keith Sykes' Scrapbook*

14 *HDE*, 16/12/1919

15 *Supplement to the HWE*, 25/01/1919

16 *HDE*, 13/11/1919

17 *HDE*, 12/11/1918; *HDE*, 21/11/1918; www.independent.co.uk/life-style/health-and-families/health-news/flu-how-britain-coped-in-the-1918-epidemic-511987.html

18 http://news.nationalgeographic.com/news/2014/01/140123-spanish-flu-1918-china-origins-pandemic

19 history1900s.about.com/od/1910s/p/spanishflu.htm

20 *HDE*, 03/07/1918

21 *HDE*, 24/06/1918

22 *HDE*, 05/07/1918; *HDE*, 08/07/1918; *HDE*, 05/07/1918

23 *HDE*, 18/07/1918

24 *HDE*, 07/0/1918; *HDE*, 08/10/1918; *HDE*, 10/10/1918

25 *HDE*, 16/10/1918; *HDE*, 24/10/1918

26 *HDE*, 29/10/1918

27 *HDE*, 04/11/1918

28 *HDE*, 07/11/1918

29 *HDE*, 26/11/1918

30 *HDE*, 12/11/1918; *HDE*, 21/11/1918; www.independent.co.uk/life-style/health-and-families/health-news/flu-how-britain-coped-in-the-1918-epidemic-511987.html

31 *HDE*, 26/11/1918, 12/12/1918

32 *HDE*, 12/12/1918

33 *HDE*, 30/12/1918; *HDE*, 31/12/1918; *HDE*, 13/03/1919

34 *HDE*, 31/01/1918

35 *HDE*, 05/02/1919

36 *HDE*, 12/02/1919

37 *HDE*, 17/02/1919

38 *HDE*, 11/02/1919; workhousehttp://historyofnetherthong.co.uk

39 *HDE*, 27/02/1918; *HDE*, 19/04/1918; *HDE*, 24/02/1919

40 *HDE*, 25/02/1919

41 *HDE*, 10/03/1919

42 *HDE*, 12/03/1919

43 *HDE*, 25/02/1919

44 *HDE*, 11/03/1919; *HDE*, 25/03/1919; *HDE*, 01/04/1919

45 *HDE*, 27/03/1918; *HDE*, 02/04/1918

46 *HDE*, 13/11/1918

47 *HDE*, 18/11/1918

48 *HDE*, 23/12/1918; *HDE*, 31/03/1919; *HDE*, 07/10/1919

49 *HDE*, 02/01/1919; *HDE*, 03/01/1919

50 *HDE*, 18/02/1919

51 *HDE*, 31/03/1919

52 *HDE*, 07/10/1919; *HDE*, 28/10/1919

53 *HDE*, 12/06/1919

54 *HDE*, 22/08/1919

55 *HDE*, 07/10/1919

56 *HDE*, 01/05/1919; *HDE*, 10/12/1918

57 *HDE*, 01/01/1919

58 *HDE*, 14/11/1918; HDE, 28/11/1918

59 *HDE*, 18/03/1919; HDE, 21/03/1919

60 *HDE*, 29/05/1919; Garside, WR, *British Unemployment 1919-1939: A Study in Public Policy*, 2002

61 *HDE*, 30/06/1919; *HDE*, 11/11/1919

62 *HDE*, 01/09/1919

63 *HDE*, 27/03/1919

64 *HDE*, 24/12/1919

65 *HDE*, 20/10/1919

66 *HDE*, 30/12/1919

67 *HDE*, 24/12/1919

68 *Women Post Office Workers in Britain*

69 *HDE*, 02/04/1919

70 *Kate Adie's Women of World War I*

71 *HDE*, 14/07/1919

72 *HDE*, 09/07/1919

73 *HDE*, 02/10/1919; *HDE*, 21/10/1919

74 *HDE*, 12/12/1919

75 *HDE*, 21/06/1919

76 *HDE*, 20/03/1918

77 *Nostalgic Memories of Huddersfield*

78 *HDE*, 26/06/1919

79 en.wikipedia.org/wiki/Sex_Disqualification_(Removal)_Act_1919

80 *HDE*, 20/03/1918; *Women Post Office Workers in Britain*; www2.kirklees.gov.uk/you-kmc/MAYOR/former/pre1974.asp?area=huddersfield; www.yorkshirepost.co.uk/news/main-topics/local-stories/the-yorkshire-lass-who-helped-make-legal-history

81 *HDE*, 14/04/1919

82 *HDE*, 27/12/1918

83 prezi.com/xdbvcs4zat_/wwi-british-literature/

84 *HDE*, 24/03/1919

85 *HDE*, 09/08/1916

86 *HDE*, 18/07/1917; *HDE*, 27/03/1919

87 *HDE*, 05/06/1918

88 *HDE*, 28/01/1919; *S Crosland School Log Book* 14/01/1919

89 *HDE*, 12/08/1919

90 *HDE*, 03/07/1919

91 *HDE*, 18/07/1919

92 *HDE*, 09/10/1919

93 *HDE*, 23/10/1919

94 *HDE*, 13/11/1919

95 *HDE*, 25/11/1918; *HDE*, 26/11/1918

96 *HDE*, 02/12/1918

97 *HDE*, 26/03/1919

98 www.arthurlloyd.co.uk/HuddersfieldTheatres.htm

99 www.marsdenband.com; www.slaithwaiteband.org.uk; www.melthamband.co.uk; www.brighouseandrastrickband.co.uk

100 www.huddersfieldchoral.com

101 www.huddersfieldsingers.com; www.mrssunderlandfestival.com

102 *HDE*, 12/02/1919

103 *Supplement to the HWE*, 13/09/1919

104 *HDE*, 18/03/1919

105 www.huddersfieldrlheritage.com

106 *HDE*, 05/05/1919

107 *HDE*, 23/04/1919

108 www.huddersfieldrlheritage.com

109 *HDE*, 04/04/1919; *HDE*, 11/04/1919

110 *HDE*, 24/12/1918

111 www.myfootballfacts.com/FA_CUP_FINALS_1871-72_to_2008-09.html; www.myfootballfacts.com/Football_League_Stats.html

112 *HDE*, 11/04/1919

113 *HDE*, 25/02/1918; *HDE*,11/04/1919; *HDE*, 07/05/1919

114 *HDE*, 31/07/1919; *HDE*, 21/08/1919

115 *HDE*, 30/01/1918

116 *HDE*, 01/08/1918

117 www.donmouth.co.uk/womensfootball/huddersfieldatalanta.html; *Bradford City Football Club: A Scheme of Work*

118 *In a League of Their Own*

119 *The Great War of Words*, Ep 2, *World War I*; Ep 10, War Without End; *World War I in Photographs; The Great War; A Pictorial History*

120 *HDE*, 25/09/1918

121 *The Great War of Words*, Ep 2, World War I; Ep 10, War Without End; *World War I in Photographs; The Great War; A Pictorial History*

122 *HDE*, 30/06/1919

123 *A Village Goes to War; World War I*, Ep 10, War Without End; *The First World War*, Ep 10, Germany's Last Gamble

124 *HDE*, 04/03/1919; *HDE*,24/03/1919; *HDE*, 27/03/1919; *All Our Yesterdays*

125 *HDE*, 29/07/1918

126 *HDE*, 29/10/1918

127 *HDE*, 23/12/1918

128 *HDE*, 20/05/1919; www2.kirklees.gov.uk/community/warmemorial/memorialdetails

129 *HDE*, 05/11/1919

130 *HDE*, 09/01/1919

131 *HDE*, 26/09/1919

132 *HDE*, 12/06/1919

133 *HDE*, 19/12/1919

134 *HDE*, 14/11/1919

135 *HDE*, 27/11/1919

136 *HDE*, 04/03/1919

137 *HDE*, 11/07/1919; *HDE*, 14/07/1919

138 *HDE*, 21/07/1919; *HDE*, 23/07/1919

139 *HDE*, 17/07/1919

140 *HDE*, 13/03/1919

141 *HDE*, 21/07/1919; *S Crosland School Log Book* 18/07/1919

142 *World War I*, Ep 10, War Without End

143 *HDE*, 18/07/1919

INDEX